THE NAZI SECRET SERVICE

THE NAZI
SECRET SERVICE

André Brissaud

TRANSLATED
FROM THE FRENCH BY
MILTON WALDMAN

THE BODLEY HEAD
LONDON SYDNEY
TORONTO

Histoire du Service Secret Nazi
© Plon 1972
English translation © The Bodley Head Ltd 1974
ISBN 0 370 10664 4
Printed and bound in Great Britain
for The Bodley Head Ltd
9 Bow Street, London WC2E 7AL
by Richard Clay (The Chaucer Press), Ltd
Bungay, Suffolk
Set in Monotype Plantin Light
First published in Great Britain 1974

TO ERIC BRISSAUD FOR
HIS TWENTY-FIRST
BIRTHDAY

CONTENTS

ILLUSTRATIONS

AUTHOR'S FOREWORD

For several reasons this book could not be published earlier. Its publication will not, however, stop my researches into the S.S. secret service. There will be, I hope, a good deal yet to discover and to say. The intention of this book is to keep the discussion of this matter open. That is why I hope that witnesses and actors not yet found or still unknown will give us all the information possible. Each item of it can be important and enable us to take a new step towards explaining the intense activity of the secret service of the S.S. (the S.D.)—probably the most complex activity of the Second World War. Too many questions remain open. Too many documents are still undiscoverable. Too many witnesses maintain silence.

I pursue every path in order to gather the testimony of the actors before they fall silent for ever. But they do not always want to speak; at times they refuse to receive me. Certain former Nazis—especially the former S.S. men and ex-members of the S.D.—consider themselves still bound by the oath of secrecy given to Hitler, though this attitude may seem anachronistic thirty or forty years afterwards. The enquirer's task is not thus facilitated. It is also necessary to overcome one's personal feelings when at times confronting genuine 'war criminals', and to eschew all notions of Absolute Evil as a principle.

The student of the history of secret services must always bear in mind that the trails are confused, that he can only approach the truth step by step, from time to time going astray, and that often he can only construct hypotheses. Occasionally I am tempted to abandon my researches in this vexed field of study until one day I discover a new document, have an unexpected meeting with an important witness who agrees to reveal what he knows, read a small press-item, receive a letter . . . and I set out on the chase with renewed enthusiasm for a while.

A book like this is not written in a few months without pausing for breath. It takes years of research. Twenty years have elapsed since my conversations with Walter Schellenberg in Italy, ten since my tête-à-tête with Heinz Jost. In entering this stealthy, twilight world of the S.S. secret service I have run into surprises—disagreeable more often than not, and sometimes dangerous. It is a heterogeneous world, riddled with inner contradictions to the point of absurdity. I found myself faced constantly with a task much more difficult than that of writing contemporary 'visible' history which is based on documents and testimony comparatively easy to find. The perfection with which, for most of the time, secrecy was observed in the Nazi Intelligence service not only explains the cloud of rumours and legends born since the end of the war but especially the near-impossibility of discovering the indispensable document or the irrefutable witness. Moreover in this domain, I repeat, all the trails are confused. Every item of information must therefore be carefully verified and cross-checked. What is one to do, for instance, when it comes from only one surviving witness? It becomes essential to check if it accords historically, politically, psychologically with what one already knows for certain, and, when possible, to conduct one's own interrogation.

Admittedly I have had luck. The few pieces of the mosaic that I succeeded in discovering have, I hope, permitted the reconstruction, if not of the entire at least of the true image of the most mysterious of secret services, that which Reinhard Heydrich founded and directed from 1931 to 1942—I limit myself to the first period, 1931–39—that which Walter Schellenberg took in hand till the end: the S.S. secret service which in many respects strangely foreshadowed all the great secret services of today.

ANDRÉ BRISSAUD

The Curtain Rises ...

'Nuremberg, Monday, September 30th 1946.

'The International Military Tribunal declares the S.S. Organisation to be criminal . . . and all the members of the S.S. to be criminals.

'The International Military Tribunal declares the S.D. [Nazi Secret Service] and the Gestapo . . . to be criminal and the members of the S.D. and functionaries of the Gestapo to be criminals . . .'

The whole world's teleprinters and radios circulated this despatch which reported the words of the President, Lord Justice Lawrence. It was the hour of the verdict. There would never be an appeal.

1

I Meet a 'War Criminal'

It was the end of February 1952. Five years had elapsed since the verdict at Nuremberg: I was doing a series of articles in Northern Italy as special correspondent for a Paris daily paper, and had just spent a Sunday with some Italian friends on the shores of Lake Maggiore. I love this region, but since morning a freezing rain had been falling with hopeless persistence. I returned to Milan by road. It was very dark, almost night. Suddenly, between Verbania and Pallanza, my hired car broke down. There was no traffic on the icy road. I had to resign myself to going to look for help on foot.

After three or four hundred metres I saw a light burning on the hillside. A large villa stood amid trees white with hoarfrost. The gate was open. I went up the central path and rang the bell. An Italian manservant opened the door. I explained my situation. He agreed to let me use the telephone in order to try to reach the local garage but did not conceal his scepticism: 'It's Sunday, and late.' After several vain efforts I got an answer but . . . they would do the repair 'tomorrow morning'. During my wrangle with the telephone the servant had disappeared. When he returned I informed him of my difficulty. He smiled and told me that the owner of the villa, apprised of my worries, offered me hospitality for the night. I was glad to accept, the prospect of setting out in the cold to search for a room being scarcely a happy one.

After retrieving my case from the car, taking a good hot bath and changing, I asked about my host. The servant led me to the drawing room. Before a wood fire two men were talking in Italian.

I learned that the master of the house was a Milanese, a lawyer. He was a tall blond chap of about forty, with an open and winning smile, dressed with quiet elegance. Turning to his companion who had risen he merely said to me, 'A Swiss friend.'

While shaking hands with him I studied him with curiosity. Not very tall, broad-shouldered. His suit of beige tweed, though well cut, hung loose on him. He had very black hair, sparse, plastered down at the sides, a penetrating glance. I was struck by the colour of his face: a dark yellow verging on brown and, particularly, by his extreme thinness, which pressed his skin against his prominent cheek-bones, and by his hollow cheeks. Large rings emphasised the brilliance of his eyes. The lips were discoloured. Obviously the man was ill, very ill.

We spontaneously adopted French as our common speech. The Italian lawyer spoke it with a Piedmontese accent. The Swiss had a very slight accent, a little harsh, which led me to think that he must come from Zurich or Constance.

During dinner I had a strange feeling that the Swiss's face was not unknown to me. Where had I seen it? When? How? Who was he? It was impossible to remember. The two men did not speak of themselves but questioned me a good deal about my present journalistic activities in Italy.

After the meal, back in the drawing room the conversation turned quite naturally towards current international politics, then we spoke of the recent World War. Presently we raised the question of Nazism and the Nazis. The Swiss spoke little, but what he said was intelligent, without passion, well informed. At a remark which I made about the S.S. which showed that I was greatly interested in the strange Black Order, he said abruptly, fixing an intent look upon me, 'For what secret service do you work?'

I burst into ringing laughter. It was not the first time this question had been put to me. I explained my previous studies, how I had entered into international journalism which had led me to follow closely the various political trials of recent years, to consult archives, to become a historian of the modern period, and so to seek out witnesses and actors in the Second World War, to meet occasionally everywhere a quite large number of former Nazis, S.S., Fascists or collaborators. I mentioned names, facts, places, dates. . . . A little nervously I ended by saying, 'What I know of the Third Reich I learned in this way. I don't work for any secret service, not even for French Intelligence. Contemporary history excites me and my trade of journalist helps me a good deal to acquire acquaintances, a vantage point, that's all.'

The Swiss, who listened attentively without taking his eyes off me, then said, 'In these circumstances I'm surprised you haven't recognised me.' He added immediately, 'My name is Walter

Schellenberg. I was head of the German Secret Service, the S.D.[1] if you prefer.'

I was dumb with surprise. Schellenberg! How should I have recognised him? His face had changed considerably since 1945. He resembled none of his photographs. My surprise was great. It was not the first time that fate had arranged for me this kind of meeting, but today my 'captive' was of remarkable size. A 'war criminal', a high dignitary of the S.S. was before me. I had just dined with him . . . a strange situation.

Schellenberg explained to me that in the last days of the war, at the beginning of May 1945, he left Himmler in Northern Germany,[2] to undertake a diplomatic mission to Stockholm with the intention of negotiating the surrender of the German forces stationed in Norway and their internment in Sweden. On May 10th the Swedish authorities placed him under house arrest. He then began his Memoirs which might serve for his defence if the victors did not delay their demand for his extradition. At the beginning of June he was transferred to Germany to the British zone of occupation; then to England, to Richmond Park near London, in the Intelligence Service's special prison: the London Cage of Kensington. There he was questioned for weeks by a commission of specialists in secret service matters.[3]

Towards the end of 1945 Schellenberg was taken back to Germany and incarcerated first in the prison at Landsberg, then in that at Nuremberg. He was to testify at various trials before being tried himself and sentenced to six years' confinement on April 14th 1949.

Two years later Schellenberg was released for reasons of health. 'I've got cancer,' he explained to me without apparent emotion. He first settled in Switzerland with the object of undergoing treatment, but the Confederation regarded him as undesirable and expelled him.

I was still under the impact of surprise and listened absently. Schellenberg went on, 'I came to Italy. I found some old friends and settled here in Pallanza. My health requires a good deal of attention and regular treatments at Milan. Very soon I am going to Turin to consult an eminent cancer specialist.'

Schellenberg died a few weeks later. He was buried on April 2nd 1952 in the public cemetery of Turin (*3ᵈ Ampliamento, Campo Est*). There he still lies but today no stone records the identity of the occupant of the *Fossa no. 1763*, deserted, covered with beaten earth.[4]

I studied Schellenberg whilst he talked. A flood of very varied thoughts overwhelmed me.

They had taken an oath to Adolf Hitler. On the dull silver of their belts was engraved the device the Führer had given them, 'Our Honour is called Fidelity'. They wore a black uniform. The white letters S.S. were their emblem. On their flat caps they displayed the badge of the Death's Head. They belonged to an élite unit, barred to the great majority. They knew that they aroused disquiet. They were proud of it. Their chief, Himmler, said, 'I know that people in Germany are uneasy at the mere sight of your black uniform. We understand that and expect in no wise to be loved.' They had the feeling of belonging to a kind of religious sect, 'the Black Order', whose existence rested on foundations and special methods which must remain secret. They did not consider themselves like others. They were the terrors of a nation over which they had spread an invisible net. They became the terrors of occupied European nations which they endeavoured to reduce to slavery. They murdered millions of human beings—men, women, the old and children—with no other motive than one founded on a racial ideology. They aroused the horror of the entire world when their crimes were revealed, when the walls fell which had been meant to enclose hermetically from inquisitive eyes the secret empire of Himmler, the Grand Inquisitor of Nazism whom Hitler called his 'Ignatius Loyola'.

We have said that their organisation, the S.S. together with the Gestapo and the S.D. (secret police and security service), were condemned as 'criminal' by the international Military Tribunal at Nuremberg. Any person belonging to one organisation or the other was declared a 'criminal', the task being left to various courts, after examining the facts, to fix the degree of criminality of each of the accused.

'The Allies' verdict sinned by omission,' rightly wrote the German historian Heinz Höhne. 'It did not explain how, in one night, a million individuals became murderers, nor whence the S.S. derived their power to transform the racial hallucination of the National Socialist regime into a sinister reality.'

Even today the stature of these black men takes on the aspect of a frightening legend, their look and expression those of terrifying masks.

I had there before me one of those S.S., one of those 'war criminals', and not just any of them: the Brigadeführer (General of Division). Walter Schellenberg, the S.S. chief who, with Heydrich, achieved the swiftest and most brilliant career within the Black Order.

I had the impression of watching a film run backwards; Schellenberg at Nuremberg, in the witness box or the dock . . . Schellenberg during the winter of 1944–45 negotiating secretly in Himmler's name with Count Bernadotte . . . Schellenberg himself arresting Admiral Canaris on July 22nd 1944 . . . Schellenberg establishing secret contact with Allen Dulles in Switzerland . . . Schellenberg having millions of bogus pounds sterling forged . . . Schellenberg causing the members of the Red Orchestra to be tracked down . . . Schellenberg himself dismantling the Soviet espionage network of the Vietinghoff brothers . . . Schellenberg attempting to kidnap the Duke of Windsor in Portugal . . . Schellenberg personally kidnapping the two officers of the British Intelligence Service at Venlo . . . Schellenberg involved in the Tukhachevsky affair . . . and all that I didn't know then!

It was enough to bowl you over. By questioning this important witness, this 'survivor', was I going at last to penetrate the mysterious S.S. secret service, more mysterious than any other Intelligence service, which had fascinated me for several years?

It was late. Schellenberg indicated his wish to retire. I asked him if he would agree to a talk with me next day about his past. He did, and left. I remained a few minutes longer with my host who, spontaneously, cordially exceeding my hopes, suggested that I stay several days in Schellenberg's company, he himself having to be in Milan next morning. I warmly thanked him, having decided to obtain several days' 'holiday' from my newspaper. I was in fact to remain nearly a week.

Alone in my room, I meditated on my unexpected encounter. This man with an unusually frank expression, with refined and captivating manners, was he the same as the 'cultured assassin', the 'sadistic gentleman' of whom Gisevius spoke?

The 'Benjamin' of the S.S. chiefs, as Himmler, whose favourite he was, termed him, had been one of the most eminent personalities of the National Socialist regime, although his activity had been firmly contained within the shadows of the secret service. I did not for an instant doubt that his brilliant career, to have been achieved essentially during the war in the very special domain of a totalitarian state's Intelligence service, must have been the fruit of an exceptional natural endowment. Neither did I doubt that he must have been gifted with a cunning sufficient to have in masterly manner avoided paying the totalitarian state the tribute which in principle it exacts of its servants and to have in a not less masterly way navigated from tribunal to tribunal at Nuremberg, sometimes as witness, sometimes as defendant, and only have collected (at what price?) a short term in prison.

The Allies, the English in particular, had been indulgent to Walter Schellenberg. Doubtless they thus rewarded him for the information he was able to give about Nazism, its chiefs and accomplices in the world, during the long years passed in the hands of the British authorities; information certainly of the first order, coming from a man who had played an essential role in the conduct of the S.S.'s secret war operations.

In bed, unable to sleep, my thoughts went back to Nuremberg, to the session of the International Military Tribunal of Friday January 4th 1946. I remembered the essence of it. Here is the exact text [5]:

THE PRESIDENT: Your name is Walter Schellenberg?

SCHELLENBERG: My name is Walter Schellenberg.

THE PRESIDENT: Will you repeat this oath: 'I swear before Almighty God to tell the truth, the whole truth and nothing but the truth.' [The witness repeats the oath.]

COLONEL AMEN (Assistant American Prosecutor): Will you speak slowly and leave a space between the questions and the answers. Where were you born?

SCHELLENBERG: At Sarrebrück.

COLONEL AMEN: How old are you?

SCHELLENBERG: Thirty-five.

COLONEL AMEN: Were you a member of the N.S.D.A.P. [the Nazi Party]?

SCHELLENBERG: Yes.

COLONEL AMEN: And of the S.S.?

SCHELLENBERG: Yes, also of the S.S.

COLONEL AMEN: And of the Waffen-S.S.?

SCHELLENBERG: And likewise of the Waffen-S.S.

COLONEL AMEN: And of the S.D.?

SCHELLENBERG: And of the S.D.

COLONEL AMEN: What was the highest position you occupied?

SCHELLENBERG: The highest post I held was that of S.S. Brigade-führer [General of Division].

COLONEL AMEN: You were the chief of Amt VI of the R.S.H.A.? [6]

SCHELLENBERG: I was chief of Amt VI and of the Military Bureau. [7]

COLONEL AMEN: For how long?

SCHELLENBERG: I was named interim chief of Amt VI in July 1941 and confirmed in June 1942.

COLONEL AMEN: Describe briefly the functions of Amt VI and of the R.S.H.A.

SCHELLENBERG: Amt VI of the R.S.H.A. was the political secret service of the Reich and in principle operated abroad.

The secret political service of the Reich had obsessed me for years. Chance and my obstinacy had enabled me to uncover not all of its activities but to penetrate some of its secrets. My luckiest encounter was that with Schellenberg; it was essential but we shall see that others less important were indispensable.

Let us return to Pallanza. On the Monday morning the sky cleared. The waters of Lake Maggiore were ruffled by a light wind. The sun was warm enough to allow us to walk in the garden. Schellenberg was wrapped up in a grey-blue cape. I questioned him cautiously; I did not want to be the inquisitor, still less the judge, I had to win his confidence. He was amiable, smiling and seemed to me happy to speak of his youth. He expressed himself with evident frankness, but I remained on my guard.

Born January 16th 1910 at Sarrebrück, he was the youngest of seven children who received a sound Christian education from their mother. The father, a piano maker, settled in 1923 in Luxembourg where Walter Schellenberg pursued his secondary studies in German and French till 1929; at the age of nineteen he entered the University of Bonn, where he studied medicine for two years, then branched off into law and political science. His studies completed, he had to go through a probationary period before being able to take up an appointment. His parents being in financial straits he asked for a scholarship from the German Government. This was the spring of 1933. Since January 30th Hitler had been in power. For this reason the professor entrusted with Schellenberg's case advised him, in order to obtain the scholarship, to enrol in the Nazi Party and also preferably in one of its organisations, the S.A. or S.S.[8] Until then Schellenberg, too busy with his studies, had been active in no political party. He decided to enrol in the National Socialist party.

'It was', declared Schellenberg, 'my financial difficulties that decided me to join the Party, though I cannot truthfully say that I took the decision reluctantly. It was obvious that a vigorous programme was necessary to palliate the worst social injustices of the

Weimar Republic, to obtain for Germany an equitable position amongst the nations and a revision of the Treaty of Versailles. It seemed to me fair that Germany should claim the rights for the attainment of which every sovereign nation, and France in particular, had always struggled.'

Schellenberg did not conceal his ambitious nature. Ideology took second place. This opportunist, emancipated from conventional ideas and methods, only thought of his career. He had the merit of frankness when he added, 'All the young people who enrolled in the party had obligations to join one of these formations. The S.S. was already considered an "élite" organisation. The black uniform of the Führer's special guard was of becoming elegance, and a number of my fellow students had joined. In the S.S. were to be found people "of the best kind" and to belong to it gave you considerable prestige, augmented by social advantages, whereas the rowdyism of the S.A. in the beer-halls was ill-seen. They were then considered the extreme elements of the Nazi movement, the most violent and fanatical. I don't deny that at the age of twenty-three the social prestige and also the attraction of a handsome uniform contributed to my choice.'

Like many young Germans of the time, Schellenberg would be loyal to National Socialism which offered him the chance of a lifetime. He would join the S.S. because he decided that the S.S. would be the greatest force of Nazism in the Third Reich. He said to me, 'Success is only attained by imagination.' But in truth he would never be an authentic Nazi, an S.S. fanatic. An accomplished actor, he would be able to acquire the confidence of Heydrich, of Himmler, even of Hitler, all three of whom praised his loyalty and his exceptional value. However, what is rare in so young a man, he would always keep a critical mind, an unfailing lucidity.

A year after his enrolment in the Nazi party and entry into the S.S., two professors at the University of Bonn spoke to him of the S.S. Secret Service, the S.D., and suggested that he enter it. He was twenty-four. He remarked, 'One would have said that, from my early youth, various influences played their part in contributing to propel me towards this particular activity, in the service of my country and my fellow-citizens.' He accepted the proposal of the two professors. He was going to enter a world where intelligence, imagination, conniving and competence play a greater part than force or mystique.

NOTES TO CHAPTER I

1. S. D. (*Sicherheitsdienst*) = Nazi Party's Security and Intelligence Service, staffed entirely by S.S.
2. Himmler, with several heads of the S.S., still hoped to play a role in the re-establishment of defeated Germany. He fled by road amongst millions of civilians and soldiers, hoping 'to offer his services' to Montgomery or Eisenhower himself . . . and not to be captured by 'anyone regardless'.
3. Colonel Scotland directed the *London Cage*. He was its absolute master. When I met him his white hair and pink cheeks made him look like a grandfather. I was told that he had a method all his own with his prisoners, wrapped in a paternal solicitude that clashed with his hard and perspicacious eyes. He was an extraordinary 'examining magistrate' and his confidences to me were very useful.
4. After the burial of Schellenberg his Italian friend had a white marble slab placed on his grave. It bore the inscription 'Walter Schellenberg, 1910–1952'. The slab has disappeared.
5. *T.M.I.* Vol. IV., pp. 386–7. (For initials, see Appendix III: Sources).
6. R.S.H.A. (*Reichssicherheitshauptamt*) = The high command of the Reich Security and Intelligence Service. See Appendix I: The Structure of the R.S.H.A.
7. The S.S. secret service comprised an Intelligence service inside Germany (S.D.—Inland, Amt III of the R.S.H.A.) and a foreign service (S.D.—Ausland, Amt VI of the R.S.H.A.). As to the Military Bureau of which Schellenberg speaks, it refers to the Abwehr (Military Intelligence Service headed from 1935 to 1944 by Admiral Canaris) which was absorbed by the S.D. in the spring of 1944.
8. S.A. (*Sturmabteilung*) = Storm-troopers. S.S. (*Schutzstaffel*) = Security forces. These two organisations were of unequal power in the bosom of the party, which was originally only a party amongst others. When Hitler came to power he would transform it.

2

The Real Boss: Heydrich

To talk of the S.S. secret service is to talk of Heydrich. The name of Heydrich is indissolubly linked with that of the S.S. secret service. One cannot be evoked without the other.

Let us go back three years before Schellenberg's entry into the S.S. On June 14th 1931, on a little farm at Waltrudering, fifteen kilometres from Munich, two men met for the first time. One, aged thirty, was short, dark, narrow-shouldered. The face seen from the front was flabby and nervous. The upper lip, high and over-hanging, was in contrast with the mouth in general, somewhat oblique in relation to the line of the eyes. The expression was attentive and cold. Behind the eyeglasses the look was slightly ironic and impenetrable. This was Heinrich Himmler, head of the S.S. for the Reich, who was resting on this little agricultural holding where his wife, Marga, reared a hundred fowls. The other, aged twenty-seven, was tall, very tall, very thin, very blond. His face was triangular in shape, with sharp features. It had a predatory nose, a large mouth with thick cruel lips. The look, blue and hard, was serious, almost grave, expressing a tense, inflexible, realistic will, devoid of any spiritual element. 'Real wolf's eyes,' wrote Himmler. 'His attitude was that of a "block of polished steel", within which neither ideologies nor emotions had any part.' Sentiments, convictions, human beings and whole peoples were only regarded as means, instruments whose use was a matter for determination. This was Reinhard Heydrich, an unknown whose friend and colleague in the S.S., Friedrich Karl, Baron von Eberstein, had sent to Himmler 'to find him a job'.

The Black Corps, so named by Himmler himself, was still, in 1931, only a small organisation within the Nazi Party, launched on a struggle for power which would not be reached until eighteen months later. The strength of the S.S. did not exceed ten thousand men in the whole of Germany. What was this beside the hundreds of thousands of Röhm's S.A. But already at this period of time the brown S.A. swamp gave out an odour of crime, blackmail, blind force, drunkenness, homosexual eroticism, while—even outside the Nazi Party—the S.S. was beginning to be considered a small army of puritans who were proposing one day to settle accounts with the group of S.A. chiefs 'unworthy of the National-Socialist revolution of the Führer, Adolf Hitler'.

Suffering slightly from cramps in the stomach Himmler had at first put off the arrival at Munich of Eberstein's protégé. He gave his health as an excuse. In fact he felt a sense of inferiority towards this career officer whom he, moreover, believed to be a member of the all-powerful Intelligence Service of the Navy (a mistaken supposition, Heydrich having belonged to the Communications Service). Yielding, however, to the solicitation of the baron, he agreed to summon the young Heydrich to Waltrudering. The latter described the meeting to his wife, Lina.

Over-awed by his interlocutor's stature, Himmler, stammering, decided to test him. He said, 'I want to create a Security and Information Service in the S.S. I need a specialist. If you believe yourself to be capable of running it, explain to me on paper how you propose to set about it. I will give you twenty minutes.'

Heydrich, surprised, had some ideas in this field, but his knowledge was limited. However, it considerably exceeded Himmler's. In half an hour Heydrich sketched a picture of what a real secret service could be within the National Socialist party under the direction of the S.S. Himmler was deeply impressed. Heydrich was the man he needed. He was fascinated. All the more so as, ironically, he typified the Nordic ideal of race so dear to Himmler but which he himself lacked. The Reichsführer's decision was immediate: Heydrich was entrusted with the creation and direction of the new organism.

So was born the S.S. Intelligence Service. On July 14th 1931 Heydrich was inscribed in the Black Order[1] and took the oath of fidelity to the Führer Adolf Hitler.

This first meeting, outwardly unimportant, was to have atrocious consequences for the history of Europe during the eleven subsequent years. In an hour the actual directive team of the S.S. was formed. The demoniac couple was united for the worst. The Grand Inquisitor had found his devil Archangel.

Reinhard Tristan Engen Heydrich was born on March 7th 1904 at 20 Gutchenstrasse, Halle in Saxony. His father, Bruno, was director of the Conservatory of Music and a composer of operas.

His mother, Elizabeth Maria Anna Amalie Krantz, was the daughter of a professor at Dresden. As with Adolf Hitler, Heydrich's origins were very troublesome: it seems that his maternal grandmother was Jewish and called Sarah.

Reinhard Heydrich did extremely well in his studies. Not only was he almost a musical prodigy, but he possessed intellectual powers well above the average; he was no less apt at sports: tennis, swimming, sailing. At the age of eleven he displayed exceptional aptitude for fencing. He became one of the most formidable swordsmen in Germany. At one moment he thought of participating in the Olympic Games in Berlin in 1936.

The internecine war which ravaged his country after the defeat of 1918 perturbed Heydrich, brought up by his parents and teachers in a fiercely nationalistic spirit. At sixteen he enrolled in the Maercker Free Corps as 'despatch carrier'. Later he became a volunteer in the Halle Free Corps. However, his intellectual and sporting activities did not suffer. At eighteen he passed his Abitur (college entrance). In the late spring of 1922 he left Halle for Kiel as a candidate for entrance into the Navy. Thanks to his exceptional gifts, his acute mathematical sense, the technical side of his studies was relatively easy and life in the open air suited him perfectly.

After a short time Heydrich embarked on the old cruiser *Berlin*, which served as a training school for officer candidates. He there quickly caught the attention of the Second in Command, a Frigate Captain called Wilhelm Canaris, future Chief of Intelligence of the German Army (Abwehr), one of the most mysterious people in history. Heydrich remained under his orders from 1922 to 1924. He was then made an Ensign Second Class. He successfully passed his examinations in English, French and Russian. Like many of his companions he showed considerable interest in pretty girls. His almost perfect Nordic type brought him numerous successes. In July 1928 he sailed as radio officer and was at the same time promoted to Lieutenant. Finally, in 1930, he became a member of the staff of the Admiral commanding at Kiel, in the capacity of Communications Officer in the Intelligence Service.

Heydrich was never to be an Admiral: who knows, he might have become a Grand Admiral? Fate decided otherwise. In April 1931, at twenty-seven, his naval career was abruptly and finally interrupted. He was expelled from the navy for 'conduct unbecoming': the daughter of a director of naval construction of the I.G. Farben at Kiel—an intimate friend of Grand Admiral Raeder—declared herself to be pregnant by Heydrich. The latter refused to admit it. Since December 24th 1930, he had been engaged to a beautiful blonde of nineteen, a last-year student at the Girls' Secondary School at Kiel, Lina Mathilde von Osten, whom he intended to marry. A military court, under pressure from the Grand Admiral, returned him to civil life.

Out of work, spurred on by Lina, a fanatical Nazi,[2] he met Himmler on June 14th 1931, two months after having suffered an 'affront' he would never forget.

Perfect technocrat prematurely, having but one idea, power for power's sake, Heydrich would ascend all the rungs of the S.S. hierarchy at dizzy speed. On August 10th 1931 he was appointed Sturmführer (Second Lieutenant), four months later Hauptsturm-führer (Captain, the rank he held in the Navy), twenty days later he was promoted to Sturmbannführer (Battalion Commander). At twenty-nine, on March 21st 1933, he would be S.S. Oberführer (General).

Throughout our conversations at Pallanza, Schellenberg spoke increasingly of Heydrich. It was plain that Himmler's formidable assistant fascinated him, was graven deep on his memory. One evening, when the sun before disappearing still illuminated the topmost peaks of the Alps, we were on the terrace waiting for the dinner hour. I could barely distinguish his face when he suddenly let himself go in confidences about his former chief.

With a sort of retrospective fear in his voice, he said:[3] 'Heydrich was a cold-blooded criminal. He had a reptile's gaze. He froze me. I knew the deadly poison in him. I have never met a similar being. His power of fascination—in altogether a different style from Hitler's —was demoniacal.'

I remarked that the word 'demoniacal' did not seem to me appropriate since one could not give a metaphysical character to his profoundly realistic will to power, free from any ideological element.

We went in to the dining room. On the threshold of the french window Schellenberg turned and looked at me intently. An ironic gleam shone in his veiled glance. My remark amused him. I felt that he was on the verge of a confidence. In fact he said, 'Heydrich's personality had certain obscure streaks. Deep down in him a certain complexity always troubled me. His cynicism seemed to me a sign of weakness, of a kind of vulnerability. His hardness and inflexi-bility were caused, as was often said, by his inclination to sadistic cruelty. There was also something else: an inner disturbance (which Himmler revealed to me after Heydrich's death, and which Admiral Canaris confirmed), set up by his Jewish origins—his maternal grandmother Sarah—and his ambition committed openly to the doctrine of an Aryan élite.'

'Did Himmler give you any proof of the Jewish origin?'

'No, but he must have had it. Canaris too, it would seem. One day Himmler said to me, "Heydrich suffers intensely and will never reach calm and relaxation. Something continuously returns to torture him. I often talked with him and tried to help him. In spite of my convictions I tried to make him believe that it was possible to overcome partly Jewish blood thanks to the superiority of the German strain, and I cited his own example . . . At the moment he seemed grateful for my help and seemed relieved, but never for long." I was quite surprised by these remarks of the Reichsführer S.S.'

'Where do you place Heydrich in relation to the other National Socialist leaders?'

Until now Schellenberg had not shown me the manuscript of his Memoirs, on which I knew he had been working every afternoon. Without answering my question he went to his room and brought back a cardboard folder, which he put on the table where we were waiting for a steaming *minestrone*. Resuming his place he said, 'I'll read you what I say on that subject.'

While the domestic was serving the Italian national soup Schellenberg read me the typewritten sheets.

'Heydrich constituted the hidden pivot around which the Nazi regime turned. The evolution of an entire nation was indirectly determined by his powerful character. He was very much superior to all his political colleagues and controlled them as he controlled the vast organisation of S.D. Intelligence. . . . Heydrich had an incredibly penetrating insight into the moral, professional and political weaknesses of his fellows and had the gift of grasping in its entirety a political situation. His unequalled intelligence was allied to the instinct of a bird of prey, always on the alert and ready, in face of danger, to act rapidly and ruthlessly. He adopted and exploited the solutions which his instinct sugested to him as useful, then, if necessary, abandoned them with an equal alacrity. Anything which seemed to him superfluous, or might present some danger, was set aside. He was extraordinarily ambitious. It seemed as if, in a band of wolves, he would always be the strongest and take command. He had to be the first, the best in everything, and by whatever means, deceit, perfidy, violence, having no pangs of conscience and served by an icy intelligence he could press injustice to the most extreme cruelty. . . .'

Let us go back to Heydrich's biography. On October 5th 1931 he was incorporated in the General Staff of the S.S. at Munich. After a short stay at the Brown House (seat of the Nazi Party) he established himself with three colleagues in a two-room flat on the fourth floor of 23 Türkenstrasse. Frau Heydrich acted as secretary.

Heydrich's ambitions were unlimited. From the end of 1931 it was certain that, sooner or later, Hitler would come to power. There was no fanaticism in this conviction but a cold assessment of political evolution in Germany at this time. He wanted his piece of the cake, the largest possible. This was why he would not only create the Secret Service organisation asked for by Himmler, but deliberately make it 'his thing', partly unknown to his chief. Already he envisaged in a future more or less distant the development of this organisation to an extent that would enable it to duplicate and, if necessary, replace the whole apparatus of Government. He thus initiated a state within the state a year before Hitler came to power.

The S.S. secret service would of course depend on Himmler; nevertheless he would enjoy an autonomy which would from the start put him in charge of the inner working of the S.S. It would be a parallel S.S. organisation, installed throughout the country, which Heydrich would set up and wholly dominate.

He left to others the ideological debates on national socialism, the ritual researches to serve the Myth of Blood so dear to Himmler, and even the foundation of the specifically S.S. Military Units (Waffen S.S.). Politician above everything, careful of efficiency, Heydrich wanted the S.S. to be ready at any instant to exercise power. This was why they had to have in their hands all the security services: (secret, criminal, public order, frontiers, etc.) and Intelligence (internal and external). But at this period the effectives of the S.S. were few and, more important, the intellectual quality of the average S.S. member was low. So for his secret service he would recruit everywhere, but especially in the universities, young people intellectually gifted and capable of executing his orders with energy, audacity and efficiency. It was thus that he little by little surrounded himself with young jurists like Walter Schellenberg, Hermann Behrends, Heinz Jost and Helmut Knochen; with brilliant economists like Otto Ohlendorf, Franz Six and Herbert Mehlhorn;

engineers like Dr. Wilhelm Albert and Dr. Otto Skorzeny; journalists like Gunther d'Alquen, etc. In a few years the S.S. secret service
would become the meeting place of the young élite of national socialism. This influx of intellectuals pleased Heydrich: the instrument
was being forged by his hands. He was to make a key force of it.
The tentacles of the black octopus would penetrate into the narrow-
est recesses of German society.

Heydrich's police concept was limitless. For him the police and
the political secret service were not simple defensive organisations,
guarantors of the security of the state, but, on the contrary, offensive
instruments which, moreover, were charged with educating the
people and ridding the nation of all ideas held to be dangerous or
unsound.

Himmler himself defined the function of the S.S. secret service
as follows: 'The S.D. unmasks the adversaries of National Socialist
ideas and thus orients the activity of the police. The executive side
is reserved exclusively and strictly for the police. Little inclined to
see themselves restricted to the role of assistants to the Gestapo, the
heads of the S.D. organisation assume a higher objective: the S.D.
will be a police of the mind, the instrument for measuring and
controlling thought.'

Without doubt the S.S. secret service would be that, but it would
be a good deal else.

During the year 1932, before Hitler came to power, the S.S.
secret service only grew slowly. Heydrich had set up his office at
4 Zuccalisstrasse in Munich. His range of action was virtually
limited to Bavaria. At Berlin the S.D. was only a little shop,
installed at 16 Eichenallee in a large, dilapidated old building
surrounded by trees and vast lawns. The head was a former Bavarian
detective called Kublinsky, of Russo-Polish origin. He was a little
under forty, but looked much more. Indisputably unattractive,
flabby, corpulent, with pink face and a soft skin like a woman's,
this homosexual was feared and detested by the dozen young
S.S. who made up the personnel of the S.D. in the German
capital.

Amongst these young S.S. figured the third young man who
would later play a decisive part at the side of Heydrich and Schellenberg in the evolution of the S.S. secret service: Alfred Naujocks. We
should remember his name. He was an 'old' Nazi militant, a Nazi
from the beginning, although he was only twenty-six. Son of a Kiel
grocer, Naujocks enrolled in the National Socialist party at the age

of fifteen, under the influence of a certain Gröthe. For three or four years he took part in many street battles. His enthusiasm for the Party increased continuously. In contrast with Schellenberg he was a fanatic and a specialist in violence. He was a welder in a locomotive factory and was drawn to Berlin which he did not know. At the end of the winter 1931/32 he left Kiel for the capital where Gröthe was inscribed in the S.D. The two friends were joyously re-united and Gröthe enlisted Naujocks on his side.

Alfred Naujocks has recounted that when he was introduced to Kublinsky the latter addressed him as follows: 'Our organisation is small but of extreme importance for the Party. You should not regard this as any old job. You must dedicate yourself to it entirely. And be warned that no one works here to make money. Our means do not allow us to pay salaries equivalent to those of a commercial business. You will only earn ninety marks a month, of which fifteen will be deducted for your meals. You will pay for your own uniform and in addition contribute to the Party chest. You see that here you will never get rich.'

After a short pause Kublinsky added, 'But we expect to grow very soon, and positions of trust await those who attract attention by their experience and good conduct. If you continue to work for the Party as you have in the past in your section of the N.S.D.A.P. I am sure that in the end you will not regret it. Without being tight-fisted we are at the moment constrained to be somewhat prudent.'

Kublinsky then looked Naujocks straight in the eyes and said, 'I must make you understand this: here I am the boss, responsible for all your acts and I have the right to require of you absolute and unquestioning obedience. You will perhaps find certain rules irritating, but they are necessary. Never forget this. I will add a word: if at this moment you feel some hesitation in binding yourself you had better leave at once, since in the future you will not be free to do so. Once involved in our kind of work you will be here for good, once and for all. Have I made myself clear? I repeat: once and for all . . . One does not leave the service of the S.D. alive.'

In fact one could not be clearer.

It was in the Eichenallee that the card-index of the secret service was born. Certain of the S.S. were delegated to the voluminous classification by card of the members of the Party. Others were busy establishing files on the Communists, the Social-democrats, the Liberals—all the opponents of National Socialism—individuals suspected of being in the service of foreigners, etc. Heydrich wanted to know everything, all that concerned their characters and weaknesses, their idiosyncrasies and habits, their past, scandals in which they had been involved, their aspirations, morals, their emotional and family relations, the places they frequented, the earnings and expenditures of individuals and of industrial and commercial firms, the movements of bank deposits, in short everything that could be used, in one way or another, against an individual, an institution or a group. All would be patiently and carefully assembled in a card-index. Such an instrument would become extremely redoubtable when the National Socialists took power on January 30th 1933.

NOTES TO CHAPTER 2

1. Card No. 10 120 in the S.S.
2. Lina Mathilde von Osten was enrolled in the N.S.D.A.P., Card No. 1 201 380.
3. At the time, 1952, I published part of my conversations with Schellenberg in *Le Phare* of Brussels, of which I had been since 1946 the Paris correspondent.

3

The S.S. Chiefs
Forgotten in Munich

1933. Hitler was in power. The black, white and red flag with the swastika floated above the Third Reich.

Goering had created the Gestapo in Prussia. Goebbels had taken the press and radio in hand. Röhm and his S.A. were masters of the streets. The Nazis were triumphant, acting, achieving, seizing everything within their reach. The new lords were called Goering, Goebbels, Röhm, Hess, Rosenberg, Ley, Frick, etc. They were the Party. They were the State.

But there were also those who seemed to be left out of the account; these were Heinrich Himmler and Reinhard Heydrich. They dreamed, planned and envisaged. They dreamed of an S.S. state; they planned to take over the whole police and Intelligence service; they envisaged methods of leaving Munich and joining the others in Berlin. For the two chiefs of the Black Order were still in Munich. They shared in the great joy but deep down they were disappointed, worse, embittered. The Führer in Berlin seemed to have forgotten 'Herr Himmler' and his ambitious assistant 'Herr Heydrich'. The men in black were not important enough to take part in dividing the cake.

For the moment they continued to discharge as best they could their police functions in Bavaria, but their gaze was fixed on the capital where stood, like a wall between them and their ambitions, Hermann Goering. The 'jolly' Goering had no intention of letting himself be stripped of his power by that 'little pawn Himmler' whom he despised. What is more, Goering had his eye on the mastery of the whole police apparatus throughout all German territory. Prussia was not enough for 'Hitler's Paladin'.

At the head of the Gestapo, Goering was solidly supported by a young bureaucrat, not a Nazi, of the Prussian Ministry of Police:

Rudolf Diels, whose acquaintance Goering had made in 1932. According to the testimony of S.S. Wilhelm Höttl, alias Walter Hagen: 'Thanks to his extraordinary abilities as an administrative technician, thanks also to the connections procured for him by his capacity as a member of an influential student body, Diels had succeeded very young—he was barely thirty-two—in carving out a very strong position before National Socialism's seizure of power.'

Elegant but sinister, an intriguer, watchful, perspicacious, without convictions, always ready to flatter the more powerful, unscrupulous, Rudolf Diels had passed from the extreme right to Socialism, then turned his coat when he sensed the Nazi wind blowing in the direction of power. He was now Goering's right hand; he had meantime married his cousin Else, who, by a first marriage, had been the wife of Goering's brother.

A detail of some importance: 'As early as 1932,' explained Wilhelm Höttl, 'Diels had got hold of the voluminous secret archives of the Prussian State Police concerning political personalities. And there the National Socialist leaders, to the extent that came within the scope of the Prussian State Police, were found described in all their aspects. All National Socialists, of however small importance, who had lived for any time in Berlin, had their card. The police had good eyes, so to speak, and nothing remained hidden from them down to the most intimate personal details.'

Moreover, his relation with the corrupt circles of Berlin had enabled Diels to buy the intimate letters of Röhm, in which the chief of staff of the S.A. revealed openly his homosexual tastes. He showed them to Goering, along with a certain number of other ultra-secret files containing details capable of disgracing his adversaries whether Nazi or anti-Nazi. Goering appreciated these revelations at their true value. Rudolf Diels was indispensable to the new master of the Prussian police.

In Berlin the Reichsführer S.S. was represented by a Prussian, S.S. General Kurt Daluege,[1] who commanded the S.S. of the capital in his name. But Daluege more and more ignored Himmler, the pale and diligent factotum of the Führer, confined to Munich. He had a good deal of ambition and dreamed of himself becoming the supreme head of the S.S. Protected by Hermann Goering, Daluege gained more important functions. He was named Commissioner of State in the Prussian Government with the rank of Lieutenant-General of the Police. As Heinz Höhne noted perceptively, 'Daluege, aware that he was, after Napoleon, the youngest general in history, did not henceforth see any valid reason to consider himself Himmler's subordinate. War was declared between the two men.'

The Reichsführer S.S. wanted to bring Daluege to his senses and to obedience. He specially despatched his dear Heydrich, whom he had made a general, to the 'rebel' with the mission to inform himself of the dealings which accounted for the attitude of his subordinate in Berlin. Heydrich proceeded to the capital, but the all-powerful Daluege did not even deign to receive Himmler's emissary. Heydrich insisted, but in vain. Worse, Goering's police, sent by Rudolf Diels, gave him clearly to understand that his presence was undesirable. Furiously angry, Heydrich returned to Munich. The two colleagues had to yield to the evidence: Goering was stronger than they.

To force the barriers, to open the road to Berlin, it would be necessary to invoke the omnipotence of Hitler himself, so Himmler multiplied his opportunities to call himself to the attention of his beloved Führer, to prove to him how wrong he was to take so little notice of him in distributing the key posts in the state.

At the beginning of March 1933, a few days after the Reichstag fire, Himmler 'discovered' two 'plots' against Hitler. From the first Himmler, as Prefect of Police for Bavaria, had placed the Count Arco-Valley in preventive arrest, the same man who in 1922 the student Himmler had wanted to release from prison where he was confined for the murder of the Bavarian Prime Minister, Eisner. This plot was, of course, imaginary. The second was no less so. Himmler 'discovered' that 'three Soviet agents' had hidden grenades near the monument to Richard Wagner, at a spot where Hitler's car passed every day.

Of course Himmler did not spare any efforts to achieve the greatest possible publicity in the press for these alleged crimes and his vigilance. He even inserted a warning: 'Information from Swiss sources leads us to fear French attempts on the Chancellor of the Reich and other eminent persons.' Himmler knew that he was touching a sensitive cord. At this period Hitler lived in constant fear of being murdered.

Himmler did not quite attain his object: to have control of the whole of the Reich police. On March 17th Hitler only asked his 'faithful Heinrich' to organise a special guard from the S.S. for his personal security, the command of which would be entrusted to the S.S. General Joseph 'Sepp' Dietrich.[2] The latter collected one hundred and twenty picked men, and on September 3rd 1933, during the Party congress at Nuremberg, the Chancellor christened his bodyguard *Leibstandarte S.S. Adolf Hitler*. The following November 9th, the tenth anniversary of the abortive putsch, the men of the *Leibstandarte* took their oath to Hitler. On this occasion the latter said to the hundred and twenty assembled S.S., 'I ask you to give your life as did the sixteen who fell at this place in 1925. For you nothing else should count in life but fidelity . . .'

'Sepp' Dietrich, just like Daluege, showed the greatest independence in regard to Reichsführer S.S. Heinrich Himmler.

At the beginning of the summer of 1933 Heydrich gained a point against his Berlin adversaries. One day when he went to the capital to inspect the S.D. service installed in the Eichenallee, he was met at the station at 3.45 in the afternoon by an S.S. chauffeur he did not know. He was young, small, nervous, with black eyes which betrayed considerable energy. While cautiously making his way through the intense traffic of Berlin the chauffeur allowed himself the privilege of asking his distinguished chief sitting in the back seat if he had had a good journey. The good-natured answer encouraged and emboldened him: 'I think you lived at Kiel for several years, General; I hope you liked the city—I was born there.'

'What's your name?'

'Alfred Naujocks.'

During the following twenty minutes they talked of people they knew, of places familiar to them, so much and so well that when the car stopped before the steps of the S.D. administration building a kind of familiarity had been established between them. The head of the office, Kublinsky, a big smile on his lips, waited for them at the front door.

When, during the dinner which he served, Naujocks again saw Heydrich and Kublinsky, he realised that their meeting had been stormy. The S.S. general, all sweetness, strongly urged Kublinsky, more nervous than ever, to take a holiday. 'You're working too hard, my dear fellow, you don't look well,' he said with false solicitude.

A little before midnight Naujocks again became chauffeur. This time Heydrich sat in front with him and asked, after the Buick had left the Eichenallee, 'Do you like your work here?'

Naujocks knew that he was being sounded out, but he affected to respond in a tone of deep sincerity. Rapidly he summed up his grievances in the form of naïve questions: 'Why don't they seem to have any confidence in us?' 'Why doesn't Kublinsky ever allow us to stick our noses out? If they think we don't deserve their confidence, why do they let us work in the S.S. secret service? After all, we're not criminals but loyal and faithful S.S. . . .'

Heydrich listened attentively. Naujocks made a discreet allusion to Kublinsky's special tastes, then suddenly dropped a bombshell by disclosing to Heydrich that ten days earlier Goering's assistant, Rudolf Diels, had come to dinner with Kublinsky. In acting as butler, serving them one dish after another, Naujocks had learned many things. In particular he had heard Kublinsky assure Diels of his entire devotion: he would regularly pass on to him all instructions he received from Munich, whether from Himmler or Heydrich.

Heydrich remained impassive but it was plain that the blow had struck home. The two S.S. separated with a handshake, a fact, thought Naujocks, of some importance.

A week went by then, without warning, a high officer of the S.D. arrived from Munich and was closeted for an hour with Kublinsky. When the latter emerged, the big man's face was disturbed and his hands were trembling. He had the look of a man hunted. He informed his staff that he was taking a holiday for an indefinite period and was led off by the S.S. man. He would never be seen again.

The next day Naujocks saw Kublinsky's successor arrive. It was Hermann Behrends. Born in 1907 at Wilhelmshaven, where his parents ran an inn, Hermann Behrends had joined the National Socialist Party and entered the S.S., where he had found his friend Heydrich, who recruited him into the S.D. We shall have frequent occasion to meet this man again; he was to discharge important functions in the S.S. secret service.[3]

Naujocks was the first to be summoned by Behrends to his office, which did not fail to rouse the curiosity of the staff. The interview was short. The new director informed him that Heydrich sent him his best wishes and ordered him to be promoted to chief of section, with a corresponding salary. In fact Naujocks became Behrends's personal assistant and his immediate task consisted of submitting a plan for the restructuring of the administration.

If Naujocks, in leaving Behrends's office, was dazed by the suddenness with which events had moved for him after his delation, in Munich Heydrich was delighted to have countered Diels by placing a sure friend at the head of the Berlin S.D. and to have discovered a young, intelligent, resourceful and unscrupulous S.S.

man. The trio Heydrich–Behrends–Naujocks would very soon become the principal axis of the S.S. secret service.

During the summer and autumn of 1933 Himmler and Heydrich remained confined to Bavaria. Heydrich intensified the work of the S.D., which now had a staff of a hundred in Munich. The two S.S. chiefs took over and demonstrated how they conceived the task of a Nazi police worthy of the name. 'Himmler', wrote Heinz Höhne, 'pursued his political opponents in the Party with the careful and cold tenacity of the bureaucrat, moderated the excesses of certain S.A. chiefs towards embarrassing and defenceless adversaries, arrogated to himself the exclusive privilege of deciding in the matter of the arrest of Catholic priests. Concurrently he built into the system the political reign of terror. He caused an enclosure to be laid out near Dachau round a group of concrete barracks and there collected the Communist and Social-Democrats arrested by his men. A new term was born: concentration camp. This term quickly became the symbol of Heinrich Himmler's political empire.'

The perfect organisation of Himmler's services drew the attention of all the German police. Amongst the most important personages in Himmler's entourage, Heydrich apart, may be named his aide-de-camp Karl Wolff, aged thirty-three, who was only a Captain in the S.S.,[4] Major Hermann Baron von Schade, who directed the 'Organisation' section; S.S. General Walter Darre, who was at the head of the Race and Population Service. More and more the general feeling grew that Himmler would sooner or later end up by imposing himself as the sole head of the Reich police. He did not conceal his intention. 'I want to put an end to the sixteen local police forces, reorganise the whole thing, create a simple Reich Police. Such a national police force is a State's best guarantee.' But Hitler, under Goering's influence, still did not budge.

Himmler and Heydrich were to find Wilhelm Frick, the Reich Minister of the Interior, an ally in their wish for expansion.[5] The reformer of the administration of the Reich, who wanted to carry centralisation to the limit, came into collision with the Prussian separatism of Goering. He needed accomplices. Himmler and Heydrich would take care of that. He summoned them to his assistance. The two confederates responded. With Frick's blessing they gradually absorbed the separate police forces of the German States. The *Länderpolizei* fell one after the other under the thumb of the S.S.[6]

In the autumn of 1933 Wilhelm Frick succeeded in convincing Hitler that the total centralisation and unification of the Reich were essential. Goering bowed to the Führer's decision. Himmler rejoiced. Involuntarily Goering would aid him to fulfil his designs.

Goering, the creator of the Gestapo, was uneasy. The growing agitation of the S.A., who spoke openly of starting a 'second revolution', threatened the established order. Röhm their chief, badgered Hitler; he wanted to incorporate the army into the S.A. Goering felt his power menaced. Röhm was a rival of great stature. Who knew what would happen if he took command of the army merged with the S.A.? Goering had need of allies to bar Röhm's path. Who? The S.S.? Why not? In Goering's mind Himmler was less dangerous than Röhm. One day he would learn his mistake.

A sensational stroke revealed the diabolic efficiency of Reinhard Heydrich. He suffered perhaps more even than Himmler from having been 'forgotten' at Munich. He dreamed of Berlin, of the capital where the new Government led by Hitler was in course of centralising the whole country. He dreamed in particular of uniting in his hands, under the theoretically supreme authority of Himmler, all the police powers and all political intelligence. He was impatient. He knew that he had first to eliminate Diels, a tough and ruthless antagonist. Two characters so similar in many respects, possessed of the same ambitions and striving for the same goal, were destined sooner or later to a violent collision.

To highlight the need for co-ordination of the police services under a single authority, Heydrich, as an expert in poisonous infection, drew attention to a so-called report by one of his S.D. agents revealing a 'Trotskyist plot' being woven—'unknown to Goering's Gestapo'—against Goering's own person! Even before the latter and Hitler had been informed, Himmler and Heydrich proceeded to make arrests and, of course, the 'plotters' made 'confessions'. Himmler and Heydrich used this pretext to entreat the Führer again to put all the police forces under the S.S. At the same time they demonstrated to Goering that the S.D. had saved his life while Diels's Gestapo were in total ignorance. They added, Heydrich's master-touch, that the S.D. had proofs of intrigue by Diels with Röhm, which was false.

Would Goering sack Diels? No. At the end of September 1933 he dismissed Diels but the same day appointed him Assistant Director of the Berlin police. Diels was not born yesterday. He clung to life and thought it prudent to leave Germany and retired to Bohemia.

To replace him in the Gestapo would Goering seek the good

offices of Himmler? Not at all. He appointed Paul Hinkler, a Nazi veteran, respected in the Party, a great friend of Wilhelm Kube.[7] But Paul Hinkler was a confirmed drinker. He had once been prosecuted for complicity in a murder case but acquitted for being in a state of intoxication.

In his new post Hinkler quickly added to his mistakes and blunders. The result was that he did not keep his job thirty days. Rudolf Diels, from his Bohemian forest, threatened painful disclosures and demanded a high price for his return to Germany. Goering submitted to his blackmail and reinstated Diels in his Gestapo post. Himmler and Heydrich did not cool down.

Then followed a tragi-comic incident.[8] Hinkler was afraid of being arrested by Diels's men and having an 'accident'. He spent his last night at 8 Prinz-Albrechtstrasse; namely the seat of the Gestapo. Naïveté? Drunkenness? No one knows. When Diels's police arrived to expel him from the premises, Hinkler took fright and, in his night-shirt, slipped out of the window into the garden. He ran to the adjacent Landtag, whose night watchman he knew, then, by way of the Potsdamerplatz, to the Tiergarten, where he made a ghostly appearance to the terror of a couple of lovers. In his anguish he approached the two young people and asked for a coin so as to be able to telephone. Frightened by the man in a nightshirt they got rid of him by generously giving him two. Hinkler wanted to summon his friend Wilhelm Kube to his assistance. He was unable to reach the nearest telephone booth: a police patrol arrested him. Despite his vehement protests he was conducted to the nearest police station. It was not easy to convince the good duty officer that he really had before him one of the high officials of the Gestapo. Here followed a series of telephone calls, the echoes of which reached Goering. It was this that saved Hinkler from a scandal.

Under constant pressure from Wilhelm Frick, Hitler finally decided on the incorporation of Prussia with the rest of the Reich. It was total unification. As a consequence Goering's Gestapo passed into the control of Himmler, who became Chief of the State Secret Police of the Third Reich.

On April 10th 1934, in Berlin, Goering assembled the members of the Gestapo in the presence of Himmler and Heydrich. He explained that all the Gestapo services would thenceforth be subordinated to Himmler, to whom he delegated his powers. He ordered his former subordinates to support their new chief loyally in the struggle he was conducting 'so courageously' against the enemies of the state.

Himmler in his turn protested his loyalty and gratitude: 'I shall always remain faithful to you,' he declared to Goering. 'You will never have anything to fear from me.'

Heydrich said nothing. He was satisfied. Had he not obtained the departure of Diels?[9]

During the Nuremberg trial in 1946, Goering stated to the Allied judges: 'At that period I did not expressly oppose the principle of surrendering the Gestapo to Himmler. It was disagreeable to me because I wanted to direct the police myself. But when the Führer asked me to agree, saying it was the right and necessary way to conduct more efficiently, throughout the whole extent of the Reich, the struggle against the enemies of the state, I placed the Gestapo in the hands of Himmler who put Heydrich at its head.'

Goering had, nevertheless, only a limited confidence in Himmler and Heydrich. So he at once set up a 'personal police', the *Landespolizeigruppe*, to assure his safety in case of trouble. This unit was stationed near Berlin at Lichterfelde, and consisted of more than a thousand men.

So one lived in the lofty spheres of the Third Reich. National Socialist Berlin strangely resembled Florence of the Medicis.

NOTES TO CHAPTER 3

1. Kurt Daluege, nicknamed *Dummi-Dummi* (imbecile in German) became chief of the Public Order Police (Orpo): *Ordnungspolizei*) in June 1939 and reached the rank of General in the S.S. (S.S. Obergruppenführer). After the assassination of Heydrich in Prague in June 1942 Daluege became unofficially Protector of Bohemia and Moravia. He was hanged by the Czechs in 1946.
2. Born in 1892, Joseph, called 'Sepp' Dietrich, held S.S. card No. 1 177, which constituted, so to speak, a title of nobility in the Black Order.
3. For his activities in Serbia in 1943, where Hermann Behrends was commanding officer of the S.S. and chief of police, he was handed over by the Allies to Jugoslavia in 1946. He was condemned to death and hanged. The records of his interrogations by the English and Americans in 1945–46 are very valuable to the historian. Behrends knew many things (*I.Z.M.*).
4. S.S. Captain Karl Wolff, card-holder No. 14 235 in the S.S., born in 1901, became in 1936 chief of staff to Reichsführer S.S. Heinrich Himmler. Appointed S.S. General and supreme commander of the

S.S. and police in Italy in September 1943, he negotiated the surrender, in April 1945, with Allen Dulles of the German armies in the Italian peninsula. Captured in May 1945, he was sentenced to fifteen years in prison, then liberated. The stenographic minutes of his trial provide a very important document for the understanding of the functioning of the S.S. organisation, the general activities of the S.S. and the psychology of the principal S.S. chiefs.

5. Wilhelm Frick, born in 1877, specialist in administration, only joined the N.S.D.A.P. officially in 1925. But already, during the Munich putsch of 1923 Frick, then an official in that city's police department, had taken sides with Hitler and the National Socialist cause. Elected a member of the Reichstag in 1924, he became Reichleiter in his capacity of head of the National Socialist group in that assembly. In January 1933 Frick became a member of Hitler's first cabinet as Reich Minister of the Interior. He occupied this important post until August 1943, when he was replaced by Reichsführer S.S. Himmler. He was then appointed Reich Protector for Bohemia and Moravia but Kurt Daluege, the vice-protector, was the real boss. Tried by the Allies as a war criminal, he was hanged at Nuremberg on October 16th 1946.

6. Himmler had himself named chief of the political police of Hamburg, of Mecklenburg-Schwerin and of Lübeck in November 1933; of Württemberg (December 12th 1933), of Baden (December 18th 1933), of Hesse (December 20th 1933), of Anhalt (December 20th 1933), of Bremen (December 3rd 1933), of Thuringia (December 28th 1933); finally, in January 1934, of Brunswick, Oldenburg and Saxony.

7. Wilhelm Kube, one of the most corrupt members of the Nazi party, former president of the National Socialist group in the Landtag of Prussia. During the war Gauleiter of White Ruthenia, he nevertheless took a stand against the S.S. by opposing the total liquidation of the Jews in his sector. On the night of September 22nd 1943 he was murdered by his young maidservant, an agent of the Russian resistance. Himmler exulted, 'Kube's death is a blessing to our country.'

8. Hinkler's melodramatic adventure was the subject of a long report to the Gestapo which has been discovered in the archives of the S.S. (*B.A.M.*).

9. Goering made Rudolf Diels security chief of the Cologne government. Diels was later made chief of the Hanover government, until Goering gave him the general management of German river navigation.

Diels drew attention to himself after the war when he published a pamphlet against Dr. Otto John: *The Otto John Case*, Göttingen, 1954.

It should be stressed that Goering rarely abandoned anyone who had at any time been one of his favourites. He displayed with respect to them a sort of 'fidelity complex' and considered himself their protector even when it was temporarily impossible for him entirely to neutralise their antagonists.

4

Heydrich's Machiavellian Game

Himmler and Heydrich moved house. They finally left Munich for Berlin. The two Rastignacs in black were going to have their revenge for having so long been kept from power. The redoubtable team had just attained its joint objective: the control of the political police of the Reich and of the Gestapo.

The Grand Inquisitor installed his S.S. general staff in the seat of the Gestapo itself, 8 Prinz-Albrechtstrasse, and the Archangel of Evil transferred to 103 Wilhelmstrasse, close by, the headquarters of the S.D. which officially became the Security Office of the Reichsführer S.S.[1] They were in the heart of Berlin's Government Quarter.

The power now held by the two S.S. chiefs was considerable. But they had no time to rub their hands and rejoice. Their task of maintaining order in the country was, from the day they took over, seriously threatened! Revolt was rumbling louder and louder in the ranks of the S.A.

What is there to say? The men in brown were discontented. The road on which Adolf Hitler had been proceeding for a year did not suit Ernst Röhm and his millions of men. They said, 'What's Adolf doing in the midst of these capitalists in morning coats and high hats, these monocled generals, these diplomatic barons, these insolent Junkers, these old conservative left-overs from the imperial regime?'

We must not forget that the S.A. were 'Left'. Many of them came over from Socialism and even from the banned Communist party. They were not all brutes, blackguards without belief or law, adventurers; a large part of them were genuine revolutionaries. For them the bourgeois world had died, definitely, on January 30th 1933. An irreversible break had to be made with all traditional values. Capitalism as an occupational system had to disappear. Socialism took precedence over nationalism.

The hostility to Hitler assumed explosive dimensions. 'Adolf is betraying us,' was the slogan running through the ranks of the S.A. Röhm had never concealed his intention to take over the army. He wanted, as we have said, the Reichswehr to be merged with the S.A. and with it form 'the great National Socialist army of the people'. The opponents of the idea said, 'Röhm is taking for his model Stalin, who has his Red Army; he wants his Brown Army'. Röhm despised the 'peacock army' and its leaders who thumbed their noses at the S.A. He defended with ferocity the idea of a national militia of which he would be the General in Chief.

It was not only a state of mind. Röhm commanded an army of five hundred thousand men, organised and quartered in barracks, in short five times as many as the existing Reichswehr. The nucleus of a general staff was made up of former officers of the First World War. Moreover it contained a gigantic reservoir of men with military training; three million S.A. could be mobilised at a moment's notice. Added to them, in June 1933, were a million 'Steel-Helmets' (the *Stahlhelm*) of whom 314 000 were ready on call.

Of course the Reichswehr took a poor view of this 'brown army'. Hitler inclined to a fusion but did not yet know in which direction. The generals of the 'old school' had not spoken their last word. One of them, the foremost man in the Reichswehr, Walther von Reichenau, an artillery general, a sporting type, a subtle politician capable of forgetting the sacrosanct principles of the Prussian military tradition if the need were felt, was chef de cabinet at the Ministry of National Defence. For him the matter was simple: the military faction of the S.A. should be absorbed into the Reichswehr. He manoeuvred in this direction. To circumvent Röhm it was better first to flatter his ambitions the more easily to get rid of him later.

But Röhm also knew how to manoeuvre. Appointed minister without portfolio on December 1st 1933, he did not stop pestering his 'old friend Adolf' to have the national defence placed in the charge of the S.A. Careful of the feelings of the military, of whom he had need in order to realise his programme of rearmament and expansion, while not wanting to disavow his friend Röhm, whose views on the subject he moreover shared, the Führer found a compromise. Von Blomberg, Minister of National Defence, and Röhm, chief of staff of the S.A., were obliged to sign a pact according to which the Reichswehr would be 'the only official armed organisation of the Third Reich': the S.A. obtained the monopoly of the pre- and post-military formations.

Hardly had the pact been signed at Röhm's headquarters after a champagne lunch; hardly had the officers of the Reichswehr taken leave of the S.A. dignitaries than Röhm gave vent to his wrath. The S.A. General Viktor Lutze listened uneasily to the explosive rage of his chief which exhaled an odour of high treason. He noted down in writing some of Röhm's ejaculations: 'What the so-called Führer says doesn't count for us. Hitler is a traitor, he'd better be sent off on a holiday ... Adolf thinks himself clever because the bankers and the military seem to support him, but he is betraying the National Socialist revolution which wc, the S.A., began ... If things can't be done with Hitler, never mind, we'll do them without him ...'

Viktor Lutze did not dare repeat these remarks directly to Hitler. He went to see Rudolf Hess, the 'Führer's representative', who was much embarrassed. He nevertheless advised him to go to Berchtesgaden and refer the matter directly to Hitler. Lutze ventured to follow this advice. The Reich Chancellor was as embarrassed as his friend Hess. 'Better to let the matter ripen,' he said. On his return to Berlin after this setback Lutze passed his information on to General von Reichenau, who lent an attentive ear. He did not hide his sentiments: 'The time is approaching when Röhm will have to pay for his flights of language and his intrigues against the Reichswehr.' The same evening the Reichswehr general had a talk with Reinhard Heydrich. It was not the first. Already for some time the two men had been conferring to find a solution to the Röhm problem. Heydrich had long been in favour of 'purely and simply liquidating Röhm and his clique'. He had a good deal of trouble convincing Himmler, who recalled 'with emotion' the time when he had fought at Captain Röhm's side for the Hitlerian cause. But Heydrich finally succeeded when he explained to the S.S. Reichsführer that everybody had an interest henceforth in eliminating the Röhm clan and dismantling the S.A.: the Führer would be able to pursue his National Socialist revolution untrammelled; Goering would be relieved of an adversary and be grateful to Himmler; the Reichswehr would have no rival and be able to bring the army to the maximum of efficiency; the party would no longer be dishonoured by this notorious debauchee; as for the S.S., not only would it finally break the last theoretical ties that bound it to the S.A., but above all, in acquiring its liberty of action, it would develop and found on a solid basis the Black Order of which Himmler dreamed.

At the end of April 1934 Röhm's fate was settled in the minds of

Goering, von Reichenau, Himmler and Heydrich. It only remained to deliver the decisive stroke and, above all, determine Hitler to act.

Heydrich's diabolic character was to reveal itself to its full extent. He went into action. He gave himself two tasks: first, to have in readiness all the means of delivering a mortal blow to the S.A.; second, to prove to Hitler that Röhm was preparing a putsch against him. He made ready commandos of killers and drew up lists of victims. On the latter he inscribed the names of the principal S.A. leaders, then added—while he was about it—those he considered the most dangerous adversaries of the regime, and also his own opponents, among them of course the former chief of the Gestapo, Rudolf Diels. But Heydrich was not alone. Each had his own list: Goering, Himmler, Theodor Eicke (commandant of the concentration camp at Dachau), the Gauleiter of Munich, Adolf Wagner, etc. There were discussions whether so-and-so should not be spared, so-and-so eliminated. It was a horrible bargaining. Goering struck off the name of Diels. Heydrich yielded.

Von Reichenau frequently conferred with Heydrich and placed at his disposition barracks, arms, ammunition and means of transport to facilitate the operation. Heydrich put the S.S. on a state of alert throughout Germany. He expected to have to break the resistance of the S.A., especially in Berlin and Bavaria, as well as in Silesia and Saxony. Everything was got ready with a view to such resistance.

To fulfil the mission he had set himself Heydrich counted on the S.S. secret service. He had to have 'proofs' capable of convincing the heads of the Reichswehr and the Führer himself that a plot was being hatched by Röhm. These items were primarily supplied to him by Sub-Lieutenant Friedrich Wilhelm Krüger, liaison man with the S.A. where he served as Heydrich's spy. The whole secret service of the S.S. and the Gestapo were put on a war footing. S.S. General Heinz Jost was to tell me that the items were at first meagre: gossip, the discovery of a few small-arms depôts, some more-or-less seditious remarks by S.A. chiefs after drinking . . . in fact nothing that could really allow Röhm to be accused of plotting or treason. Heydrich fumed.

Then came the climax: on June 4th 1934 Hitler received Röhm. Heydrich learned from his Gestapo men that the two old comrades met for five hours and reached an understanding to put off until later the solution of the S.A.–Reichswehr problem. It was agreed that Röhm should send his men on leave for a month from July 1st. In August they would see . . .

This information from the Gestapo seems more reliable than the official version later issued by Hitler himself on July 13th according to which he had tried 'in vain to bring the S.A. leader to a compromise'.

The day after this meeting Röhm in fact sent the S.A. on leave for the whole of July and himself decided to take a cure at Bad Wiessee in Bavaria. Was Heydrich's criminal design to come to nothing? It would be most difficult for him to assert that the S.A. was preparing a coup while they were scattered all across Germany and even abroad to enjoy their month's holiday. But Heydrich's devilish genius did not lack resourcefulness. He had no proofs? He would fabricate them. Hitler, indisputable champion of what might nowadays be called brainwashing would—by a stroke of irony—allow himself to be brainwashed by his young pupil Heydrich. The latter would demonstrate that he was a past master in the art of inserting in someone's brain—in this case Hitler's own—a fixed and false notion (Röhm's putsch) which would cause him to take decisions and perform a desired action—the physical elimination of Röhm and the heads of the S.A.

With the support of Goering and the complicity of Goebbels and Hess, all three of whom feared Röhm's excessive power, Heydrich set on foot the preparations for the suppression of the S.A. and, at the same time spread and caused to be spread by the S.D. a whole series of faked news and forged documents. Rumours of the imminence of an S.A. putsch began to circulate in army circles, and came, carefully guided, to the ears of Hitler.

Hitler, however, still seemed undecided. Doubtless he feared his too zealous colleagues, Goering as well as Röhm. As was his wont, he was not displeased to play the rival forces against each other so as himself to remain the supreme arbiter. But Heydrich was too deep in to draw back. He knew that the development of the S.S. was only possible at the expense of the S.A. so the purge of the S.A. had to be accomplished, and accomplished before July 1st.

Today we ask the question, did Röhm have a plan for a putsch in mind? It cannot be excluded, though we have no proof one way or the other. The trial, which I attended and which took place in Munich from May 6th to 14th 1957, regarding 'The Night of the Long Knives' threw no light on this important point.[2] It is nevertheless quite conceivable that Röhm toyed with plans the realisation of which would have brought about sooner or later the elimination of the Führer. Many historians, wanting to blacken Hitler in this business, have too much whitewashed Röhm. The chief of the S.A. was no 'little saint' and it is possible if not probable that at this turning point in his political ascent Röhm gave way once more to his natural inclination which was to conspire to attain his own destiny, his loyalty to the Führer taking second place.

All witnesses are unanimous in affirming that Röhm had only contempt for the hierarchical and despotic Reich that Hitler was constructing and fiercely opposed the mystical Order of the Blood inspired by Hitler's 'visions', the ramblings of Rosenberg and the 'mad pride' of Himmler. 'These Teutonic reveries,' said Röhm, 'are destined to impotence.' What he wanted was a kind of pretorian republic, socialist and military, an S.A. state in which the Brown Shirts wielded the power directly. The Hitler–Röhm conflict, polarised by the Reichswehr, was thus a good deal deeper than it appeared. This said, had Röhm the intention of acting swiftly, as Himmler and Heydrich declared to Hitler? That's another story. On the other hand, what is certain is that the little camarilla which had gathered round Röhm was methodically preparing the necessary psychological atmosphere for the proclamation of a 'second revolution', Röhm's own favourite expression. There was the danger for Hitler; and there Heydrich's opportunity.

After June 4th Heydrich brooded in bitterness. His efforts had had no result. What was to be done if Hitler continued to hesitate and, worse, reject the idea of the liquidation of Röhm and the principal S.A. chiefs? Did not the operation put in hand risk turning against its authors? Heydrich had reason to fear the Führer's reaction. He knew him to be an opportunist, surprising in his audacities and capacity for instantaneous action, capable of anything. Heydrich played a great and highly risky game, dragging with him Himmler, Goering, Goebbels, Hess and . . . von Reichenau. A combination of circumstances was to favour his bloody designs. Events were to take a leap forward.

First, Röhm imprudently stuck his neck out. Doubtless regretting having given in to Hitler at their interview of June 4th, which resulted in the sending of the S.A. on holiday, on June 8th he published a threatening communiqué in the entire press: 'The enemies of the S.A. will get the answer they deserve at the appropriate moment and in due form. If our enemies think that the S.A. will not return from their leave, or return only in part, they are mistaken. The S.A. are and remain the masters of Germany's destiny.'

This fanfaronade delighted Heydrich. Hitler would obviously not relish the challenge.

An international event would also play its part. On June 14th Hitler flew to Venice via Padua where he would hold his first conference with Mussolini. The announcement of this meeting produced considerable agitation in international circles and aroused enthusiasm in Germany. But for Hitler the journey was a fiasco. He returned humiliated, deeply wounded. On June 14th and 15th Mussolini treated him with condescension, like master to pupil, lavishing advice and multiplying edifying examples. He recommended him 'to begin by dismissing from time to time the members of his entourage to prevent them from becoming more powerful than himself'. Mussolini had pronounced the name of Röhm for whom he did not disguise his antipathy: 'Begin', he said to Hitler, 'by putting a little order in your house. Get rid of individual mischief-makers who compromise the National Socialist regime on the international level.'

Two days later, Franz von Papen made an important speech at the University of Marburg, naturally Christian in inspiration but also monarchist and violently critical of the Hitler regime which he accused of allowing the proliferation of 'the fanatics and chatterboxes who talk heedlessly of unleashing a *second revolution*'. He did not cloak his criticisms of 'the confusion between brutality and virility' of the National Socialists, 'the terrorist methods in the domain of justice as well as that of the police . . .' Although censored by Goebbels, the speech had the effect of a bomb.[3]

Hitler replied the same day during a meeting of the Party at Gera (Thuringia). '. . . All the dwarves who imagine that they have something to say will be swept away by the power of our common idea. For all the dwarves forget one thing, whatever criticisms they think they can formulate: where is the Better that can replace what exists? What have they got to put in its place? Absurd, the little worm who wants to fight so powerful a renewal of our people!'

All the other Nazi leaders reacted violently against Franz von Papen's speech and warned the enemies of the regime—those of the Right (von Papen) as well as those of the Left (Röhm)—that they would be wrong to count on protracted impunity: Rosenberg, on June 20th in the *Völkischer Beobachter*; Goebbels on June 21st, in a big speech in Berlin; Himmler and Heydrich's two accomplices, Hess and Goering, fired the last salvo. On June 25th Rudolf Hess, on Cologne radio, prepared the country psychologically by demanding unconditional loyalty to Hitler: 'Woe to him who thinks he can serve the revolution by organising a revolt (. . .) Hitler is the great strategist of the revolution (. . .) Woe to him who tramples on the subtle threads of his strategic plans in vain hope of getting there before him. He is an enemy of the revolution, even if he is in good faith.' The challenge to Röhm was clear. On June 28th, in a no less violent discourse at Hamburg, Goering declared, 'He who does not give his trust to Hitler commits an act of high treason. He who destroys this trust destroys Germany and should fear for his head.'

In this atmosphere Goering brought Hitler a new and thick file assembled under the supervision of Heydrich and Daluege on the state of mind of the S.A. throughout Germany. Did Goering know that the file was bogus? It is probable but not certain. It is possible the Führer's Number Two had also let himself be infected by the redoubtable fox Heydrich. The latter had not been niggardly. The file was composed of many letters intercepted by the censor, recordings of telephone conversations between the S.A. chiefs, denunciations more or less anonymous, reports of agents of the S.D. and the Gestapo assigned to keep an eye on the S.A. leaders. The whole file had been carefully 'arranged' by Heydrich and his colleagues of the S.D. under Behrends's direction. There was no overt question of a putsch against the Führer, nor of assassination, not even of rebellion, but the reading of the whole plainly allowed the worst to be feared: never would the S.A. tolerate being stripped of their power but on the contrary showed that they had every intention of breaking willy-nilly 'the chains which the reactionary parties and big industry have imposed on Hitler'.

When he read the report, in which several offensive epithets, adroitly inserted by Heydrich and Behrends, wounded him personally, the Führer considered that the attitude of the S.A. was rapidly leading to civil war. He said so to Goering who mentioned this reaction at Nuremburg in 1946. At the prospect of returning to the dark and bloody days of 1918/19 Hitler saw red. The regime was in great danger. He decided that he had better smother this revolt in the egg as he had smothered the Communist opposition and not be satisfied with half measures. He would act while the S.A. was on leave; a complete change in the S.A. organisation would be effected. He told Goering that he would give his assent to the operation prepared by Heydrich against the S.A. but did not set the date of execution. 'He still hesitated to strike down his old comrades,' said Sepp Dietrich.[4] 'He preferred in fact that it should happen without blood-letting.' This was to reckon without the Goering–Himmler–Heydrich trio, who were growing impatient. Heydrich made ready the final details of the purge.

On June 23rd Hitler went to Neudeck to inform Marshal Hindenburg of the decision he had taken. Even before he could open his mouth Hitler heard the old soldier reproach him in forceful terms 'for having allowed certain young people to raise the possibility of a second revolution'. Then, in shaking his hand in farewell, without Hitler having even given his explanation, he said, 'It is high time for you to put a little order in the house.'

After Mussolini, Hindenburg. And now the third: General von Blomberg, whom Hitler passed in leaving the old Marshal's. The Defence Minister said to him, 'The Army needs time and thought to achieve its transformation. If the Party must merge with the State, it still should not be to the detriment of the State. It's time to put an end to this agitation and bring the extremists of your Party to their senses.'

Hitler swallowed the reprimands without saying anything. He had need of the army. He had need of its heads. He had need of von Blomberg. But he would never forget. When he could he would rid himself of the 'old rubber lion'—von Blomberg's nickname in the Army.

In the S.S. camp the last preparations were made, everything was in readiness on Thursday June 28th. They were only waiting for the green light from Hitler. Would he finally decide to go into action?

1. Nevertheless it was not before November 7th 1934 that the headquarters staff of the S.S. left Munich for Berlin.
2. *Protokoll des Schwurgerichts in dem Strafverfaheren gegen Joseph Dietrich und Michaël Lippert* (Munich Trial, May 6th to 14th 1957).
3. Only the *Frankfurt Gazette* printed it before the prohibition.
4. See note 2.

5
The Night of the Long Knives

Throughout the whole of Germany the flags were at half-mast. Fifteen years earlier, on June 28th 1919, Erzberger had had to sign in Germany's name the Treaty of Versailles, to accept the victors' Diktat. In all the barracks in Germany an officer read a text to emphasise that there was no possible forgetting such an affront: 'Fifteen years ago the glorious German Army, your comrades, were betrayed, stabbed in the back; that will never happen again.'

At Tempelhof aerodrome the flags were likewise at half-mast. At nine in the morning, while a heavy rain began to fall, an S.S. guard of honour in parade uniform, black with white gloves and belts, formed rank up to a large three-engined aeroplane. The crew at full strength was grouped near the little iron ladder which gave access to it. A command resounded. The S.S. stiffened with a click of boots and presented arms. Adolf Hitler, in a leather coat, cap in hand, walked to the 'plane accompanied by Hermann Goering, in the dress uniform of an Air Force General, a light cape over his shoulders. There followed the aide-de-camp Brückner, S.S. General Schaub and Dr. Otto Dietrich,[1] the Führer's press secretary. They were going to Essen, capital of the Ruhr.

When the aeroplane landed on the Essen–Mülheim aerodrome it was raining hard. All along the ten kilometres which separated Mülheim from Essen a dense crowd lined the road to acclaim the Führer. In the city the national day of mourning was not observed. It was decked everywhere with flags and garlands displaying the swastika in honour of the marriage of Joseph Terboven, Gauleiter of the Rhineland, which Hitler and Goering had come to attend.[2]

At the Town Hall Ilse Stahl, the bride, in a long, form-fitting embroidered dress of white silk, a large diadem in her hair, pressed a sumptuous bouquet of red roses to her bosom. When Hitler advanced towards her, her cheeks flushed, her look became ecstatic. At her side, his black hair slicked down and parted at the side, his face clean shaven, Gauleiter Joseph Terboven stiffened to attention, right arm extended.

Dr. Reismann-Grone, Mayor of Essen, presided over the civil ceremony and delivered an allocution which was punctuated by the hurrahs from the crowd packed in the square. In the hall S.A. and S.S. sat side by side, impassive or smiling; amongst them could be recognised S.A. General Karl Ernst, head of the Berlin S.A., who had postponed his own honeymoon in order to be present.[3]

The ceremony over, the official cortège proceeded to the cathedral for the religious service. It was still raining but the crowd was as compact as an hour earlier.

At the wedding breakfast, served at the Hotel Kaiserhof in the Lindenallee Goering offered the address of congratulation to the newly wedded pair; S.S. General Zeck then made a short speech during which he particularly stressed that 'I here celebrate the old, the good old comradeship between the S.S. and the S.A., the good old companionship which unites the S.S. and the S.A. to the manual and intellectual workers.' This sentence was loudly applauded by those present, led by the Chancellor, Adolf Hitler.

A little before five, whilst S.A. General Karl Ernst was in his 'plane on his way back to Berlin where together with his young wife he was to pack his bags, Adolf Hitler paid a visit to the Krupp factories. In the hall of honour Baron Krupp von Bohlen und Halbach and Miss Irmgard von Bohlen welcomed him. After a long visit and a talk with the German steel magnate, Hitler returned to the Hotel Kaiserhof. Goering was waiting for him there. He showed him the numerous messages from Berlin. Himmler and Heydrich had been working well: the despatches all stressed the preparation for the S.A. putsch, some brought details of the armament of such and such assault section. One of them confirmed that the S.A. would direct its action against the Reichswehr and gave the list of generals who were to be killed. Another message, the last, gave the date of the putsch; Saturday June 30th, and the time five o'clock in the afternoon. Hitler said nothing but he was pale. He paced the grand salon of the hotel which had been transformed into an office. The telephone rang; Brückner answered. The call ended, he turned to the Führer and told him that the S.D. Rhineland service announced that a foreign diplomat had been molested by the S.A. at Cologne. Hitler exploded, 'The S.A. has become a danger to the Reich. Get me Röhm at once at Pension Hanselbauer in Bad Wiessee.'

Turning to Goering he said, 'I've had enough. An example must be made. These lunatics must be arrested. Go back to Berlin. Judge the situation and call me before taking action.'

Goering understood that the fruit was ripe and left content.

When Hitler had Röhm on the wire he confirmed the need of an urgent clarification of the S.A.–Reichswehr conflict. For this purpose he requested him to convene all the principal S.A. leaders at Bad Wiessee on June 30th at eleven o'clock for a plenary session at which he, Hitler, would be present. Röhm was not surprised. When he hung up the receiver the S.A. chief turned to von Epp, who was standing beside him and said, 'All the misunderstanding with Hitler will soon be cleared up. I'm going to order a big banquet for the evening of the 30th at Munich, in the Hotel Vierjahreszeiten. There will be a vegetarian menu for the Führer's benefit.'

On Friday June 29th the sun gave way to rain when Hitler and his suite went to inspect the work camps in Westphalia. Round ten o'clock, while they were visiting the Regional School of the Reich Work Corps, at Buddenberg Castle near Lünen, the rain started to fall again, but as on the previous day an enormous crowd shouted, 'Heil Hitler! Sieg Heil!' The Führer seemed to hear or see nothing. He was preoccupied. He then went to the Camp at Olfen but cut short his inspection. Abruptly he decided to go to Godesberg, eighty kilometres to the south, near Bonn.

Hitler installed himself at the Hotel Dreesen. It was a quiet, modest hotel, well known to the burghers of Bonn and the Ruhr. From there he exchanged messages all afternoon with Goering in Berlin either by telephone or air. Planes took off from the Essen aerodrome or Bonn-Hangelar for Berlin Tempelhof. From there a courier hastened to Goering who communicated with Hitler in the same way, the chief concern being secrecy and speed.

From Berlin arrived increasingly serious news emanating from Goering or Himmler, stressing the growing nervousness of the S.A., its warlike preparations. Hitler did not speak; he appeared distrait. He was sitting in an armchair facing the view. In the hotel and its garden police inspectors in long leather coats and S.S. in black uniforms watched over the Führer's security.

Amongst the S.S. present was one who came from Bonn, a man with very bright dark eyes. It was young Walter Schellenberg, doing his last policing operation before entering the S.D. Nearly twenty years later, at Pallanza, Schellenberg recalled it. 'Throughout the whole day', he told me, 'strange and disquieting rumours reached my S.S. unit. They pictured a plot, divisions in the Party leadership, imminent catastrophe and radical decisions by the Führer.

'I was on guard duty inside the hotel, near the french windows leading from the terrace to the dining room; from there the view extended to the heavy waters, powerful and Wagnerian, of the Rhine and the rocky, wooded slopes of the Massif of the Seven Mountains with the fortified summit of Petersberg. In the same room preparations had been made for a conference and after a little while 'they' arrived. Amongst these high dignitaries of the Party I recognised Adolf Hitler. He looked gloomy, scowling, shut in on himself. There was also Dr. Otto Dietrich. Later S.A. General Viktor Lutze, chief of the Hanover Gau, came to join them. A little after that Dr. Joseph Goebbels arrived from Berlin.

'Suddenly the sky darkened. The air became suffocating. With astonishing violence the storm broke. When it began to rain I was on the terrace and pressed against a french window to get what shelter I could. Flashes of lightning zig-zagged across the sky, illuminating the scene with a strange and sinister light, the valley resounded with the fury of the storm which poured down cataracts lashed by insane gusts of wind. From time to time the Führer approached the window where I was standing and watched the storm, his eyes lost in a reverie. It was obvious that he was overwhelmed by the weight of the grave and difficult decision to be taken.'

Lieutenant Brückner, the Führer's aide-de-camp, came and went with the succession of despatches. The conversation between Hitler and Goebbels was animated. Suddenly through the storm a motorcyclist appeared at the bottom of the hotel steps. He left his machine, rapidly climbed the steps and hurried towards Brückner, who had been alerted by Schellenberg. The motorcyclist brought a message from Goering. Brückner passed it to Hitler, who read it and without a word handed it to Goebbels.

In Berlin Karl Ernst had placed his men in a state of alert since that afternoon, Friday 29th, Goering's message confirmed one from Himmler which arrived a few minutes earlier. Hitler was little by little convinced, under Goebbels' influence, that the S.A. had definitely decided to go into action in the capital.

This Karl Ernst, whom Hitler had seen the previous day at Terboven's wedding, was a resolute man who was under thirty-five and commanded 250 000 men as resolute as he. Hitler knew him well. He knew that this former hotel porter, former café waiter, who now sported flamboyant uniforms weighed down with medals, insignia, gew-gaws, was strikingly cynical. He had a powerful and vulgar head and a thick mouth which betrayed his lust for pleasures and violence. In Berlin he was feared. His S.A. were 'taboo': they could steal, rape, kill and Ernst would shield them. For some he was only a sadist, a common criminal transformed into a responsible official representing order and the state. The file collected by Heydrich on Karl Ernst, of which Hitler had knowledge, was overwhelming. But Ernst was Röhm's right hand. To strike Ernst was also to strike Röhm.

And it was this Karl Ernst who, according to Goering's message, had just put his S.A. in a state of alert. Hitler's brow was careworn. He hesitated what decision to take. He could take no chances. The S.A. were not choir boys—Röhm liked to say, 'The S.A. are not an uplift society for the education of girls but an association of tough fighters.' Their fate was at stake there in the grand salon of the Hotel Dreesen. The Führer could not but think of all those men whose rule was obedience to his person to the death. Must these 'political soldiers' who, as Röhm said, 'had battered the way with their fists to the National Socialist idea of the future, the way to victory', now be decapitated? Hitler remained tight-faced. At his side Goebbels was silent. 'I was full of respectful admiration,' he was to say, recalling that evening at Godesberg, 'for this man on whom sat the responsibility for the fate of millions of human beings and whom I saw in the process of weighing a painful choice: on one side the tranquillity of Germany, on the other, those who had until now been his intimates.'

'Until eight in the evening,' Schellenberg told me, 'there was no let-up in the storm. Then it moderated; the massed clouds drifted away and little by little all became quiet and serene, as if pacified by magic.

'After dinner, at about ten-thirty, I saw Sepp Dietrich, commander of the Leibstandarte S.S. Adolf Hitler, arriving from Berlin.'

Sepp Dietrich, square-jawed, powerful, with glistening teeth, was of medium height, but looked taller in his black uniform on which shone the gilded oak leaves of an S.S. General. He was a faithful executive who lived in the Führer's daily entourage. The latter could have complete confidence in him. Sepp Dietrich's eyes showed clearly enough the fanaticism which would lead him to die or kill for the Führer.

'S.S. General Sepp Dietrich saluted the Reich Chancellor,'

Schellenberg went on, 'the latter gave him an order which I heard perfectly, "Return to your 'plane at once, go to Munich. When you get there, telephone me here at the hotel. I will then give you my detailed instructions." '

When Sepp Dietrich telephoned from Munich a little before midnight he received a second order from the Führer, 'Go at once to Kaufering to lead two S.S. companies to Bad Wiessee. I am coming,' he added.

Fresh news had precipitated Hitler's decision. Adolf Wagner, Bavarian Gauleiter and Minister of the Interior, had notified him by telephone that the S.A. had 'emerged into the streets of Munich during the evening shouting slogans hostile to Hitler and the Reichswehr and singing revolutionary songs'. One of them had as a refrain the significant verse, 'Sharpen your long knives on the kerb-stones.'

Wagner's information was in part true but, an accomplice of the S.S., the Gauleiter exaggerated the incident and Hitler believed Wagner. It was then that the Führer decided to go to Munich himself, then to Bad Wiessee.

'Hardly had the conversation with Sepp Dietrich ended,' Schellenberg then told me, 'when the telephone rang again. Berlin was asking for Hitler. It was the Reichsführer S.S. Heinrich Himmler who wanted to speak to the Führer in person. Hitler took up the telephone. As he listened to Himmler his expression changed. He could no longer control his nervousness. He answered in monosyllables and nearly dropped the telephone. Suddenly his eyes glittered. He hung up and turned to Goebbels. Himmler had told him, he said, the general alert to the S.A. was in fact set for Saturday, June 30th and that the Gestapo had just learned that at five p.m. the S.A. was to occupy the Government buildings. "It's the putsch!" exclaimed Hitler, who several times repeated the word "putsch".'

'Hitler was increasingly nervous,' Schellenberg stated. 'Violence and disquiet could be read on his face. At no moment did he appear to doubt the news transmitted by Goering, Wagner and Himmler.

' "Ernst", Himmler said to Goebbels, "did not leave for Bad Wiessee as he should have done; he must therefore be going to direct the putsch in Berlin." '

'Goebbels did not contradict Himmler,' Schellenberg emphasised, 'though he knew that Ernst had left the capital for Bremen where he was to take a ship for Teneriffe and Madeira to spend his honey-moon. Goebbels's object in this stands out very clearly.'

It was now the hour for action. The Reich Chancellor had made his decision. The 'Night of the Long Knives' was about to begin. It was to be a major turning point in the history of Nazism.

Walter Schellenberg gave me further details, 'It was about one in the morning. Lieutenant Brückner, an imposing figure, came directly towards me. He told me that it was necessary to ensure security as far as the airport of Bonn—Hangelar, at least fifteen kilometres from Godesberg. The Führer was leaving and wanted to waste no time. I at once transmitted this order to my superior. Already men were running to the garages where the cars were drawn up. Two despatch riders started. Hitler came out with his companions. At his side Dr. Goebbels was waving his hands and talking to him, at times in a low voice.

'Hitler shook hands with Dr. Anton Dreesen, owner of the hotel and a former comrade-in-arms. The Führer, with Goebbels, got into the back of the first of the Mercedes which waited at the bottom of the little colonnaded flight of steps; Brückner got in front, next to the driver. The Chancellor's car and those of his suite started off immediately.

'The lorries arrived for the guards and we took our places. We followed the cars to the airport. There the Führer's personal pilot, Hans Baur, waited on the sodden runway near his machine, a heavy three-engined Ju-52. When he saw the group of six men accompanying the Führer, Baur leapt into the cockpit and started his motors roaring. Hitler took with him Dr. Joseph Goebbels, Dr. Otto Dietrich, the S.A. leader Viktor Lutze and three bodyguards, Brückner, Schaub and Schreck. The big machine lifted off heavily and climbed through black clouds in the direction of Munich. It was two in the morning.'

According to the testimony of Dr. Otto Dietrich: 'Sitting up front, near Hans Baur, Hitler kept his teeth clenched and the pilot respected his chief's silence. His features drawn and puffy from lack of sleep, an untidy lock of hair on his forehead, he held his flat cap on his crossed knees and turned up the collar of his crumpled leather coat. His eyelids half closed, sunk in his thoughts, more enigmatic and remote than ever, the Führer stared silently into the expanse before him. With all the power of its three engines the Junkers flew towards Bavaria. Slowly the June 30th sky began to pale before us. The weather was very good. We put down at four in the morning at Munich airport.'

Fifteen hundred kilometres from Munich, at 8 Prinz-Albrecht-strasse, headquarters of the Gestapo, two men had been in their offices since eleven the previous evening: Himmler and Heydrich. The aide-de-camp Karl Wolff saw to the liaison between the different sections of the S.S., which were all on 'a war footing'. For the last time he examined the long, very long, list of the men they were going to have assassinated. They were awaiting the signal from Munich. At 3.45 the telephone rang in Himmler's office. It was the Gauleiter Wagner, who announced from Munich that the Führer would arrive in a few minutes and that Hitler himself would give his instructions to the head of the S.S. When Himmler reported this information to Heydrich the latter smiled coldly and made only a brief comment: 'The Führer will be obeyed beyond his hopes.'

In the Hotel Hanselbauer at Bad Wiessee, on the shore of Lake Tegern, near the frontier between Germany and Austria, a man with a naked torso was living his second-to-last night, without of course knowing it: Ernst Röhm.

After staying up late to empty countless brimming tankards of beer, burst into marching songs and anthems with his officers, aides-de-camp, chauffeurs and bodyguards, all from the S.A., Ernst Röhm, the pretorian, the centurion, had retired to the balcony of his room. An S.A. on guard outside the hotel noticed him, naked to the waist. The light from the room illuminated his profile, accentuating the vulgarity of his fat face, seamed by a large scar from nose to chin, and also his protuberant stomach freed from the S.A. belt which always seemed to have difficulty in containing it. A fresh breeze, as every night at this season, blew from the hills covered with forest and pasture, along the valley of the Wiessach and raised ripples on Lake Tegern which glistened under the moon. Röhm must have been pondering over his old friend Adolf's phone call. No shadow of suspicion crossed his mind. He had given von Epp his last instructions for the dinner at the Vierjahreszeiten Hotel which he would offer the Führer and seal the accord, as he thought, on the resolution of the S.A.–Reichswehr conflict.

The tough warrior with the square neck and bull's shoulders shivered and left the balcony. He went in to go to bed; as usual he only put on the trousers of his pyjamas and so threw himself down on his bed and fell asleep immediately. It was four in the morning. Hitler had just landed at the Munich–Oberwiesenfeld aerodrome.

He hurried out of the 'plane, quickly descended the metal steps and went directly in long nervous strides to the waiting cars. He greeted no one. Far behind because of his awkward limp, Dr. Goebbels tried to catch him up. Near the cars the Führer noticed a military lorry also parked. Soldiers of the Reichswehr, in steel helmets, rifles between their knees, were there to ensure the protection of the Reich Chancellor, as were two military armoured vehicles. When the officer commanding the detachment went forward to salute the Führer, the latter declared in a tone that permitted no answer, 'You will thank General Adam, commander of Wehrkreis VII, for the military protection he is offering me. But the Reichswehr must remain totally apart from what is happening and will happen. It is not to be involved in it. I insist: it is not to be involved in it.' Then he added in a lower tone, 'It's the worst day of my life—the hardest. But believe me, I shall know how to execute justice. I'm going to Munich then to Bad Wiessee . . . I'm going to see to these swine.'

He took a few steps, then before getting into the car, gave the order, 'Notify General Adam at once of our intentions.'

Dawn brightened the sky. Objects, forms, trees took on definition but the sun had not yet risen. The light was cold. Hitler got into the car with Goebbels and called to the driver, 'To the Ministry of the Interior.'

The doors slammed, the cars moved off. In a few minutes they reached Munich's first buildings. The shutters of the houses were still closed, the shops shut, passers-by rare. When the convoy stopped before the Ministry of the Interior, Hitler was again the first to get out. The S.S. were there, faithful men who had been warned of the Führer's arrival. They were not unaware that the hour of action had come and they were with Adolf Hitler. There were Emil Maurice, Buch, Hesser and others. Hitler greeted them, Brückner at his heels, and entered the building. The Gauleiter Adolf Wagner, at the Führer's left, summed up the situation; for the moment at least, no rising was to be feared in Munich.

On the second floor, in an anteroom to Wagner's office, the S.A. General Schneidhuber waited dozing in a chair. When he saw Hitler he tried to get up but the former was already upon him shouting, 'Traitor . . . traitor . . . arrest him!'

In Wagner's office Hitler, Goebbels and the Gauleiter drew up the list of names of the men to be arrested. Wagner himself telephoned to S.A. General Schmidt to report at once at the Ministry of the Interior 'where the Führer was expecting him'. When Schmidt entered the office Hitler pounced on him shouting, 'Traitor: You're under arrest. You're going to be shot.'

He tore off his insignia of rank. Astonishment was visible on the face of Schmidt, who could only open his mouth without making himself heard over Hitler's shouts. While Schmidt was being led away, to join Schneidhuber, Hitler kept shouting, 'You're going to be shot. You're going to be shot.'

Hitler asked Wagner to telephone Berlin: Rudolf Hess must come at once to Munich.

It was nearly six o'clock. The sky over the city was blue. Having settled the urgent problems—the arrest of the S.A. leaders in Munich, the arrest of those who would arrive in the morning by train, their incarceration on Stadelhelm prison—Hitler left the Ministry of the Interior and got into his car. Gauleiter Wagner, who accompanied him, remained at the top of the steps; his task was to remain in Munich to control the situation there, to see to the arrests and prevent any action by the S.A.

The Führer's car, Schreck with him, set off in the direction of Bad Wiessee by the broad Avenue Thal, the bridges over the Isar and Rosenheimerstrasse. Behind was Goebbels's car, then those of Walther Buch, head of the Nazi Security Court, of Emil Maurice and Hermann Hesser, as well as requisitioned taxis packed with armed S.S. men. It was six in the morning. Half an hour later the convoy ran along the shore of Lake Tegern, quiet and iridescent in the light of daybreak. Then appeared the first houses of Bad Wiessee. The cars slowed down. At the last bend a lorry carrying S.S. of the *Leibstandarte S.S. Adolf Hitler* and their chief, Sepp Dietrich, was waiting for them. The convoy did not stop but pressed on to the Pension Hanselbauer.

The S.S., revolvers in hand, leapt out and ran for the building whose shutters were still closed. The grass and moss muffled the sound of their boots. The encirclement was quickly completed. Hitler was at the front door, surrounded by Brückner, Maurice and several S.S. Suddenly he gave a sign. The action was unleashed. The door was kicked open.

Goebbels was to narrate, 'Without encountering resistance, we were able to enter the house and surprise the gang of conspirators still sunk in sleep and put them under immediate arrest. It was the Führer himself who did the arresting.' An S.S. trooper declared, 'I would have liked the walls to fall down and the whole German people to become witness of these events. They could understand how right the Führer was to settle accounts, pitilessly and rigorously, with the guilty. How right he was to make them pay with their lives for their crime against the nation.'

The first room into which the S.S. penetrated was that of Count Spreti, an S.A. General at Munich, who, having no time to get up, was dragged out of his bed and, half naked, thrust in to the corridor with insults.

In the next room the S.A. General in Silesia, Edmund Heines, former killer from Sainte-Vehme and an old Nazi who had taken part in the Munich putsch of November 9th 1923, was sleeping naked, intertwined with his young chauffeur. Emil Maurice and Brückner broke down the door, revolver in hand, taking the couple by surprise. Heines, with the face of a girl but the body of an athlete, made to reach for a pistol on his night table. Emil Maurice fired. Heines collapsed. He and the chauffeur were seized, bound and dragged from the room. They were taken outside, in front of the pension, where they were killed by a bullet in the head.

Nearby the members of Röhm's staff underwent a similar fate. In a corner of the hall S.A. Colonel Julius Uhl, chief of Röhm's personal bodyguard, lay tightly bound to another aide-de-camp, Lieutenant Reiner. Their faces were bloodied by kicks from the S.S.

Whilst these scenes were unfolding another was taking place, tragic and ignoble. Hitler knocked on Röhm's door. He drummed his fists against the wood crying, 'Open!'

Röhm's drowsy voice asked, 'Who is it?'

'Me, Adolf. Open!'

'What, you already?' Röhm exclaimed. 'You're already here? I didn't expect you till noon.'

'Open!'

Röhm slid back the bolt and appeared, massive, torso naked, his face red and swollen by his curtailed sleep, his eyes questioning. Hitler, convulsed and frothing, his hippopotamus-hide whip furiously lashing the tails of his long leather coat, poured out invectives and insults on his aforetime comrade, who remained stupid, dumb, only partly awake. Röhm had often been the witness of Hitler's angers, but never of such a rage, of such hysteria. He tried to protest. The other's fury redoubled. He pushed Röhm into the room. The door shut on the two men. Quickly the Reich Chancellor's voice lost its intensity. One could hear the sound of a lively discussion between the two but not distinguish the words. No one will ever know the secret of this last dramatic interview. Suddenly, Röhm having doubtless got a grip on himself and answered Hitler sharply, the door of the room opened. The Führer was livid. In a paroxysm of exasperation he shouted as he went out, 'This swine is lacking in respect for me. Arrest him at once.'

On the threshold of the room Röhm mechanically scratched his shaven head. He had a dressing gown over his arm but was still in pyjama trousers, torso and feet bare. Two S.S. men took hold of him and drew him towards the hall. The operation was over. There was nothing left but to return to Munich with the prisoners and the bodies.

It was a quarter to eight. An unexpected incident then occurred. A shock commando of the S.A. arrived at Bad Wiessee, summoned by Röhm to form a guard of honour for Hitler and the S.A. chiefs who were to have taken part in the conference. Hitler went up to the Commando leader and in a tone that admitted no answer, gave him the order to turn around and go back to Munich. The Commando leader hesitated, looked round him, fixed his eyes on the Führer. Then, without understanding, he complied.

The S.S. and their prisoners also returned to Munich. During the journey they passed the file of cars bringing the S.A. chiefs to the reunion. Hitler had them stopped and the occupants questioned. If to the question, 'Are you with Röhm?' they answered, 'Why, of course,' they were abused, seized, disarmed and taken aboard. In the opposite case, which was less common, they were invited to follow on behind.

During this time Wagner and Lutze, whom Rudolf Hess had joined, arriving by air from Berlin, had laid a trap at the Munich railway station. On the arrival of the train from Berlin, the S.S. arrested all the S.A. leaders, who were too astounded to react. The same happened during the morning on the arrival of other trains from various directions. All the S.A. dignitaries were conducted directly to the Munich–Stadelheim prison where Sepp Dietrich's black-clad men maintained order and crowded them into cells.

On his arrival in Munich Hitler went to the station where he heard the report of the S.S. and of Gauleiter Wagner. Hess, Goebbels and Lutze were there too. Everything passed off normally, without difficulty. Hitler then decided to go to the Brown House, situated a few hundred metres from the station in the Briennerstrasse.

It was exactly ten o'clock when Hitler entered the Party head-quarters. The building was guarded by S.S. men and in the neighbouring streets were posted soldiers of the Reichswehr, armed and helmeted, but they did not intervene.

The Führer scanned the despatches from Berlin. In conformity with the instructions issued, in accordance with the 'Colibri' plan, Goering and Himmler had 'suppressed' the so-called 'insurrectionary movement'. Throughout the country as a whole the regional commanders of the S.D. and the Gestapo broke the seals of the envelopes containing the confidential instructions drawn up by Heydrich. The commandos of death were everywhere let loose.

In Munich the bloody suppression began early in the afternoon. After a short interrogation, the S.A. leaders were led one by one into the courtyard of the prison where a suffocating heat prevailed. The firing squads were composed of eight picked S.S. men. They obeyed at the command, 'It is the Führer's will. Heil Hitler! Fire!'

A first salvo destroyed August Schneidhuber, S.A. General in Bavaria and prefect of Munich police. There followed General Hans Hayn (Saxony), Hans Peter von Heydebreck (Pomerania), Schmidt (Munich); then General Fritz von Kraussner, Colonels Lasch, Kopp and Erwin Count von Spreti, Colonel Uhl, Lieutenant Reiner and still others.

'And Röhm?' asked Hess.

'I have reprieved Röhm by reason of past services,' answered Hitler, his face rigid.

In Berlin terror was let loose also. In the palace on the Leipzigerplatz, Goering, Himmler or Heydrich gave precise orders. Thus, for example, Goering summoned S.S. Captain Gildisch and simply said to him, 'Find Eric Klausener, President of Catholic Action, and finish him off.'

Gildisch clicked his heels, extended his right arm, saying 'Heil Hitler,' and went off to the Ministry of Transport in search of this new victim. When he found him he fired a single bullet into his head.

Whilst footmen in livery were regularly bringing Goering, Himmler and Heydrich sandwiches and bottles of beer, the Gestapo men were depositing on Goering's desk little white slips of paper which bore one or more names of men arrested and taken to the Cadets' school at Lichterfelde. Goering responded with gleeful violence 'To be shot . . . to be shot . . . to be shot . . .'

Gisevius, who was then in Goering's palace, was much upset by

Himmler and Heydrich: the great manipulators.

Goering (right) makes a gift of his Gestapo to Himmler.

Above The S.S. police chiefs: Huber, Nebe, Himmler,
Heydrich and Müller. (*Ullstein*)

Below left Dr. Werner Best, head of the S.D.

Below right Walter Schellenberg in 1945.

the atmosphere there. He was to write, 'A sudden anguish seized me by the throat. I breathed an air of hatred, tension, civil war and especially blood, a great deal of blood. On all faces, from the sentinels' to that of the lowest orderly could be read that terrible things were happening.'

It was learned that amongst those slaughtered were General von Schleicher, former Chancellor of the Reich and his wife; Councillor von Bose, chef-de-cabinet of Vice-Chancellor von Papen; General von Bredow, anti-Nazi and former head of the Abwehr; Edgard Jung, one of von Papen's advisers; Walter Schotte, Dr. Voss, Col. von Detten, the ace flyer Gerd and many others.

At the Lichterfelde barracks, as soon as the prisoners arrived, handcuffed, they were without delay bound to the wall from which the firing squad was never more than five or six metres distant. The wall was soon spattered with blood. And in his palace in the Leipzigerplatz Goering kept shouting 'To be shot . . .'

Into the Prinz-Albrechtstrasse gaol a prisoner of note had just been taken. Heydrich, immediately notified, smiled. He announced the good news to Goering and Himmler: 'My men have just got hold of Gregor Strasser. He's at the Prinz-Albrechtstrasse. At last the swine will die.'

'Shoot him,' said Goering.

'No,' said Heydrich. 'If you agree it would be better to finish him with a bullet in the head. A firing squad is too great an honour for swine like that.'

Gregor Strasser, one of the earliest Nazis, the one to whom Hitler perhaps owed the most, was a former Socialist, brimming with activity, endowed with great brilliance. He was a fine politician. He had broken with Hitler because he was not a man for nice distinctions: when he condemned, he did not mince his words before Hitler himself as well as Goering, Goebbels, Hess or Himmler. They had an account to settle, they settled it.

He was arrested while lunching at home with his wife and their twins, whose godfather was none other than Adolf Hitler. The eight Gestapo detectives put no question, gave no explanation. They handcuffed Strasser and led him off to the Gestapo prison. He was thrown into a cell with a window looking out on an internal corridor where an S.S. man kept watch. He stayed there several hours without knowing what it was all about, with no one to answer his questions.

Suddenly Strasser discerned a shadow behind the window.

Instinctively he leapt to one side. A revolver shot sounded. The bullet flattened against the wall a foot from his head. Strasser tried to reach the wall into which the window opened, the only place where he would be out of the line of fire. A second shot resounded. He was hit in the shoulder and fell across his bed. Two more shots hit him in the stomach and the thigh. His blood spread round him. At this moment the door opened and three S.S. men[4] entered the cell. They bashed in the face and head of the wounded man with their boots and then left. Gregor Strasser suffered long death pangs, Heydrich having ordered, 'Let the pig bleed.' During the evening, however, an S.S. man returned to the cell and finished him off with a bullet in the nape of the neck.

Throughout Germany the blood bath spread and the repression began to extend beyond the framework assigned to it. Goering liquidated all who had inconvenienced him or whose life seemed a threat. Himmler and Heydrich did the same for the same reasons. Therefore the S.S. chief Anton, Baron of Hohberg und Buchwald, was killed; also von Kahr, former head of the Bavarian government who had played a conspicuous part in the 1923 putsch, Dr. Fritz Beck; Dr. Gehrlich; Dr. Willy Schmidt (killed by mistake); Fr. Stempfle, who knew too much about the 'suicide' of Hitler's niece Geli Raubal; and others.

This 'Night of the Long Knives', as it was called, seemed to have no end. No one has ever been able to construct an exact list of the victims of the massacre. Hitler put the number at seventy-seven, but it is thought that it reached about five hundred.

In the course of the afternoon of Saturday, June 30th, Hitler left Munich for Berlin. At Tempelhof airport, whilst they were waiting for Hitler's plane, the officials saw a small Junker put down at the end of the runway and taxi slowly towards the control tower, then stop near a black Gestapo Mercedes. Captain Gildisch leapt to the ground, then, flanked by two of the S.S. revolver in hand, came S.A. General Karl Ernst whom Gildisch had arrested in Bremen at the moment of his embarkation with his young bride for the Canaries. Gisevius noted, 'the chap seemed to be in good humour. He bounded from the 'plane to the car and smiled on all sides as if wanting to show everybody that he did not take his arrest seriously.' Plainly the S.A. leader did not understand what had occurred. He was to be shot at Lichterfelde crying 'Heil Hitler!' convinced that he was the victim of he did not know what 'reactionary plot'.[5]

Hitler's big three-engined Junkers appeared in the sky. After circling, it landed heavily and taxied towards the officials. When the engines stopped, the S.S. guard of honour stiffened. An oppressive general silence reigned.

H. B. Gisevius relates that 'Hitler got out first. Everything about him was sombre: brown shirt, black tie, leather coat, high regulation boots. His head was bare, his face dead white, he was badly shaved, his features at the same time hollow and swollen, his eyes blank, looking straight ahead and half concealed by a drooping lock . . . Without a word he exchanged salutes with his entourage. Meanwhile, the passengers got down from the plane: Brückner, Schaub, Sepp Dietrich and others. They seemed grave, depressed. Lastly a sinister figure made its appearance: that of Goebbels. Slowly, ceremoniously Hitler passed before the guard of honour. He moved painfully, with heavy steps, from one puddle to another. One had the impression that he was going to sink in. While proceeding towards the row of cars drawn up a few hundred metres away, he stopped with Goering and Himmler. He required a report from these two acolytes, although he had certainly been in touch with them all day by telephone.'

Gisevius continues, 'Then Himmler drew from his sleeve a long tattered list. Hitler went over it, whilst the two men murmured in his ear. One could see Hitler following the reading with his finger, lingering from time to time over a name. The whispering became more animated. Suddenly he threw his head back, with a gesture of such deep emotion, not to say rebellion, that all present noticed it. We glanced at each other significantly, Arthur Nebe[6] and I. We had the same thought. They had just informed him of Gregor Strasser's "suicide".'

A sombre red twilight, very Wagnerian, gave an exceptional character to the scene, its true colour to this day of blood. Was it over? No, Röhm was still alive, in his cell in Munich, under stay of execution, like many others on this night of June 30th/July 1st who feared to be amongst the next victims designated. Fear, terror, anguish placed their stamp on these hallucinatory hours.

The chief of the Prussian police, Kurt Daluege, did not avoid this anguish though apparently nothing threatened him since he had been on the side of the killers, one of them. However, he preferred to set up a camp-bed in his office at the Reich Ministry of the Interior. Gisevius misunderstood. As he was conversing with Daluege's aide-de-camp he said, 'What fine proof of zeal our chief shows by spending the night in his office.'

The other interrupted, 'Zeal? What zeal?' He suddenly turned crimson and his voice shook, 'He's in a funk. A funk. That's why he doesn't go home.'

Ernst Röhm had thus been spared by the Führer.

The night of June 30th/July 1st Goering, Himmler, Sepp Dietrich and Heydrich (it does not seem that Hess was present) gathered in Goering's office. Hitler had to be made to order Röhm executed.[7]

All morning of July 1st, at the Reich Chancellery, Himmler and Goering strove to convince the Führer. In vain. The two sinister confederates persisted. They knew well that Röhm alive was a weapon against them. Hitler knew it too. It was why he evoked the years past, the services rendered. What new arguments did Himmler and Goering find to make Hitler yield step by step? This is unknown. A little before one o'clock they had won. A few moments later the Führer spoke with the Minister of the Interior at Munich. He gave specific orders to S.S. General Theodor Eicke: get rid of Röhm by inducing him, if possible, to commit suicide. Hermann Goering glowed with satisfaction. Heinrich Himmler hid quite well the pleasure he felt.

When he had replaced the receiver Theodor Eicke chose two dependable officers, S.S. Major Lippert and S.S. General Schmausert.[8] All three went to Stadelheim prison.

Twenty-three years had to pass before the exact circumstances of Röhm's murder were put together. I remember the Munich trial in May 1957, of which I spoke in the preceding chapter. Sepp Dietrich and Michael Lippert were in the dock. Both, especially the second, reported for the first time in detail how Röhm was killed.[9]

It was 2.30 p.m. on Sunday, July 1st 1934. In cell 474 Röhm was seated, naked to the waist, on an iron bed. The door opened, Eicke entered, put on the table a revolver loaded with one bullet and a special edition, fresh from the press, of the *Völkischer Beobachter* announcing in large type Röhm's removal from office. He told him, 'You have ruined your life, but the Führer has not forgotten his old companion in arms. He is giving you a chance to draw the necessary conclusions. You have ten minutes.'

Röhm did not answer. Eicke left.

At the end of a quarter of an hour, not having heard a shot, Theodor Eicke drew his revolver from its holster and Michael Lippert did the like. The two S.S. men again entered Röhm's cell;

S.S. General Schmausert, also with revolver in hand, remained in the corridor. Eiche called out, 'Röhm, get ready.' The founder of the S.A. was holding the *Völkischer Beobachter* in his hand. He was standing, still naked to the waist. Lippert, whose hand was trembling with emotion, fired two shots. Röhm fell on his back, between the table and the bed, stammering, 'Mein Führer, mein Führer!' Theodor Eicke then finished him off with a bullet in the chest.

The S.A. was neutralised. Its head lay in a pool of blood, dead. That night Röhm's body was carried, according to some, into the courtyard of Stadelheim prison for burial, according to others to the crematorium in the East Cemetery at Munich.

That Sunday afternoon, July 1st, in Berlin, the Führer gave a tea-party in the gardens of the Reich Chancellery attended by diplomats, ministers, deputies to the Reichstag, high dignitaries of the Party and the S.S. The crowd massed before the Chancellery could be heard acclaiming the Führer. The latter, aglow, went to the window and saluted the crowd, which shouted 'Heil Hitler!'

Gisevius, who was observing him when he returned to the garden, noted, 'I understood at this moment how much the man was on edge that day and that he was trying to escape from his inner trouble by taking refuge in the pose which from then on became his most efficient weapon.'

Surrounded by diplomats and elegant women, Goering, in a magnificent pearl-grey uniform covered with decorations, did not look at all troubled. He was radiant, triumphant. Less conspicuous, surrounded by several S.S. officers and Party dignitaries, Heinrich Himmler, the man in black, was smiling circumspectly. Heydrich was absent, at Gestapo headquarters. He rounded off the 'Night of the Long Knives' which would give the S.S. in general, that is to say Himmler, and the Gestapo in particular, in other words Heydrich, increasing power. More men were to die during the night of July 1st/2nd.

When a young S.S. officer handed Hitler a message announcing that Röhm had refused to commit suicide and been killed, the Führer turned very pale. He put the message in his pocket and a few minutes later withdrew to his own apartment.

In the evening Hitler received a telegram of congratulation: 'It appears from reports that I had rendered to me that you have crushed all the seditious intrigues and attempts at treason thanks to your energetic, courageous personal intervention. You have delivered the German people from a great danger. I offer you my profound gratitude and my sincere regards.

Von Hindenburg.'

It was only at 3.30 on the morning of Monday, July 2nd 1934, that Hitler finally ordered Heydrich to stop the executions. A few hours later the Führer addressed an order of the day to the S.A. demanding of them 'the most perfect discipline, a loyalty and fidelity without reserve to the Army of the Reich'. He had succeeded in liquidating internal opposition as he had a year earlier liquidated the Socialist–Communist opposition.

The heads of the Reichswehr had obtained what they wanted. They forgot the spilling of Generals Schleicher's and Bredow's blood. They wanted to forget the part played by the S.S. Had not General von Reichenau been charged with re-organising, at the military level, the S.A. troops? Ten years later, on July 20th 1944, these same generals would try to assassinate Hitler. They would fail and the result would be *their* Night of the Long Knives, but that one would be marked by nearly ten thousand executions.

During the summer of 1934 blows rained upon the men in brown. The total of S.A. effectives was progressively reduced from three million to little more than one million. The S.A. was no longer armed. The new chief of staff, Viktor Lutze, issued an order of the day on July 3rd confirming the thirty days' leave prescribed and requiring that the name of Röhm be obliterated from the blade of the S.A. dagger of honour, the blade of the 'long knives'.

'From a military the S.A. became a militant formation,' observed Jacques Benoist-Méchin. In the French weekly *Candide*[10] Jean Fayard wrote, 'Physically a militiaman of the S.A. is the instrument of political power. Morally he is a minor priest of a new religion.'

The S.S. became the major priests. It was they who were the real victors of the Night of the Long Knives. They had strictly applied the motto Hitler had given them, 'My honour is called fidelity' . . . at the price, if the Führer required it, of his brother's blood. In every city in Germany the men in black were fêted. The Gauleiter Terboven declared to the crowd assembled in the Adolf-Hitler Platz in Essen; 'Fidelity is something fundamental, the abscess has been lanced; there existed elements of corruption as there exist everywhere. But what matters is to know how to react against gangrene.' And 'Sieg Heil!' greeted the men of the Black

Order who marched preceded by music, acclaimed, flattered, triumphant, more disquieting than ever.

In Berlin, Heydrich congratulated Hermann Behrends and Alfred Naujocks for their 'excellent work of preparation'. The two S.S. secret service men were promoted. Himmler congratulated Sepp Dietrich and Theodor Eicke for their 'efficiency' at Munich. They too were promoted to a higher grade in the S.S. As for Reinhard Heydrich, he was rewarded by Himmler in July 15th for 'the capital role' he had just played and promoted to General of an army corps (S.S. Gruppenführer) as of June 30th 1934. He had won the confidence of Hitler. Goering, Hess and Goebbels, who had been his accomplices and henceforth regarded him as one of themselves. The real rise of Reinhard Heydrich began, that of the S.S. secret service and of the Gestapo as well.

NOTES TO CHAPTER 5

1. No relation to Sepp Dietrich, commander of the *Leibstandarte S.S. Adolf Hitler*.
2. In April 1940 Joseph Terboven was appointed Commissar of the Reich in occupied Norway. He became an alcoholic and had difficulties with Heydrich and Schellenberg. After Germany's capitulation he committed suicide (May 1945).
3. Hermann Goering and Ernst Röhm were witnesses at Karl Ernst's wedding in Berlin.
4. According to Gregor Strasser's brother Otto, who claimed to have the information from the warden who wiped up the blood in the cell and was instructed to remove the bullet marks from the walls, two of the S.S. men were called Reinhard Heydrich and Theodor Eicke. As to the former it was possible but improbable, as to the latter it was impossible since he was then in Munich.
5. Karl Ernst was executed, according to some (without proof), for having 'participated in the Reichstag fire' in order to suppress an 'embarrassing witness'. It will never be known.
6. An S.S. General, chief of the Criminal Police, who was to become fiercely anti-Nazi and was ultimately hanged by the S.S. in 1945.
7. In May 1957 Sepp Dietrich told me that he had not been present at this meeting.
8. Deposition of Michael Lippert. *Cf*. Chap. 4, Note 2. Theodor Eicke was killed on the Eastern Front in 1943.
9. I followed the proceedings from May 6th to May 14th 1957 as special correspondent of a Paris daily. There were only two French journal-

ists, the correspondent of *Agence France Presse* and myself. One of my colleagues, the American John Dornberg, gave an excellent analysis of this trial in his book *Schizophrenic Germany*.

10. *Candide*, October 7th 1937.

6

One Name Too Many on the List

Schellenberg entered upon his functions in the service of the S.D. at Bonn on July 2nd 1934. He was still, he told me, 'fascinated by his sight of Hitler at Bad Godesberg three days earlier'. The bloody purge seems not to have shocked him. He was only twenty-four and had no rank, no responsibility in the S.S. He did not know what had happened in the higher spheres. He believed Goebbels's propaganda: there had been an attempt at a putsch, but the Führer had nipped it in time, thanks to the S.S. Schellenberg asked himself no further questions. A wind of victory blew over Himmler's Black Order.

On the morrow of the Night of the Long Knives the S.S. soared, as it were with its own wings. Its prestige grew. The Party directorate commissioned the S.S. secret service—the only centralised organisation of Intelligence—to follow, in fact to frustrate, the intrigues of the lesser Nazi potentates; to keep informed, in that jungle of hostile clans, of all the rivalries, open or underground. Rudolf Hess as 'Führer's representative' proclaimed the S.D. to be 'the Party's sole official Intelligence service'.

The spirit that ruled the S.D. attracted the young and ambitious Schellenberg. Those round him were animated by the same feeling and thought as he did. Disgusted by the Weimar Republic, partisans of a regime specifically German, of which the first condition was the omnipotence of the state, to which 'any sacrifice was owing', they were fiercely National Socialist, anti-capitalist, steeped in hatred of anything that might recall the social catastrophe of the bourgeoisie, the economic crisis of the 1930s. Their anti-semitism was born of their resentment of the trusts and the banks. For these 'aristocrats' of National Socialism the vulgar ideology of the veterans of the Party (especially of the S.A.) was out-dated. The National Socialist revolution must be 'reasonable', ruled by a clear and healthy intelligence. It is enough to say that they had little appreciation of

73

the gulf between the ideas they held and developed, and the reality with which they were daily confronted: the arrogance and fatuity of the Party bosses, the opportunism of the big and little Nazis, the quarrels of the factions, the corrupt practices of all sorts. It was not thus that they imagined the Third Reich. The nation had to be put into good order. 'The S.D.', said Himmler, 'is the ideological information service of the Party and the state . . . It must struggle against the enemy . . . against the Communists, the Jews, the Free-masons, the reactionaries, against confessional or politicising groups.' Tireless, the agents of the S.S. secret service went about fulfilling their immense task, uncovering the least ideological irregularity, noting down the smallest organic defect in the course of their clinical scrutiny of the nation put in their charge. Schellenberg said, 'Information flowed in increasingly to the headquarters of the S.S. secret service in Berlin where it was recorded, examined from all angles, and instigated orders which kept the police and the Gestapo perpetually on the alert.'

Events followed at an accelerated rhythm. Barely twenty-five days after the Night of the Long Knives the S.S. participated in a sensational murder committed beyond the German frontiers. It was on the occasion of an attempted National Socialist putsch in Vienna during which the Austrian Federal Chancellor, Dr. Engel-bert Dollfuss, was assassinated by Austrian members of the 89th S.S. regiment. The *coup d'état* failed. World opinion was roused to indig-nation. Mussolini massed his troops on the Brenner. Hitler dis-avowed the murderers and performed a thorough 'cleansing' on Himmler and Heydrich. It seems, however, that the 'cleansing' was pure form. After the *Anschluss* with Austria in 1938 he had a com-memorative plaque attached to the Federal Chancellery in Vienna on which could be read, 'Here on July 25th 1934 German soldiers of the 89th S.S. regiment fought. Seven of them were hanged.'

On August 1st 1934 the Minister of Defence, von Blomberg, signed a decree entitled, 'The law concerning the supreme head of state of the German Reich.' Its first paragraph stipulated that 'The functions of President of the Reich are added to those of the Chancellor. Consequently the powers at present vested in the President of the Reich. . . .' The second paragraph stated, 'This law will take effect on the date of the death of President of the Reich von Hindenburg.'

The next day, August 2nd 1934, Field Marshal Paul von Hinden-burg, President of the Reich, died. A few hours later the soldiers of the Reichswehr, officers and general officers first, took an oath of loyalty to Hitler as Commander in Chief of the armed forces.

Schellenberg quickly became adept in the working of the S.S. secret service at Bonn. After a few weeks he left for Frankfurt where he was to undergo a course of training at police headquarters. His abilities were soon recognised by his superiors, who entrusted him with the most interesting and important cases. 'I had the impression that my acts and doings were ruled by some invisible hand.' He was not long in discovering this 'invisible hand'.

In the autumn of 1934 Schellenberg was charged with a delicate mission. He was sent to Paris for a month 'with orders to bring to light the political aims of a certain professor at the Sorbonne', he writes in his Memoirs. When I saw Schellenberg in Italy I did not know about this mission and so could not question him about this Frenchman. Since then no testimony or document has turned up to clarify this point.

Back in Frankfurt he drew up a report on his mission. A few days later he was congratulated. He was appointed to Berlin, where he was to receive training in different services of the Gestapo and the S.D., then closely intertwined, before receiving a definite post. At Berlin he first worked under Dr. Oswald Schaefer, former director of the Criminal Police and head of the Gestapo at Munich.[1] He later observed, 'This was an extremely interesting period for me. Officials of all ranks could not have been more agreeable and courteous, and all doors opened before me as if some invisible power were silently at work in the complex processes of this gigantic machine.'

One day he received an order to report to S.S. General Werner Best. For nearly an hour the two men discussed a purely technical dossier. As Schellenberg was leaving Dr. Best said to him, 'I don't know what Heydrich has in mind for you. Probably he will explain it to you one day.'

Schellenberg was surprised. 'This remark of Dr. Best's', he told me in Italy, 'left me deeply thoughtful and in particular uneasy. I didn't know Heydrich and he didn't know me. We had never met, not even in a corridor. Why should the supreme head of the S.S. secret service and of the Gestapo be interested in me? I didn't dare to question Dr. Best, one of the most eminent heads of the S.D. Was it a good thing or a bad?'

Dr. Karl Rudolf Werner Best, a native of Hesse, was in truth a strong personality. A disciple of Ernst Jünger, he was a convinced nationalist and uncompromising defender of the overriding reason of state. In 1930 he published an essay in which he wrote in particular 'The object of every power within the state is to dominate all the other powers. In this struggle each power tries to identify itself with the state, whose basic tendency is total power; the wider the power of the state extends, the nearer the state is to perfection.' Chief of police in Hesse in 1933, he was not long in coming into conflict with the Gauleiter, Sprenger, and Himmler then appointed him head of the S.D. in Bavaria. At the end of 1934 he was put in charge of the S.D. in the capital. On January 1st 1935 he was named Superior Government Councillor and chief of the judicial and administrative section of the Gestapo in Berlin. He engaged also in certain matters of espionage and counter-espionage abroad. His influence was great in the S.S. secret service. We shall have further occasion to speak of him.[2]

On leaving him, still for service reasons, Schellenberg paid a visit to S.S. Colonel Heinrich Müller, who was already virtual head of the Gestapo. Schellenberg said, 'The contrast between these two men [Best and Müller] was very striking. Best was a cultivated man, with an excessive leaning towards intellectuality, whilst Müller was dry and laconic. Small and stocky, with the square skull of a peasant and a protruding forehead, he had thin lips and penetrating brown eyes veiled by heavy lids which quivered nervously. His hands, with square fingers, were broad and massive. This man, who began his career as a simple detective, was to play a preponderant role in my life . . . He ended our first conversation by saying, "Heydrich appreciates your reports. If you were sent to us it was not only through routine. You are in fact going to work at the central office of the S.D., which depends on the Party rather than the Government. A pity! I would make better use of you in my administration." Despite his friendly farewell, his eyes and his expression remained cold. I did not then know of his profound resentment towards the S.D.

'The mystery of my promotion was thus made a little clearer. Best and Müller had both said that Heydrich took an interest in me. So the formidable head of the S.D. himself represented the invisible force which had guided me, like a pawn on a chessboard through all the windings of the Nazi secret police. The next day I reported to the central office of the S.D.'

Schellenberg was enrolled in the service of S.S. Colonel Herbert Mehlhorn who was charged with the secret surveillance of all spheres of German life. This gigantic task would require the creation, in September 1939, of a special department of the S.S. secret service: The internal S.D. (*SD—Inland*) which would be placed under the direction of Otto Ohlendorf.

Herbert Mehlhorn was a strange character whom Schellenberg quickly learned to know well and to esteem.[3] Born into a rich industrial family, he had studied law and practised as a lawyer in a large industrial city in Saxony. Schellenberg thus describes him:

'Not very impressive in appearance, almost ugly, he possessed an extraordinary intelligence combined with remarkable gifts as an organiser. His chief defect was a lack of decision in his attitude towards others and his great tactical mistake was to try to manoeuvre against Heydrich within the S.S. itself. Soon the latter set to work to eliminate this adversary and bring about his fall. Mehlhorn was certainly not a Nazi, since he did not profess an absolute loyalty to National Socialist ideas, which the Party required. Later, when I knew him better, he said to me in the course of one of our long conversations, "National Socialism is only one of many stages in the history of the German people. It is merely how the eternal German idealism today expresses itself. Whether this new stage will end in success no one knows. But to talk of a thousand-year-Reich is pure absurdity." Herbert Mehlhorn thus rejected one of Hitler's favourite themes.'

When welcoming Schellenberg to the central office of the S.D. Mehlhorn told him, 'Heydrich seems to be much impressed by your activity. He warmly recommended you to me. Do you know him?'

'No,' answered Schellenberg frankly.

'It's odd . . .' said Mehlhorn, shaking his head.

'I've never seen him.'

Mehlhorn said nothing and looked at his new colleague with an evasive air. He was only half convinced.

It was at this period that Schellenberg made the acquaintance of Alfred Naujocks, of whom we have already had occasion to speak. The two young S.S. men of the secret service were not in sympathy. Of Schellenberg, Naujocks said to the English journalist Gunther Peis, 'He is a fusspot, a swaggerer. He has a brilliant mind but he's artful and too ambitious to be honest. He is a master of the art of deceit. From our first contact I distrusted him.' On his side Schellenberg said to me of Naujocks, 'He was brave and full of ardour. His fanaticism irritated me. He was violent, proud of his former brawls with the Communists and of his exploits in the boxing ring. He was a secret service technician, a specialist in the surprise attack. His intelligence was lively but limited. He had no culture. I don't know why, but he always seemed to have an inferiority complex with me. Our relations were always friendly but cold.'

Naujocks, who always worked under the direct orders of Behrends, was in high favour with Heydrich. The latter entrusted him with secret dossiers concerning Soviet agents discovered in Germany and neighbouring countries. The young S.S. man daily saw the dossiers swell. The German–Soviet relations were officially friendly but the secret services of the two countries were engaged in a relentless struggle. Every episode in this war enriched Naujocks's files—within the S.S. secret service he figured as 'specialist in counter-espionage of the Russian section'. He did not conceal his pride. He was however only an administrative agent. Heydrich decided to put his promising youngster to the test and 'launch him in the field'. An occasion arose. A new name appeared incessantly in the reports transmitted from sources as distant from one another as Leningrad, Warsaw, Bucharest and Vienna: that of Anton Horvath.

The S.D. dossier concerning him stated that he was a Major in the Czechoslovak army, a farmer's son, aged thirty-three, a bachelor. This calm efficient, cultured and ambitious man had been, in 1931, sent on a mission to Moscow. He was on friendly terms with a certain number of Red Army officials and had often been seen in the company of Marshal Tukhachevsky, with whom, it appeared, he had been in constant relations. Two years later he was chosen by Prague for a period in Berlin in the office of the Czechoslovak military attaché. His intelligence and charm opened the diplomatic and military circles of the German capital to him. He consorted with the officers of the general staff of the Reichswehr. He was even several times received by Generals von Blomberg and von Reichenau. Of course, Major Anton Horvath was, during his stay in Berlin, the object of constant surveillance by the Abwehr (the Intelligence Service of the Army, then commanded by the naval Captain Patzig) and from another side by the S.S. secret service. Nothing suspect was then recorded. His departure from Berlin at the beginning of 1934 was marked by a brilliant reception at the Czechoslovak embassy and the many officers from the general staff of the Reichswehr present expressed their regrets to him.

At the beginning of August 1934 Naujocks met a double agent from Prague, Joseph Borg, who, working alike for the Russians and the Germans and receiving large sums from both, informed the S.S. secret service that Major Anton Horvath was receiving more or less secret intelligence from the German High Command, from officers he had known during his stay in Berlin. Borg's information was meagre but it revealed to Naujocks that the German High Command harboured traitors. From another source Naujocks learned that Major Anton Horvath in reality was working for the Soviets. Before speaking of it to his superiors, Naujocks studied the matter carefully. He had a presentiment that it was important. He first found out all he could about Joseph Borg. The latter seemed to him to be the archetype of double agent, that is, a spy who works for everybody and is a danger to everybody. One could not, obviously, have confidence in him. However, moved by some sixth sense, Naujocks reckoned that Borg was not lying. Why then did he denounce to the Germans an agent of the Russian espionage for which Borg himself was working? It was another story that Naujocks promised himself to clear up. Information on Horvath poured in. It cross-checked with Borg's. Naujocks decided to go to Heydrich with the Czecho-slovak Major's dossier. He handed his chief a resumé of the situation which he had composed, saying 'I consider that we should take a very close interest in this Major Horvath.'

When Heydrich had finished reading, Naujocks added, 'This may be the new Soviet agent who seems so well versed in the dispositions and the slightest movement of our forces in the East.'

'It's possible,' said Heydrich, 'what exactly do we know about this Soviet agent?'

'Practically nothing, except that he is remarkably well informed and that on the evidence he has access to the Reichswehr's files. As you have always recommended me not to get the people from "the house opposite"[4] mixed up in our affairs, I have no idea what the Abwehr on its side knows. So far as we know the documents he has transmitted in the course of recent months were not top secret, but all the same unpleasantly near to being. It may also be that we only have knowledge of a quarter of these messages. In any case he must be a terribly busy man.'

Heydrich opened the dossier and ran through it rapidly. He asked, 'Is it your belief that the new Soviet agent in question and Major Anton Horvath are the same person?'

'To be convinced,' replied Naujocks cautiously, 'I should need other proofs. Nevertheless, I think it is the same.'

'Have you shown this dossier to Behrends?' pursued Heydrich.

'He has been informed of everything from the start, and it was he who suggested that I talk to you if any new element should appear.'

'Well, if he can spare you for a few days I'd like you to pay a visit to Major Horvath and see what you can get out of him.' Heydrich added the stipulation, 'Careful! No violence and don't be disappointed if this journey to Prague leads nowhere. We'll say that it is actually only a routine check.'

Before Naujocks left Heydrich said, 'Make no mistake, Naujocks, I am not so much interested in Horvath as in his sources of information. I want to know who the traitor is in the German command.'

The same evening Naujocks took the train for Prague. He was delighted to escape from the administrative routine but he realised that for this first mission his instructions were rather vague.

Naujocks told Gunther Peis, 'I advanced into the enemy camp without a weapon, without a plan. Doubtless I would first have to meet Borg, but even this interview would have to be maturely thought out, the chap being not very estimable. In any event, without Borg's help at the beginning it was obvious that I would not get very far. The information from this double agent had been accepted. It didn't matter much whether one placed confidence in him, a little more or a little less . . . I had to run the risk of every spy in a foreign city, of being arrested, of having an "accident", being kidnapped or at least subjected to strict observation. In short, I was convinced that a meeting with Borg would inevitably have repercussions and whatever happened was better, all in all, than a sterile wait. I didn't sleep much that night in the train, and it was a rather disillusioned and nervous spy who turned up at the Central Hotel in the early morning.'

After a copious breakfast Naujocks telephoned Joseph Borg and asked him to come to his hotel immediately.

'Impossible before lunchtime,' answered the agent.

Naujocks was a little surprised. All right! To master his impatience, he went for a walk in the centre of Prague, which he did not know. At noon he found Borg in the hotel bar. He was a small man, heavily built, carefully dressed. 'He's a man,' thought Naujocks, 'who should be robust but good cheer has softened him a bit.' His face was furrowed with wrinkles. His look was curiously intent. His lower lip drooped. Naujocks felt ill at ease. However, he made the opening move. 'Your note,' he said, 'was very interesting. Have you had further news of your friend?'

Borg shook his head and asked, 'Have you any instructions for me?'

Naujocks plunged his nose in his glass to gain time. It was

precisely the question that troubled him. What the devil could he give him in the way of instructions? The other drank also, in silence. Naujocks took the plunge. 'I'd like to meet him,' he said in a voice as firm as possible.

Borg started. 'It's not impossible,' he said, 'but—whom are you going to pass yourself as?'

On the impulse of the moment Naujocks had conceived a plan. He took a swallow of alcohol and replied, 'Tell him that I am an important person working for Moscow and charged with a special mission. Tell him that I may have need of him and that in any event I should like to meet him to thank him for his excellent work.'

Borg gave a furtive smile. 'It's an unsubtle ruse,' he said, 'but good luck to you.' He added with a touch of contempt in his voice, 'It may work since he's not a real professional.'

The remark got on Naujocks's nerves. Neither was he a real professional! He felt it only too keenly in the face of Borg's placidity. The latter, on leaving, said, 'I'll telephone you about six. I don't promise anything, but I'll do my best.'

After lunch in the hotel restaurant, Naujocks went to his room to get a raincoat; he wanted to take a walk and it was raining. On opening the door his glance fell on the suitcase he had left on his bed. It had been moved. He quickly noted that it had been searched: his razor, which he had put in one of his shoes, was now wrapped in a washing glove. All sorts of ideas swirled in his brain. He had no documents or compromising objects. The fact was, nevertheless, that someone had been interested in his case and searched it. Who? A Czechoslovak agent? A Soviet agent? He bitterly blamed himself for the negligence. In the future he would lock his case with a key. He felt deeply, deeply humiliated that a bell-boy or a chambermaid had been able to take advantage of his stupidity. He had nothing to hide, but all the same! He had just learned a lesson he would never forget.

Naujocks returned from his walk a little before six and had tea brought him in his room. He was waiting for Borg's telephone call. A quarter of an hour passed, a half hour . . . nothing. Naujocks paced his room like a lion in a cage. 6.45, nothing. It was nearly seven when the telephone finally rang. The voice on the other end of the wire said laconically, 'In a half hour at the same place.'

Naujocks did not open his mouth. Borg had already hung up. For the first time that day Naujocks felt gripped by excitement. He went down to the bar and ordered a double whiskey on the rocks which he drank at a gulp.

At 7.30 Naujocks saw Borg coming towards him accompanied by a couple. He had eyes only for the man, tall, thin, prematurely grey, a handsome face lighted by smiling eyes. He had a distinguished bearing in his Major's uniform. Naujocks was tormented by a doubt: this man was far from the classic image of a spy as he in his innocence had imagined him. He would have sworn that he was a brilliant officer and a man of the world.

Joseph Borg made the introductions. It was then that Naujocks took note of the very dark and very pretty young woman introduced to him as Paula, the Major's sister. Her black eyes had an extraordinary sparkle as she said, 'I'm delighted to meet you. I hope you are not angry with me for coming. My brother never takes me anywhere. But I'm proud to go out with him. He's so good looking in uniform, isn't he?'

Her voice sent a shiver up the nape of Naujocks's neck. Major Horvath laughed. 'Joseph assured us that you knew nobody in Prague, so Paula at once insisted on coming.'

'I'm delighted she did,' murmured Naujocks, who admired this magnificent girl dressed and hatted with such rare elegance. He noticed a curious and amusing dimple at the end of her nose, small greedy lips, the delicate ears adorned with ear-rings set with diamonds, and especially a breast 'to damn a whole monastery of monks' (an expression familiar to him).

Beyond doubt Naujocks was charmed: Paula for her part did not have the air of finding the young German uninteresting. She threw him a troubling glance.

After having had a quick drink Borg, with a glance at his wrist watch, said, 'I think it's time for me to go. I've an appointment. Do forgive me . . .' He disappeared after a brief exchange of courtesies.

Naujocks suggested dinner. His companions took him to a restaurant in the Old City, calm, candle-lit. In the taxi he had time to take stock of the situation. It was somewhat unusual and, by and large, he still did not feel sure of himself. Nothing indicated that this man was a secret agent, as Borg had assured him, except for the fact that he was there for a discussion with 'a special envoy of the Soviet espionage'. But if he wanted to talk 'business' why was he accompanied by his sister, if sister she was? Naujocks felt the warm body of Paula close to him. He was extremely troubled. She wore an intoxicating perfume. The evening promised to be not unpleasant. Naujocks decided to let himself be guided by the Major's conduct.

In the restaurant they seated themselves at a secluded table. Paula was opposite Naujocks who, overcome by her beauty, did not take his eyes off her. At the beginning of the meal Paula excused herself for a moment. Major Horvath leaned over towards Naujocks and said in a low voice, 'I have the impression that you are rather taken with Paula.'

'Extremely,' returned Naujocks with a half smile.

'It's enough that one of us is mixed up in this,' said the Major soberly, 'but now she is too. Though God knows I didn't influence her. She is very valuable to us and her efficiency is great.'

Naujocks stiffened with surprise. Could Paula likewise be working for the Soviets? Quickly getting his expression under control he mumbled, 'No doubt, no doubt.'

It was with relief that he saw Paula return. He studied her with fresh interest. It was Paula who, with the smoked salmon, began openly talking 'business'. She asked Naujocks, 'Now long do you expect to stay in Prague? If we can help you in any way, just tell us.'

'I expect to stay a few days,' he replied evasively. 'Thank you for your offer but I don't need anything. I merely wanted to meet you to chat about things in general.' But he added, 'It's for me to ask if I can help you. Have you any complaints to make about us?'

Major Horvath hastened to answer, 'Not in the least, everything is going splendidly. Nevertheless, I should like to devote some money to exploiting a possible contact. It has to do with a Luftwaffe man whose mother is a Czech. He works in a secret German enterprise near Lübeck. He is in difficulty at the moment and I'd like to come to his help.'

Naujocks nodded, 'Good enough. We can arrange that.'

He now knew what he wanted to know about the precise role of Major Horvath. He no longer had any trouble in carrying on the conversation. He had entered into the skin of his character as a special Soviet emissary. His guests did not for an instant suspect him. They were at his mercy. He exploited the situation to the limit. Two bottles of Tokay made them agreeably familiar. At the end of the meal he had gathered a number of very useful bits of information. In particular he had learned the name of the Luftwaffe man in Lübeck, the names of three Soviet 'converts' in Germany as well as the cover name of their messenger. He knew also, and this was less agreeable, that Paula at times effected the liaison between Prague and Berlin. The idea that Paula was mixed up in all this continued to disconcert him somewhat.

After a final glass in Major Horvath's flat, Naujocks accompanied Paula home on foot through the deserted streets. She gave him her arm, pressed against him. He felt an irresistible need to ask her why she had chosen this dangerous life, but did not succeed in finding an excuse for broaching the subject. He thought with regret that they would have to separate. Arrived at the block of flats in which Paula lived, it was she who offered her lips, she who proposed that he spend the night with her. Thirty years later Naujocks retained a wondering memory.

The next day he returned to Berlin. He drew up for Heydrich a long detailed report with many notes as well as his interpretation of his conversations with Major Horvath and the list of names he had collected. All the names except one.

Heydrich and Behrends were delighted: they had out-stripped the counter espionage services of the Abwehr and, in particular, won the first round in their contest with the High Command: three officers of the General Staff traitors,[5] it was a good bag! Schellenberg, who had recently been performing a period of service with Behrends, was informed and the dossier opened to him. He studied it and then had quite a long conversation about it with Naujocks.

Three weeks later Naujocks received a copy of the list of six arrested persons. Five, amongst them the three officers of the Reichs-wehr general staff, were taken as the result of his information, the sixth was removed from a train going from Prague to Berlin and found to be in possession of a microfilm. Her name was Paula Horvath.

Naujocks was never to know who added this sixth name to the list. Was it Joseph Borg, who had communicated it directly to Behrends? Was it Schellenberg, who had guessed everything when questioning Naujocks?

Several days later Schellenberg was summoned by Heydrich. The latter did not speak of the Horvath affair. Schellenberg wrote in his Memoirs: 'It was with real apprehension that I passed through the Gestapo building where he had his office. Perhaps I was at last to know what designs he had for me.

'When I entered his study Heydrich was sitting behind a desk . . . His voice was much too high for so strong a man and his speech nervous and jerky. Although he almost never ended his sentences, he always succeeded in clearly expressing his thought. My first interview with him went quite well. He first spoke to me of my family, then of music. He questioned me about my legal studies, my career as a lawyer . . . When he began to talk of the organisation and extension of the counter-espionage system in Germany, as well as of the political secret service, his voice took on a grave and urgent tone; I at once realised that he was talking to a subordinate and criticised strongly certain aspects of my reports, warning me against a tendency to treat judicial questions too conventionally. At the end of an hour and a half he terminated the interview and I left his office greatly impressed by the force of his personality, developed to a point I had never before encountered and have never encountered since.'

After this interview Walter Schellenberg's career was to take a new turn. The young S.S. man was to be placed under the orders of Dr. Werner Best and devote himself more and more to counter-espionage.

NOTES TO CHAPTER 6

1. Dr. Oswald Schaefer, member of the N.S.D.A.P. (No. 1 772 081) and of the S.S. (No. 272 488) was in his capacity of *Obersturmbannführer S.S.*, at the head of the 9th intervention commando (*Einsatzkommando*) which operated in the U.S.S.R. from June 1941. After 1945 he underwent two years of preventive detention but was not involved in the Nuremberg trial devoted to the *Einsatzgruppen* which took place between July 25th 1947 and April 9th 1948. He was acquitted in two trials (1950 and 1966) for 'insufficient evidence'.

2. Werner Best, *Die deutschen Aufsichtverwaltungen, vergleichende Ubersicht (Manuskript, 1941)*: The German surveillance services—a comparison. Manuscript to be found in the Institute for the Problems of Occupation at Tübingen (*Institut für Besatzungsfragen,* Tübingen). Cf. Also *T.M.I.N.,* Vols XVII, XX and XXI.

3. *T.M.I.N.,* Vol. XX and Document D-419.

4. In the language of the S.S. secret service 'the house opposite' meant the rival service, namely the Intelligence service of the Army (Abwehr). In the Abwehr the same expression was used to designate the S.S. Secret Service.

5. The names of the three officers are unknown. Naujocks never divulged them and they do not figure in the dossier of this affair which was found in the archives of the Gestapo (Bundesarchiv, Coblenz).

7

The Polish Spy Sosnowski

We now go back five years, to 1929, to the Ministry of the Reichs-wehr, in the Bendlerstrasse, and an office of the General Staff, that of Lieutenant-Colonel Bender.[1]

For two hours he had been dictating to his secretary, Benita, some new notes which substantially modified the ultra-secret document on which he had been working for a week. He was satisfied with Benita's work. Her typed text was a masterpiece of clarity, cleanliness and form. After an attentive re-reading he shut it away, with the rest of the dossier, in the large safe built into the wall.

Returning to his seat behind his desk, Bender could not help admiring once again the pretty girl who had been working for him for nearly eight months. Quietly made up and scented, she had long black hair rolled into a tight coil on the nape of her neck which rounded off her face and set off her brown skin, her well-formed ears and warm look. She had a small nose above a large mouth with full sensual lips. Dressed in the latest fashion copied from that of Paris, she often wore those odd straight skirts which ended above the knee and slid back over her thighs when she was seated.

Bender was not in love with his secretary. This brilliant officer of the First World War, who had won his officer's braid under fire, was still young, forty, but he was married to a magnificent woman aged thirty, a tall blond Pomeranian who had given him two fine children. For ten years they had lived together lovingly in untroubled fidelity. But Bender could admire beauty and his secretary was beautiful, of high breeding, distinguished. He entertained a great respect for her. She was a brave girl, energetic, with real intelligence and of a noble family. In his eyes Benita was a rare pearl, a dream of a secretary.

In this year 1929 Benita, née von Zollikopfen-Altenkligen—a family celebrated since the Middle Ages for the grim warriors it had bestowed on Germany—had just divorced Count Kurt von Falken-hayn, son of one of the Kaiser's Field Marshals. She was twenty-eight. She had married after receiving a superior education, finishing her studies in Switzerland and England. An excellent horsewoman, a good swimmer and a tennis champion, she also was a good painter. Unfortunately her father, a high officer in the imperial army, had died leaving only a meagre pension. Since her divorce she lived with her mother in precarious circumstances.

In the Weimar Republic of the Thirties poverty amongst the daughters or wives of officers was not a blemish. The Treaty of Versailles had limited the Reichswehr to a hundred thousand men; pay and pensions were at a derisory level; and, since there was a lack of man-power, the daughters of the military caste accepted beggarly salaries to fill the void in the establishment. Benita became one of them at the General Staff in Berlin's Bendlerstrasse.

An enthusiastic equestrienne and horse-lover in general, Benita went as often as she could to horse shows. One afternoon, in the bar at a race course, she met an extremely attractive Polish officer, Jurik von Sosnowski, the Chevalier von Nalecz. Then aged thirty, he still had the charm of youth. Tall, extremely well-mannered, he had large blue eyes half-veiled by short sensuous lids under arched brows. His small mouth seemed set in a mocking kiss. A keen woman chaser, Sosnowski soon captivated Benita.

The young divorcée introduced him to her mother. He treated Frau von Zollikopfen-Altenkligen with chivalrous tact and soon re-established the ladies' way of life in its former level of splendour. Their debts were paid and they again led an existence corresponding to their social rank. The old lady came ardently to wish that this rich and brilliant officer should become her son-in-law. The more she saw the sentimental links between him and her daughter tightened, the more she gained confidence in the future.

Lieutenant-Colonel Bender had observed the transformation in his secretary, for Sosnowski had asked Benita to keep her job in the Bendlerstrasse 'till our wedding day'. She was smartly dressed, her hair, make-up and perfume elegant. Her face radiated happiness. Her affair with Sosnowski was marvellous and madly passionate.

Benita and Jurik had been in love three months when one evening she made a curious discovery. They had gone for supper to a large restaurant in the Kurfurstendamm with some aviation officers. The conversation seemed to have excited Sosnowski. He was gay and lively when he took Benita back to his flat. While he was changing in the bath room into a luxurious green silk dressing gown embroidered with gold, she set to work to tidy up his clothes which he had scattered round the room. She was intrigued by the shirt cuffs covered with pencilled notes. She was about to put it into the wash basket when she suddenly heard Sosnowski, back in the room, roar, 'Where did you put my shirt? I need it at once.'

She kept her calm and answered, 'Do you want the shirt or the cuffs?'

'My cuffs,' he said without noticing the suggestion.

She handed them to him. Her lover's activity in Berlin had just been made brutally plain to her.

'You've got a bad memory,' she exclaimed.

He looked at her in surprise. Her expression was tense, her hands shook. She went on, 'A secret agent compelled to take notes like a common race-goer!'

The blow struck home. He attempted a denial, but his position was untenable. Benita was intelligent. The whole night they had a passionate discussion which their embraces only renewed. In the early morning Benita ended by telling him that his work as a spy did not appeal to her. She felt no special interest in Poland. So far as she knew, the Polish peasants had everything to gain by living under German rule. However, she loved Sosnowski and that was all that mattered: she belonged to him wholly, she would be his accomplice. She agreed to serve him thenceforth as secretary, as messenger. She would do anything to help him.

'That night,' Sosnowski stated several years later to the English spy E. H. Cookridge, 'I destroyed the woman I loved most in the world.'

No doubt, but that night he demanded nothing less of her than a guarantee more solid than a passionate vow. He extracted from her an acknowledgement of the debt of which mention has been made in a form highly compromising to the borrower. 'Received from the Intelligence Officer—the Polish Major Jurik von Sosnowski, Chevalier von Nalecz, the sum of two thousand marks.'

When Benita was later in the clutches of the Gestapo she wrote out her confession and alluded to the conclusion of the pact with a sincerity that admitted no doubt. 'I loved him,' she wrote. 'He had a weakness for smart women of refined elegance. To please him I accepted money, all the more readily because he continued to tell me that barely a year later I would be his wife and it was necessary that I do him credit in Poland. He ruled out the possibility of a war between our two countries . . . He gave me to understand that his profession was as good as another, that the information he collected was of no importance in peacetime, and that the Treaty of Rapallo had consecrated, alas, a Russo-German friendship which time had only confirmed. I felt horror for the Soviets . . . The hatred I felt for the Soviets, the caresses of the man I loved overcame everything. I was as if intoxicated. He asked this proof of love from me, he gave me the paper to sign, I obeyed.'

At the beginning of 1935, when Walter Schellenberg read this passage in Benita's confession, he composed a very short note to serve as a report on 'the Sosnowski affair' to his chief, Heydrich. 'Political infantilism. Benita was totally subjected to Sosnowski sexually. She abandoned any personal judgement, renounced her self and rejected all responsibilities. Doubtless a masochist since obedience seems to be inseparable from her voluptuousness.' At the bottom of the note Schellenberg added, 'Irredeemable for our purposes.'

A few days earlier, Schellenberg had been telephoned by Heydrich, who said, 'I am sending you today the dossiers of an important espionage affair conducted by a Polish officer called Sosnowski. The preliminary investigation is ended and the indictment drawn up. The trial will begin in February. I want you to probe the matter to the bottom. You will learn a great many things. Find out if amongst the scoundrels charged there are any recoverable for our secret service. You've got ten days to send me your report.'

It was in this way that Schellenberg was led to take an interest in 'the Sosnowski affair'.[2] The first question Schellenberg asked himself when the dossiers were in his possession was, 'Who is this Sosnowski?'

He noticed at once that the thick dossier concerning Jurik von Sosnowski, Chevalier von Nalecz, had not been compiled by the Gestapo but the Army Intelligence Service (Abwehr). A note was attached to it: 'Jurik von Sosnowski is not a professional intelligence agent. Rotten through and through, with no political ideals. Money, women, horses and social life with him take the place of ethics. He caved in during interrogation without there being much need to press him. Attached is a schedule of the information he sold, to our knowledge, to the Polish secret service, the French and the English. It is possible that he has been in contact with Czech Intelligence.' This note was signed by Corvette Captain Richard Protze, of Army Intelligence III-F, the army's counter-espionage service.[3]

A cavalry officer in the Polish army, Jurik von Sosnowski was from his youth a breaker of hearts, a dashing frequenter of horse-shows and race-courses. He had fallen madly in love with a ravishing countess, Maria Wlotny, avid like him for luxury, the fox-trot, the tango, jewels, horses and sexual pleasure. But Maria was, to the Polish secret service, agent Z 30, called 'Antoinette'. One evening she admitted to her lover the reasons for her frequent travels from Warsaw to Berlin, from Berlin to Paris, Danzig or Budapest. From then on he accompanied her on her 'missions' as often as he could. He was, unfortunately, always simultaneously the prey to the feelings of the jealous lover when he saw her leave on the arm of a foreign officer, to the disquiet of the accomplice and the stupid vanity of the protector.

One night at the Warsaw railway station, while Sosnowski was saying goodbye to the countess in a compartment of the train leaving for Paris, an officer came for him. He was to report immediately to the military office in the station. He obeyed. It was a simple identity check. When he returned to the platform he saw with horror that the compartment in which he had left Maria was on fire. His mistress called through the window, 'Jurik! Jurik!' But the door was locked and the window stuck half-way. Sosnowski wanted to jump in but two officers with strong arms held him saying, 'There's nothing more can be done.' When the fireman arrived to put out the blaze, Maria was dead.

It was only a few years later, on a February day in 1926, that Sosnowski acquired an explanation of this strange death, of this crime, from Colonel Lipinski, chief of Polish Intelligence, who disclosed to him that 'Countess Maria Wlotny, who was our agent Z 30, was an incomparable associate. Only the profession, the dealing in secrets, her luxurious tastes, turned her head. She sold the French to the Poles, the Poles to the French, the Germans to the Poles and the French. The accident of which she was a victim in Warsaw station spared her a trial for high treason, this was better for her.'

'And for the Polish counter-espionage service,' observed Sosnowski hoarsely.

But on that February day in 1926 Sosnowski was a poor judge. He was at the end of his tether. Colonel Lipinski held his fate in his hands. After the countess's death he had squandered the money she had left him, risked his military career by debauching the wives of his colleagues and superiors, run into debt to acquire an expensive racing stable. His latest feat had turned out a catastrophe. At Cracow he seduced the wife of the commanding officer of his regiment, eighteen years older than himself, the Baroness Anna Romel. To suppress the scandal the Baron obtained from Rome an annulment of his marriage and obliged Sosnowski to pay a tidy sum in damages and interest—and marry Anna. Sosnowski was completely ruined. The evening he was summoned by Colonel Lipinski he had had to sell his racing stable at auction. The head of the Intelligence Service told him that he would have to leave the army, and ended with the words, 'You're done for, Jurik von Sosnowski, Chevalier von Nalecz.'

Sosnowski was an utter wreck. The colonel went on, 'To escape disaster . . . there may be a solution . . . yes, there may be . . . You might accept a transfer into my service . . . If you do, you can still use your gifts as a horseman, a tennis player, man of the world . . . and heart-breaker. But I warn you there is no question of staying in Poland. It is a post abroad that's waiting for you and it will not be the safest.'

Sosnowski, who had the impression of waking from a bad dream, accepted. Colonel Lipinski smiled faintly. 'I was so sure that you would agree to co-operate with me that yesterday, at the sale of your horses by auction it was one of my confidential agents who bought them. All you need do is to transport your thoroughbreds to Berlin, for instance, to train them for the next Olympics of 1932. Well? Yes or no?'

Sosnowski accepted everything. Horses, women, balls, restaurants, money, pleasures and luxuries. The good life was to begin again.

In 1928 Sosnowski settled in Berlin with his wife. After a short time he supplied some diplomatic information of high importance. In return he demanded a considerable increase in salary and, especially, the repatriation of his burdensome spouse who at fifty looked sixty and turned out to be a nuisance in present circumstances. Colonel Lipinski in his turn proved co-operative. He came to Berlin to judge the situation and had the unfortunate Anna Sosnowski's passport revoked and herself recalled post-haste to Poland. Free, without money worries, Sosnowski plunged into the fashionable pleasures of Berlin high society. Three months after his wife's departure he met Benita, 'the woman of my life'.

Benita, the slave of her 'lord and master', was ready for anything to keep him. Their passion remained ardent as ever, but Sosnowski had need of 'fresh meat' to verify his power of seduction and also to obtain 'information'. Benita transformed herself into a procuress. According to her written confession, it seems that she was able to overcome all jealousy, even with the confused feeling that she possessed other women by means of Jurik. She furnished him with all those he wanted, provided of course that they were capable of affording interesting intelligence. Amongst these 'victims' Irene von Jena was to play a principal role.

Irene, who came of a poor family, was the daughter of a General. I have seen a photograph of her with Benita and Sosnowski, taken on the Côte d'Azur. Irene was as blond as Benita was dark but both possessed an undeniable sensual beauty. Irene also worked at the Reichswehr ministry in the Bendlerstrasse in Berlin as a junior official for a meagre monthly salary of 225 marks.

It was Benita who introduced Sosnowski to Irene. In a few days the latter succumbed to the spy's charm. He opened to her a gilded life such as she had never imagined even in her wildest dreams. Benita was no obstacle to her love for Sosnowski. The Polish officer was able to corrupt this young mistress whom he had known as a virgin. She had at first rebelled against the tortuous demands of her lover, then had submitted and quickly proved to have a volcanic temperament. It was then that Sosnowski brought Benita into their erotic games. Little by little the couple became a drug to Irene; they created a *ménage à trois*. By way of celebration they left for Nice where, for two weeks, Benita and Sosnowski inducted Irene into their wildest debauches. It was at Nice that Sosnowski revealed his real occupation to the girl. Subjected mentally and physically, she was now incapable of reacting. To complete his domination he offered her four hundred marks for every document she provided.

Back in Berlin Irene gave proof of exceptional qualities. She supplied Sosnowski with a detailed diagram of the Reichswehr, a list of the Abwehr's chief officers and agents working against Poland, and soon a series of documents on the German military budget, which showed that at the time Germany was claiming to be crushed by the Dawes and Young plans, she was actually starting to re-arm. Certain of these documents were passed on by the Poles to Paris, London and Washington, which were considered interested in this question of Germany's military revival.

Benita and Irene . . . Sosnowski pursued his conquests and his search for information. 'Benita the intermediary' flushed another rare bird in the person of Renate von Natzmer who also worked (she was the third) at the Ministry of the Reichswehr in the armoured vehicle department. She was far from being as pretty as Benita and Irene but she had a certain charm and showed herself in Sosnowski's hands a voluptuous partner. Shy and poorly dressed, she was transformed under the supervision of Sosnowski who, always using the same scenario, first made her his mistress then his Intelligence agent. The task was made easier for him by a recent disappointment in love which had broken Renate and by attacks of sciatica which added to her despair. Sosnowski appeared a knight of legend to her dazzled eyes.

Renate, too, soon showed herself to be an accomplished associate. Not only did she supply much detailed information on the German motorised forces, but disclosed that her supervisor had entrusted her with a highly confidential task: every Wednesday she assembled in an iron-bound chest documents intended for destruction (shorthand notes, rough drafts, typed carbon copies, duplicates, revised reports, etc.) which she, accompanied by a non-commissioned officer, was to consign to an incinerator. So that the maximum secrecy might be preserved, the non-commissioned officer stayed outside the room during the operation. What Renate proposed was simple, and Sosnowski naturally agreed, namely that she keep and pass on to him the most interesting items in the collection. Thus she transmitted to her lover an incredible number of highly important documents. If one believes the indictment drawn up against her in 1934, Renate offered even, for a very large sum—she had acquired a taste for money—the detailed plan for the deployment of the German army and its invasion of Poland in the event of war. The Polish Intelligence service may have found the sum too great. However it was to be, with a few modifications, the plan followed after the declaration of war on September 1st, 1939.

One may rightly wonder: how could a Polish officer thus launched into Berlin society, having his connection in high military circles, flaunting himself everywhere with girls like Benita, Renate or Irene, not to mention more transitory but equally conspicuous mistresses— how could he not have aroused the attention of the German counter-espionage services?

In fact Sosnowski was actually under suspicion. The former heads of the Abwehr to whom I put the question have assured me so. Colonel Oscar Reile, who was during the occupation to be one of the heads of the Abwehr in France, but was at this period employed in the 'Polish' section, confirmed to me that Corvette Captain Richard Protze was having Sosnowski watched from the beginning of 1932.

The dashing Polish officer was also exciting the interest of the capital's journalistic circles. I have discovered an article published in the *Berliner Tribune* on May 10th 1932 entitled, 'Who is Cavalry Captain Sosnowski? On a secret mission? His relations with Benita von F——' But if the article dilates on the social and amorous activities of the handsome Pole, there is little about his real past and nothing at all about his 'secret mission'. These bits of gossip did not seem to worry Sosnowski who, informed, sustained, protected, adulated, also exhausted, by a band of amorous women, seemed more and more to lose a sense of danger. However, Richard Protze was becoming convinced that the Polish officer manipulated his harem in his capacity of secret agent more than he played the secret agent to manipulate his harem. One does not provoke fate indefinitely. Sosnowski was to become the victim of those who served him so well.

At a brilliant Berlin reception to which he was accompanied by Benita, Sosnowski made the acquaintance of a striking Iranian, Katia Berberian, who came with her current lover, Joseph von Berg. The two couples found themselves so drawn to one another that they ended the night together in Sosnowski's flat. The result was an interchange: Katia became Sosnowski's mistress, Benita became Joseph von Berg's, whom she married a few weeks later, without ceasing, however, to love Sosnowski and work for him.

'I led a double life,' Benita wrote in 1934. 'Forced to hide my terrible secret from a man I was learning to love the better I knew him . . . If only I had confessed everything to my husband! But I always hoped things would change and I kept silent . . . Sosnowski had a lasting affair with that Persian, Frau Berberian, whom he met the same evening that I met Joseph von Berg . . . She introduced him into the world of mannequins, actresses and women of the demi-monde. She ran a large, very fashionable, dress shop. . . . Sosnowski had dozens of mistresses in addition to Renate von Natzmer. The Persian encouraged them all . . . Parties of a very special character were given in Sosnowski's flat. The men usually came without their wives . . . I never went myself . . . All Berlin was talking about it. Sosnowski boasted of having possessed at least a hundred women in the single year 1933. . . .'

Katia Berberian was complaisant and did not interfere in Sosnowski's secret activities, in which she did not participate but of which she was not unaware. Lea Niako, a star dancer, of whom Sosnowski had made a conquest during a trip to Budapest, was to prove more scrupulous. Daughter of an actress from Hamburg and a merchant from Odessa, she began a career full of promise when she met

Sosnowski. Like the others she fell madly in love with him. He already imagined that she might become his Mata Hari but made the mistake of unmasking his batteries too soon. Lea fell into a panic. Moreover, back in Berlin, she very soon learned that she was not the only favoured one, far from it, and suffered the worst tortures of jealousy. Chance brought her into contact with an agent of the S.S. secret service, to whom she presently disclosed various things. When she discovered her confidant's real functions, it was too late.

It was at a moment when, on her side, Renate von Natzmer committed one of those rank errors which must always be expected from amateur agents. In the autumn of 1933 she went on holiday in Bavaria, near Garmisch, in her family's modest residence, and found it quite natural, she who was but a needy salaried employee of the Reichswehr ministry, to wear clothes with the labels of the grand fashion houses, to sport costly furs and jewels. Her parents were astonished to see her arrive like this. What had happened to Rennie? The latter had at once to invent a tale. She explained to her parents that her immediate superiors, General von Hollmann and General Hans Guderian, held her in high esteem and had royally recompensed her, so good was the service she rendered them.

The father was proud of his daughter. He recalled that General von Hollmann had forty years earlier been a cadet with him at the Military Academy of Potsdam. Without saying anything to his daughter the older von Natzmer decided to write to his dear Hollmann to thank him for an 'honour that reflected on the whole family'. He also reminded him that he had been 'his comrade in the glorious era when we both served the Emperor'.

When General Hollmann received the letter he failed to understand it. He vaguely remembered Cadet von Natzmer. He also knew vaguely that a certain Renate von Natzmer was employed in the Ministry but would not have been able to recognise her if he met her in a corridor. On the other hand he knew perfectly well that neither he nor any member of his staff had bestowed on the person in question the smallest recompense, certainly not one that reflected 'on the entire family'. General Hollmann found all this rather fishy. He ordered an enquiry. The Abwehr unleashed its bloodhounds on Renate's trail. Corvette Captain Richard Protze took charge.

One evening one of the Abwehr agents noticed a light in Renate's office. She should have left more than two hours earlier. When he opened the door he saw the girl sitting in front of her typewriter. She started, but recovered herself quickly and complained of all the work she had to do. The Abwehr agent saw the safe open and detected a look of fear in Renate's eyes. He pretended to have noticed nothing and withdrew.

The next morning Captain Protze, who had been told of the incident by his agent, had a conversation with the Colonel for whom Renate worked as secretary. The Colonel at first seemed irritated, then remembered that his safe at the moment contained the latest plans for an eventual operation against Czechoslovakia and Poland, statistics on the present state and the importance of various armaments of the Reichswehr, the state of production, the plans for new arms, etc.

In the days following, the Colonel watched attentively his young secretary's behaviour. On three different occasions he returned to his office late in the evening and verified the contents of his safe. Everything was in perfect order. But at the end of the week, on a Friday evening, the last ten pages of an important study relating to military operations were missing. He had worked on this plan during the day and Renate still had several corrections to type. Nevertheless this did not give her the right to leave the document outside the safe. On the Saturday morning he found the ten pages in their place. He could still not bring himself to assess fully the import of his discovery. Nevertheless he spoke of it to Richard Protze.

The Abwehr agents delegated to watch Renate had not wasted their time. They had discovered the relations existing between Renate von Natzmer, Irene von Jena, Benita von Berg and Captain Sosnowski. Without these latter knowing, the net was closing around them.

On its side the S.S. secret service, alerted by Lea Niako, pursued its investigation. Lea, alarmed by her own imprudence, had indeed retracted, but the agents of the S.D. had been unleashed. They felt themselves to be on a good trail, and their discoveries, if not as exact as the Abwehr's, were no less interesting. Fourteen friends of the handsome Sosnowski were shadowed night and day.

Who would deliver the fatal blow, the Abwehr or the S.D.?

In sporting jargon, Richard Protze was several lengths ahead. In fact, apart from the enquiry into the Renate–Irene–Benita–Sosnowski doings, Protze had a stroke of luck when he succeeded in arresting at Stettin in the autumn of 1933 the Polish spy Helmut Zühlker, whose real name was Walter Kudzierski. The latter had finally 'come clean'. His admissions had led to the arrest in Berlin in December 1933 of two other Polish spies, Casimir Zielinski, porter at the Polish

Wilhelm Frick,
Minister of the Interior.

Left Kurt Daluege, head of Orpo.

Below Hitler holding his audience.
(*Bundesarchiv Koblenz*)

Above left Otto Strasser, founder of Nazi dissident group, The Black Front.
Above right Röhm, head of the S.A., with his lieutenant Karl Ernst.
Below Bad Wiessee, with the lake-front Pension Hanselbauer
on the right. (*Engel-Sonnfeld*)

embassy, and Leopold Langer. At the end of January 1934 the last two admitted that they had links with Sosnowski. By then Protze had sufficient evidence to warrant taking action against all the suspects of German nationality, and he would, certainly, have had them arrested, but it was Sosnowski who interested him most particularly. To justify the arrest of an officer of Polish nationality he needed proofs. At present he might take action. However, the Abwehr did not possess the power of execution. It was the Gestapo who possessed this power. So Protze alerted the Gestapo. The Superintendent of the Criminal police Joseph Kubitzky was charged with the operation.

Who warned Sosnowski? Was it Lea Niako, stricken with remorse? Was it the Polish Ambassador in Berlin, Jan Lipski who, though quite ignorant of the Cavalry Captain's activities, had probably seen through Sosnowski's game and, foreseeing an imminent scandal, intimated that he had better get back to Warsaw at once? The answer is unknown. All one knows is that Sosnowski actually resolved to leave Berlin. But before doing so he organised a grand farewell evening. Lea Niako was to give a programme of Spanish dances. Sosnowski had decided to disappear at the height of the party, get into a Nash he had left in a nearby street already loaded with the necessary luggage. A few hours later he would be in Warsaw.

Superintendent Kubitzky was no child and knew his job perfectly. Sosnowski's stratagem had not escaped the Gestapo's agents. The Superintendent took his precautions, determined to act in the course of the evening of February 24th. The waiters hired by Sosnowski were in reality agents of the Criminal police and the Gestapo, the cloakroom women as well. As for the Nash, it was unusable. As soon as Sosnowski had parked it an agent of the Criminal police had removed the distributor.

In Sosnowski's flat, full of guests from seven o'clock onward, the party was in full swing. The long report drawn up by the pseudo-waiters would be the delight of an author of erotic thrillers. At the beginning the evening seemed a little stiff, but the enormous cold buffet, the abundance of alcohol and the music from an orchestra hidden behind a large tapestry warmed the atmosphere. New guests never stopped arriving. The atmosphere grew more and more electric. There were too many young and pretty women, too provocative. From time to time a couple left the room arm in arm.

Round ten o'clock Sosnowski had all the lights extinguished. Only two lamps diffused a little illumination and defined the space where Lea Niako would give her 'recital' of Spanish dances. When she appeared she was greeted by general applause. The ballerina was dressed, or rather undressed, in an ensemble that passed itself off for Spanish: a wide skirt of red silk, slit up the sides like those of professional dancers, which exposed her leg to the hip, and a bodice of white silk, completely transparent which allowed a view of her small high naked breasts whose nipples were emphasised by lipstick the same colour as her skirt. She had shaken out her hair which fell on her shoulders and naked back. She was very pretty like this. She smiled, sure of herself, sure of the effect she was producing on the company. The dances began.

The atmosphere changed from minute to minute. Men were sitting even on the floor round Lea, clapping their hands in rhythm, their eyes riveted on her body which unveiled itself at every movement. She drank glass after glass of champagne. She was unrestrained, her dances became frankly erotic. She did not draw back when men's hands caressed her in passing. She grew hot and her bodice stuck to her breast, augmenting the eroticism of her attitude. In the comparative obscurity couples fondled one another, embraced on all the sofas, the poufs, even the carpet.

It was nearly midnight. The orgy had begun. Sosnowski, who seemed to have kept full control of himself, got ready to slip quietly away. Superintendent Kubitzky then moved in.

The surprise was complete. The lights were turned on, the waiters drew their pistols and, aided by police in uniform, collected all the guests in the drawing room, hands in the air and facing the walls. Some had to be routed out of the bedrooms, others from the kitchen and domestic offices. Amongst them Kubitzky discovered the Baroness Amelia Fregewang, utterly drunk, taking a shower in her evening dress. He chased her out, her clothes clinging to her skin, and made her join the others penned in the drawing room.

'At least allow Baroness Fregewang to go home,' Sosnowski requested, 'she'll catch her death on your premises.'

'Possibly,' answered Kubitzky. 'We are in the process of arresting other ladies, here and elsewhere, who may well have caught their death on yours.'

On Monday morning at seven Benita was arrested at home. It is reported that she received the police jauntily. Superintendent Kubitzky himself performed the arrest.

'You are under arrest, Baroness von Berg.'

'On what ground?'

'Presumption of spying for a foreign power.'

'Oh, good! What a relief! I was afraid it was for having slandered Goering.'

It was only on February 27th that Irene von Jena was arrested, on her return from Czechoslovakia where she had gone on holiday. Renate von Natzmer was apprehended in Pomerania, where she had been taking a sentimental journey with her fiancé, Erich Gruse.

Schellenberg now had a quite ample grasp of the matter. One point, however, puzzled him; the attitude of the ballerina Lea Niako.

At the beginning of their detention Sosnowski and his mistress began by fiercely denying every item of the accusations resulting from the enquiries of the Abwehr and the S.D. But Sosnowski's confrontation with Lea, who had been left at liberty, proved decisive. The ballerina was panting, frantic. When the Polish officer found that his mistress, through jealousy, had turned informer, he went over to the counter-attack and, abandoning all gallantry, accused the poor girl without stint. Now that he was caught, he was determined to drag her with him. He disclosed that Lea, floundering in the meshes of a double game, had tried to save him after doing everything possible to ruin him.

'So, Captain Protze,' demanded Sosnowski, 'isn't your car licence number IA 4683? Didn't the S.D. agent who looked after this charming child arrange an appointment with her at the *Rodeniele* café? Didn't you know, Captain Protze, that she warned us of your intentions and enabled me to send away three of my principal agents, X4, Y7 and XY? Look for them, gentlemen, keep on looking.' And he added ferociously, 'Now I'd like to know what you paid for this dove's information? I rewarded her royally. Isn't that so, Lea?'

'Yes,' answered the girl, sobbing.

None of the investigators had hitherto acknowledged that cupidity had been Lea's decisive motive. They had to yield to the evidence and Lea was arrested on the spot. Her 'patriotic motives' melted into thin air.

This was not altogether Schellenberg's opinion. He composed a long note on Lea Niako and asked permission to question her in her cell. After also studying the Iranian Katia Berberian's dossier he came to the same conclusion. Heydrich procured the necessary authorisations for him. Conversations with Lea Niako and Katia Berberian led Schellenberg to believe that they could both be 'salvaged'. Heydrich himself intervened with the Ministry of Justice to have the tribunal separate their case from that of the others and suspend any prosecution of them. His wish was granted. Both passed from prison directly to Schellenberg's office. He informed them the prosecutions could be resumed at any time if they did not co-operate with him. They understood very well. Their eyes were opened during their months of incarceration and their love for Sosnowski was changed into savage hatred. Both promised to take an implacable revenge on the Polish secret service.

I don't know what became of the pretty ballerina. I suspect that Schellenberg was at one time much smitten with her. In any event he does not mention her in his Memoirs. On the other hand he writes of Katia Berberian, 'Following our instructions she continued to work for the Poles who, after having her carefully watched, took her back into their service. She became one of our most valuable and surest helpers, and finished by delivering into our hands more than ten Polish agents.'

During the investigation into the affair, which lasted more than a year, Sosnowski acted with complete chivalry towards the mistresses imprisoned because of him. He tried to clear them all—except Lea Niako, naturally. But he did not succeed. There was far too much proof against them. He also tried to marry Benita, whose marriage with Joseph von Berg had been annulled, to give her Polish nationality, which would have saved her. But Anna von Sosnowski, who now hated him savagely, refused a divorce.

The trial began at the beginning of February 1935. The three principal accused were Benita, Renate and Irene. Although the facts were plain and unarguable, the charges crushing, Sosnowski tried one last time to save the three women. He declared that Benita knew nothing of his activities, it was only 'by chance' that she had put him in touch with the girls at the Reichswehr ministry. He also accused himself of having submitted Renate von Natzmer to an odious blackmail to obtain from her the documents of whose importance she was quite ignorant. Finally he tried to establish that he had drugged Irene von Jena to impose his desires on her and force her to work for him. Nothing helped. The prosecution found it easy to demonstrate the opposite. Worse: the prosecutor, Kempter, flung at him:

'Defendant Sosnowski! You accepted from Miss Renate von Natzmer cuff-links worth four hundred marks, more than her monthly salary at the Ministry. You satisfied your taste for luxury and debauchery by using the money your country sent you. You, a military agent of the Intelligence? An officer of the Polish secret service? Not a bit! You wanted to play the part of a hero, you're nothing but a vulgar spy. A patriot? Never! A bought man, therefore venal, that's what you are.'

Pale with rage, Sosnowski leaned over to his lawyer, Ludwig, who asked to address the court. 'The client I am defending, Captain Jurik von Sosnowski, chevalier von Nalecz, raises no objection to what has been said here of his activity. He will not protest against the verdict that may be rendered. He cannot in this place defend himself against the attacks made by the prosecutor Kempter against his honour as an officer. But if he should meet him later wherever he may be he will answer weapon in hand.'

Those present noticed the flash of pride in Benita ex-von Berg's eyes. Since Sosnowski had been enclosed, like herself, within the four walls of a cell she loved him as madly as in 1929. She had been overcome and her admiration for him multiplied tenfold on learning of the efforts he had made to marry her.

On February 16th 1935 the president of the tribunal read the sentence:

'Benita von Zollikopfen-Altenkligen, death.

'Renate von Natzmer, death.

'Irene von Jena, penal servitude for life.

'Jurik von Sosnowski, chevalier von Nalecz, penal servitude for life.'

To justify the indulgence to Sosnowski the tribunal's verdict, in stating its reasons, alluded in contemptuous terms to the spy's origin, he being born in Polish territory formerly annexed to Austria; 'Sosnowski is not a German of the Reich; he was born an Austrian, one of those inhabitants of the frontier who today works for his new country, Poland. Consequently we have thought it just to substitute life imprisonment for the capital penalty.'

Sosnowski did not remain long in prison. In May 1935 a German spy, Lydia Orzoreck, was arrested at Czenstochowa, a frontier town where the Poles were building a line of fortifications. The Polish Intelligence Service thought they might propose to the German Government the exchange of the spy for Sosnowski. The Polish Ambassador in Berlin, Count Lipski, was entrusted with the negotiations. Lydia Orzoreck was not as important as Sosnowski, but it was found that the German spy was on intimate terms with one of the top men of the S.S. He intervened and, after some bargaining, the exchange was accomplished in the spring of 1936. It was a broken creature who returned to Poland, a wreck, an old man with white hair, whose hands constantly shook.

Six years later, in February 1942, in German-occupied Poland, he died of dysentery in the concentration camp of Saratow.

Sosnowski had played the part not only of lady killer but of executioner too. The evening of February 17th 1935 Hitler rejected Benita and Renate's petition for a reprieve. Next morning at six they were brought into the courtyard of Blötzensee prison at Charlottenburg. It was bitterly cold. They shivered in their dresses of sackcloth, the necks of which had been cut away by scissors. As a signal favour their hands had not been fettered. It was still night but the courtyard was lit by powerful floodlights. In a corner stood two coffins. Renate von Natzmer had her hands over her face. Her shoulders were shaking with sobs. Benita held herself erect. She radiated beauty, though her hair had turned grey.

Pushed and sustained by three gaolers, Renate climbed the steps of the scaffold weeping, then suddenly screaming that she did not want to die. These agonising cries chilled the bystanders and must have shaken the black-masked executioner whose hands trembled; the first blow was not enough to sever Renate's head and the bloody axe had to be raised a second time.

Benita, her eyes wide open, witnessed this massacre but did not flinch. Her face seemed to express an intense mystical communion with an invisible being. Whilst the magistrate read the sentence concerning her, before a crucifix framed by two candles, Benita walked calmly to the scaffold without a glance at the cross. Her bearing froze the gaolers, who let her proceed alone to her doom. Calmly she knelt and put on the ground a photograph of Jurik von Sosnowski. The two assistants bent her body in order to place her neck on the block. She looked intently at the face she had loved. The executioner performed his task. The head rolled near the little photograph which slowly became covered with blood.

NOTES TO CHAPTER 7

1. Pseudonym. He did not consent to reveal to me certain aspects of this affair except on the condition that I would not divulge his real name. Although he has died since our conversations I am keeping my promise.

2. Personal testimony of Richard Protze and Heinz Jost. In his memoirs —but was it he who composed this chapter strewn with improbabilities

and errors?—Schellenberg indicates that he was 'given charge of the matter from beginning to end'. The truth is different, we have ascertained. The investigation by the counter-espionage services took place in 1933, while Schellenberg was a student at Bonn; the legal proceedings began in February 1934; Schellenberg, as we have seen, only entered the S.D. in Bonn on July 2nd 1934, and was not posted to Berlin until the late autumn of 1934. He could not therefore have conducted the affair 'from beginning to end', as he is made to say.

3. An excellent intelligence officer, Richard Protze, called 'Uncle Richard', ended his career as a Naval captain. He directed Amt III-F (counter-espionage) of the Abwehr until 1935. He was very close to Captain (later Admiral) Conrad Patzig, Admiral Canaris's predecessor at the head of the Abwehr. Richard Protze died in 1955. His evidence on the Sosnowski affair was of prime importance to me.

8

The Skiers of Death

January 19th 1935, in Berlin. It was a little after four p.m. when
Alfred Naujocks opened with his key Tania's door on the third floor
of an expensive block of flats in the Derfflingerstrasse. Tania, his
mistress of three months, a pretty twenty-four-year-old brunette,
had a post in the Ministry of the Interior, where she really worked
for the S.S. secret service. Their affair was for the present clandestine as their work. Tania nevertheless regarded herself as his fiancée
but Naujocks always maintained a prudent silence when she spoke of
marriage. In fact, he loved her a great deal. The idea of marrying her
attracted him. However there were many obstacles to overcome and
Heydrich was not the least of them. At the S.S. one could not marry
without the Reichsführer S.S. Heinrich Himmler's personal
authorisation, after a strict enquiry into the qualities and the antecedents of the two 'postulants', their ancestry and parentage. When in
addition one belonged to the S.S. secret service, one had first to
obtain Heydrich's consent. Everybody at the S.D. knew that if
Heydrich had a frenzied appetite for women he was none the less
misogynous and the bonds of marriage—although he was himself
married—seemed to him a danger to his agents.

Naujocks went towards the kitchen, which had the light on. He
heard the clatter of dishes. A tall blond girl, dressed in a black
woollen suit, with fine fleece-lined black leather boots, was clearing
up. It was Edith Karlebach, aged twenty-seven, who shared the flat
with Tania. After shaking hands with her Naujocks asked, 'Isn't
Tania here?'

'No. She oughtn't to be on duty this afternoon but was called to
the Ministry about an hour ago. She's left you a message. Here it is.'

Naujocks took the note, which he read swiftly. It ended, '. . . Take
care. I've confidence in you both. I love you. Kisses. Tania.' He
tucked it carelessly into his pocket and asked, 'Are you ready? Have
you got your luggage?'

'Two bags strapped up in my room.'

Naujocks carried the bags down and loaded them into his car. Edith had put on a coat and a black fur toque. She was carrying a pair of skis which he secured on the roof of the Mercedes next to his own. 'Well, let's go,' he said unsmilingly as he took the wheel.

They rode through Berlin, weighed down by an embarrassment which only lifted a little when they turned south to the main highway. Edith asked cheerfully, 'Where are we going? Is it a surprise?'

Naujocks, on edge, did not answer. After a moment he asked brusquely, 'What did Tania tell you?'

'Tania is an adorable girl. She has been a real sister to me. She told me that she expected to leave with you for a few days and was very pleased, but at the last moment was kept by urgent work at the Ministry. Since she knew that you really needed a few days' relaxation in the open air she didn't want to postpone your short leave. I was astonished when she suggested that I should go with you.'

Naujocks interrupted, 'Why did you agree?'

Edith answered, 'Tania insisted strongly. She didn't want you to go alone. She said I could be useful to you because you needed physical exercise and, as I am a good skier, I could give you some skiing lessons.'

'You haven't answered me. Why did you agree?'

'Does it offend or displease you?'

'Answer me.'

'I must admit that I don't really know. I hardly know you, except through some confidences of Tania's. We've only met two or three times . . . I'm never there when you come to dinner at Derfflinger-strasse.'

'And?'

'You didn't seem to me particularly agreeable. Nevertheless there must be something odd about you since I admit that I always wanted to know you better, to understand your attitude.'

'And it's for that, out of curiosity, that you accepted Tania's proposal,' he said laughing.

'Not exactly. I haven't had a holiday for months and the idea of getting away for some skiing delighted me. It was almost too good to be true.'

Naujocks smiled. 'I like that better,' he said.

Edith bent towards him. 'If Tania hadn't proposed it herself insistently, I might believe you had an idea at the back of your mind.'

'I've no idea at the back of my mind,' put in Naujocks a shade

impatiently. 'I'm going for a little relaxation and some skiing with
. . . with a good companion. That's all.'

'Fair enough,' she replied without noticing the sudden gravity of
Naujocks's expression. 'So let's enjoy ourselves like two pals.
Incidentally, where are we going?'

'To Czechoslovakia, south-west of Prague.'

'Splendid! I've never set foot in that country.'[1]

Night had fallen. Naujocks seemed concentrated on driving his
car. He did not speak. Whatever Edith thought, he did have an idea
in the back of his mind, but it was not at all what she imagined. Ten
days earlier, on January 9th precisely, Heydrich had summoned him
to his office and without a word handed him a photograph. It was the
picture of a man with the physique of the hero of a novel for dreamy
girls: tall, slim, a very attractive face, bright masterful eyes, a
sensual mouth and dazzling teeth.

'Who is it?' asked Naujocks.

'Rudolf Formis,' replied Heydrich. 'He is doing clandestine radio
broadcasts against National Socialism.' As Naujocks raised enquiring eyes—the name meant absolutely nothing to him—the S.S.
chief added, 'the Führer himself gave me instructions to track this
man down. I promised to have him brought back alive. Do you
understand? Alive. All I can tell you. . . .' Heydrich turned towards
an immense map of Europe which covered a wall of his office and
placed his finger on a region of Czechoslovakia: 'It is there that he
operates, about forty or fifty kilometres south-west of Prague, probably near the small town of Pribram. We can't determine his position
more exactly, since our direction-finder specialists are working from
too far away. Formis makes two broadcasts a day, at eight p.m. and
ten p.m. which can be heard perfectly throughout southern Germany.
It is open propaganda for Otto Strasser's Black Front.'

The 'Strasser Brothers', as they were known, namely Gregor and
Otto Strasser—the former five years the elder—played an important
part in the birth and development of National Socialism between
1920 and 1932. Originally Socialist, they moved rapidly into doc-
trinal opposition to Hitler, especially Otto, who tried to give form to
an obscure concept of National Socialism on economic and social
principles, first according to what was called the Bomberg Programme, then in the *Fourteen Theses of the German Revolution* and
finally in the *Construction of German Socialism*, published in 1930.

When Hitler, after the failure of the Munich putsch on November
8th/9th 1923, left prison, he finished *Mein Kampf* and only resumed

the leadership of the N.S.D.A.P. on March 15th 1925. He then offered the direction of the Party in north Germany to Gregor Strasser. The latter, with his brother Otto and their secretary Heinrich Himmler, future Reichsführer S.S., rapidly created an organisation in the north which, while recognising Hitler's authority in theory, soon took on the character of a separate party. The Strasser brothers, who held themselves out as 'proletarian Socialists', identified opposition to the Treaty of Versailles with opposition to capitalism and advocated the alliance of Germany—'the first proletarian nation in the world'—with 'the other proletarian nations oppressed or unrecognised by the capitalist powers of the West: the U.S.S.R., China and India.' In Berlin they founded the daily *Berliner Arbeitszeitung* and a weekly intended for the nucleus of the Party, the *Nationalsozialistiche Briefe*. Otto directed the papers, assisted by a young Rhinelander under thirty, who had a sound university education, was a doctor of philosophy of the University of Heidelberg and had written novels and scripts. His name was Paul Joseph Goebbels. He became private secretary to Gregor Strasser when Heinrich Himmler elected to join Hitler in Munich where the latter appointed him a little later Gauleiter of Lower Bavaria. Goebbels would soon feel the way the wind was blowing, and attached himself to Hitler with fidelity so lasting, enthusiastic and unconditional that he preferred suicide to surviving the Führer in 1945.

The Hitler–Strasser conflict first came into the open on November 22nd 1925 at the Party congress in Hanover, organised by the Strassers, to which Hitler sent Gottfried Feder to represent him. The congress adopted the Socialist programme of the Strasser brothers and decided to supersede twenty-five points of Hitler's programme, adopted in February 1920. It was open revolt. But Hitler restored the situation on February 14th 1926 at the Bomberg congress: Gregor Strasser was defeated. Two years later Otto Strasser left the Party; Gregor, a Deputy, remained. In 1930 Otto Strasser formed the Black Front with members of the Party who had openly broken with Hitler, the youth of the Steel Helmets, the Werewolves, the *Jung Deutsche Orden*, the Peasants' Revolutionary Movement, the *Tatkreis*, etc. The Black Front was in its origins a school for nuclei or cells. It became a half-official, half-clandestine power (reflecting in this the Communist Party) whose badge was a sword and hammer. Its activity was essentially journalistic but 'centres of action' were formed. The Black Front developed in 1931 and 1932 but much less spectacularly than Hitler's N.S.D.A.P.

In December 1932 Gregor Strasser was prepared to accept Chancellor Schleicher's offer to enter his cabinet as Vice-Chancellor. But Hitler, pressed by Goering and Goebbels, accused him of betraying the National Socialist Party. Goering told Hitler, 'Gregor Strasser wants power so as to supplant you and then destroy you.'

On December 9th 1932 Hitler convoked in the offices of the Presidency of the Reichstag the heads of districts, the inspectors and the deputies of the N.S.D.A.P. He pronounced a crushing indictment of Gregor Strasser. The latter's supporters, even the most faithful, refused to break with Hitler. Strasser then lost his sang-froid and capitulated. Without even an attempt at resistance he gave up and retired to private life. He sank into oblivion and would be, as we have said, one of the victims of the Night of the Long Knives.

Otto Strasser recognised that his life was in danger when Hitler took power on January 30th 1933. On February 28th he left Berlin for Thuringia, then for Vienna. But in the Austrian capital the Nazis were already very strong and the S.A. wanted to strike down the leader of the Black Front. Even in Prague, where he sought refuge under a pseudonym, he was not safe from the Nazis. Spurred on by Hitler himself the Gestapo men tried twice to lay hold of Otto Strasser and bring him back to Germany. Both efforts failed.

During the spring of 1934 the Gestapo ring closed round the head of the Black Front. The action was directed from Berlin by a certain 'Frank'. Two of Otto Strasser's colleagues, Kritsche (alias Hildebrand) and Adam (alias Mohr) were contacted and bought by the Gestapo. The latter passed on to 'Frank' an important piece of information; the name of the man who had built the Black Front Radio transmitter and operated it in Czechoslovakia: Rudolf Formis. When Heydrich was notified he at once summoned Naujocks, as we have seen.

Until the suburbs of Dresden Naujocks, still at the wheel of his car, ran over in his mind the principal points of the Strasser–Formis dossier. Edith was silent and somnolent. Her perfume flooded the car and disturbed Naujocks, who from time to time cast a glance at his companion's lovely face. She was as pretty as Tania but a totally different type. He then thought of his 'little Tania' . . . Saw her again at Derfflingerstrasse, the evening he had acquainted her with Heydrich's orders regarding Formis and invited her to accompany him.

Tania was at first delighted with the idea of going off with him for two or three days or perhaps longer. She had a right to a week's leave whenever she wished. But the more Naujocks entered into his explanation, the more uneasy he saw her become. She finally said, 'I didn't realise the scope of this mission, Alfred. You must understand me. Not that I'm afraid—though I'm afraid for you—but I'd be so anxious not to make a mistake that I'd be bound to be exposed at once.'

'Don't talk nonsense.'

'It's true. I've nothing of the vamp about me. And I'm no good at lying. I'd spoil everything. The more I think of this business, the more it terrifies me. I couldn't bear the idea of being a source of additional danger for you.'

He did not answer. He was disappointed.

'I've got an idea,' she said, 'why don't you take somebody who really knows nothing about this undertaking?'

'Another woman?'

'Yes. Edith, for instance.'

'Edith?' echoed Naujocks, astounded.

'Why not? She's intelligent, she can interrupt what she's doing for a few days and she's one of my best friends.'

He looked at Tania for a moment. That she should suggest his going off with this sparkling young blonde was a sign of confidence which filled him with wonder.

'All right,' he finally said, 'but it would be better if the suggestion came from you. I can't decently telephone and ask her to go abroad with me for a few days.'

'I'll talk to her myself tomorrow morning,' said Tania simply.

When he knew that Edith had agreed, Naujocks talked to Heydrich about it. The latter said with a sarcastic laugh, 'A brilliant idea, my dear Naujocks. I am convinced that you—if not the Service —will benefit greatly from this journey. However, try not to forget that you also have a little job to do.' Although with bad grace, the permission was granted.

The details of the mission were arranged during a conference which Naujocks had with Joseph Huber.[2] A Mercedes, licence number IP 48259, was supplied. The luggage was the usual sort a couple carried for a mountain excursion: skis, knapsacks, baskets of provisions, two cameras, a pair of powerful binoculars, a gramophone and records, two or three bags with clothes. A passport was issued in the name of Alfred Gerber, business man, and the car's papers bore the same name. Large scale maps of the area to be explored were obtained.

'Once you've located Formis,' Heydrich told him, 'you will at first keep an eye on him for a while. Then you will return to Berlin where you will be furnished with the equipment to sabotage his transmitter. We don't want to take the risk of hiding this material in your car before knowing where Formis is.'

Naujocks would have need of money. He would have to smuggle it out since the Germans at this time only had a right to enter Czechoslovakia with a minimal sum. With the help of his old friend Gröthe he hid bundles of hundred-mark notes distributed practically everywhere in the car: in the seats, under the floor mat, in the rear luggage compartment, even the instrument panel. 'Even if you are caught,' Gröthe told him, 'you can simply say that your pretty blonde is a great spender.'

Naujocks, when parking his car in front of the Hotel Continental in Dresden, looked at his watch: 6.30 p.m. He had done an average of ninety kilometres an hour. This put him in excellent humour; when the reception clerk offered him two seats for the opera, he consulted Edith with a look and gladly accepted.

After the evening at the opera, where they saw a production of *Faust*, Naujocks and his companion returned to their hotel for supper. Edith was hungry. She ate with a youthful and healthy appetite. He looked at her with an admiration she pretended not to notice. They chatted gaily. At a sudden movement she made, a button on her bodice slipped out of the too large buttonhole. Alfred noticed that she was not wearing a brassière. Before she could button up again, he had time to observe that her breast was bronzed. She must have taken sun-baths entirely naked. As if divining his thought, Edith spoke of her last holiday on the shores of the Baltic. Without embarrassment she explained that she had been there with one of her clients, a keen amateur of nudism. She had spent a marvellous fortnight. She added, 'Since I was sun-burnt all over, I have since tried to keep this colour. One of my friends, an electrical engineer, made a cabin for me, at home, in which he installed ultra-violet lamps which exercise a revivifying effect on the whole organism. Vitality and physical resistance are considerably increased by ultra-violet rays. They activate the circulation of the blood, soothe pain and hasten the process of recovery in many cases of illness.'

Interested, Alfred asked, 'Do you also do that for your clients?'

She smiled. 'Only certain clients . . . Those who really have need of a revitalisation.'

'I see.'

He said nothing more, but he was beginning to wonder if Edith's gymnastic course was not a somewhat 'special' course. She realised this and with surprising frankness, undertook to undeceive him. 'Don't imagine something that isn't. It's a matter of helping industrialists, businessmen, politicians who don't take enough exercise, to lose a few kilos. I choose my clientèle. My prices are high but my treatments are effective. It happens that I allow a client to make advances to me, to go out with me to the cinema, a concert or theatre, and even to sleep with me if I want to, but it is no more frequent than if I ran a picture gallery, a barber's shop saloon for men or a restaurant.'

'And your employees are feminine, I believe?'

'I am very strict with my girls and watch them closely. There are no doors to close and so I can see what's going on. The slightest indiscretion and the masseuse is at once in the street. Since they are well paid and get big tips, they don't take the risk of possible advances from the clients. Of course what happens outside my gymnastic course is not my business. I believe, however, that the behaviour of my eight girls cannot be criticised. . . .'

Naujocks was on the point of saying what he knew on the subject but pulled himself up in time. Had he not had Arthur Nebe, chief of the Criminal police, communicate to him the result of the enquiry ordered by Heydrich on the activities and morality of Edith's courses? To admit it would reveal his membership of the S.D. He therefore changed the conversation. They were in the café. The orchestra was playing a fox-trot and several couples were dancing.

'Would you like to dance?' asked Naujocks.

'No, I don't feel like it.'

'Good. Nor I, I don't find it very amusing. But when I must I know . . .'

'Me too . . . this evening I don't want to. Doubtless it's the change of air and the car ride . . . I'm worn out.'

'We'll go back to our rooms when you like,' he said in a tired voice which betrayed his own great weariness.

They left Dresden next morning, January 20th, after breakfast. The Mercedes travelled slowly, the icy surface making the road difficult. Shortly before the frontier, at Attenberg, Naujocks stopped the car at an inn and ordered coffee. He had some urgent explanations to make to his companion. 'By the way,' he said in a natural tone, 'when we arrive at the frontier don't show any surprise if you learn that I am called Alfred Gerber. It's the name of the friend who lent me the car, and he warned that I'd have endless trouble if I were caught driving a car that didn't belong to me. The Czechoslovaks won't let me go before alerting the German police to make sure the car isn't stolen. The Mercedes' papers are all in the name of Alfred Gerber.'

She glanced at him in surprise. 'Isn't all that a little dangerous?'

He shrugged his shoulders. Edith's surprise was perfectly justified, but she in fact made no objection. 'No,' he said, 'don't worry.'

'In that case . . .'

They got back into the car which, a few kilometres further on took its place in the queue of vehicles waiting to pass the customs. The frontier post consisted of a group of cement buildings flanked by casemates on both sides of the road. The barrier was raised and each car, after a short stop, hurried away. A half dozen guards in heavy cloaks with rifles over their shoulders checked the papers. When his turn came Naujocks took Edith's passport and accompanied the guard to the inspector's office while other guards took the licence number of the Mercedes. All went quickly. They were now in Czechoslovakia.

'You didn't have any trouble?' Edith enquired.

'No,' he replied curtly as the car moved forward on the icy road.

The country was covered in snow. The sky was grey, low.

'At what time do we reach our destination?'

'We'll lunch on the bank of the Elbe, then spend the afternoon in Prague. We'll leave in the evening for Pribram.'

The pair lunched without hurry in an inn at the village of Steti. Naujocks then took the road which follows the Elbe to Melnik. There he turned right on to the arterial road leading to Prague, thirty kilometres distant. The streets of the capital were also covered with a thick layer of snow.

It is hard to explain why Naujocks dallied so long between Dresden and Prague. Even with the icy roads and the crossing of the frontier he could easily have covered the one hundred and fifty kilometres in the morning. However that may be, he strolled with Edith through the Czechoslovak capital until night fell. In those streets he had traversed a few months earlier was he looking for the ghost of the lovely Paula Horvath, now stagnating in some Gestapo cell?

They made some purchases then went to dine at the most luxurious hotel in Prague. At nine they left in the car to cross the city in the direction of the trunk road which would take them to Pribram. The first hills appeared on their right as soon as they left the suburbs. A crescent moon spread a ghostly light on the road glistening with frozen snow.

'Will it take long?' asked Edith.

'We're not far from Pribram,' answered Naujocks. 'Just think, when you wake up tomorrow morning you will see a snow-covered mountain from your window.'

Naujocks drove carefully and in silence. He was haunted by one worry: where was he to begin his search in a region so vast? Edith, whom the landscape enchanted, attributed her companion's silence to the beauty of the place. Five minutes from Pribram Naujocks stopped at a crossroads. Three directions were offered him: Pribram to the right, Dubenec one kilometre ahead, Obory twelve kilometres to the left. Why did he turn his car in this last direction? He didn't know. He was to say, 'I was irresistibly drawn to the left.' They passed through Obory, a village asleep under the snow. Suddenly they saw below them on the left the wide ribbon of the River Moldau which stood out against a landscape of fields and woods uniformly white. A small road descended to a few buildings huddled together. A sign indicated that there was an hotel there. Naujocks decided to make for it.

'I get the impression that they hadn't had one single guest for years,' said Naujocks, stopping in front of the hotel whose two-storey façade showed no light. 'And I who thought that Bohemia was the land of dancing and cheerful wood fires. Let's wake them up.'

'Remember it's after ten.'

'A hotel you see is worth two you don't see. Even if we were near a place where joy reigns, here I'm sleeping tonight.'

He rang once, twice. An incredibly thin old woman opened without enthusiasm and admitted that she had two rooms free. The formalities were completed in the presence of a husband even thinner than his wife. Slipping between icy sheets, Naujocks reflected that he would not bring Formis back to Berlin before catching a bad grippe, indeed pneumonia. He stated that he did not sleep well that night.

In the morning, when Naujocks flung open the shutters of his room, he was dazzled by a bright sun shining in a clear blue sky. A mountain was visible from Edith's window. A pleasant odour of coffee brought a smile to their faces. Shaving and dressing quickly he hastened downstairs. The proprietress appeared and wished him an almost cordial good morning which contrasted sharply with her welcome of the evening before. She led him into the dining room where he was soon joined by Edith, resplendent in form fitting scarlet skiing trousers with a white pullover, a chamois-skin jacket thrown over her shoulders. He looked at her with frank admiration.

'Thanks for the mountain,' she said laughing, 'it was there waiting for me. Do we climb it now or after breakfast?'

'Thank you for being so beautiful,' he laughed in return. 'But let's have our coffee.'

They were served a copious breakfast. 'It's a wonderful day', he said, 'in which nothing can go wrong.'

He persuaded Edith to renounce her skiing and take a walk along the river, which she did not consider a sufficient compensation. They decided in the end to traverse the valley by car. Before leaving he was assured by the proprietress that there were no other guests in the hotel. They slowly followed a small narrow road alongside the river, enjoying the increasing warmth of the sun. Naujocks watched for a sign indicating the proximity of houses and wondered if he should consider himself lucky that they were so few. He stopped two or three times to photograph Edith and the landscape, being careful to include the only buildings they had seen so far. These photographs might be useful later.

They had been travelling an hour when at a turning in the road Naujocks noticed an hotel whose chimneys gave out thin spirals of white smoke. It was a comparatively large building which seemed to have been the home of some rich farmer. Pines surrounded it, and, nearby, an old bridge prolonged the road towards the plain, through a thick forest.

'Wouldn't you like a coffee?' he asked Edith.

Without waiting for an answer he turned the car into a broad lane which descended towards the hotel. On the façade could be read Hotel Zahori. Naujocks noticed a garage, fresh tyre tracks and a pair of skis against a wall. The square hall was furnished with old furniture; on the walls were stags' heads, guns, sporting prints. A very dark-skinned chambermaid carrying a tray smiled in sign of welcome and invited them to go into the sitting room. Naujocks observed her Asiatic physiognomy—doubtless she was of Hungarian origin.

Edith entered the room first. When she drew up to the fireplace where a large wood fire was burning, Naujocks discovered a man drinking his coffee in small sips. He was astounded. The man was tall, thin, with a very attractive face, sparkling, domineering eyes, a sensual mouth and glistening teeth. No doubt of it: it was Rudolf Formis.

Naujocks had difficulty in mastering his emotion, concealing his immense surprise. He observed with satisfaction that Formis had not yet looked at him. He was fascinated by the beauty and grace of Edith who was arranging her hair in front of a mirror. A thousand questions occurred to Naujocks: did Formis live in the hotel? Under what name? Did he work alone or with accomplices? Was the hotel-keeper involved with him? Did he broadcast from the hotel or another place? Perhaps he was only passing through? In that case, where did he live? How to find out without arousing his attention?

As Edith came back to Naujocks, who had taken a few steps towards the table where Formis was sitting, the latter rose and said, 'I believe you are Germans like me. Would you take your coffee with me? I am at the moment the only guest in the hotel and the tourists are very rare, except at weekends.'

The waitress appeared and took their orders. Having done so she asked, 'Another white coffee, Mr. Formis?'

'Why yes, of course,' he answered with a smile.

Naujocks wondered if he were awake or dreaming. So Formis was using his real name. In other words he thought himself perfectly safe in this remote corner of Czechoslovakia.

What sort of man was he really? Speaking of Formis to my friend Victor Alexandrov, Otto Strasser said, 'He's a first-class chap. During the war he had been a brilliant officer; with the return of peace he resumed his work in electronics. In it he showed himself highly gifted and the author of several inventions in the field of radio. His professional advancement was swift. Appointed director of the radio station at Stuttgart, he was very successful, but his ability was only equalled by the hatred he felt for Hitler. His first exploit, in 1933, was the cutting of the principal cable of the trans-mitter one day when Hitler was making an important speech at Stuttgart. It was impossible to transmit it. An enquiry was insti-tuted, but he was not suspected. However incidents multiplied every time a speech by the Chancellor had to be broadcast by his station and it ended with his falling under suspicion. He succeeded in escaping. After many adventures he turned up at Prague where he put himself at my disposal. I forgot to say that he had long been a member of the Black Front.'

Otto Strasser went on: 'I then asked Formis to construct a transmitter. He made one so perfect that this gem is now in the Postal Museum of Prague. The second phase of our broadcasting enterprise was the discovery of a safe place from which we could transmit unknown to the Czech authorities. It was incumbent on us to keep up appearances. The third point to settle was the choice of a speaker. Formis decided to take this on himself. Each week I sent him a speech I had recorded on a disc. The place chosen was the Hotel Zahori, near Pribram, sixty-five kilometres from Prague. This hotel was patronised at weekends by the citizens of Prague. The rest of the time it was practically empty and the proprietor was not curious. The transmissions began in September 1934. It was the first example of a clandestine broadcast, of a "pirate radio".'

Let us return to the Hotel Zahori. Addressing Edith, Formis told his 'story' in a warm, pleasant voice: 'I chose this hotel by chance to live in. My doctor in Stuttgart advised me to take a rest. I at once packed some suitcases which I put in the boot of my car and started out. I drove as far as Nuremberg. It was raining. I started again for Pilsen. Hardly had I crossed the frontier than the sun came out. I took this for a favourable sign. A friend I met by chance at Pilsen suggested to me the neighbourhood of Pribram. I passed this way and stopped at this hotel. It suited me perfectly. I was lucky.'

'Do you ski?' asked Naujocks.

'Yes, a good deal, but I am clumsy at it. I brought a little work with me in case I should be bored.'

'What is your trade?' asked Edith innocently.

'I am an electrical engineer. But the weather has been so good I've only had one desire: to sit in the sun after an hour or two of skiing. I try to get through some work in the evening, you know how work piles up when you're away.'

After a short silence Formis turned to Edith. 'Do you expect to stay here?' It was like a ray of hope in Formis's eyes.

It was Naujocks who answered, 'What do you think, Edith? Would you like to go on? I admit this hotel seems charming to me.'

Edith asked Formis, 'The hotel seems charming to me too but are there good ski runs hereabouts?'

'There are no "runs" but you can make some very fine excursions. You can go over the Krana-Hora, about ten kilometres from here, or else the Pisek or the Tok, twenty kilometres away. There are very easy slopes and some hard ones. They're all pleasant and picture-esque.'

Edith turned to Naujocks. 'I'd like very much to stay here. Are there any rooms available?'

'Oh yes,' said Formis. 'There's one right next to mine.'

'Does he think we're married?' Naujocks wondered. Edith still had her glove on so one could not tell if she were wearing a wedding ring. Naujocks got up. 'In that case,' he said, 'while we're waiting for the coffee let's go and see the proprietor about a booking.'

Edith followed him to the reception desk in the hall. A large jovial man received them cordially and tendered them the register. 'Yes,' he said with an understanding smile, 'I have a very nice room looking on the river, the best, number 3.'

He also took them for a honeymoon couple. Edith opened her lips to undeceive him and ask for two rooms but Naujocks stepped roughly on her toe and said, 'Perfect. We expect to stay a week.'

He squeezed the girl's arm hard to make her keep quiet whilst the hotel keeper, noticing nothing, said, 'I'll have your luggage brought to your room. Can I have the key of your car?'

'Here it is,' said Naujocks, handing him a bunch.

'Thanks. If you will follow me I'll show you your room.'

'There's no hurry,' said Naujocks. 'We'd rather have our coffee first, wouldn't we, Edith?'

Squeezing even harder the arm of his companion, whose face was red with anger, he led her into the hall. There she disengaged herself and ejaculated furiously, 'Will you explain yourself?'

'Hush!' he ordered her. 'I can't tell you anything now but I had to act as I did.'

'*Had* to!'

'Yes. Your admirer in the sitting room is a traitor. His picture has been in all the German papers. I'll explain by and by. Keep calm and give the impression that you're my wife. And above all, for heaven's sake, avoid arousing his suspicions. Leave it to me. . . .'

Edith's anger gave way to amazement. Before giving her time to recover herself he steered her into the sitting room. She leaned towards him and said in a low tone, 'I'll turn my ring around, it can pass for a wedding ring.'

'A good idea,' he returned in the same tone, admiring Edith's sang-froid and the speed with which she adapted herself to an extraordinary situation.

'All right?' asked Formis with a smile. 'Good! Then we'll meet at lunch. Goodbye.' He went out and a moment later they heard him going upstairs.

As Edith started to speak Alfred put a finger to his lips. 'Sh! Let's finish our coffee and take a stroll by the river.'

After drinking up quickly Edith and Naujocks went out and leaned on the parapet of the bridge, looking down at the water which swirled below them amidst the ice-floes. He finally broke the silence: 'Edith, I'm very sorry but I couldn't tell you anything in Berlin. In coming here I was not at all sure to track down this Formis . . .'

'Are you from the police?'

'If you like; I belong to the Party secret service, the S.D.'

'Who is Formis?'

Alfred explained what he had himself learned from Heydrich, and added, 'The man is dangerous and pernicious. For four months, every day he has used a powerful transmitter to flood the Reich with fake news and Otto Strasser's anti-Nazi commentaries.'

'What are you going to do, now you've located him exactly.'

'I must go back to Berlin for one day to receive instructions from my chief, Heydrich. It is most important that you should help me, Edith—more important than you can imagine.'

'What should I do?'

'I like your question, Edith. It means that you are ready to collaborate with me in the interests of the Great Reich.'

'Of course.'

'Yet you don't belong to the Party?'

'No, but. . . .'

She did not finish her sentence. Her look betrayed a growing feeling for Alfred, who, concerned with his mission, paid no attention to it. He then said, 'Edith, you're to keep an eye on him. If, during my short absence, he decides to leave, telephone me at once in Berlin at a number I'll give you presently. You will merely say, "Uncle Otto has the grippe." I will then give you all necessary instructions. Do you understand?'

'Perfectly. "Uncle Otto has the grippe."' She burst out laughing.

He smiled and said, 'For the moment I'd like you to go to your room. Unpack our luggage and put things in order as if we were going to stay a week.'

'Aren't we staying a week?' she asked in disappointment.

'It's unlikely. When you've finished tidying up come down and wait for me in the sitting room.'

She nodded, still smiling and turned towards the hotel. Alfred this time noticed the smile. He followed her with his eyes, admiring her easy sportswoman's gait.

She took five steps and turned. 'I'd better wear a real wedding ring and play at being really Frau Naujocks,' she said simply.

He corrected her with a laugh: 'No! Not Frau Naujocks, Frau Gerber!'

'True!' She burst out laughing and ran on to the hotel.

Naujocks lit a cigarette. He too went towards the hotel. From the window of 'their' room Edith called out happily, 'Hoo-hoo!'

He raised his head and made her a friendly gesture. Suddenly he felt the blood beat in his veins. Up above, over the roof top, a few centimetres from a dormer window, at the edge of the roof, appeared a short cylinder which his experienced eye recognised at once: it was a telescopic antenna for a high-frequency radio transmitter. A white wire, virtually invisible, connected it with Formis's room. He analysed his discovery with lucidity: Formis transmitted from his room and must certainly be obliged to mount to the attic to deploy his antenna. In order to destroy the set, he must procure the key of Formis's room, at least an impression of the key. To do that, Edith must encourage her admirer's advances and even allow herself to be drawn into the room. 'She is big enough', he thought, 'to know how far to allow Formis to pursue his amorous offensive.' All this was clear in his mind. He went up to rejoin Edith and in a low voice told her of his discovery. She knitted her brows when he explained that she should respond to Formis's advances.

'Should I encourage him—very far?' she asked, unsmiling.

'As far as you like,' Naujocks replied. 'The important thing is to obtain an impression of the key before leaving for Berlin. I've got wax for the skis which will substitute for the soft wax which I haven't got.'

The three lunched together. Their conversation was gay, carefree. Formis made circumspect advances to Edith, who seemed to encourage him. Without quite understanding why, Naujocks thought that she lent herself a little too easily to the game he had urged her to play. It was worse during the afternoon. They went to ski a few kilometres from the hotel. The two men were markedly less good skiers than Edith, who gave them lessons. But why did Formis always contrive to fall near Edith, who helped him to get up? To see them clasped together irritated Naujocks, who had several spectacular tumbles, provoking outbursts of laughter from the other two.

Back at the hotel they had several drinks. At eight, when they were about to go into dinner, Formis excused himself and was away for a quarter of an hour. At ten, the same. This time Naujocks followed him discreetly at a distance. He then made a discovery which confirmed what he thought: the transmitter was undoubtedly in Formis's bedroom. Naujocks had time to return to Edith before Formis rejoined them.

When they separated it was past midnight and they had drunk several bottles of Tokay. For Edith and Naujocks, face to face with the door shut, it was the moment of truth. It was to be a night of love.

The next morning the weather stayed good and all three had an hour of skiing near the hotel. Formis announced that he was lunching in Prague but would be back by the end of the day: a little after eleven he got into his car and was seen off by his new companions. He had hardly gone when Naujocks and Edith went up to their room. They noticed with pleased surprise that Formis's key had remained in its lock. The chambermaid was in the act of doing out the room. Naujocks dexterously slid the key silently from the lock, drew a lump of wax from his pocket and took a perfect impression.

Naujocks changed his clothes. Edith was silent, disappointed at being left alone. He had just told her that he was leaving immediately for Berlin and would be back in time for dinner. A feeling of anxiety overcame her. She accompanied him to the Mercedes and flung herself in his arms. 'I'm afraid,' she said in a low voice, 'I feel something terrible is going to happen.'

'Be sensible. It's your feminine intuition, eh?' he said lightly. 'Well, I don't believe it.' As he was letting in the clutch he added, 'We'll see each other at dinner. Be nice to Formis if he gets back before me—but not too nice.'

'Idiot! Remember to buy me a wedding ring.'

He gave her a troubled look. Edith . . . Tania . . . He no longer knew just where he stood. He left with a heavy thrust on the accelerator.

Naujocks reached Berlin by the regular air service. Before going to the headquarters of the S.S. secret service he bought two wedding rings, one for Edith, one for himself. Heydrich listened to his report in silence. He finally allowed a thin smile to flit across his lips. 'So luck has not stopped being on your side?'

'I think so.'

'It's a good beginning. But don't be overcome by an excess of optimism. Don't forget that your mission will be a failure unless you bring Formis back alive. It's the most important thing from every point of view. . . . Is your friend Edith a girl to show herself "amiable" to Formis?'

Heydrich's eyes glittered. His smile became equivocal. Naujocks replied, 'I don't know . . . Maybe . . . But it may not come to that.'

'For greater security take Gert Gröthe with you. He is reliable. He has a cool head. I'll keep the impression of Formis's key. You'll have a duplicate in an hour.'

Naujocks and Gröthe finalised the details of the operation, equipping themselves with phosphorus, chloroform and pistols. Formis's key in his pocket, Naujocks and his companion reached Tempelhof airport, where they took off at 6.15 for Prague. Gröthe had become Gert Schubert. In the 'plane he said to his friend, 'Till now you've had the devil on your side. Let's hope my presence doesn't break the charm.'

'I'll leave you at the hotel where I spent my first night. I'll come for you tomorrow. Don't leave the hotel on any pretext, and avoid all contact with strangers.'

On landing Naujocks felt himself becoming nervous. Was it his imagination or did the police examine his passport with special attention?

'Your journey has certainly been quick, Mr. Gerber,' said the policeman at last as he handed him back his passport with a smile. Naujocks made a polite murmur and breathed more freely.

The two men regained the Mercedes in the nearby car park. The engine being cold, hiccuped and refused to start. Naujocks frowned. 'It's the first time it's played this trick on me . . . Ah, at last.'

'Better not have such a hitch tomorrow,' Gröthe advised, 'You'd best stop at a garage and buy a heating lamp to keep the motor warm.'

Alfred did so. An hour later he left Gröthe at the first hotel then at speed went on to his own. Again he was anxious.

Edith, who had heard the Mercedes arrive, ran to meet him. She embraced him lengthily, impetuously. 'I'm happy you're back,' was all she said.

They went up to their room, passing Formis who was coming down. He greeted them with a nod but did not stop. Naujocks was nonplussed. When they were alone Edith said, 'He knows everything, I'm sure. He was almost rude to me when he returned from Prague. He went straight up to his room and didn't come down until now.'

Naujocks pondered. Had Formis discovered their identity or did he simply distrust them? How had they aroused his suspicions? What had he gone to Prague for?

'Everything's in order for tomorrow evening,' he finally said. 'It would be foolish to try to hurry things on now, unless he plainly decides to leave this evening, but I don't think he will.'

Observing that she did not understand, couldn't understand, he resumed, 'I can't tell you any more, but don't worry; there won't be any trouble.'

Had Edith told Naujocks the truth? If the testimony of one of the chambermaids is to be believed, when Formis returned from Prague he met Edith in the hall. They chatted for a moment, then went for a walk. When they returned an hour later they were laughing uproariously. They asked one of the hotel waiters to photograph them arm in arm 'to make my friend jealous', in Edith's words. Then she and Formis settled down in the sitting room to have tea with rum. The chambermaid declared in her testimony, 'No honest woman ever made such advances to a stranger; one wondered if she was not going to plump herself on his lap.' [3]

To explain Formis's change of attitude we have other testimony, that of Otto Strasser whom he had gone to see in Prague. Here is the dialogue between the two men:

'All going well? Nothing suspicious, Formis?'

'No, nothing. Just a bogus married couple, from Germany, on a pseudo honeymoon. A harmless young pair.'

'Germans? Aren't you afraid that . . .?'

'I'm armed, and anyway I don't think that the girl wishes me ill, quite the contrary.'

'Have you been able to find out who these people are?'

'Yes. He's a young businessman of twenty-four who comes from Kiel and is called Alfred Gerber, she's a teacher of gymnastics in Berlin, charming, a very good figure. She's called Edith Karlebach, is twenty-seven but looks twenty.'

'Be careful, Formis. If you discover anything suspicious notify the aliens' department of the police. Stay on your guard.'

Had Formis alerted Strasser? Did he realise that Edith was playing a game? Was he alarmed?

When Naujocks and Edith descended to the dining room only two places were laid. Formis was not to be seen. The dinner passed in silence. Edith, more and more nervous, barely touched her food. Naujocks ate like an automaton. He was thinking that, when the moment came, he should remove Edith out of danger. Why had he dragged her into this business? And if it failed? He realised that he was more or less in love with her . . . What a time to choose! The last train for Berlin left Prague at 11.25 p.m. Naujocks would attempt the impossible to have her take it next day while he, Gröthe and a chloroformed Formis sought to cross the frontier by car. He had to find out how long it would take him to get from the hotel to Prague railway station. Next day he would make a trial run. This would also enable Gröthe to familiarise himself with the road. One never knew!

After dinner they found Formis sitting in the bar before a large glass of brandy, looking gloomy. On seeing them enter he emptied his glass at a gulp, rose and vaguely wished them good evening. 'He must be a bit drunk,' thought Naujocks.

In their room Naujocks had a good deal of trouble in calming Edith, whose unease had turned into fear. Kisses and caresses, love-making, seemed finally to dispel her black thoughts. Naujocks shut his eyes and immediately fell asleep. Edith, twisting and turning in her bed, only succeeded in sleeping towards three in the morning. In his hotel Gröthe, full of optimism for the morrow, rested tranquilly.

Naujocks was the first to rise. Before eating breakfast with Edith he took a short walk in the sun along the river. He was calm, but all his nerves and muscles were tense. It was today or never. To destroy the transmitter and kidnap Formis was only half the battle. He had next to get Edith to Prague and then dash for the frontier . . . and cross it. How much time would he have before the alarm was raised? Between two or three hours? It wasn't much. Was Strasser's organisation in Czechoslovakia strong, well organised. If so, did not Formis possess a system of alert in case of danger? Naujocks estimated the risks. The best course, it seemed to him, was to act between Formis's first and second transmissions, namely at nine, at the latest nine-thirty. He would then have an hour to go to Prague and would need an hour and a quarter or an hour and a half to do the ninety kilometres on snowy roads which separated the capital from the frontier. Emphatically, the more Naujocks considered his plan the more he realised that the time would be terribly short: the whole operation had to be completed in under three hours.

Edith was a nervous wreck. She had rings under her eyes. Her mouth was contracted. She seemed lost and defenceless. Plainly she was in a hurry for this 'holiday' to end. Formis put in only a brief appearance. He gave them a vague smile when they passed one another at the entrance to the hotel. They took the Mercedes and went for Gröthe. Naujocks said to him while they were making for Prague, 'My little finger tells me that at this exact moment Formis has slipped into our room to look for daggers, pistols and bombs . . . All he'll find is that Edith isn't Frau Gerber; her bags and dressing case carry the initials E.K. That may re-assure him a little. He must know that two lovers not united by the bonds of marriage always behave oddly.'

Edith seemed not to hear. 'What time do you want me there this evening?' asked Gröthe.

'Be on the other side of the bridge at nine, it will take you about an hour's walk from your hotel. I'll give you a signal: I'll turn out the light in my room three times. You will climb up by a rope I'll leave hanging on the river side. No one at the hotel ought to see you.'

Naujocks drove fast but he was calm. He was in his element: he fixed his plans, left nothing to chance and gave his orders. The S.S. training produced its results. He was now an agent of the secret service in action. He discussed matters with Gröthe altogether indifferent to the effect of their conversation on Edith. She was silent but seething with anger. It was the first time that Naujocks' designs were revealed to her in so detailed a fashion. What contempt for her, as woman and as friend, she was thinking. When she imparted her recollections of this adventure she said, 'Naujocks used me without even showing me sufficient trust to let me entirely into the secret. I was caught between two fires. I was too afraid to show my anger and could only keep my feelings to myself. Naujocks was a man exquisite in intimacy, a perfect lover, but in action he was hard as steel, ruthless, devoid of all sentiment. He terrified me . . . he was a magnificent killing machine.'[4]

When Naujocks parked his car in the front of the station he looked at his wrist-watch: fifty minutes since leaving. He reckoned that at night there would be less traffic and he would doubtless make the journey in a little less than three quarters of an hour. He was well satisfied. He went into the station, checked the time of the train's departure for Berlin and took a ticket for Edith but kept it in his pocket.

They lunched at a restaurant in the old city then all three went to a cinema. On the return journey they remained silent. The tension increased as evening drew on. Edith and Naujocks left Gröthe at his hotel after having taken his bag and returned to their own. It was six but already completely dark. Arrived at the top of the slope leading to the Zahori, Naujocks turned the car round and descended in reverse. He shut off the ignition, and let the vehicle roll silently then braked into a deep-shadowed corner, under the pines, on the roadside. They got out without shutting the doors, and Naujocks swiftly installed the heating lamp he had bought on Gröthe's advice under the bonnet. The Mercedes was now in position for departure on the main road and its motor ran no further risk of starting trouble.

While crossing the courtyard Naujocks noticed that Formis's car was in the garage. The large thermometer of enamelled iron hanging at the entrance to the hotel showed 4 °C, below zero. He went in without attracting attention and ascended silently to their room. There was nothing to do but wait. Edith packed the bags without a word. When she had finished she stretched out on the bed still saying nothing. Naujocks took up a detective story which he read in an armchair.

The total silence which reigned in the hotel was broken a little before eight. Naujocks went noiselessly to the door and listened. He heard steps in the corridor. There was a pause, then the light sound of a door gently shut and a key turning. Someone, Formis, had gone to the attic and an instant later come down again. He should be transmitting. A quarter of an hour later, approximately, the same sounds occurred. Then again silence.

A little after nine Naujocks decided to call Gröthe. He made the agreed signal and, opening the window, threw out the end of the rope. He felt two short tugs then one long. He drew up the rope, attached two suitcases to it and let them out of the window. He repeated the operation. Gröthe went to put the luggage on the back seat of the Mercedes. Finally he appeared, panting, on the window ledge. When he was in the room Naujocks explained to him in a low voice: 'I don't think they've seen us come in. We'll wait till ten o'clock for Formis to go up to the roof. I'll then hurry to his room and wait behind the door, the pad of chloroform in my hand. You will come along a moment later, or even earlier if you hear the sound of a struggle. Bring the bottle of phosphorus for the set. We'll bring it here and let it out of the window. And particularly, for heaven's sake, not a sound! Give me the key and the chloroform.'

Naujocks looked at his watch. It was 9.45. He went on, still in a low voice, 'Now listen. If he is punctual he won't be long before going to the attic to let out the antenna.'

Naujocks stood still by the door, one hand on the knob which he turned noiselessly to be able to spring out when the moment came. Edith was sitting on the bed, eyes shut, hands clasped, her face as white as her pullover. Gröthe, erect behind Naujocks, bit his lips till they bled.

Suddenly came the expected sound. They were steps mounting the stairs, stopping a fraction of a second at their door, then continuing deliberately down the corridor, passing their door and Formis's, and up the stairs to the attic. Formis must have gone down to dinner without their realizing it, probably at the time of Gröthe's arrival. Naujocks counted the steps: one, two, three, four, five . . . He knew there were six. The sixth creaked. Naujocks, without a sound, was already outside before Formis's door. He slid his false key into the lock, pressed it, turned it, trying to make the least noise possible, and suddenly he had a shiver of fear. He understood: on the other side there was a key in the lock! Formis was therefore in his room and someone else had gone to the attic.[5]

Naujocks's head swam. 'Who's that?' Formis shouted.

Naujocks, his throat dry, answered, 'It's me, your neighbour Gerber. Could you . . . could you . . . lend us . . . some soap?'

There was a silence, the sound of a footstep, another silence then the door opened very slowly, a few inches. An intent, questioning eye appeared and two fingers proferred a piece of soap.

Everything then happened with vertiginous speed. Naujocks threw all his weight against the door, hand extended towards Formis's throat; the latter lost his balance and dragged his assailant with him as he fell.

The two Germans struggled frenziedly, overturning everything in the room. The bottle of chloroform broke. In a flash Naujocks saw Formis draw a revolver from the pocket of his dressing gown. Three shots resounded. Naujocks felt an acute pain in his left hand and foot. Then there was another shot and Naujocks felt the body with which we was struggling relax and sag. In the doorway stood Gröthe, revolver in hand. Formis had been killed with a bullet in the head. Naujocks cried, 'Look out! They'll be here in a second. Where is Edith?'

She appeared, her eyes starting out of her head. Seeing Formis on the ground, she opened her mouth like a drowned person and fainted.

All Naujocks's plans were annihilated. He was suffering from his wounds but, with what was left of his presence of mind, he snatched the bottle of phosphorus from Gröthe, leapt to the open case containing the transmitter and poured the contents of the bottle into it. A violent explosion resounded while a huge flame swept the room: the phosphorus had ignited the chloroform-laden air. Naujocks realised too late that the yellow powder had at the same time set fire to his bleeding hands. He regained his room choking, moaning, reeling and opened the window wide.

Gröthe, revolver in hand, held back the personnel of the hotel who had come running, terrified. He made them line up against the wall, then descend to the cellar where he shut them in, saying, 'No one is to leave under penalty of being shot down without warning. You will be released at dawn.'

Before rejoining Naujocks he tore out the telephone wires. Helped by Gröthe, Naujocks carried Edith to the bed and slapped her to bring her back to her senses. She recovered consciousness. An expression of horror covered her face. Gröthe stood her on her feet. Naujocks ordered, 'Quick! We'll go out by the window.'

'Why not by the door?' asked Gröthe in surprise.

'Idiot! Because the ground floor entrance has a burglar alarm which they connect every evening after dinner. We've no time to disconnect it. If we go out that way they'll probably hear it ring and realise that we've gone and hurry to raise the alarm. By going through the window we may perhaps gain an hour or two.'

Gröthe slid first down to the courtyard, followed by Edith then Naujocks. The latter leapt to the steering wheel. Edith sat next to him, Gröthe in the back with the bags. Naujocks started the engine, which responded at once. The journey to Prague was a nightmare for him. His wounded left foot was numb, but he succeeded in moving it sufficiently to be able to use the clutch. His hands troubled him even more: the left one bled continuously and they were both swollen by the phosphorus burns, the right one being the more affected. He had great difficulty in keeping them steady on the wheel.

The ride to the station took fifty-three minutes. When stopping, Naujocks said to Edith, 'Take your ticket from my right hand pocket. You've got seven minutes till the train leaves. Good luck.'

Edith did as she was told with a trembling hand. Still silent, she got out and banged the door to violently. Gröthe just had time to hand her her two bags. She ran to the big staircase without turning round. Naujocks started off again at high speed, lurching across the icy snow, barely avoiding a tram whose bell clanged angrily. He got the Mercedes on to the road to the north and pressed the accelerator down flat once they had left the suburbs behind.

It was twenty-five minutes past midnight when the lights of the frontier became visible. They had taken less than an hour to do the ninety-six kilometres. Naujocks stopped fifty metres from the barrier, parking the car at the roadside. They would do the rest on foot. Gröthe helped Naujocks to put on his ski-mittens in order to hide the state of his hands. The two men went to the gate reserved for pedestrians. Gröthe tendered the passports, which the customs-officer stamped and returned without raising his head. A few steps and they were in Germany.

They made for an hotel. Drops of blood were dripping from Naujocks's hands. To the manager he explained, 'We've had an accident. Our car is immobilised the other side of the frontier. Can we spend the night here? Can you call a doctor?'

The manager told them to come in. A doctor came to examine the wounds. He asked no questions but took their names and addresses, saying he would have to notify the police.

The next day, having recovered the car, Naujocks and Gröthe sped to Berlin without a stop. When Naujocks reported to Heydrich and told him the story of his adventure he received no compliments. The head of the S.D. was furious. The destruction of the transmitter delighted him, Formis's death left him indifferent, but what would the Führer say?

The Führer didn't say anything and congratulated Heydrich on having silenced the voice of the Black Front. Heydrich was careful not to inform Naujocks. So things went in high Nazi circles.

On January 25th 1935 the teleprinters of the German newspapers linked with the German press service (D.N.B.) carried the following bulletin: 'During the night of 23rd/24th January a German emigrant in Czechoslovakia by the name of Rudolf Formis was found killed by a bullet from a revolver in a hotel near Pribram. The Czech authorities say they suspect two men and a woman of German nationality of being the authors of the crime, but no further details have been supplied.'

The German reporters who tried to find out more were requested by Dr. Goebbels's office to busy themselves with something else: 'There is nothing more to be said on this subject.'

Following an approach by the German Ambassador to the Prague Government, the Czechoslovak press also maintained silence in the matter. But the Czech authorities had succeeded in identifying the assassins after a long and careful enquiry conducted jointly by the Criminal Investigation Bureau and representatives of the military counter-espionage section. In a report from the Criminal Investigation Bureau can be read:

'The three Germans implicated in the murder of the emigrant Rudolf Formis at the Hotel Zahori near Pribram arrived in the country on January 20th. They were Alfred Gerber, twenty-three, from Berlin, and Gert Schubert, twenty-four, likewise from Berlin. Edith Karlebach left the country by train. The two men had a Mercedes, licence number IP 48259, crossed the frontier at Teschen and succeeded in getting away. The proprietor of the Hotel Zahori has been arrested and accused of complicity.[6]

If the Allies had known these facts when they arrested Alfred Naujocks in 1945, he would no doubt have been hanged without further ado. In 1935 he simultaneously lost Edith and the love of Tania. A mild punishment for such a crime.

NOTES TO CHAPTER 8

1. Statement of Edith Karlebach in 1948 to a Czech journalist, Miroslav Vozka, reproduced in *Der Spiegel*.
2. N.S.D.A.P. card No. 4 583 151 and S.S. No. 107 099, Joseph Huber, former militant of the Bavarian Popular Party (*Bayerische Volkspartei*), was at this period councillor of the Criminal Department and chief of the Gestapo section for the supervision of the non-Marxist parties, Catholics, Protestants, the *Black Front* and the dissident *Steel Helmets*.
3. Colonel Moravec, of the Czechoslovak Secret Service, a refugee in London after March 15th 1939, told me after the war that an investigation by the police and the counter-espionage service had been conducted jointly in January 1935 into the Formis affair. The hotel-keepers, the chambermaids, the waiters, the inspectors and superintendents of police and customs at the airport and the frontier had been questioned at length. The voluminous dossier of this enquiry has disappeared. But I was able to consult the notes of the summary Colonel Moravec brought with him to London three years after the Formis affair.
4. *Cf.* Note 1.
5. It was never discovered who had ascended to the attic. Possibly one of the hotel staff, an accomplice of Formis.
6. Colonel Moravec explained to me after the war that the proprietor had been accused because he had raised the alarm too late for the police to lay hold of the criminals. We have seen that he could not have acted otherwise.

9

Secret Rivalries:
Canaris–Heydrich–Schellenberg

The 'house opposite', the Abwehr, changed heads. On January 1st 1935, Wilhelm Canaris officially succeeded Conrad Patzig in the direction of the S.R. (Intelligence Service) of the land forces. When he heard of this appointment Heydrich confided to his wife, 'Lina, Patzig's departure delights me. With him no collaboration was possible. I'm surprised that the choice of his successor should have fallen on Canaris. Well! Personally I'm very pleased. I hope we'll be able to understand each other. I've never forgotten, you know, the time I served under him as a cadet at Kiel. He admitted me to his intimacy. For two years I played the violin with his wife Erika. . . . What a musician! I haven't seen the Canarises for ten years, I think we'll re-establish friendly relations. You'll see, Erika Canaris is a marvellous woman.'

At that time Heydrich had serious worries. His secret service was at a turning point. It was no longer the little Munich shop of 1931– 34. The organisation had developed considerably since its installation in Berlin. The spider's web woven all over Germany grew tighter and tighter. The recruitment had improved, young intellectuals flowed in. However the S.D. was not yet, as Heydrich wanted, an organism comparable to the great secret services such as British Intelligence, the Soviet N.K.V.D. the French Deuxième Bureau or even the Abwehr; all the less in that the police apparatus of Heydrich (Gestapo and S.D.) had a tendency to paralyse itself. The jurisdiction of the S.D. too much overlapped that of the Gestapo. The repeated orders from Heydrich regarding a necessary division of duties were insufficient to settle the problem. Moreover he was not unaware of the personal rivalries; the ponderous Bavarian, Heinrich Müller, virtual chief of the Gestapo, was too often in conflict with the distinguished Werner Best, Heinz Jost, Herbert

Mehlhorn or Walter Schellenberg, who were themselves far from being in harmony with one another.

The S.S. secret service had a trial run in preparing the Night of the Long Knives, in conducting the Horvath and Formis affairs, in intruding into that of Sosnowski. But these were only amateur jobs. Of this Heydrich was perfectly conscious. His 'colts', Schellenberg, Naujocks, Jost, Mehlhorn, Rasch, Behrends, were not yet professionals in Intelligence work like the officers of the Abwehr. Their training had to be intensified, their capacity increased. All the directives of the period show that he was striving to open up for the S.D. new perspectives, give it vaster fields of action. His intent was clear: that the S.D. secret service should become the unique and mighty secret service of the Third Reich.

On this ambitious road he had already encountered and knew that he would constantly encounter a tough adversary: the Abwehr. To absorb the Abwehr, 'supreme hope and supreme thought', would be no easy task. Military Intelligence had adopted the device of Colonel Nicolaï: 'The Intelligence service is the appanage of gentlemen; if it is entrusted to others it will collapse'. The S.S. had no citizen rights in this domain, neither did the Party members. And it is known that the Abwehr was the most active hotbed of all the conspiracies against Hitler. Moreover, *officially*, espionage and counter-espionage, military as well as political, were the preserve of the Abwehr agents alone.

The intrusion of the S.S. into the Horvath, Formis and Sosnowski affairs only increased the tension between the Abwehr and the S.D.

Throughout the year 1934 Heydrich multiplied the occasions for eliminating Captain Conrad Patzig, avowed enemy of the S.S. He knew that he could not attack frontally this organ of the all-powerful Reichswehr, coddled by Hitler. He had sought to provoke incidents, so much so that the Führer himself had been informed and ordered the Minister for the Reichswehr, von Blomberg, quickly to find a *modus vivendi*. The 'old rubber lion' had understood and hastened to obey his master. He summoned Patzig to tell him, 'Your presence at the head of the Abwehr is incompatible with the needs of the Party. I must find a successor for you.'

Patzig, weary of perpetual conflicts with Heydrich, hoped for nothing else. He proposed his friend, Captain Canaris, to succeed him. Despite strong opposition from Grand Admiral Raeder, Canaris was named to and accepted the formidable post.

The first meeting of Canaris and Heydrich as equals took place on 'neutral ground', in a Berlin restaurant. It was very friendly, at least on the surface, and evident that the ex-cadet, then thirty, was very pleased to see again his former superior whom he had much admired. But Heydrich had developed. He now judged men cynically, dividing them into two categories: those who had to be handled with care until he became stronger than they, and those who had to be destroyed in one way or another as soon as possible. He thought he recognised in the man nicknamed the 'little admiral' one who belonged to the first category. He knew him to be intelligent and adroit, but considered him more a worldling than a man of action, quite timorous, indeed timid. He believed it would be comparatively easy to manoeuvre him in the jungle that was the Third Reich where he, Heydrich, was one of the largest of the beasts of prey.

To attain his end, the absorption of the Abwehr, Heydrich was helped in his ambition by the fact that Army Intelligence Service had to work with the police (Gestapo), directed by himself, to make arrests, searches and other activities of that sort. The Abwehr, as we have seen in the case of Sosnowski, possessed no executive organ of its own. Heydrich furthermore knew—and it was important—that Canaris's superiors, General von Blomberg and General von Reichenau, were, as the expression went, 'tinged more brown than black'.[1] But they wanted at all costs to avoid a conflict with the S.S. chiefs. In this state of mind they awaited a new chief of the Abwehr who would find common ground with the S.D. and the Gestapo.

Vis-à-vis Canaris, Heydrich thus felt himself in a strong position. But he underestimated his adversary. Later, when he saw the admiral at work, his eyes were opened. He warned his subordinates against him: 'He's an old fox with whom you have to be very careful.'

Canaris on his side treated Heydrich with all the cordiality of 'an older friend': nothing could have provoked greater satisfaction in the other, who had never forgiven the Navy for expelling him. In this respect he had, as is known, an inferiority complex, sublimated into fierce aggression, especially against the officers of all arms. Also he was flattered by the attitude of his former chief.

Canaris very soon saw that the ex-cadet had changed greatly since the time he had been under his orders. Today, it was plain, the man was voracious and looked formidable. However Canaris could not avoid being fascinated by his keen intelligence. At the same time he felt something like fear, instinctive, physical. The slightly mongolian appearance of Heydrich's eyes, his cold and piercing gaze, almost reptilian, were disquieting. He was an adversary of exceptional quality, with whom it was necessary to play a continuous game to avoid being caught in his claws. The succession to Conrad Patzig was likely to be burdensome. The same evening Canaris noted in his diary, 'Heydrich is a barbarous fanatic with whom it will be very difficult to co-operate frankly and straightforwardly.' Canaris understood that he was going to have to 'navigate' very carefully: his course would be strewn with hidden and most unexpected reefs.

In the course of his negotiations with Heydrich, or with the latter's assistant Dr. Werner Best, he gave proof of diplomatic talent. He yielded to the S.S. one position after another of small importance, but obstinately stood his ground on vital matters. He had been ordered to reach a compromise with the S.S.: therefore they came to an agreement. But he knew well how to arrange that decisions should not be formulated too precisely so as to be able later to interpret them in a sense most favourable to himself.

At the end of 1936, after two years of negotiation, Canaris and Heydrich finally reached accord on ten points—they would later be called the 'Ten Commandments'—which defined the new limits. The protocol was signed by Canaris and Best on December 21st 1936.

In this adjustment of reciprocal fields of activity the Abwehr would keep, in principle, control of counter-espionage while the Gestapo would continue to look after all operations resulting from judicial decisions. In the long run this basis of agreement would not lead to better relations between the two services. There had for one thing been no exact definition of counter-espionage. An unambiguous definition is obviously difficult. But distrust existed, and was to increase in this case. It was only a reflection of the very great tension between the Reichswehr and the S.S. It would soon become dramatic. Apart from the distrust, there would enter in the Gestapo's surveillance of and spying into every politically suspect element, which would lead to frequent encroachments in the counter-espionage sector.

Under the 'Ten Commandments' the Abwehr kept the monopoly of espionage. Nevertheless, at Heydrich's insistence, the latter remained strictly confined to the military sphere: the Abwehr agents were not to interfere in matters of politics. In return the S.D. would transmit to the relevant services of the Abwehr any military information it might incidentally obtain.

The frontier between political and military intelligence is movable and it is practically impossible to define the exact point marking the boundary between the politico-military and the purely military. Canaris did not delude himself about Heydrich's intentions. He well knew that the signature to the agreement would scarcely be dry before his adversary would launch into military espionage without regard to the Abwehr. In fact Heydrich imposed no restriction on his S.D. men. But Canaris was just as artful as Reinhard Heydrich if not more so. He had no intention of confining himself to military intelligence. It was a long while since the politician and diplomat had supplanted the naval officer in him. He was quite convinced that he could operate on the political terrain with a competence and prudence sufficient to keep himself well informed on political problems abroad and at the same time to give his military superiors the authentic intelligence of which they might have need. Subsequent events were to prove his confidence in himself justified.

At the beginning of the spring of 1936, shortly after the occupation of the Rhineland by the Reichswehr, Canaris bought a small house in Berlin in the Schlachtensee neighbourhood, in the elegant and quiet Zehlendorf quarter bordering on the Grünewald forest. The Heydriches, who had established regular and friendly relations with the Canarises, found Zehlendorf extremely agreeable and settled there in their turn. By a curious chance the Schellenbergs lived there, as well as the Chief of Police of Berlin, Wolf Heinrich Count von Helldorf, the head of the Criminal police Arthur Nebe, the Abwehr Colonel Hans Oster and the Government counsellor Hans-Bernd Gisevius.[2] Frau Canaris was delighted to have rediscovered the excellent violinist Reinhard Heydrich and resumed their musical evenings together as in 1922–24. Lina Heydrich and she struck up a close friendship. They quickly fell into a routine.

'Sunday evenings, sometimes at the Canarises, sometimes at our house, were devoted to music,' writes Frau Heydrich. 'My husband and the Admiral never discussed politics in my presence. The conversation between the four of us was given over to literature, philosophy, the arts, anecdotes of the Admiral's voyages and, particularly, music. My husband and Frau Canaris would discuss Haydn and Mozart for hours on end. Reinhard enjoyed them profoundly, I think. It was his only real relaxation, since he worked practically twenty-four hours a day, managing to find only a little time for fencing, riding and flying his aeroplane. Moreover he had a great admiration for Frau Canaris who was truly a very fine musician.'

At this period Walter Schellenberg had entered the circle of Heydrich's intimates. 'Intimates' does not mean 'friends'. The

Archangel of Evil was a lone wolf. He had not, he never would have, one real friend. Hitler in delivering his funeral oration said, 'He was a man with an iron heart.'

Schellenberg was the only one amongst the dignitaries of the S.S. to participate closely in his family life. For more than seven years a curious relationship, half official half personal, linked these two young S.S. leaders who cherished the same burning ambition. It comprised mutual admiration, affection and hatred all at the same time. It would often be agitated, indeed dramatic, but remained solid. It offered Schellenberg the chance to know Heydrich better than anyone. At Pallanza the latter was often at the centre of our talks. Schellenberg's appreciation of his character—even if at times the details cited were not altogether in conformity with the truth—assume a genuine historical importance.

From the beginning of spring, 1935, Schellenberg went out regularly into the best Berlin society with Lina and Reinhard Heydrich. Together the three visited concerts, the theatre, the cinema, art galleries. They often passed the afternoon or evening playing bridge in what Heydrich with a touch of irony called, 'the gentle intimacy of the family circle'. In fact the Heydrich household was often stormy. Lina had character and a lively intelligence. If she was justifiably proud of the position occupied by her husband, she did not enjoy very great conjugal happiness. Heydrich admitted it himself, at least in a private letter, and, knowing what one does of his uncontrollable sexual appetite, it could not have been otherwise. His wife did not hide it. In the summer of 1961 she stated in all frankness to the English historian Charles Wighton, 'Yes, there were always girls, many girls, in my married life.'

Schellenberg said to me of Heydrich, 'This man with a heart of ice could not resist his sexual thirst. He abandoned himself to it without the least restriction or slightest precaution. He then altogether lost the calculating prudence which characterised all his other actions. Nevertheless he always regained sufficient self-control in time to avoid too serious incidents. The number of women he had is incalculable. He was the king of the cabarets and nights clubs of the Kurfurstendamm and Alexanderplatz. All the managers, barmen, barmaids and dance hostesses knew him. He was one of their best customers. He seldom went out alone. Most often he took me with him or had Alfred Naujocks, sometimes Heinrich Müller, Gert Gröthe or Hermann Behrends accompany him. It was for us a frightful drudgery because one had to put up with his false gaiety, his false cordiality and especially his perverse and tasteless caprices.'

It is understandable that the expression 'the gentle intimacy of the family circle' took on a cruelly ironic sense when uttered by Heydrich. Also understandable is his widow's bitterness, even thirty years later. And one can't help wondering about Schellenberg's role with regard to Heydrich and his wife.

In 1935 Reinhard Heydrich was turned thirty-one, his wife four years younger, and pretty, very pretty. Walter Schellenberg was twenty-five. He had fine dark eyes and a smile which easily charmed the so-called weaker sex. He was nearly always in civilian dress, elegantly cut of choice material. He made Lina his confidante in his love affairs. He found her an attentive and thoughtful listener, less preoccupied than her husband. It would not appear that their relations were more than friendly, but the friendship became very intimate and deep. Despite a probably mutual tenderness, I do not believe that they yielded to any stronger inclination. They both knew only too well Heydrich's devouring jealousy, although he did not deny himself any deviation from conjugal fidelity. He was capable, in his own words, of 'pursuing his mortal enemy to the tomb'. An anecdote related by Schellenberg illustrates this.

Heydrich had, in 1935, had a house built for Lina—with a mortgage of thirty-five thousand marks—a charming thatch-roofed chalet on the Baltic coast on Fehmarn Island.[3] Until the annexation of Schleswig-Holstein by Bismarck her ancestors were liberty-loving sailors and merchants who felt at home in all Nordic countries from Scotland to Russia. Lina so loved the island of Fehmarn that she lived there with her two children from the end of spring till the end of autumn. Her husband came to see them nearly every weekend. In his own 'plane he landed near Lübeck then took the ferry to Fehmarn. The former naval officer, who had a little boat, often sailed in the waters of the Baltic. He too loved the house.

At the end of September 1936 he called a conference here of the chief Gestapo and S.D. leaders. Schellenberg was amongst them. After the conference the latter, having still a day's leave, remained a further twenty-four hours at the hotel in which he had been staying while Heydrich and the others left for Berlin.

Four days later in Berlin he was telephoned in his office by the head of the Gestapo, Heinrich Müller. Heydrich desired that they should all three do a tour of the night clubs. Schellenberg imagined that it was one of his usual escapades and accepted without further thought although he was not at the moment on very good terms with Müller. 'As often happens with people whose life is constantly in danger,' wrote Schellenberg, 'I was superstitious and had a presentiment that the evening would turn out badly. But I found Heydrich in one of his best moods and my fears were soon dissipated. He did not want to hear, as was usual, about the latest espionage matters, saying that for once there should be no shop talk. After dinner in a well-known restaurant we adjourned to an obscure bar near the Alexanderplatz.'

Of the sequel Schellenberg gave me a version not exactly that which was to be published in his Memoirs several years after our conversation. Knowing that Schellenberg's manuscript had been altered before publication, I will adhere to what I noted down in 1952.

'It was nearly midnight when we went into the "Frida" bar, where I had never been before,' Schellenberg told me. 'The barman who greeted Heydrich as an habitué was a sinister type. A "night bird", young and quite seductive, perched on a stool, saw us enter. Her face, at first smiling and inviting, froze when she set eyes on our chief. Obviously she knew him well, too well. He did not notice her until he sat down with us at a little table in the darkest corner of the room. In a crisp tone of command he snapped one word at the girl: "Out!"

'She reacted as if stung by a scorpion, took up her handbag, made a sign to the barman and disappeared. This incident, which I still can't explain, made me uneasy. Meanwhile Müller had ordered three cocktails. The conversation was at first commonplace. We spoke of Heydrich's personal aeroplane, its performance, its manoeuvrability. I had just taken a large swallow of my cocktail, which had a sweetish taste, when Müller said to me, "Well, old man, I think I know that you had some fun the other day after we left Fehmarn. Is Lake Plöner as pretty as they say?"

'Heydrich interposed, "Schellenberg, don't try to fool me. You've just drunk poison. It can kill you in six hours. If you'll tell me the whole truth, the absolute truth, whatever it is, about your excursion with my wife on Lake Plöner, I'll give you the antidote. I want the truth. You understand me: I want the truth."'

'At the moment I didn't much believe in the story of poison, for Heydrich was perfectly capable of playing such a sinister joke with an impassive face. All the same I must admit that my heart began to beat heavily. What if it were true? Succeeding in controlling my feelings, I told him in a voice as calm as possible how the afternoon had in fact been spent.

' "After our conference I asked you, since I had a free day, if you would allow me to stay on for twenty-four hours at Fehmarn. Not only did you agree, for which I thanked you, but when I was saying goodbye you said, "If you have a few minutes, go and see my wife, it would give her pleasure to have a chat with you." '

' "That's right," said Heydrich, "what I want to know is what then happened between my wife and you." '

' "But. . . ." '

' "I want the truth." '

' "Nothing happened. I went to see Lina after lunch and we had coffee, talking about art, literature, music, subjects which you know greatly interest her." '

'Müller listened attentively, his forehead wrinkled, his eyes malevolent. He must have looked like that when he interrogated one of the Gestapo's victims. With the evident intention of impressing our hierarchical superior he said to me, "After coffee you both went to Lake Plöner. Why do you hide the fact? You must know that, without being aware of it, you were being observed the whole time." '

' "In fact I didn't know. I willingly believe you. I have nothing to hide and am hiding nothing. In what way was this outing blameworthy? Did your spy also tell you that we went bathing? Did he tell you that afterwards we played ball, volley-ball to be exact, with other bathers?" '

'I took an aggressive tone,' Schellenberg told me, 'more and more aggressive against Müller. I felt that I wasn't far from throwing the contents of my glass in his face. Before Müller had time to open his mouth to answer me Heydrich said, "What you've just said is correct. I telephoned Lina, who gave me the same account and . . . the information given me by Müller is identical." '

'Heydrich was silent for a moment, then went on, "When did you leave Fehmarn?" '

' "About an hour after accompanying Lina home I took the ferry. I arrived in Berlin at eight and went to my office to lock up in my safe the dossiers I had brought to the conference. Is that all you want to know?" '

' "Well, I suppose I have to believe you," said Heydrich. "But give me your word of honour that you will never attempt a similar escapade with Lina." '

'I rebelled and answered, "A word obtained in this way is pure extortion. First give me the antidote to your poison and I will then give you my word of honour. As a former naval officer, do you deem it honourable to proceed otherwise?"'

I don't know if Schellenberg really spoke in this way to Heydrich, but if he did he had courage. Heydrich didn't like an appeal to his honour as an officer and still less a reminder of his time in the Navy from which he had been expelled. His reaction might have been very violent. One must believe that it was not. According to Schellenberg, Heydrich regarded him attentively before making a gesture of acquiescence and ordering another glass, the famous 'antidote'. The barman, who only seemed to be waiting for this order, hurried over to the trio and presented a full glass which Schellenberg drank at a gulp with a grimace. The drink seemed to him to be a dry Martini with a special taste—the effect of his imagination, or more bitter than usual? No one can say. Schellenberg gave his word of honour to Heydrich, then offered his excuses for 'this innocent outing'. Heydrich declared that he wanted to hear no more of apologies and ordered another round of drinks. The night culminated without further incident in a fashionable night club. Schellenberg never knew if the first glass was really poisoned.

A few months earlier, in the spring of 1936, Schellenberg had made the acquaintance of Canaris during a dinner at the Heydriches. The young S.S. man had been captivated by the personality of the 'little admiral', the head of the Abwehr. He wrote, 'Canaris is a remarkably intelligent and sensitive man, full of excellent qualities. He loves his horse and his dogs. "Schellenberg," he often said to me, "look at the superiority of animals. My dog is discreet, he would never betray me . . . I can't say as much of men!" . . . Canaris was a charming travelling companion, and always showed himself kindly and paternal to me . . . In many respects he was what one would call a mystic. Although a Protestant he admired the Roman Catholic Church, its organisation and the power of its faith. Italy and the Vatican exercised a great influence on him, traces of which can be seen in his acts as a conspirator.'

During the summer Schellenberg participated regularly in the croquet games on the Canarises' lawn. The civil war which had begun in Spain on July 18th was their principal topic of conversation. Canaris knew Spain and the Spaniards extremely well, and was moreover a friend of the chief of the Nationalists, General Franco. Schellenberg was fascinated by the 'little admiral' who knew how to endow his stories with a passionate and convincing warmth.

Schellenberg also came upon the Abwehr chief regularly riding in the Tiergarten, where they often rode side by side talking of the affairs of their respective services. Schellenberg played an odd role. Heydrich used these meetings to sound out Canaris on his intentions and doings. Canaris on his side did the same. Schellenberg, in whom both had confidence, acted as a buffer. The rivalry between the Abwehr and the S.D. in fact worsened from week to week. But one may wonder which of the two Schellenberg served better. His supple disposition, scheming, cunning, helped him to mislead Heydrich and Canaris simultaneously. He succeeded to the end in maintaining this delicate balance and most friendly relations with both men. It was not one of Schellenberg's most engaging aspects.

That said, I now understand why a man like Canaris, endowed with an exceptional loftiness of spirit and a rare sensibility, could form a friendship with the young S.S. man who was after all his adversary. Schellenberg exercised a real power of seduction. Even knowing what I did of him in 1952—I was ignorant, it is true, of certain of his past activities—my feelings towards him were at least cordial. Strange. It was not because of his tragic physical condition, which might have inspired me with pity. There was something else. Yes, Walter Schellenberg was a 'War Criminal'. Yes, he had been one of the most important S.S. leaders. Yes, he had been Himmler's favoured junior and Heydrich's intimate . . . But if I compare him with the rest of the S.S. I find it hard to imagine him in the black uniform. I know that he had great gifts as an actor, yet he had those accents of sincerity which do not deceive. In his Memoirs he pleads his own cause, obviously, and too often veils the truth. But in the course of our conversations he never once tried to exonerate himself. What he told me sounded convincing. It was impossible for me not to believe him. I am today convinced that he then spoke to me frankly and I must yield to the evidence: Schellenberg, the upstart, the realist, the intriguer was not a vulgar being, still less a black-guard; he possessed a certain moral sense—due no doubt to his profoundly Catholic education—and also certain undeniable human qualities which rendered him sympathetic to me. This must be said, it seems to me.

NOTES TO CHAPTER 9

1. Brown, the colour of the S.A. uniforms, applied to Nazis in general, while black, the colour of the S.S. uniforms, applied to Himmler's Nazis.
2. Colonel Hans Oster, a fierce anti-Nazi, ended by being hanged by the S.S. on the same day (April 9th 1945) as his chief, Admiral Canaris, at the concentration camp of Flossenburg. Count von Helldorf, a member of the plot against Hitler in 1944, was also hanged by the S.S. Nebe suffered the same fate in January 1945 for the same reasons. As for Hans-Bernd Gisevius, he survived and at Nuremberg was a terrible and implacable witness for the prosecution.
3. After the war this house constituted Frau Heydrich's sole resource—she opened a small guest-house there.

10

A Forger's Masterpiece—
the Tukhachevsky Affair

Riding boot to boot, Schellenberg and Canaris brought their mounts to a walk. In the snow-covered Tiergarten the sounds from the city only reached them muted. The cold was keen at the beginning of January 1937. The east wind lowered the temperature well below freezing.

'It's a wind from the steppes,' remarked the young S.S. officer.

In a way that seemed quite natural he dilated on the immensity of Poland and Russia. The geographical conversation turned political. Schellenberg questioned the admiral on the current state of German–Soviet relations. But the other did not seem talkative. Plainly, he observed, Canaris did not like this subject broached. He knew the 'little admiral' to be deeply anti-Communist and did not understand his reluctance to speak of the U.S.S.R.

The reasons for this attitude were explained to me by former associates of the head of the Abwehr, notably Colonel Oscar Reile.

Canaris, of remote Italian origin, was only attracted by the Mediterranean countries. The Slavic world seemed to him mysterious and without great interest. His knowledge of the countries to the east was relatively slight. Finally, anti-Communist since witnessing the revolutionary attempts in Germany between 1918 and 1920, he had always disapproved of certain Germans' policy of rapprochement with the Soviets. In particular he had been in disagreement with Colonel Nicolaï, former chief of the Kaiser's Intelligence Service, who had tenaciously urged from 1920 a policy of military collaboration between the Reichswehr and the Red Army.

It should be recalled that this collaboration had been pushed very far under cover of absolute secrecy and with the total agreement of the Soviet Government. In 1923, the year of the Treaty of Rapallo, the Reichswehr–Red Army collaboration had begun under the orders of the Defence Minister, Gessler, and General von Seekt, seconded by Colonel Nicolaï. The first result was that German officers went to the U.S.S.R. to be initiated into the use of arms like aircraft and tanks which had been forbidden to the Germans by the Treaty of Versailles. In return the Germans transmitted to the Red Army their technical expertise and the strategic as well as other knowledge of the German General Staff. Later this co-operation was extended to armament.

Today we know that the aviation centre was established at Lipetsk, in the province of Tambov, between Moscow and Voronezh, for eleven years. The testing ground for armour was near Kazan on the Volga. According to General Ernest Köstring who published his Memoirs in 1953, 'We had available for our experiments in chemical warfare a vast area all of whose villages had been evacuated.' This is understandable when one realises that 'chemical warfare' was nothing other than poison gas.

Round 1930 the staffs of the Reichswehr and the Red Army began to organise joint war games and manoeuvres for staff officers. Amongst others, Generals von Blomberg and Köstring participated on the German side, Generals Voroshilov and Tukhachevsky on the Russian. This curious Russo-German military symbiosis produced its fruits. Thanks to it the bases were laid for the new German offensive strength which from 1938 would threaten Europe and in 1941 come close to annihilating Soviet Russia. General Köstring writes, 'Long after Hitler came to power, the Chief of Staff Goering stated that the Luftwaffe would never have reached its acknowledged high level of efficiency in 1939 if it had not been able to undergo an intense preparation and formation at this period. The same remark applies to the armour, which was confirmed to me by the specialists in this arm, amongst others General Guderian.'

As the German journalist Sebastian Haffner emphasises, 'Even the greatest geniuses in military organisation would have been incapable of creating in six years, 1933 to 1939, the most powerful Air Force, the most efficient armoured divisions of the time. The apparent "miracle" of the German remilitarisation under Hitler was only rendered possible by the patient, diligent, dogged, groundwork performed during eleven years in Russia.'

It should be recognised that this paradoxical secret military collaboration between Germany and the Soviet Union, which lasted from 1923 to 1933, is without precedent in history, even between allies. 'To find the equivalent of what happened in the Twenties and

Thirties in the depths of the vast Russian spaces', writes Haffner, 'unknown to the whole world, including the German public, we must for an instant imagine the Federal Republic in the act of perfecting, in the heart of Mao Tse-tung's China, and in conjunction with Chinese specialists, a nuclear strike-force.'

But to return to January 1937. Admiral Canaris and young Walter Schellenberg discussed the re-establishment by Stalin of the traditional ranks in the Red Army and the institution of the grade of 'Marshal of the Soviet Union'. Schellenberg mentioned the youngest of the Marshals: Mikhaïl Nikolaivitch Tukhachevsky. Canaris said he had never had the opportunity to meet him. He had heard him much spoken of by different German generals who had accompanied him when he came to Germany in 1923 and 1932 to take part in the Reichswehr large-scale manoeuvres with a group of Soviet officers; also by those who had known him as a student in a Red Army officers' training course with the General Staff of the German army; and by those, finally, who had been in contact with him on the Russo-German military commission charged with supervising the execution of the 1923 conventions.

'Yes,' said Schellenberg, 'Tukhachevsky knows our country well. He came to Berlin five times between 1925 and 1932. He established friendly relations with some of our generals. He seems very Germanophile . . . What's your opinion?'

'He made an excellent impression on von Blomberg,' Canaris replied non-committally, 'less, doubtless, for his professional abilities than for his social manners, which contrast sharply with the crude deportment of his colleagues in the Red Army.'

There the conversation ceased. The admiral knew when to let matters rest.

A few days later, on some pretext, Heydrich invited the head of the Abwehr to lunch. Canaris described to his friend and assistant Piekenbrock the details of this strange tête-à-tête. At the end of the meal Heydrich turned the conversation to the U.S.S.R., manifested his ignorance of its political and military structure and said he would like to be briefed. He was particularly 'desirous of being informed about the present chiefs of the Red Army'. He knew that the admiral had easy access to the archives of the Reichswehr's General Staff. Could he not transmit to him 'for several days' the dossiers of 'some Soviet generals who had spent some time in Germany before the advent of Nazism'? Tukhachevsky interested him especially. Canaris pricked up his ears. He remembered then

Schellenberg's remarks. What was the S.S. hatching? Was Heydrich wanting the documents to compromise certain German generals hostile to Nazism and accuse them of treason or had he some other idea in mind? The admiral was evasive. Heydrich insisted. It was important to him. Canaris dodged adroitly. Yet he could without difficulty have satisfied his interlocutor. He possessed an interesting dossier concerning precisely Tukhachevsky, and various items of information, odd to say the least, from London and Paris. But Canaris, in the two years he had been dealing with Heydrich, had begun to know that tortuous spirit well and his mistrust was increasing. Confronted by the admiral's attitude the S.S. chief did not hide his disappointment.

'I know, Admiral, that by our Ten Commandments agreement military espionage and counter-espionage are exclusively under your jurisdiction. But this is no military matter. The Führer wants to have intelligence on the political plane on the present heads of the Red Army and has charged me with supplying it to him. Not having the necessary elements I turn to you.'

'I'm sorry,' said Canaris, 'but without a precise and imperative order signed by the Führer, I cannot circulate the dossiers of the General Staff of the Reichswehr.'

'A spark of hatred seemed to flash in Heydrich's eyes,' Canaris told his friend Piekenbrock, 'but he quickly controlled himself.'

Heydrich in fact confined himself to saying, 'Very well, Admiral, I'll report to the Führer.'

For several days Canaris heard no more of the Russian dossiers. Suddenly he was told one morning that a fire had broken out on the premises of the Abwehr and Reichswehr General Staff in the Bendlerstrasse. There had been serious damage. When he arrived at the spot Canaris observed without excessive surprise that among the offices burned were those of service T3 where were stored the dossiers concerning Russian affairs, especially those pertaining to the Soviet generals who had had contact with the German army. There was no doubt that the arson was signed Heydrich. Rage and disgust assailed him. What should he do? Complain to the Führer? He would not be believed. Better wait to see what Heydrich was hatching. He would then see what steps were appropriate.

What Heydrich was hatching turned out to be an astounding masterpiece—I use the word with reluctance—of political poisoning, one of the most extraordinary secret service affairs ever known, one of the bloodiest also, which historians call the Tukhachevsky affair.

I have to state that we shall doubtless never know the whole truth. Not only are all the protagonists dead, but one cannot refer to the Kremlin archives to put an end to uncertainties and clear up a problem in which the motives are tangled and inextricable. The more I have studied this affair, over a period of twenty-five years, the fewer certainties have I acquired. In all honesty, it is impossible to adduce the beginning of a solution. One can have an impression but not an opinion. Let us limit ourselves to mentioning the indisputable facts, the evident, probable or doubtful ones.

To understand the meaning of Schellenberg's and Heydrich's conversations with Canaris we must go back a little, to the first days of December 1936.

Heydrich received in a private dining room of the Hotel Adlon in Berlin a very curious person. Thin, wearing a close-fitting suit of good Parisian cut, a triangular face, short hair parted in the middle, with a small moustache, he was an important personage in the world of the Russian emigrés in France, the White Army General Nicolas Skoblin. He was then forty-two years of age. In Paris he was the assistant to General Miller, the successor to General Kutiepov (who disappeared mysteriously in January 1930), at the presidency of the World Organisation of Russian emigré soldiers.

Skoblin had been introduced to Heydrich a few months earlier by a common friend, Baron Wrangel.[1] The Germanophilism and fierce anti-Communism of Skoblin had attracted the head of the S.S. secret service. Heydrich's intelligence and energy had conquered Skoblin, all the more easily because the least information was always well paid for by the S.D.

The meeting at the Hotel Adlon having taken place in secret, its tenor is obviously unknown. But from four testimonies (those of Schellenberg, Behrends, Naujocks and Jahnke) the essential is known: Heydrich received from Skoblin a detailed report according to which the Soviet Marshal Tukhachevsky was plotting with the German General Staff with the aim of achieving a double military putsch: in Moscow to get rid of Stalin, in Berlin to get rid of Hitler.

Heydrich, who as we know had a revenge to take on the 'Military', jumped at the proferred opportunity. Did he for a moment believe in the veracity of Skoblin's detailed report? It is hardly probable. He was going to act as if he believed it and not for an instant suspect the real origin of the information.

The day after his interview with Skoblin, Heydrich summoned to his office the chief of the Eastern Service of the S.D., S.S. Colonel Hermann Behrends and the great specialist in international affairs, S.S. Captain Erich Jahnke. He told them what he had just learned and ended, 'Properly used, this intelligence will deliver a blow to the High Command of the Red Army from which it will certainly not recover for many years. So far as the German General Staff is concerned, it will rid us of elements which remain hostile to National Socialism.'

Erich Jahnke's reaction was immediate. He represented to Heydrich that Skoblin could easily be playing a double game and that the information could have been forged entirely by the Soviets and passed on to Skoblin by Stalin's orders. Jahnke reckoned that there might be a double corruption: to weaken the German General Staff by arousing the S.S.'s suspicion of its members, the external poisoning: and at the same time to permit Stalin to act against the military clique at the head of which was Tukhachevsky who would be charged with high treason—the internal poisoning. Jahnke stressed that 'By reason of the internal difficulties of the Soviet Government and the Russian Communist party, Stalin obviously does not want to start an action against his generals himself and prefers that the incriminating documents should come from abroad.'

Heydrich, irritated by these subtleties, fell into a rage and declared that even if Jahnke were right, the result would be the same and serve National Socialism. When Jahnke insisted, Heydrich ordered him out of his office, putting him under three months of house arrest. Then he said to Behrends, who had not opened his mouth, 'I'll talk to the Reichsführer S.S. Himmler about it, then we'll go and warn the Führer.'

Walter Schellenberg, who had been secretly apprised of the matter by Erich Jahnke, told me, 'At the moment I did not see at all clearly into the intrigue in question. Heydrich had the air of knowing perfectly what he wanted. On Christmas Eve Heydrich and Himmler called on the Führer. Heydrich informed me that Hess and Bormann were present when he divulged his plan: to produce enough documents to prove indisputably that Marshal Tukhachevsky and several of his colleagues in the Red Army were conspiring with certain German generals to seize power in their respective countries, and find a means whereby these documents would fall into Stalin's hands. Heydrich told me that Hitler had been quickly convinced of the utility of such an operation, but had insisted that the German generals implicated should not seem to be conspiring too directly against him, Hitler. Obviously he did not want to tempt Providence.'

In his Memoirs Schellenberg adds this comment: 'Hitler was at this moment confronted with the gravest possible decision, whether to align himself with the Western powers or against them. And within the framework of this very grave decision he had also to choose the way of using the dossier brought by Heydrich. On the one hand, to support Tukhachevsky would have meant the end of Russia as a world power. But a miscarriage would have dragged Germany into war. On the other hand to unmask Tukhachevsky ran the risk of helping Stalin to reinforce his power, or, equally, involve him in annihilating a good part of his General Staff. In the end Hitler decided against Tukhachevsky and intervened in the internal affairs of the Soviet Union on Stalin's side. This decision to support Stalin instead of Tukhachevsky and the generals determined the whole course of German policy until 1941; it may be considered one of the most fateful decisions of our time. It ended by leading Germany to conclude a temporary alliance with the Soviet Union and encouraged Hitler to attack the West before turning against Russia.'

The day after New Year's, 1937, Heydrich summoned Schellenberg, Behrends and Naujocks. He placed before them Hitler's decision and the general lines of his plan. He explained, 'The Führer has given me a formal order to leave the General Staff of the German army completely ignorant of what we are arranging against Tukhachevsky, for fear that our officers, more or less Russophile, should warn the Soviet Marshal.' Then he turned to Schellenberg and said, 'To contrive the false documents we need we must have the dossiers in possession of the General Staff concerning Tukhachevsky's various contacts with our generals in the past. For this we require the help of Admiral Canaris. Prepare the ground, my dear Schellenberg, and I will undertake the rest.'

Heydrich then addressed Behrends and Naujocks: 'The work you are to accomplish must be done very quickly, perfectly and in the most absolute secrecy. You must dig out the best engraver in Germany to counterfeit letters and documents. They must look as if they had been stolen from the files of the S.D. and the Abwehr. We must likewise give the impression that we are conducting an investigation into the German side of the treason—without mentioning names, the Führer forbids it.'

Heydrich ended, 'If Stalin obtains this dossier through the agency of his own secret service, the N.K.V.D., and is convinced that it is genuine, he'll break Tukhachevsky like that'—and he snapped his fingers for emphasis.

After taking leave of Heydrich and Schellenberg, who had other matters to settle together, Naujocks accompanied Behrends to his office. When the latter's door was shut Behrends said with a half-smile, 'I must admit that dear Reinhard gets up to some remarkable tricks.'

'And doesn't anyone at the General Staff know?'

Behrends smiled ironically. 'My dear Naujocks, in which member of the Bendlerstrasse do you think that Hitler, Himmler or Heydrich place their confidence. Name one general.'

Naujocks dropped his voice: 'But . . . Marshal von Blomberg. . . .'

Behrends burst into laughter. 'The "rubber lion"? You're joking. The old blockhead's days are numbered. His dossier at the S.D. is crammed. One day we'll lay a snare and there won't be any more "Rubber lion".' Turning serious, Behrends went on, 'In any case this business is not altogether fictitious. There can be no doubt that certain members of our General Staff are a little too friendly with the Russians—a number of them were in the U.S.S.R. between 1923 and 1933—and moreover our generals' distrust of the National Socialists is notorious. It's just this that's the beauty of the plan. It contains an element of truth that makes it plausible. The documents we are going to fabricate will only—what shall we say?—precipitate events a little.'

A few days later Naujocks's old friend Gert Gröthe was summoned in his turn by Heydrich. The latter unfolded a plan which he was to execute with the minimum of delay. Gröthe could not believe his ears. It amounted to no more or less than burgling, by night, the premises of the Ministry for the Army! Heydrich gave Gröthe a detailed plan showing the offices of the relevant services. The orders were simple: open the safes and lay hands on the largest number of documents possible.

Gröthe at once went into action. His team was divided into three groups, each to be accompanied by an expert safe-breaker from the Department of Criminal Investigation. The operation once accomplished, a fire was to be started to obliterate any trace and spread the greatest possible confusion. Gröthe gave no explanation to his agents who wondered, when they left the room where they had been assembled, what would happen to them if they were caught. No one was, though, and the operation succeeded completely. However, once it was over, the S.D. agents, perhaps too conscientious, did so well that the fire rapidly became a major one. An important mass of papers was irremediably destroyed by the flames and by the water from the firemen's hoses summoned from all Berlin's fire-stations. In the confusion the S.D.'s special brigade got away without being seen, carrying off important spoils which filled Heydrich with joy. What did it matter to him if a floor of the Abwehr was practically demolished, if long cracks appeared in the walls of the structure: the end justified the means.

In his Memoirs Schellenberg writes, 'It has been said that the documents collected by Heydrich to implicate Tukhachevsky were to a large extent forged. In fact very few of them were forged, no more than was necessary to fill certain gaps. This is corroborated by the fact that the whole dossier, a voluminous one, was ready and presented to Hitler in the brief space of four days.'

This is likewise what he told me during our conversations at Pallanza. At the time I had no ground for contradicting him. It may be that on this point Schellenberg's memory was bad. In any event, the statement is untrue. Nearly two months elapsed between the burgling of the Abwehr and the transmission of the dossier to Hitler. This interval is very short when one thinks of the amount of work the forgery entailed.

Let us have a look at this dossier which, in its definitive state, runs to thirty-two pages. Amongst the dossiers stolen by Gert Gröthe and his team there are no proofs of a German–Soviet military plot but studies, reports, working hypotheses, copies of letters exchanged at the time of the German–Soviet military collaboration. To transform this material by a clever forgery into a conspirators' dossier would have needed thought, knowledge, technical means, able forgers and—a good deal of time.

After examining the stolen dossiers, Heydrich and Behrends decided that the 'Tukhachevsky dossier' should contain a number of 'documents', letters and memoranda purporting to be in large part reports from an S.D. agent charged with enquiring into the links existing between the German and the Red Armies; transcriptions of telephone conversations between officers of the German staff indicating presumed relations with Russian officers, copies of 'intercepted letters', various stolen notes . . . the whole to be crowned by a choice tit-bit, a letter from Tukhachevsky himself. This letter would be quite long and mention a previous secret correspondence. The various documents would name Russian officers who were partisans of Marshal Tukhachevsky and a certain number of German officers arrested during the previous four years—since Hitler's coming to power—for having manifested 'anti-National-Socialist views'. The whole of the dossier would bear the seal of the S.D., but the majority of the items would appear to originate from the Abwehr. Heydrich was even in favour of attaching a personal note—forged of course—from Admiral Canaris addressed to Hitler.

'This dossier', Heydrich stated, 'will be found in my office. Several members of the S.D. have access to it. One of them—it might be Naujocks—having doubtless an urgent need of money, will be prompted to take a photocopy of it and sell it to the Soviet secret service.'

'It's brilliant!' exclaimed Behrends with deep sincerity when reporting this conversation to Alfred Naujocks. 'Now let's get busy.'

Although the prospect of entering into direct contact with the Soviet secret service did not enchant him, Naujocks was excited by the scope of the work to be accomplished.

'Now let's study the signatures your engraver will have to reproduce,' said Behrends.

'But I haven't got an engraver,' Naujocks protested.

'Find one, old man.' And Behrends continued, 'First we must have Tukhachevsky's signature. That's easy. We've got letters of his as well as the protocol he signed in 1926. Then there's Canaris's. No problem. Those of our Reichswehr colleagues who are in prison will be equally easy to obtain. But we need the signatures of several officers still active. That will be more delicate. We haven't a lot of correspondence with the Tirpitzufer and the Bendlerstrasse.'

'We can't go and coolly ask those fellows for their autographs,' remarked Naujocks.

'Of course not, but there are ways. They all sign letters and cheques. However, it's probable that we shan't have all the signatures we need. The more complicated problem is that of official seals. Each document must give the impression of having gone through the usual channels with the stamps and initials *ad hoc*. And for that we must have the "Top secret" and "confidential" seals used by the military, as well as a half-dozen other stamps. Think about it. And telephone me as soon as you've found your forger. What else do you need to know?'

Naujocks rose, eager to begin: 'Must all these documents be typewritten?' he asked.

'Yes, or at least most of them.'

'In that case we'll need an assortment of machines. Those of the

Great General Staff only strike capitals. I must also try to find a machine with Russian characters for Tukhachevsky's letter.'

'Perfect!' said Behrends as he shook Naujocks's hand. 'But don't panic, we shan't have need of them for about a week. It's the minimum necessary to get ready the rough drafts of the documents with Schellenberg.'

Naujocks easily procured the necessary typewriters. There remained to find a forger. Neither the S.D. nor the Gestapo could supply him with the man he needed. He then referred to the head of the Party's archives office who gave him a list of five names and addresses. The first four were of no use. The fifth, Franz Putzig, who ran a small printing plant founded in 1909 in Zehlendorf, turned out to be the virtuoso hoped for.

The welcome Naujocks at first received was frosty. The old, white-haired printer had distrustful eyes and brusque manners. He was not especially communicative. Naujocks then offered him his S.D. card which he studied carefully, turned round, then gave back. 'What do you want of me?' he merely said.

In a low, even voice Naujocks answered, 'Your name has been given me as that of a man who can be trusted to do a job of vital importance to the Party.'

The printer's face displayed no reaction. Naujocks went on, 'Needless to say the work is highly confidential and personal. Even your most trusted employee must not be let in on the secret. I understand that, as an engraver, you have immense experience.'

'Thirty years,' said Putzig briefly.

Naujocks sighed happily. 'Would you be disposed to undertake this work for the Party?'

'Of course. What's it about?'

'You would reproduce seals, signatures, etc. Will you agree to?'

The answer came slowly and hesitantly. 'It's a strange request. You put me in a delicate position. This type of engraving is not my field; it is highly specialised work and I doubt if I am capable of undertaking it. Finally, even if I accept this commission for whatever reason—and in any case, sir, I must be in possession of a formal order—what guarantee have I, what certainty that I won't be prosecuted? Who will assure me that your request is not a trap? These things happen, you know.'

Naujocks at once responded, 'What kind of guarantee do you want?'

Old Putzig thought a moment before answering. 'First, I must have a guarantee from my local superior in the Party, and next one from yours, whoever he may be. I want it clearly stated in writing that I am doing this work by order and shall receive no remuneration. If you first fulfil these conditions I may perhaps be able to help you. I shall, of course, be very glad to put my modest talent at the disposal of the Party.'

Naujocks hid his joy as best he could. He had at last found his man.

During the following days Behrends, with the collaboration of Schellenberg and Jost, worked steadily to prepare the texts of the forgeries for Naujocks to bring to Putzig's workshop every evening. The engraver had real talent. Each signature, every seal, was a masterpiece of precision and exactness. As each forgery was handed to him Naujocks exclaimed, 'Marvellous! You're a genius.'

All was soon done. Heydrich himself, though thrifty of compliments, paid tribute to Putzig's splendid work when scrutinising the papers spread out on his desk, Behrends and Naujocks being with him. For the tenth time he examined Tukhachevsky's pseudo-letter which Schellenberg and Naujocks had composed, then the signature over which he paused a long time. 'Absolutely remarkable,' he murmured.

Turning to his two accomplices he said, 'And now affix the appropriate seals on all this and make the photocopies yourselves. Use a sufficiently bad light to show that Naujocks, who is presumed to have made away with these documents, had little time at his disposal.'

Heydrich re-read Tukhachevsky's pseudo-letter. Excellent work, down to the paper with a Russian water-mark, and the document was composed in the Soviet Marshal's characteristic style. In the left margin were scrawled notes in pencil more damning than the letter itself.

Heydrich said to Naujocks, 'We have discussed with Behrends the way in which the dossier should fall into the hands of the Russians. He suggests letting Benes know in Czechoslovakia through his secret service. It's not a bad idea because Benes will doubtless warn Stalin, with whom he is on friendly terms, of a plot led by Tukhachevsky. And the Czechs will probably enter into negotiations with us on behalf of the Russians. However, I prefer you to deal directly with them. We will alert them discreetly in different ways. When we have divulged your name they will arrive at the gallop. From then on you must not forget that you control the over-all situation; it will be you who choose the date and place of the meetings. . . . Of course your chief preoccupation will be to see the colour of their money before handing over the least important document. Don't forget you are supposed to demand something like three million roubles. Bargain, if necessary, but that figure is neither too high to be unreasonable nor too low to be suspicious. Those roubles will be useful to pay our agents in the U.S.S.R.'

And, shaking hands with his two colleagues, Heydrich said, 'This evening I will have Skoblin warned, and my other "contacts", to lay the trap for Stalin.'

One wonders if Heydrich was really unaware that General Skoblin, intelligence agent for the Germans, had also long been a Soviet agent. We have said that in Paris he was assistant to General Miller, head of the World Organisation of Russian soldiers in exile. He was married to an ex-prima ballerina of the Petrograd Opera, the beautiful Nadezhda Vassilievna Plevitskaya. Although she had married a White general, Plevitskaya had always worked for the Reds, at first for the O.G.P.U., then the N.K.V.D. We know this thanks to documents which the French police seized in 1937 at the Skoblin residence in Paris. We know also, from the same source, that Skoblin himself had in about 1930 become a spy in the pay of the N.K.V.D. In fact in that year, after a long period of poverty, he had bought a small property in the country, at Ozoir-la-Ferrière in the Seine-et-Marne, and in Paris the couple led a social life they had not been able to lead previously. The heroic fighter in the White Armies, the proud patriot, had morally disintegrated under the double influence of poverty and, especially, of the too beautiful Plevitskaya who in self-defence had remained in the service of Moscow and drawn along her husband.

But we must not judge Skoblin too quickly. Guilty though he was of betraying his own for the benefit of Moscow and Berlin, it seems certain that he nevertheless remained thoroughly anti-Communist. This is less paradoxical than it appears. Skoblin nourished in secret strange ambitions. He, who had been 'the youngest general in the White Armies', was the sworn enemy of Tukhachevsky, 'the youngest general in the Red Army', whose adherence to the Revolution he regarded as a felony. Skoblin dreamed of nothing less than to lead a 'crusade against Bolshevism', to avenge the defeats of Denikin and Kolchak, have Tukhachevsky shot and drive Stalin from the Kremlin. Once he had sincerely counted on France and England to destroy Bolshevism, but he had witnessed the decline of the two great Western nations and understood their powerlessness while Nazi power grew. At present he based his hopes on the support of the Germans, avowed anti-Communists since Hitler's coming to power, who would launch their victorious Panzers on the road to Moscow.

At the same time, and to attain the same result, Skoblin wanted to get rid of General Miller and take his place. Once chief of the World Organisation of Russian soldiers in exile, Skoblin would lead the White Armies to the reconquest side by side with Hitler's armies. Five years later this was to be the dream of General Vlassov.

These are the reasons why at the end of November 1936 on the terrace of the Hôtel des Voyageurs at Egreville (Seine-et-Marne) he met two agents come from Moscow, Alexander Spiegelglass and Vassily Sarovsky,[2] to whose proposals he listened attentively. The bargain was quickly concluded. The N.K.V.D. undertook to cause the disappearance of General Miller, in return for which Skoblin would help them to destroy Tukhachevsky by supplying them with proof of his collusion with the Trotskyists and certain members of the German General Staff.[3]

Skoblin immediately saw his opportunity: to have the Soviets destroy his hated enemy, Tukhachevsky and his partisans, and make the Germans understand that, in these circumstances, an attack on the U.S.S.R. would pay. He, Skoblin, would then form a government which would wipe out all traces of Communism and conclude a Russo-German alliance making Russia and Germany the two dominant powers in Europe.

Without loss of time Skoblin drew up a report, based on the grounds suggested by Spiegelglass and Sarovsky, denouncing the collusion of Tukhachevsky with members of the German General Staff and, incidentally, with the Trotskyists; then, for Heydrich's benefit, he added various items of information in his possession relating to Tukhachevsky's discussions in London and Paris in January–February 1936. That done he had, as we have seen, gone to Berlin where his report gave Heydrich his 'genius' of an idea.

At this point the question arises why Stalin charged the N.K.V.D. with a double poison-spreading task: on the one hand to compromise Tukhachevsky so deeply that he would necessarily be executed, on the other aggravate the hostility between Hitler and his generals most favourable to a German–Soviet understanding.

For some time, in this year 1936, Stalin had been wondering about the state of mind prevailing amongst the generals of the Red Army, by now one of the strongest on the continent. On November 20th

1935 he had conferred the dignity of 'Marshal of the Soviet Union' on Voroshilov, Blücher, Boudienney, Egorov and Tukhachevsky but he divined amongst them, especially Tukhachevsky, an independence of spirit and a sort of 'class consciousness' which considerably worried him. The Red Army did not seem sufficiently integrated into the Party. What would happen if these marshals and generals contested his authority? The future relations between the U.S.S.R. and Germany were high on the agenda of the Supreme Soviet. Stalin inclined to an understanding with Hitler, all the more since he felt an armed conflict rapidly approaching. He wanted to turn Germany against the West, and, according to his own expression, use her as an 'ice-breaker' to dislocate the capitalist world. He had to persuade Hitler that he had less to fear from the U.S.S.R. than from the West. Reassured in the Moscow quarter, Hitler would doubtless launch his armies against Austria and then Czechoslovakia, which would provoke the intervention of England and France. The result would be a long and costly war which would exhaust his adversaries. The hour for a Soviet intervention in Europe would then strike.

This line of thought was not shared by all the Red Army chiefs, and especially not by Marshal Tukhachevsky who wanted a 'preventive war' against Germany, whose rearmament alarmed him. Tukhachevsky did not hide his view, even in official meetings, even in the Supreme Soviet. Stalin exploded. Who was master of the Kremlin? Who controlled the policy of the U.S.S.R.? The dictator felt a double danger looming: internally, the threat of a military *coup d'état*, externally the launching of a preventive war he did not want at any price since it would automatically group all the capitalist countries round Hitler to help him crush the 'Bolshevik aggressor'. A recent tract by the exiled Trotsky haunted Stalin, especially the two sentences: 'By his baneful policy Stalin is facilitating the task of the Bonapartist elements. If a military conflict breaks out, some Tukhachevsky or other will have little trouble in overturning the regime with the help of all the anti-Soviet elements in the U.S.S.R.'

Who then was this emulator of Bonaparte, this Marshal Tukhachevsky with whom we have been concerned since the beginning of this chapter?

Born in the Smolensk region on February 16th 1893, Mikhaïl Nikolaivitch Tukhachevsky sprang from a family of lesser nobility enamoured of French culture; he began his schooling at Penza, then, after 1909, went on to Moscow. Endowed with extraordinary physical strength, an all-round health which impelled him to sport, to bodily activity, he felt the awakening of a military vocation. He entered the Cadets' School in Moscow. After graduation he opted for the Alexander Military Academy. Promoted to Second Lieutenant on the eve of the 1914 War, he chose the infantry of the Semionovsky Guard, in which Suvarov had once served.

During the Great War, Tukhachevsky gained attention by his dynamism, his exceptional qualities as a leader and his gallantry in action.

Taken prisoner by the Germans in February 1915, he was sent, after several attempts to escape, to the camp at Ingolstadt in Bavaria, and interned in Fort 9 along with several French officers. Two of them were destined, like the future Soviet Marshal, to enter into history. One of them was already celebrated at this time for his exploits as an aviator. He was called Roland Garros.[4] As for the second, he was a graduate of St. Cyr, at present a young captain of twenty-six, captured at Verdun in 1916. Still unknown at that time, he had to wait twenty-five years to become world-famous. This French captain was called Charles de Gaulle.

Tukhachevsky in the end succeeded after several failures in escaping and regaining Russia. When the young officer returned to his country in the autumn of 1917 the vast Empire of the Czars was in full revolution. At first hesitant which side to take, Tukhachevsky allowed himself to be seduced by the propaganda of the Russian Communists, who proclaimed the abrogation of feudal privileges, the abolition of landed property, the division of the soil amongst those who cultivated it, the nationalisation of capitalist enterprises, the cessation of hostilities, the institution of a just peace 'without annexations or indemnities', etc.

From then on, despite his aristocratic origins, while the former nobles and 'bourgeois' were mercilessly tracked down Tukhachevsky rallied with sincere enthusiasm to the regime Lenin had installed. He enrolled in the Communist Party in April 1918 after a face to face meeting with the new master of Russia.

Since February 23rd, Leon Trotsky, Commissar for Defence, had been organising the first units of the Red Army of Workers and Peasants. On June 19th, Tukhachevsky was posted to the eastern front, the first to be opened on the Volga. On June 26th, at the age of twenty-five, he assumed command of the First Army, the first large operational unit created within the framework of the new Red Army. After that until 1920 he occupied more and more important positions of command.[5]

With peace restored Tukhachevsky became a hero. In the highest echelons of command, in the field and at an age of particular receptivity he had acquired an exceptional experience amongst the Soviet military chieftains. He was thus quite naturally associated with the groups of officers and politicians to whom Lenin entrusted the overhaul of the Russian military apparatus after the upsets and extraordinary 'mutations' of recent years.

For ten years, first under Lenin then under Stalin, Tukhachevsky rose to more and more important commands, sat on numerous special commissions and various Party organisms, delivered speeches, published countless articles and various military works. In 1931 he passed another stage in his career by attaining a position at Government-level itself. He was appointed Assistant Minister of National Defence and chief of armaments of the Red Army. The work he did then was considerable. His worth was recognised by all, at home as well as abroad.

Stalin had supported this military reorganisation. Was not his propaganda centred on the slogan of the 'encirclement of the Soviet Union by capitalist powers'? But his distrust, always on the alert, instigated him to worry about any 'Bonapartist' symptoms in his marshals and generals. He had made up his mind to take precautions in time against a military coup. A recent example haunted him: Hitler had been able to smother in the egg the plans for an eventual putsch by his lieutenant, Ernst Röhm, in June 1934. Was he, Stalin, incapable of doing what Hitler had done? He would have his Night of the Long Knives, but after his own fashion. He knew how to wait for the favourable moment to strike.

Tukhachevsky was to commit a certain number of errors which would decide Stalin to take action.

On June 19th 1936, Tukhachevsky represented Stalin at the funeral of King George V in London. During his stay in the British capital, the marshal had arranged, through the medium of General Putna, military attaché at the Soviet embassy, several secret interviews with the British chiefs of staff. Convinced of the need of a 'preventive' war against Hitler's Germany, Tukhachevsky found his opposite numbers reticent. They did not believe in the Nazi peril. To convince the British that a coalition of England, France, Czechoslovakia and the U.S.S.R. would serve to eliminate the danger of a German military revival, the marshal gave them a comprehensive insight into Russian military thinking. He did not hesitate to let them know not only the exact quantities of effectives and armaments that the Russians could make available from the beginning of war as well as the delays entailed by a general mobilisation, but went on to explain the main elements of the strategic plan worked out by the Soviets' Supreme War Council. The English remained sceptical. Tukhachevsky then offered them the exact figures of his country's war potential as well as the monthly production of guns, tanks, 'planes and warships. All this was so astonishing that the English did not believe a word of it. They thought that the figures put forward by the Soviet marshal were deliberately exaggerated to advance his case, since they did not correspond with the estimates supplied by the agents of the Intelligence Service in Russia. So they listened with polite attention and the most extreme reserve.

Tukhachevsky left London for Paris on February 9th. He was deeply disappointed. Would he receive a warmer welcome from the French? He made the same statement to the Chief of the General Staff of the French army, General Gamelin, as he had to the British and urged him to make his dispositions before it was too late. Gamelin coldly replied that France could not depart from her defensive attitude so long as Germany did not commit an act of aggression.

'But then it will be too late,' exclaimed Tukhachevsky.

'A preventive war would not only be contrary to the principles which inspire French foreign policy,' answered Gamelin, 'it would be disapproved by majority opinion.'

The somewhat rigid attitude of Gamelin, although perfectly polite, is easily explicable. The English had informed him of the tenor of the conversations in London and their report was marked by a total scepticism. Gamelin could then only show himself circumspect; all the more in that in the matter of 'preventive war' the French were no more eager to be involved than their allies across the Channel. They did not want 'to be Russia's cat's paw'.

Tukhachevsky returned to Moscow profoundly discouraged. The West was blind! What he had revealed to them had been to no purpose. But he clung to his opinion and was to commit a fatal error at the next meeting of the Supreme Soviet.

One of the principal items on the agenda was the question of German–Soviet relations. The interventions of Molotov and Litvinov were very moderate. They signified in general that it was essential to persuade Hitler that he had less to fear from the U.S.S.R. than from the West. It was Stalin's own thesis. When Tukhachevsky rose to address the meeting his speech had the effect of a stone in a pond. Stalin could not hide his anger. Tukhachevsky attacked the Hitler regime root and branch, denounced Germany's accelerated re-armament and quoted the passage from *Mein Kampf*: 'Destiny seems to show us the way: by delivering Russia to Bolshevism it deprived the Russian people of the intelligence necessary for the creation and maintenance of a State organism . . . The immense Empire to the east is ripe for collapse. The end of Jewish domination in Russia will be the end of Russia as a State . . .' Addressing the governments of London and Paris over the head of his audience, Tukhachevsky declared that 'war has become inevitable' and that 'the wisest thing is to get ready for it at once'.

It is obvious that if Tukhachevsky spoke in this way it was his intention to add weight to his secret talks in London and Paris. It is also because he was expressing publicly the opinion of the majority in the Red Army. In making himself their spokesman he hoped to influence the members of the Politburo and induce them to change their attitude.

Did he realise what reaction he was provoking in Stalin? It is unlikely. Tukhachevsky was so convinced that he forgot all prudence. For to Stalin these resounding remarks had a precise meaning. He knew too well how a conspiracy is prepared. In his eyes all these words, all these acts, proved that Tukhachevsky and his friends were getting ready to overthrow the regime and take his place in the Kremlin. Trotsky's sentence rang in his ears like an alarm-signal: 'If a military conflict should break out, some Tukhachevsky or other. . . .' The more he reflected, the more he was convinced that it was imperative to strike quickly and ruthlessly. But he was aware that he could not attack the Marshal frontally. Nor could he dismiss him because the entire army would make common cause with him, even, without doubt, Voroshilov. Equally he could not openly resort to lying and calumny. At that period, when his dictatorship was not yet totally secure, he had need of a 'moral cover'.

With his habitual duplicity he found the solution, the vilest one: have Tukhachevsky condemned by the Army itself by supplying it with 'proofs of his treason'. Accusations had to be brought against the Marshal of so criminal a character that Voroshilov and the others would refuse to defend him, better yet accuse him. A plot with the Trotskyists and the German military chiefs would to the trick.

Stalin proceeded by stages. He began for various tactical reasons

Marshal
Tukhachevsky.

General Skoblin,
the double agent.

Otto Ohlendorf, head of counter-espionage, with the spy-chief Heinz Jost.

Marshal von Blomberg and General von Fritsch confer with Hitler. (*H. Hoffmann-Zeitgeschichlichttes Bildarchiv*)

Hitler enters Vienna, March 1938. (*Presse-Photo*)

inside the Party by turning his guns on Yagoda, head of the
N.K.V.D. whom he replaced by Iezhov.

The dictator called in the said Iezhov on September 26th 1936.
According to the deserter from the N.K.V.D. Walter Krivitsky,[6]
Stalin revealed to the new chief of the secret service his suspicions
with regard to the Red Army in general and Tukhachevsky in
particular. He delegated him to go ahead with the enquiry himself in
a tone admitting of no answer: 'I've had enough of all this prattle, of
all these conspiracies. I want to get it all clear. But mind one thing—
the only means of deserving my confidence and keeping the post to
which I have appointed you is not to come and tell me that the plot
doesn't exist. You must, you understand, you must bring me the
proofs of it.'

Iezhov understood. If he wished to save his skin he must get busy
on the production of his 'proofs'. He would bring home the bacon,
would Comrade Iezhov. Stalin had chosen well, knowing him for
what he was: a dwarf, consumptive, asthmatic, suffering from morbid complexes and pathological repressions, embittered, spiteful,
hypocritical to the point where he could have given lessons to the
great Jesuit inquisitors, but capable of obedience and animal docility
to his master.

Iezhov had in his possession a fantastical report composed by
Alexander Orlov[7] on a conversation between Karl Radek and the
German Colonel Nicolaï at Oliva (on the free territory of Danzig)
which had remained amongst the dossiers passed on by Yagoda. It
should be noticed that Karl Radek was arrested on September 22nd,
the same day as Sokolnikov, Serebryakov and Pyatakov, all old
Bolsheviks, former partisans of Trotsky, accused of wishing to ruin
industrialisation and collectivisation 'with the help of the German
and Japanese Governments'. According to Orlov's report 'a conspiracy, directed politically by Radek and Pyatakov and linked with
the military group Tukhachevsky–Putakork–Gamarnik is being
woven against Stalin. . . . Radek has met Colonel Nicolaï to put the
finishing touches to the collaboration between the German and the
Red Armies . . . Pyatakov went to Norway to see Trotsky to obtain
his approval and also went to Copenhagen to meet Trotsky's son
Sedov . . . The conspirators have proposed to the German Government the conclusion of an economic and political treaty on the
condition that the said Government does not launch an attack
against the U.S.S.R. under cover of the trouble which may arise
during the projected *coup d'état*.'

Iezhov 'arranged' the Orlov report and charged Vassile Sarovsky and Alexander Spiegelglass with transmitting it to General Skoblin in Paris in order that the latter might communicate it as coming from himself to the S.S. secret service.

We have seen how the 'bull' Heydrich had charged the concealed rapier proferred by Skoblin. Iezhov did not suspect that Heydrich, inspired by Hitler, would purloin the rapier and turn it against the Soviets, persuading them that their lie was true and that the Red Army really was getting ready to liquidate Stalin.

Iezhov, informed of the fabrication of the forgeries by the Nazis, rubbed his hands and made ready to buy them through one of his agents. However, he was a cunning person and knew Stalin's entourage well; he knew that Marshal Voroshilov might cast doubt on the value of these documents. What he needed to buttress the theory of treason and conspiracy was a high foreign personality, not implicated in the affair, but who had good relations with Moscow, to warn Stalin by a message informing him of a plot directed by Tukhachevsky. This message would reinforce the authenticity of the German documents. And—astonishing fact—just like his German counterpart Heydrich, he reckoned that the man best qualified for this role would be the Czechoslovak President, Edward Benes.

Benes had great confidence in the Intelligence service which functioned in Geneva under the direction of a Czech, Nemanov. It was therefore to Nemanov's office that Skoblin, on Iezhov's order, transmitted the following information: Radek had plotted with the Germans against the Soviet Government; Tukhachevsky had conspired with Radek; therefore Tukhachevsky was a German agent. Another agent of the N.K.V.D., established at Prague, fortified this syllogism by instilling poison into the Nemanov office: the Trotskyists and their accomplices of the opposition had concluded a treaty with the Germans; the members of the Trotskyist Czech opposition were about to organise strikes to paralyse the war industry.

But it was essential that the information passed to Prague via Geneva be blended with information coming from other sources. At Paris a colleague of Skoblin, Nicolas Alexeiev, who worked for the N.K.V.D., contrived to have himself caught while trying to steal the secret plans of a French submarine, the project for which had been abandoned. He was accused of espionage and committed to the Cherche-Midi military prison. In the course of questioning he 'confessed' that 'a deserter from the Soviet network' had confided to him 'secrets originating in the Muscovite General Staff'. Amongst authentic information of no great value, and which confirmed his statements, Alexeiev also 'let drop' the name of Tukhachevsky, whom he accused of collusion with the Nazis. The French Intelligence apprised, not the Soviets, but—they too—the Czechs, by way of their military attaché in Paris, who sent it on to Benes.

Finally, on Heydrich's initiative, von Weizsäcker, Under-Secretary of State at the Reich Ministry for Foreign Affairs, 'revealed' in confidence to the Czech Ambassador Mastny that certain Soviet military circles had contemplated with the leaders of the Third Reich the liquidation of the tension between Moscow and Berlin, and that the policy of the U.S.S.R. towards Prague might change from one day to the next if the Tukhachevsky group came to power in the Kremlin.

This time, strengthened by the sheaf of concordant information, Benes decided. At the beginning of March he called Alexandrovsky, the Ambassador of the U.S.S.R., into personal and secret conference and communicated to him the information which had reached him by different channels. The 'military plot' inspired by Tukhachevsky was thus confirmed without possible argument. Without losing an instant Alexandrovsky sent off a long and confidential report to Stalin.

The trap had worked, and Iezhov had at this point gained the start on Heydrich, who during this time was polishing off his fraudulent dossier.

Stalin set in motion the second part of his plan. On March 20th 1937 Tukhachevsky, having returned from a holiday passed at Gagri on the shore of the Black Sea, resumed his duties in Moscow. On April 5th he was informed that, contrary to what had been agreed, he would not go to London on May 12th to represent Stalin at the coronation of the new King of England. Already affected by the mention of his name at the trial of Radek in January 1937 and by the rumours circulated about him on that occasion, Tukhachevsky sensed that something was being prepared against him. He was all the more alarmed because during recent months the N.K.V.D. had caused a number of generals to be arrested or to disappear. On April 12th, Tukhachevsky was sent for by Voroshilov, who received him coldly and notified him that he had been relieved of his post of Assistant Commissar for Defence and transferred to the Volga military sector.

At the May-day parade Tukhachevsky arrived first. Alone, his thumbs clasping the back of his belt, he moved towards the rostrum reserved for generals and marshals. Jegorov took his place after him but did not salute him. Gamarnik joined them, then the other army chiefs. A sinister and icy atmosphere weighed on the generals. At the end of the military parade Marshal Tukhachevsky left Red Square without waiting for the civilians' procession.

The N.K.V.D. men lay in wait for their prey.

Let us return to Berlin, at the beginning of this May 1937, where we left the trio of confederates, Heydrich, Behrends and Naujocks. The last-named was to get in touch with the N.K.V.D. and hand over the Tukhachevsky dossier for three million roubles. After mature reflection Heydrich decided to make contact with Stalin through the following channels: a German emigré who lived in Prague and worked under the orders of S.S. Colonel Böhme put the last in touch with a friend and confidant of Dr. Benes to whom he confided that a certain Alfred Naujocks in Berlin was ready to sell the Soviets a dossier which would destroy Marshal Tukhachevsky. President Benes, already alerted to the scent, fell into the new trap and told Stalin in a personal letter.

The response from the Kremlin was immediate. Two of Iezhov's agents came to Prague, made contact with Böhme and went to Berlin where Naujocks, forewarned, awaited them. Three million gold roubles in banknotes and the Tukhachevsky dossier changed hands.

A small detail: if the Tukhachevsky dossier was bogus, so were the three million roubles. Schellenberg in fact wrote in his Memoirs, 'I had personally to destroy most of the three million roubles paid by the Russians as they consisted of large notes whose numbers had obviously been noted down by the N.K.V.D. Each time that one of our agents tried to use them inside the Soviet Union he was arrested with record speed.'

The day of King George VI's coronation in London, May 12th, Iezhov passed the Tukhachevsky dossier on to Stalin.

The possession of this decisive 'proof' of treason seemed then to guide Stalin in his choice of the manoeuvre he would employ against the generals. On May 20th the news of the discovery of a military plot began to circulate inside the N.K.V.D. Krivitsky, who left Moscow on May 22nd, reported that at that period the officers' corps was prey to a veritable panic. On the same day General Eideman, one of the alleged leading spirits of the plot, was arrested during a Party conference in Moscow. Two days later it was the turn of army corps General Feldman. When he learned of this arrest Tukhachevsky, his face dark, said to one of his officers, 'It's an odious provocation!' In reality Tukhachevsky knew that he was lost. On May 26th, the day he arrived at Kuibischev to take up his new post, he made a short speech at a conference of the military district. One of the officers present, Koritski, remarked that since their last meeting Tukhachevsky's hair had curiously turned white. The next day, May 27th, he did not turn up at the conference. He had been arrested.

On June 1st it was announced that 'Y. B. Gamarnik, former member of the Central Committee, having compromised himself with anti-Soviet elements and in fear of certain arrest, has committed suicide.'

From Lubjanka prison General Iakir, arrested on May 31st, addressed a letter to Stalin in which he protested his innocence. He wrote, 'I am a loyal soldier, devoted to the Party, the State, the people . . . All my conscious life has been passed in honest work, filled with self-denial, under the eyes of the Party and its leaders . . . I am honest in every word. I shall die pronouncing words of love for you, for the Party, the country, with unshakeable faith in the victory of Communism.'

On the original of this letter Stalin wrote, 'Scoundrel and prostitute'. Marshal Voroshilov added, 'A perfectly exact description'. Molotov also affixed his signature. Kaganovich finally wrote in his turn, 'For the traitor, the blackguard and the [an obscene word follows] . . . there is only one punishment: death.'[8]

Late in the afternoon of June 11th 1937 Radio Moscow broadcast the text of an official communiqué: 'After investigation, the matter of Tukhachevsky, Iakir, Uborevitch, Kork, Eideman, Primakov, Feldman and Putna, arrested at various times by the People's Commissariat of the Interior has been referred to the special judiciary tribunal of the Supreme Court of the U.S.S.R.

'The prisoners are charged with breach of military duty, of treason to the country, of treason to the peoples of the U.S.S.R., of treason to the Red Army of Workers and Peasants.

'The facts collected in the course of the investigation have established the participation of the accused, as well as of Gamarnik, who recently committed suicide, in an action against the State in conjunction with high military circles of a foreign state which follows policy hostile to the U.S.S.R. Being in the service of the military espionage of the State, the accused systematically delivered secret information on the condition of the Red Army and performed works of sabotage for the weakening of Soviet military power; they attempted also to contrive, in case of military aggression against the U.S.S.R., the defeat of the Red Army, with the ultimate aim of contributing to the re-establishment in the U.S.S.R. of the power of the great landed proprietors and the capitalists.

'All the defendants admitted being entirely guilty of the accusations brought against them.

'The trial of this matter will take place today, June 11th, in camera, by the special judiciary tribunal of the Supreme Court of the U.S.S.R. under the presidency of the President of the Military Tribunal of the said court, Ulrich . . .'

Next day, June 12th, another, laconic communiqué announced that Tukhachevsky, Iakir, Uborevitch, Kork, Eideman, Feldman, Primakov and Putna had been executed by firing squad.[9]

The execution of Tukhachevsky and his co-defendants marked the beginning of a massive purge in the ranks of the Red Army. We should notice, by the way, that of the nine judges constituting the special judicial tribunal of the Supreme Court of the U.S.S.R. seven would be shot in their turn in the course of the following weeks. Amongst them were Marshals Egorov and Blücher, and General Alksnis, head of the Red Army Air Force. The 'Stalin purge' eliminated the eleven deputy Defence Commissars as well as three out of the five marshals, seventy-five out of eighty members of the Supreme War Council, thirteen out of fifteen army commanders, fifty-seven out of eighty-five corps commanders, one hundred and ten out of one hundred and ninety-five division commanders, two hundred out of four hundred and six brigade commanders . . . It is estimated that thirty thousand to fifty thousand officers were physically eliminated during this period, which must represent about half of the body of specialist officers.

That was how one proceeded in the Stalin era.

Even Hitler in his boldest imaginings would not have conceived this orgy of individual tragedies and crazy scenes in the U.S.S.R. The Red Army was decapitated, and thoroughly. The effects of this unprecedented purge would be felt until 1943.

The question remains why Stalin conducted such a barbarous operation. One could at a pinch understand a modest purge—accept his shooting a few marshals and generals not submissive enough, not sufficiently intimidated and obedient. But such a carnage; a belated revenge? A despot's megalomania? Blood-lust?

No. Stalin was not afflicted with insanity. He was a cool-headed calculator who joined the power of decision with patience to an extraordinary degree in the art of setting up a smoke screen at the opportune moment, which enabled him to survive a series of difficulties before the final victory. This man of unbreakable will, this astute politician undertook nothing without a valid motive, even if no scruple, no humane consideration, no moderation deterred him from the accomplishment of what he had decided. Stalin was doubtless a monster, but he was not mad. So then what?

It is odd that Stalin never produced the famous 'dossier' fabricated by Heydrich, which had required from the forgers so much patience and skill! From June 1st to June 4th, during an extraordinary assembly of the Soviet revolutionary military Defence Committee, whose agenda comprised only one item, the denunciation by Stalin in person of 'the Fascist counter-revolutionary military organisation', the dictator used only the depositions, falsified by the N.K.V.D., of the arrested soldiers. He demanded the execution of the accused, but did not speak of the 'dossier' which 'proved the treason'. According to several testimonies, amongst them Nikolin's, the 'dossier' seemed to have served to provoke the required indignation, especially from Marshal Voroshilov. And Stalin may then have utilised it to 'incite the judges to pronounce the death sentence against Tukhachevsky' (still according to Nikolin). It is therefore probable that the judges took cognisance of the documents; but they were not mentioned officially. The accused were pronounced guilty on the ground only of Stalin's statements to the Military Soviet.

This attitude of Stalin is surprising since he was not ignorant of the origin of the famous dossier and the falsification of the items it contained. Unless . . . Stalin, at sight of Heydrich's 'documents', reckoned that smoke attested the presence of fire, that Tukhachevsky and his companions were not 'innocent' in the sense Stalin understood, in other words that they were really meditating a *coup d'état*.

It follows that, through elementary auto-suggestion, Stalin's morbid suspicion towards 'two-faced people', towards 'spies in foreigners' pay' extended from one to the next to the point of obliterating thousands, tens of thousands of human lives.

They were not all 'guilty', it will be said. It mattered little to Stalin that a great number of innocent people should also perish. What was guilt! To Stalin justice did not enter in, only the existence of Stalin's U.S.S.R. The horror that the monstrosity of these acts inspires in us should not prevent us from separating the motives founded on reason.

In 1944, after the 20th of July plot, Hitler did not proceed otherwise. He also would have his Tukhachevsky, the illustrious Marshal Erwin Rommel; and his purge of the army, though less vast than Stalin's, was not less bloody and atrocious.

The question that remains, one which doubtless will never be answered, is whether Heydrich bamboozled Stalin and brought off a master stroke in causing him to behead the Red Army, or whether Stalin used Heydrich to eliminate a rival in the person of Tukhachevsky, and dominate his army. Whichever way, it is only the result that counts. It is evident that, without spilling a drop of German blood, Heydrich had presented Hitler with a great military victory, four years before the celebrated Operation Barbarossa.

The whole story is fantastic but, in the history of the secret service, the Tukhachevsky affair is one of the peaks.

NOTES TO CHAPTER 10

1. Not to be confused with the general of the same name.
2. Spiegelglass, second assistant to the head of the executive department of the N.K.V.D.; Sarovsky, Commissar 3rd grade for State Security. The two Russian agents worked under the direct orders of Iezhov, Yagoda's successor at the head of the N.K.V.D.
3. General Miller disappeared in mysterious circumstances on September 23rd 1937, kidnapped in broad daylight in one of the quiet streets of the sixteenth Arrondissement in Paris. Skoblin, who seemed deeply involved in the kidnapping and was questioned by National Security, suddenly fled and disappeared in his turn. La Plevitskaya, abandoned by her husband, was tried and sentenced to twenty years imprisonment. She died in 1940 in Rennes prison. As for Skoblin, he was never seen again. He may have been put by Soviet agents aboard a cargo vessel plying between Barcelona and Sebastopol.
4. French aviation officer, born in 1888, Roland Garros was one of the most brilliant pioneers of French aviation. In September 1913 he made the first flight over the Mediterranean from St. Raphael to Bizerta. Having established the altitude record he was also the inventor of shooting through propeller-blades. After escaping from the Ingolstadt camp he resumed his place in Guynemer's celebrated Stork Squadron and was killed in combat in 1918.
5. Commander of the First Army on the Eastern front; then second-in-command, Northern front; commander of the Eighth Army on the Southern front; commander of the Fifth Army on the Eastern front;

commander of the Thirteenth Army on the Caucasian front; temporary commander-in-chief on the Caucasian front; finally commander-in-chief on the Western front.

6. Walter Krivitsky, real name Walter Ginzburg, left the U.S.S.R. on December 5th 1937. He wrote his memoirs in exile (re-written by American journalists more solicitous for publicity than history), *I Was Stalin's Agent*.

7. Alexander Orlov, former assistant chief of administration of the O.G.P.U., was in close relations with several agents of the N.K.V.D. and especially with Mironov, Yagoda's chief collaborator in the Zinoviev trial. He defected to the West in June 1938 and wrote *Histoire Secrète des crimes de Staline*.

8. Details revealed by A. N. Tchelepin in his speech to the XXIInd Congress of the Communist Party of the U.S.S.R.

9. It seems, according to several testimonies, that Tukhachevsky and his companions were shot, not in the execution cellars, but by day in the courtyard of the N.K.V.D. building at 11 Dzerjinsky Street, and surrounded by lorries whose engines drowned the noise of the shots. The chief of the firing squad was Serov, a young officer recently transferred from the Red Army into the N.K.V.D. who later became head of the K.G.B. (until 1948) and subsequently (in 1959) chief of the Red Army's secret service. Nikita Khrushchev, who violently denounced Stalin's crimes and the 'cult of personality' at the Party's XXIInd Congress in 1961, shouted during a meeting of the Moscow party in 1937, 'Stalin is the greatest genius, the master and chief of humanity. Under his unshakeable leadership we shall destroy our enemies to the last man and throw their ashes to the winds.'

11

The Devil's Workshops

The bloody conclusion of the Tukhachevsky affair was helpful to the S.S. secret service. Heydrich, who had already acquired the confidence and gratitude of Hitler at the time of the Night of the Long Knives, now saw his prestige grow in the Führer's eyes.

Alfred Naujocks was the first to benefit from this mood. Heydrich in fact, at the beginning of the summer of 1937, instructed him to create inside the S.D. 'a technical department capable of supplying anything from miniature cameras to a Turkish cookery book'. Heydrich explained, 'The S.D. depends much too much on the other Intelligence services for some of its most secret activities. Not only do I detest asking a favour, but I don't want the other services to stick their noses into our business, especially the Abwehr. The people of the Canaris household end up knowing of every S.D. undertaking. We have only to ask them for a document for them to know at once what purpose it's for. We've got to put an end to that. It's you, Major Naujocks, who will look after this technical department.'

'But General, you've just said Major . . . I'm only a Captain.'

Heydrich smiled, 'My dear Naujocks, Reichsführer S.S. Heinrich Himmler has this morning signed your promotion to the rank of Major S.S. and you become the chief of the S.D. technical department!'

'I'm very touched and honoured,' said Naujocks, 'I am deeply grateful for this proof of your confidence . . . What powers shall I have?'

'You shall have a free hand. As for expenses, submit the accounts directly to me. Your assistant will be S.S. Captain Bernhard Krüger.[1] I hope you will form a good team.'

Naujocks himself reported this conversation in 1945 to Colonel Scotland, who questioned him in the famous 'London Cage' in Kensington where he was imprisoned. He then insisted at length on the 'semi-scientific' nature of his activity within the S.S. secret service, keeping carefully quiet about his work as strong-arm man in Slovakia, Gleiwitz, Venlo, which, if it had then been known, would have brought him straightaway to the gallows. But we are now perfectly informed about the unusual activities of the technical department of the S.D.

Naujocks launched with enthusiasm into his new job. He recruited whomever he liked and gave orders as he pleased. He installed his department in the old S.D. training centre in the Dellbrück-strasse where, as we have seen, he made his debut as a secret agent. Now he was the boss. He had a large office comfortably furnished with sofa and easy chairs fitted out on the first floor, with a powerful wireless receiver and several works of art. Next door his bedroom was furnished with taste. He was especially proud of his private bathroom, glittering with chrome pipes, the floor and walls covered with tiles of black mosaic. On the same floor he had the bedrooms of the resident personnel installed, the radio workshops and store-rooms. The ground floor was reserved for the administration, archives and the office of his assistant, Bernhard Krüger. The basement was occupied by an ultra-modern printing works. Finally, the top floor of the huge building was devoted to photographic studios and laboratories of all kinds. Naujocks was not dissatisfied with himself.

Barely was he installed than he received his first order from Heydrich: radio transmitter-receivers which must have three precise characteristics: they must be the smallest possible, very simple and capable of being made in large quantities. Naujocks quickly recognised that these sets were intended for the secret organisation of the S.S. in the Balkans, where the postal and telephonic communications, often deplorable, were under government control.

Naujocks set to work. He visited countless factories and discussed his problem with the directors and technicians. He had to submit to the evidence: Germany certainly possessed the best wireless sets in the world and their technique was unequalled, but never before Naujocks had anyone asked the technicians for a miniaturisation of the apparatus they designed. No industrialist, no engineer, no technician told Naujocks that what he asked was unrealisable, but 'we need time, research . . .' Naujocks and the S.D. could not wait. And the problem was solved as follows: Naujocks ordered one of the best radio models already in production, but he had it made in the most reduced form, then his men hid it in objects of apparent insignificance such as refrigerators, lawn-mowers, clocks, stoves, gramophones, etc.

At the end of a year forty transmitter–receivers were functioning in the Balkans and were in permanent contact with the principal S.S. radio centre, situated near Berlin and known by the name of *Funkstellen Wannsee*. This centre could establish perfect contacts not only with all the countries of Europe but with those of Asia, Africa and the two Americas as well. Naujocks described the place not without humour:

'It was a charming house, at the western end of the lake, in the midst of thick greenery, so perfectly camouflaged that it seemed a simple holiday villa. On the magnificent lawn, carefully tended, and on the terrace, there were chairs and tables of iron painted white under gay umbrellas. A child's swing was well in evidence. At the water's edge was moored a small boat, freshly painted. Unluckily all this splendid camouflage clashed strangely with the gigantic antenna which rose from the garden well above the height of the tallest trees.'

In spite of this 'imperfection', the *Funkstellen Wannsee* can be considered the first installation of the kind in the world. The S.S. secret service did a pioneer's work. For the first time in the history of Intelligence, this wireless network replaced the old system in use until then: telegrams apparently innocent but in reality coded, special emissaries recruited from amongst the pages and sleeping car attendants of transcontinental trains, of steamers and aeroplanes.

But in the Dellbrückstrasse they were not satisfied to perfect transmissions. The demands of the different sections of the S.S. secret service were more and more numerous and diversified. The devil's workshop supplied strange varieties of explosives, new types of invisible ink, special movie-cameras, microphones hidden in the most ordinary objects, bullet-proof pullovers and even a collection of poisons. In this last category of 'supplies' Naujocks had recourse to the collaboration of an eminent Munich toxicologist, Dr. Schalberg. This former lecturer at the university was at first surprised to be invited to change his role: to manufacture poisons instead of discovering them. But he very soon grew enthusiastic about his new task, which consisted of producing fatal substances capable of remaining stable, that is, not changing colour with variations of climate, heating, mixing or with time. They had also to be completely odourless. Dr. Schalberg discovered several varieties fulfilling the specifications. What were they to be used for? I admit that I don't know. On the other hand, Dr. Schalberg's most important contribution to the S.S. secret service was the conception and fabrication of a small capsule capable of containing poison and being secreted in a false tooth. Hundreds of these capsules were made and some utilized not only by agents captured by enemy secret services but also, in 1945, as we know, by several Nazi leaders including Hitler, Goering and Himmler.

The photographic section at the Dellbrückstrasse for its part, performed several technical exploits. It did so with the help of two factories. Leica, Franke and Heidecke perfected a camera five centimetres high and two centimetres and a half thick, provided with the most perfect lenses and a special shutter of very great precision. This camera could be used without difficulty by amateurs and allowed reasonable results to be obtained in almost any conditions, so much had their margin of error been reduced.

Still in the field of photography Naujocks one day paid a visit to the Agfa establishment and discussed with their technicians the type of film to be used in these very small cameras. He then obtained information which was to become one of the most extraordinary new devices in the equipment of the perfect secret agent. Naujocks, having put the question, 'What are the smallest dimensions to which a photograph can be reduced?' was told, 'To the size of a pinhead'. When he showed his incredulity they displayed photographs so reduced. He was astounded. They explained that these micro-photographs invented by Professor Zapp could be enlarged by using the current type of apparatus and give pictures of normal dimensions. The use and advantages of these micro-photographs leapt to Naujocks's eyes: no more rolls of cumbersome film, but a thing hidden between the pages of a book, in a watch-case, sock-suspenders, tubes of shaving cream, handles of umbrellas hollowed out for that purpose, etc. One could even in most cases transmit coded messages. Intelligence agents need no longer fear a search. The Agfa scientists further explained to Naujocks, what seemed to him incredible, that the reduction to the size of a pinhead would swiftly be improved to the dimensions of a full stop on a typewriter. It would be ready a few weeks later. From then on the German agents throughout the world would send to the S.S. secret service in Berlin perfectly innocent letters, minutely examined but in vain by all the counter-espionage services on earth. Hundreds of messages would thus arrive at the S.D.—and also at the Abwehr, let into the secret—without attracting attention. The secret of the 'full stop' would only be discovered in September 1941 by the American counter-espionage.

Parallel with these various technical services Naujocks had developed another, born of the Tukhachevsky affair, of which the masterpiece was the fabrication of counterfeit pounds sterling during the war, the service of counterfeits which the head of the Dellbrückstrasse christened 'The Naujocks Travel Agency'. He recounted to the British investigators of the 'London Cage' how this 'Agency' was born:

'One day I learned of the arrest in France of one of my colleagues in the S.D. whom I knew personally, a highly intelligent man who spoke many languages, who had until then had a brilliant although short career in the S.S. secret service. I was much grieved. This agent had been long and carefully trained, provided with an expensive equipment and a large sum of money. An imperfection detected in the false papers with which he had been supplied had been his downfall. I was deeply troubled by this defect in our services.

'I went to Prinz-Albrechtstrasse where for a whole morning I put questions right and left. In the afternoon I arranged to see Heydrich and spread out before him a collection of passports intended for the S.S. secret agents.

"Have a good look at them," I told him, "they're so badly made they wouldn't deceive a child."

"Well then," said Heydrich. "We can do better."

"Where do they come from?"

"They belonged to people who are dead or in concentration camps. In any event, they don't need them any more." Heydrich studied a page of a passport. "You see that it is sometimes necessary to efface certain stamps and alter a name. This can never be a perfect job in view of the special quality of the paper used: it is chemically treated to discourage forgers."

"Nevertheless I'm convinced we can do better."

"What do you suggest?"

"That we fabricate new passports exactly similar to real ones."

Heydrich shook his head slowly. "It's not as simple as you think. We have already studied this question and I'm told it's impossible."

"I'm convinced it's not."

"Well, try. Have the dossier I collected on the problem sent you. Study it. Talk to me about it again."

Continuing his confidences Naujocks told the British inquisitors, 'I must admit that, back in Dellbrückstrasse, having studied

Heydrich's dossier, I was a little discouraged. I had doubtless been too enthusiastic in affirming that it was possible to fabricate passports so exactly similar to real ones that no one could detect the forgery. In fact I realised that a passport is the fruit of years of work and thought. Its conception is such that it should render the forger's job impossible. For instance a chemical analysis indicates that several countries use a special quality of hand-made paper. An enquiry amongst German paper makers revealed that it was practically a lost art and that orders for this kind of paper went customarily to rare specialised enterprises in Switzerland or Great Britain. However the firm of Spechthausen, near Berlin, accepted my request to study the possibility of making a small quantity of paper and to this end made numerous experiments. Chemical enterprises co-operated with them in the analysis of special substances, intended to baffle forgers, which were notably present in the paper of Swiss passports. The formulae for these substances could be discovered; but the work took weeks and I had incurred heavy expenses.'

Naujocks had another problem to solve; the counterfeiting of the stamps used by the most widely diverse frontier posts. First he had to have every page of his S.D. colleagues' passports photocopied. But he quickly realised that to do this work suitably he needed not one hundred or two hundred passports but many hundreds, preferably of the most diverse nationalities. He quickly found a solution. He obtained Heydrich's consent—given with bad grace—then went to the central passport bureau where he had a fruitful meeting with the director. A few days later all travellers arriving in Germany were asked if they had been registered 'according to the new regulations'. No, of course. They did not know about them. Their passports were then kept for twenty-four hours, 'a simple formality'; they were given a receipt and after the stated interval their passports were restored to them. During the interval the S.D. photographers hurried to take pictures of each page on film of extra-fine texture.

Naujocks was not long in plunging into the midst of the thousands of photocopies, which were carefully cut up and each stamp thus obtained classified. Thousands of names of frontier posts, well or little known, of all Europe, of the whole world, packed the filing cabinets of Naujocks, who said to his friends, 'My collection of stamps is the largest in the world.' And it was true. It was an operation without precedent successful in all respects.

Naujocks was not satisfied with passports; he likewise collected identity cards, residence permits, official formularies, letter heads, etc.: anything that could be printed and of use to a spy. 'The Naujocks Travel Agency' worked all out and employed forty-five persons in the Dellbrückstrasse when fully staffed.

When the quality of the paper and the negatives was right, the last material obstacles overcome, Naujocks decided to try an experiment by creating a difficulty. He found an S.S. sergeant employed in an administrative section of the secret service and offered him a fortnight's holiday in Switzerland as well as a large sum of money on condition that he pass himself off as a Swiss subject and use a Swiss passport. The sergeant agreed and set out.

Before he had reached the frontier Naujocks had a telephone call put through to the Swiss police to warn them that an individual with such a name would next day try to cross into Switzerland with a faked passport. The expected happened. The S.S. sergeant was arrested at the frontier. The passport was examined from every angle, was subjected to ultra-violet rays and in the end was returned with apologies. He had no doubt been the victim of an unscrupulous person or of a sinister joke. The sergeant returned to Germany at the end of the fortnight by another route and another frontier post minutely examined his passport. He passed without difficulty. When the sergeant came to narrate his misadventure to Naujocks the latter thanked him warmly: the test was conclusive.

While Naujocks was perfecting the various technical arms of the S.S. secret service, Schellenberg was attempting, at Heydrich's order, to reorganise its structure (see Diagrams, page 300). In the mind of Heydrich, eager to strengthen the bases of an S.S. empire whose limitations he knew, it was a matter of forging a unique and homogeneous group out of his two principal elements, the Sipo and the secret service, into one service of National Security (*Reichssicherheitsdienst*, R.S.H.D.).

To understand the problem laid before Schellenberg, it should be recalled that since June 17th 1936 Himmler was the head of all German police.[2] The police department, properly speaking, an organism of the State, was divided into two principal bureaux (*Hauptämter*):

1. The guardians of the peace in uniform (*Hauptamt Ordnungspolizei, Uniformierte Polizei* or *Orpo*) which embraced the communal police, the gendarmerie, and the *Schutzpolizei* (*Schupo*) and was directed by Kurt Daluege;

2. The Security Police (*Hauptamt Reichssicherheitspolizei* or *Sipo*), which included the Criminal Police (*Kriminalpolizei* or *Kripo*), commanded by Arthur Nebe, and the State Secret Police (*Gestapo*), commanded by Heinrich Müller. The Security Police or Sipo was commanded by Reinhard Heydrich.

But Heydrich also directed the S.S. secret service (S.D.) which was an organism of the Party.

The objective allotted to Schellenberg was (1) the assumption by the State of the S.S. secret service, whose employees, unlike Sipo's, were not civil servants; (2) independence of the S.S. secret service with regard to the Party, on whose goodwill it was, in Heydrich's view, too dependent.

Schellenberg did not have an easy assignment. In fact, he had to take account, in elaborating his project, of Himmler's general conceptions which tended to a fusion of the S.S. with the whole of the Reich police forces and with those, especially Heydrich's, which would lead to the fusion of the S.D. and Sipo in one unique body.

The chief danger to avoid was the dissolution of the secret service into Sipo. 'The secret service,' declared Heydrich, 'must at all costs keep its own distinct character'. The danger was obvious: in becoming an institution of the State, the S.D. effectively freed itself from the heavy tutelage of the Party, but greatly exposed itself to bureaucratic contamination by Sipo. Schellenberg, like Heydrich, was a fierce antagonist of traditional administrative norms and jurist-bureaucrats who represented them. Schellenberg's aim was unequivocal: 'The new administrative apparatus must be relieved of all restraints of out-of-date thinking, it must possess the qualities of flexibility, efficiency and mobility, required in a Reich of the dimensions of the one our Führer is in the act of creating.'

The technocrat Schellenberg's ideas were not shared by Dr. Werner Best, a Nazi and S.S. certainly, but a jurist before everything. He thus described the police, 'The action of the police is necessarily in conformity with the law, since it is the expression of the Führer's will,' but, implacable defender of the Reason of State, he thought that the affairs of state should not be entrusted to people who were ignorant of or despised the law.

Prodded by Heydrich, Schellenberg engaged in war against Best. But the latter was not easily influenced and knew how to manoeuvre. Against Heydrich's ambitious project he adroitly gained the support of Hess, for the Party was determined not to let one of its organisms, the S.D., fuse with a State institution, Sipo. Still more adroitly he ranged Himmler against the fusion. The reorganisation was consigned to oblivion.

Dr. Best succeeded all the more easily with Himmler because at this time the latter was becoming more and more uneasy about the independence of line taken by Heydrich. The clashes between the two major chieftains of the S.S. were then frequent. Lina Heydrich herself bore witness after the war that the relations between her husband and 'Dear Heinrich' were disturbed with storms. On every occasion Heydrich remained calm but Himmler often exclaimed in an unsteady voice, 'You, you . . . Your logic! Always your logic. Everything I suggest you counter with your logic. . . . I've had enough of you and your captiousness.'

Heydrich then retreated, at once gave way, allowed himself to be forgotten for a while. More often he won. Himmler confided to his masseur, Keresten, that a veritable sickness overtook him every time that Heydrich came to make his report: 'They are', he said, 'masterpieces of concision; a brief description of the person or the situation, arguments presented in increasing order of importance, conclusion drawn like a line under a sum. After which he gives his opinion on the problem and suggests the solution which ought to be adopted.'

Himmler froze before such clarity. He was powerless to resist these assaults. He accepted everything, though ready later to telephone Heydrich to tell him that before undertaking whatever it might be, he must talk to the Führer. A little later, if a different solution was adopted by Himmler, the latter, face to face with Heydrich, of course too sheltered behind so-called 'Führer's Orders'.

Himmler's was an elusive personality to grasp. Those who knew him in his lifetime had trouble, after seeing him, in describing him. There are as many portraits as witnesses. 'The application of a limited scholar but also something methodical as an automaton might be' (Karl J. Burckhardt). 'A good schoolmaster but certainly not a principal' (General W. Dornberger, 'Father of the V-I'). 'Cold, calculating, avid for power, Hitler's evil genius, the individual most devoid of scruples in the Third Reich' (General Friedrich Hossbach). 'Never was I able to catch his eye, always shifty and flickering behind his pince-nez' (Alfred Rosenberg). 'There was nothing diabolic about this man. Courteous, not without humour, he liked to throw in a witticism now and then to lighten the atmosphere' (Count Folk Bernadotte). We might add the testimony of a man who knew Himmler well: Sepp Dietrich.

On May 4th 1957, in Munich, Dietrich agreed to receive me on the eve of the trial for the affair of the Night of the Long Knives, which I have already mentioned. Dietrich was a fanatic with a complete loyalty to his Führer; in 1957 he still spoke of Hitler with a quivering admiration—even while recognising certain of his mistakes—but of Himmler he spoke to me in these terms: 'He was a profound dissembler, hypocritical, venomous, animated by a mad ambition which only vanished in the presence of Adolf Hitler. When the Führer addressed a criticism to him, Himmler remained trembling, with the air of a beaten dog, incapable of uttering the slightest word in his own defence; he was as if thunderstruck. I had several memorable slanging matches with this bogus tough. He always threatened me with his thunderbolts but he never dared to do anything to me. . . . He knew I'd smash his mug.'

A few years earlier one of Himmler's former secretaries, Frau Josefa R., had drawn me this other likeness: 'The Reichsführer S.S. was capable of enormous routine work, performed with a routine automatism that exhausted us. He often betrayed an extreme inner hyper-tension by flushes on his cheek-bones and forehead. His fanaticism, in appearance icy, was deep, tumultuous, burning with sincerity. His fidelity to the Führer seemed unshakeable. When he spoke of him he often had tears in his eyes and imperceptibly stiffened his attitude into that of physical and moral standing at attention.'

For my part I believe it is enough to read his speeches, letters, directives, his intimate journal, to hear the recordings which exist of his voice, to realise that the fanatic of the myth of blood believed with all his being in what he said, in what he did, and that he would not have flinched from anything, any crime, to attain the objects designed by his Führer.

At Pallanza I often questioned Schellenberg about Himmler. He eluded nearly all my questions. Embarrassment? Concern not to repudiate one he had admired and supported to the end? Admiration still keen which he didn't want to admit? I don't know. My notes of the period on this subject are contained on a single sheet. 'He was changeable and readily influenced,' Schellenberg told me, 'but his loyalty to the Führer was absolute. It was only at the end, round March–April 1945, that he dared ask himself questions about Hitler's mental state—under my influence and that of Professor von Crinis— but he was paralysed at the notion of acting alone, without "an order from the Führer" . . . Even after the latter's death he remained bewitched.'

One day, as I was talking to Schellenberg of the strange mixture of racial theories, pagan beliefs and naturist doctrine which constituted 'the Himmlerian ideology', he smiled and said, 'Yes, Himmler sometime lacked a sense of reality. It was in this way that he considered himself the reincarnation of the Emperor Henry I who had fought against the Hungarians and the Slavs. He recommended us to take exercises in concentration in order to be able to exert our will at a distance . . . He was very credulous and superstitious . . . He believed in horoscopes, seers, hypnotists, wizards of all sorts. It was his childish side. With me, in our work, he was never like that.'

In his Memoirs Schellenberg writes: 'This Himmler, with whom I now daily found myself face to face, was, after Hitler, the most powerful man in the Reich. Nevertheless I can only describe him as the typical German schoolmaster. He graded his pupils' studies with precision and for every answer he would have liked to give them a mark in their reports. His whole character exhibited a great deal of application and loyalty combined with bureaucratic exactitude. Nevertheless to judge Himmler only by this carefully maintained façade would have been a mistake. I recognised this later.'

And Schellenberg goes on, 'He never expressed praise or blame directly to anyone. Later I understood this peculiarity of his behaviour better. It was, at bottom a kind of cowardice—not that he would have been afraid to praise or blame (he could show himself extremely courageous on certain occasions). But to express an opinion was against his nature: he preferred to leave to others the disgrace of being in the wrong. If time revealed an unjust criticism or misplaced blame, it was thus always possible to find the subordinate to whom was attributed the errors. This system gave Himmler an attitude of extreme detachment, the air of looking down on ordinary conflicts. This made him the final arbiter.'

It is difficult if not impossible to disentangle the exact relations between Himmler and Heydrich. What is obvious is that the former had need of the latter. One may well ask to what extent the dreaded Himmler feared the redoubtable Heydrich. In the beginning Himmler might have believed he had in the person of Heydrich a companion extraordinarily gifted but encumbered with a racial flaw (the Jewish grandmother, Sarah), an ideal partner capable of opening the way for him to the highest spheres of power without any risk of his ever becoming a rival. From 1934–35 Himmler knew that he had been mistaken but it was too late, their union was indissoluble. They were bound together for the worst.

With the exception of Martin Bormann who, thanks to his confidential position with the Führer—especially from 1941 onward—had the right to consider himself invulnerable, all the Nazi chiefs feared Heydrich, even if they occupied a post superior to his in the hierarchy of the Third Reich, and did so with a mixture of fascination and impotence, like the herald of an irreversible doom.

In the years 1936–39, and it would be worse after 1939, the mere mention of Heydrich's name and, even more, his appearance in person, was enough to throw a cold douche over any Berlin gathering, especially a Nazi one. However, Reinhard Heydrich observed the greatest discretion, never thrusting himself forward in public. He was not Goebbels, Goering or Ribbentrop. He disdained personal publicity and seemed content to remain a sinister personality in impeccable black and silver uniform by the side of the Reichsführer S.S.

From the beginning of his career at the head of the S.D., Heydrich had recognised the value of the personal card-index thought up by Himmler, and from that moment began to collect information concerning 'domestics as well as ministers', convinced that only the knowledge of the weaknesses of others would enable him to establish sure connections.

His real power reposed in the big safe in his office at the S.D., of which no one but he possessed the key. There were the dossiers on the origins of various Nazi personages. He knew all about the uncertain genealogy of Adolf Hitler as he did those no less uncertain of Rosenberg, Hans Frank, General Milch and Robert Ley. He was not unaware of any of the private doings of Goebbels, Streicher, Bormann, Hess, Ribbentrop or von Papen nor of Goering's corrupt propensities. Better than any other of his partners or rivals Heydrich knew how to gain an indirect but effective influence and discreetly provoke the overthrow of power which did not become apparent until the moment of the victim's downfall.

Heydrich did not confine himself to assembling the means of blackmailing individuals. Every group or organisation which he judged to offer some danger to the Third Reich, in a near or distant future, or to himself, at once became the object of his attention. Of course after the elimination of Röhm the General Staff occupied one of the first places on his list of suspects.

NOTES TO CHAPTER 11

1. Bernard Krüger, N.S.D.A.P. card No. 528 739 and S.S. card No. 15 249 became chief of Amt VI-F, the technical service of the S.D. abroad when Naujocks fell into disgrace during the war and was sent to the Eastern front as a private in Sepp Dietrich's *Leibstandarte S.S. Adolf Hitler*. After the war, which Krüger finished with the rank of *Sturmbannführer S.S.* (Major), he worked at the *Standard-Elektrik-Lorenz AG* in West Germany.
2. Reichsführer S.S. und chef der Deutschen Polizei (R.F.S.S.).

12

The S.S. Spies Are Everywhere

<hr>

Heydrich was patient. Since he had been expelled from the Navy he had, as was known, an account to settle with the reactionaries of the Officers' Corps. He was determined to settle it sooner or later. For this 'inverted' Christian there was no worse sin than the sin of intention: he suspected all the generals of the worst intentions with regard to National Socialism. He was not entirely wrong. Their loyalty was only on the surface.

When the July 1934 sun had dried the blood of the S.A. chiefs struck down by Hitler's orders, the 'war lords' rejoiced. The Führer had chosen the Army as against the Party. Germany's true strength no longer belonged to the 'street bravos', to three million of the S.A. humbled and consigned to the role of 'minor preachers', but to the military and to them alone. The generals had not understood that their real enemy was perhaps not Ernst Röhm—an authentic front line officer with his scars and mannerisms—but the man who had supplied the execution squads: Heinrich Himmler, seconded by Heydrich.

On March 16th 1935, like a clap of thunder came an announcement of crucial importance not only for Germany but for Europe and the world: Adolf Hitler had just signed the *Law for the Reconstruction of the Wehrmacht*. The Reichswehr is dead, long live the Wehrmacht! It was a decisive turning point. Compulsory military service was re-instituted. Henceforth the Army was no longer a state within a state. In restoring their effectives the Nazis fully intended to control the military. The duel between the S.S. and the Army was to begin.

Adolf Hitler gave his generals a poisoned gift. But the proclamation that accompanied it sounded a solemn note: 'From today the guarantee of the honour and security of the Reich is again entrusted to the strength of the German nation.' The new army, contrary to what Germany had known until then, was a national army.

On May 21st 1935, a new law definitively fixed the place of the Wehrmacht in the being of the Third Reich. It began with the statement that military service was not an exaction but an honour. It affirmed that in time of war every man and every woman must share in the defence of the Fatherland. There was no longer any question of a professional but of a national army.

As to the supreme head of the Wehrmacht, he was henceforth to be the Führer and Reich Chancellor. The command was to be exercised by the War Minister, von Blomberg, assisted by General von Fritsch for the Army, Admiral Raeder for the Navy and General Goering for the Air Force.

During a reunion at the famous Bürgerbräu beerhouse in Munich amongst his first companions in arms of the 1923 putsch, Hitler alluded to the relations between the Party and the Army.[1] 'Of all that I have accomplished, that of which I am proudest, and for which posterity will be most grateful to me is not only not to have destroyed the Reichswehr of a hundred thousand men, as certain ill-advised minds pressed me to do, but to have made it in less than four years the framework of a new popular German army, with which all can co-operate who might otherwise have become our enemies.'

For him the tasks of each were plain: 'The Party is the guarantor of the nation, our army its protection. Either the German is the first of soldiers or else he is not a soldier. We want to be the first of soldiers.'

All was then for the best in the new National Socialist Germany.

This was not the opinion of Himmler nor of Heydrich.

In the Third Reich, where everything was political, the non-political character of the army had become an absolute rule. The law was specific. Soldiers were not permitted to pursue any political activity. Membership of the National Socialist Party or of one of the formations or groups affiliated to it was suspended for the period of active military service, as was the right of soldiers to vote or take part in a plebiscite. The Army seemed so independent of the Party that certain opponents of the regime agreed to enter the Officers' Corps which appeared to them a kind of interior emigration. There they benefited from freedom of thought and even, in some cases, of word. The military had their own courts. The laws of state regarding the supervision of administration and the promotion of civil servants did not apply to the armed forces.

Theoretically Adolf Hitler placed a blind confidence in the political loyalty of the army. Was he sincere, or did he shut his eyes because he had need of the army for his policy of expansion, called 'lebensraum'? Himmler and Heydrich were resolved to open the Führer's eyes when the time was ripe. They waited two years.

We are at the end of 1937. If conscription had brought into the Wehrmacht a large number of soldiers recruited from the S.A. and even the S.S., if the young officers were for the most part converted to the new regime, there nonetheless existed in the higher levels a spirit of revolt. Certainly it was equivocal for at bottom the generals were in agreement with the Führer's aims and also dreamt of world hegemony. But they were in complete disagreement on the means.

The revolt issued in an odd approach of several generals to Marshal von Blomberg: 'We are uneasy. The Führer's policy entails grave risks which we cannot ignore. You alone can intercede with him.'

The marshal frowned and put his subordinates in their place. 'The Wehrmacht has no business in the political field. Its mission consists of executing orders transmitted to it, not arguing about them. Go back to your work and stay clear of politics.'

Himmler was of course aware of this démarche. He was a little reassured by the marshal's attitude, but Heydrich observed to him that the 'old rubber lion' was weak and would not always maintain the Führer's point of view. Himmler took this line all the more easily because he knew exactly where he was aiming.

At a recent meeting of the leaders of the Black Order, in the medieval and unusual setting of the castle of Wewelsburg, he permitted himself a few confidential remarks. 'Every revolution endeavours to control the army and breathe its spirit into it. Only when this end has been attained can a revolution claim to be triumphant.'

Immobile round the long table the S.S. generals, whose oak-leaves glinted on the collars of their black uniforms, remained silent. They knew very well that the new German army was not profoundly National Socialist despite the oath of fidelity to the Führer. So there were only two solutions and Himmler unfolded them in the tone at once cold and debonair which he affected. 'The first solution consists of entirely liquidating the corps of officers. That would be the better method but we haven't got the time to replace them, before the grave happenings now being prepared.' He let a long silence elapse and added in a very low voice, 'But these gentlemen will lose nothing by waiting. And we shall not be long in taking care of some of these titled reactionaries.'

Inscrutable, Reinhard Heydrich smiled faintly. He had in his dossiers enough with which to blow up the whole General Staff. And what didn't exist he well knew he would have no trouble in inventing. Had he not proved it in the Night of the Long Knives or in the Tukhachevsky affair?

After having reassured himself by a quick glance round the assembly of all the high dignitaries of the S.S., Himmler went on, 'The second solution will in the long run be the more rewarding. We are going to develop in the midst of our Order an armed force which will incarnate the ideas which it is the task of National Socialism to inculcate in the Wehrmacht.'

So the method was defined. To men like Heydrich and like 'Müller-Gestapo' fell the work of removing the reactionary and conservative heads of the army; to men like Generals Haussner, Dietrich or Steiner that of creating a new revolutionary army which would one day become the Waffen S.S., the S.S. army.

Each henceforth knew his mission. It only remained to get down to work.

Heydrich was ready. He had spread his nets. Those he had decided to destroy would blindly flounder into them.

The infection of Hitler was ingeniously performed by Heydrich throughout the months from October to December 1937. There was not a week in which he did not supply Himmler with a dossier crammed with information from the Gestapo or the S.D. about 'the revolt of the generals'. The Reichsführer S.S. passed them on regularly to his Führer, who grew more and more agitated. He even said to Goebbels in speaking of the generals, 'They have for generations received an utterly wrong education and today we see the sad results.'

To Hans Frank he was even harsher: 'This presumptuous Junker caste is nothing but a pack of empty heads, triflers and useless trouble-makers . . . I was mistaken about them . . . They haven't a single idea and think they know everything . . . The General Staff is the last freemasonry I haven't dissolved.'

'Has the time come?' Heydrich asked himself as these remarks were repeated to him.

The marriage of the War Minister, Marshal von Blomberg, a widower, father of three children, with the young blonde Eva Gruhn on January 12th 1938 in Berlin was, despite the presence of Adolf

Hitler and Hermann Goering as witnesses, surrounded by a singular discretion: a few lines in the papers and not even a photograph of the ceremony. A marked contrast with the staging which characterised the least event in the Third Reich.

A few days later strange rumours began to circulate in Berlin. The War Minister had made a 'terrible misalliance'. In the high military spheres, great sticklers for conventions and precedence, an officer had no right to marry 'a nobody'. And, according to the rumours, Eva-Gruhn-become-von-Blomberg was worse than 'a nobody'. Before marrying the 'rubber lion' the pretty Eva had intensely indulged, for money, in what is nowadays called 'group sex'. Scandalous photographs existed in the files of the police Vice Squad. It was alleged that Blomberg's new mother-in-law had herself incited her daughter to debauchery. Was not the mother manageress of a 'massage parlour' whose activity had cost her two sentences for prostitution and the organisation of prostitution?

When the chief of the criminal police, Arthur Nebe, notified of these rumours by Count von Helldorf, Prefect of the Berlin Police, had Eva Gruhn's dossier brought him, he could not believe his eyes. But this subtle fox quickly perceived that it was a diabolical scheme. The dossier was perfectly faked, so perfectly that Nebe had not a second's hesitation as to its author: it could only be Heydrich himself. Count von Helldorf was of the same opinion: 'It is designed to destroy Marshal von Blomberg. That is evident. It is probably a plot set up, well worked out and perfectly executed by the Gestapo. When the most important person in the German army marries an unknown, you can be sure that Heydrich knows who she is.'

'So what?' asked Nebe.

'I'd like to know who thrust a prostitute into the arms of an amorous marshal.'

Thus the Blomberg affair began. Helldorf told Goering who told Hitler. But that wasn't all.

Tuesday, January 25th, a visitor was announced to the Führer. It was Himmler. The Gestapo had a new dossier to pass to the Chancellor. The interview lasted over an hour. In the ante-room Colonel Hossbach wondered what the S.S. could now be up to. They had 'trapped' Marshal von Blomberg. On whom were they now going to direct their fire? He would not be long in finding out. The victim was General von Fritsch, Army Commander-in-Chief. The motive was as artful as it was ignoble. Since the Röhm affair Hitler had an explosive horror of homosexuals. What he had just learned about von Fritsch infuriated him. He called Hossbach and to him expressed his anger: 'After the scandalous conduct of the first marshal of the Third Reich I should have expected anything . . . But this? No! This time it's too much.'

Colonel Hossbach then learned what the dossier brought by Himmler contained. General von Fritsch was a moral pervert and in the grip of a blackmailer.

'May I see the dossier?'

Hitler handed it to his aide. It was an ordinary police dossier and not very convincing. It was made up of insinuations rather than proofs. Hossbach did not seem convinced and tried to defend von Fritsch. But Himmler's arguments had evidently already decided the Führer. He brutally broke off the interview with, 'I ask you not to warn von Fritsch.'

'My conscience forbids that. He must be told of what he is accused.'

Hitler looked exasperated but did not answer. Colonel Hossbach at the end of the day went to General von Fritsch and told him everything. The Commander-in-Chief was indignant: 'It's unspeakable, nothing but a tissue of lies. . . . I well recognize Himmler and Heydrich's dirty paws. . . .'

It was also the opinion of Colonel Hossbach, who detested the S.S. and thought the dossier a gross fabrication, straight out of the offices of the Gestapo.

What was to be done? Counter-attack. In what quarter? Hitler himself. Hossbach promised von Fritsch to see Hitler next morning and try to reverse the situation.

To his great surprise Hossbach found Hitler more understanding than he had expected. The Chancellor's anger seemed to have somewhat diminished and he listened attentively to his aide-de-camp's explanations. He even used an odd sentence: 'If von Fritsch is innocent why shouldn't he succeed von Blomberg as War Minister?'

But two visitors were waiting outside the Führer's door who were once again to alter his judgement. Booted and belted in their black uniforms, Himmler and Heydrich were walking up and down the marble corridors of the Chancellery waiting to return to the attack. This time it would be the kill.

In the afternoon Hossbach was again summoned into the presence of the master of the Third Reich. He was in a very had humour. 'You're wrong. Von Fritsch is not only a pervert but a liar. Besides, all homosexuals are liars.'

Hitler's rage was fearful. Hossbach felt that he could no longer save the commander of the land forces. He made a final suggestion: 'Couldn't we convoke a court of honour?'

'It seems to me useless. In any event I am relieving von Fritsch of his duties. But he can't say that I am condemning him without a hearing. Summon him to the Chancellery.'

'When?'

'This evening.'

The interview was dramatic. Hitler was not alone. He had asked Hermann Goering to be with him. He wanted to have a genuine soldier near him to settle his account with the head of his land forces. Goering was annoyed. The role did not please him, even if the new Luftwaffe was jealous of the traditional army and much more impregnated with National Socialist doctrines.

Goering remained silent, his look dim, his pout stern. As for Hitler, he wore the expression of his worst moments. At von Fritsch's entry he said brusquely, 'You are accused of a breach of Article 175 of the penal code.'

'It's untrue. You have no proof.'

Hitler did not answer. He knew that the 'proof' was in the room next to his office. This witness for the prosecution, brought by the Gestapo, was a confirmed criminal. For Hitler the word of a blackguard was equal to a general's. The man came in. His name was Hans Schmidt, a notorious pervert.

He repeated his story in a monotonous voice: 'One evening in November 1934 this man [indicating the general] followed a young homosexual prostitute near the Lichterfeld Station. The nature of their relationship in that waste ground was beyond doubt. I decided to blackmail this person [another gesture towards the general]. He promised me money. Next day he in fact gave me fifteen hundred marks. For several weeks I succeeded in getting him to give me further sums. I remember his name, von Fritsch, and I recognise him perfectly.'

The general was white with anger. 'I swear on my honour that I have never seen this man.'

The Führer cut him short. 'I have no belief in what you call your honour. Get out of my sight.'

'I'm innocent and ask to appear before a military court.'

'I place you on indefinite leave and you shall be answerable only to civilian justice.'

The interview was over.

General Beck tried to intervene with Hitler, throwing all his prestige into the scales, but in vain. It was explained that there was a confusion of names, that there existed a Captain von Frisch without the 't' who was a homosexual. Hitler declined to listen; he had decided to be rid of Marshal von Blomberg and General von Fritsch. The former defended his wife's honour less heatedly—he did not even raise the subject in his last meeting with Hitler—than did the latter his own honour. The generals all reacted in the same way. That von Blomberg must go caused no regret, but von Fritsch's honour was another matter. The war lords counted. They wanted a court of honour to be set up. General von Brauchitsch particularly urged it. His was a voice that carried weight. He did not keep silent in private about the 'S.S. thieves' kitchen'. Himmler and Heydrich felt that they had gone too far, that a trial would establish von Fritsch's innocence with certainty. But were they to back-pedal? It was Hitler who extracted them from the hornets' nest they had stirred up and in which they let themselves be caught. The Führer was aware of the generals' discontent and wanted at all costs to avoid an Army–S.S. confrontation, as he had four years earlier an Army–S.A. confrontation. He accepted the generals' proposal to set up a court of honour presided over by Dr. Sellmer, assisted by Goering, General von Brauchitsch and Admiral Raeder. But, not without forethought, he set the trial for . . . March 10th 1938.

On February 4th 1938, Adolf Hitler promulgated a major decree which marked the triumph of the National Socialist ideology over the conservative spirit: 'As from today I shall personally exercise the command of all the armed forces. The former General Staff of the Wehrmacht at War Ministry becomes the High Command of the armed forces (*Oberkommando der Wehrmacht*: O.K.W.) and comes directly under my orders as my military staff.'

New chiefs had now to be designated. For Commander-in-Chief of the land forces (O.K.H.) Walter von Brauchitsch was chosen. He was still a Prussian nobleman but he had the reputation of docility towards the political power. He would be, with Admiral Raeder for the Navy (O.K.M.) and General Goering promoted Marshal of the Luftwaffe (O.K.L.) under the orders of the Chief of the General Staff of the O.K.W., Wilhelm Keitel.

Hitler knew he could count on Keitel. His devotion was unqualified. He would give the regime the armed strength it needed to conduct his policy.

The *gleichschaltung*, the subordination, of the Army had been achieved. There was no question of 'liquidating', as Himmler and Heydrich had dreamed of doing, the whole of the officers' corps. But the purge made itself felt: sixteen generals were retired and forty-four transferred.

The military operations could begin. Even if the first was a mere 'promenade' into Austria.

As announced, the von Fritsch trial actually began on March 10th 1938. The first session was taken up with the witness for the prosecution, Schmidt, who maintained his testimony and whom the lawyers for the defence did not succeed in leading to contradict himself. Goering, at the end of a few hours, suspended the hearing. When it was resumed he announced that the court would have to adjourn its deliberations for 'important reasons which concerned the interests of the Reich'.

Hitler had just given the order to invade Austria. It was the Anschluss.

The von Fritsch trial was blurred over.[2] On March 11th the German armoured divisions dashed for Vienna and at their head, by the Führer's wish, marched the black giants of the *Leibstandarte S.S. Adolf Hitler*, commanded by Sepp Dietrich. The S.S. opened the way for the Wehrmacht. It was more than a symbol, it was the sign of victory.

The annexation of Austria was a personal triumph for Heydrich. Largely thanks to him and the S.S. secret service Adolf Hitler's country was delivered over to the Third Reich without a single shot being fired.

For four years Heydrich had used with success the technique of the Trojan horse to destroy the equilibrium of Austria and infect it from within, Goebbels's intense propaganda rounding off the work. It was on the morrow of the failure of the Nazi putsch in Vienna in July 1934—during which the Austrian Chancellor Engelbert Dollfuss was assassinated—that Heydrich, having learned his lesson, began his operation of infiltrating and undermining 'by order of the Führer'.

With the help of a Linz lawyer, Dr. Ernst Kaltenbrunner, and of an assassin from Trieste, Odilo Globocnik[3], he patiently organised a powerful fifth column which would penetrate into every sphere of Austrian life.

A reorganisation within the Nazi Party facilitated Heydrich's work. Since 1933 there existed three services detailed to look after Germans resident abroad: the Foreign Organisation (*Auslandsorganisation, A.O.*) directed by Gauleiter Wilhelm Böhle; the Foreign Political Office (*Aussenpolitischeamt*) of Alfred Rosenberg, whose field was German students abroad; and lastly the Committee for Germanism Abroad (*Verein für das Deutschtum im Ausland, V.D.A.*) which maintained relations with Germans everywhere in the world.

The rivalry between these groups became so acute that in 1936 Hitler entrusted Hess with looking after all the interests of Germans resident abroad himself. For this purpose Hess created an Office for Germans by Origin Resident Abroad (*Volksdeutsche Mittelstelle, Vomi*) which was at first placed in the charge of Otto von Kursell. The latter rapidly revealed his incompetence. Hess then turned to Himmler who grasped the chance on the wing, seeing the opportunity to make a place for himself in the Reich's foreign affairs. The direction of *Vomi* was given by Himmler to one of his most brilliant S.S. leaders, a former aviation officer, Werner Lorenz.

The new head of *Vomi* took up his post in January 1937. Heydrich at once took advantage of the situation to install, under cover of Lorenz's emissaries, a discreet network: centres of S.D. intelligence, directed from Berlin by Heinz Jost, which covered the whole world. The right hand of *Vomi*'s chief was no other than Dr. Hermann Behrends, friend of Heydrich's youth, whom we have met in previous chapters. By this expedient the S.S. secret service organisation participated actively in the foreign policy of the Third Reich, notably in the centre of Europe, in Austria, Czechoslovakia, Hungary, etc. The men of the Black Order more and more occupied key positions.

In the S.S. secret service it was Schellenberg who was given particular charge of Austrian problems. He writes in his Memoirs: 'The information coming from Austria itself was so abundant that the principal difficulty arose from its very quantity. The thousands of Nazis who had recently fled from Austria supplied us with all the contacts we could desire.' Officers of the S.D. paid numerous clandestine visits to Vienna and other Austrian cities to prepare the ground. S.S. espionage was at its height. Although Schellenberg has always denied it, I have good reason to believe that he himself went at least once to the Austrian capital, at the end of November or beginning of December 1937.

At the beginning of 1938 Schellenberg was instructed to collect

Above Henlein's guerrillas in manoeuvres on Sudeten border. (*C.T.K.*)
Below Sudeten Germans rapturously acclaim their Führer,
October 1938. (*Presse Diffusion—Lausanne*)

Mgr. Joseph Tiso in 1938. (*C.T.K.*)

Karl Hermann Frank: Heydrich's man in Czechoslovakia, he was used to oust Henlein, the Sudeten leader.

Himmler, Hitler and Sepp Dietrich consider Czechoslovakia (January 1939). (*Bundesarchiv Koblenz*)

and have printed all reports relating to the attitude of Italy and the Western powers towards the plan for the annexation of Austria and its eventual incorporation into the Third Reich. The dossier thus compiled was to be submitted to Hitler.

The process of infiltrating Austria was further intensified by the creation of the Union of the East Marches (*Ostmärkischeverein*) controlled by Glaise-Horstenauy, who had become Minister of the Interior.

The story of the Anschluss is too well known to be repeated here. We shall limit ourselves to recalling that Chancellor Schuschnigg was compelled to obey the summons which Hitler sent him for a meeting at Berchtesgaden on February 12th 1938. At the end of the meeting he had, under threat of an immediate military invasion, to accept three provisions which meant the end for him: (1) Dr. Seyss-Inquart, a member of the Austrian Nazi Party since 1931, was named Minister of the Interior and of Security; (2) a general political amnesty to free the Nazis condemned for crimes; (3) the Austrian Nazi party to enter the Patriotic Front. Less than a month later, on March 11th, Schuschnigg had to resign. The same evening Hitler issued an ultimatum to the President of the Republic, Miklas. At dawn on Saturday March 12th the German troops crossed the Austro-German frontier.

The S.S. secret service had of course been the first to go into action. Walter Schellenberg relates: 'On the night of March 11th/12th I received the order to proceed to Vienna with Himmler by 'plane. We were accompanied by a company of the *Leibstandarte S.S. Adolf Hitler* and by some members of the 'Austrian Legion' which had been formed in Germany. We left Berlin–Tempelhof in two large transports. It was a very disagreeable flight. The two machines were overloaded and the atmospheric conditions bad. During nearly the whole of the flight we lost sight of the ground and could not maintain radio contact with Vienna.

'During the flight Himmler discussed various administrative problems with me which were raised by the new statute which would be imposed on Austria in becoming the Eastern March (*Ostmark*). We had withdrawn to the rear of the 'plane to get away from the noise of the motors. Himmler was leaning against a door when I saw that the safety catch had not been closed. Any moment the door threatened to open under the weight of his body. Seizing him by the jacket I drew him sharply forward. He glared at me but, after I had explained, thanked me warmly, saying he would be glad,

if the occasion arose, to do as much for me. We landed in Vienna at
4 a.m. The signing over of the administration to German authority
occurred at that same moment, by which Seyss-Inquart's Government was firmly established.'

This Seyss-Inquart Government comprised conspicuously Dr.
Ernst Kaltenbrunner, the leader of the Austrian S.S., as Minister
of Security, and Dr. Hüber, notary and Goering's brother-in-law,
as Minister of Justice. The Reichstatthalter Seyss-Inquart had,
moreover, two important members of the Party at his side: the
chargé d'affaires Wilhelm Keppler and the Reich Commissioner
Bürckel 'a hard nut'.

Contrary to what has been stated by a large number of historians,
the S.S. secret service did not lay hold of all the archives of the
Austrian secret service. At Nuremberg, Kaltenbrunner and Seyss-
Inquart passed this over in silence. As for Schellenberg he got out
of it, with his usual cunning, by an aboutface. 'I received', he said,
'an order from Heydrich to place all the files, all the documents of
the chief of the Austrian secret service, Colonel Ronge, in safety.'
In his Memoirs he was a little more precise: 'The papers I found
had little relation to current events; they were in particular information useful for the deciphering of codes. Colonel Ronge himself
declared his readiness to work in the future for the S.S. secret service.'

The man who was at this time Colonel Ronge's assistant, Lieutenant Colonel Erwin von Lahousen Vivremont, and who was a
few months later to become a principal assistant to Admiral Canaris,
chief of the Abwehr, told me after the war what had occurred.

When Schellenberg met Ronge, he was surprised to learn that
Admiral Canaris, accompanied by the Abwehr section chiefs had
already paid him a visit two hours earlier. He had taken away some
dossiers which seemed to interest him keenly. Lahousen did not
hide his smile of satisfaction at sight of Schellenberg's anger. Yes,
the Abwehr had beaten the S.D. to the post. 'The four dossiers
which so greatly interested Heydrich and Schellenberg,' Lahousen
told me, 'and which are at present in the "little admiral's" hands
are no other than the dossiers "Hitler," "Goering," "Heydrich"
and . . . "Canaris", drawn up by our Intelligence Service during
the preceding years. The "Hitler" dossier contained in particular a
certain number of documents on the Austrian origins and youth of
the Führer.'

This disappointment of the S.S. did not calm its repressive fury
but excited it. From its temporary headquarters in the Hotel Metro-

pole, Heydrich sent his Gestapo bloodhounds in search of all enemies, real or assumed, of National Socialism while he ordered the docile Austrian police, taken in hand by Kaltenbrunner, to make a gigantic round-up in order 'to avoid any untimely demonstration which might risk disturbing the popular enthusiasm'.

In two days in the capital alone seventy-six thousand people, approximately, were arrested. Most of them were sent to concentration camps, especially the Mauthhausen camp, erected on Austrian soil in the spring of 1938, the sinister reputation of which would extend across the whole world. At the same time an obscure S.S. officer, Adolf Eichmann, laid the foundations of what would become, after August 20th 1938, the Central Office for Jewish Emigration and would have as its primary object the preparation for the expulsion from Reich territory of 250 000 Austrian Jews. To complete the bringing of the Austrians into step an order issued on March 18th 1938 by the Reich Minister of the Interior, Frick, authorised Reichsführer S.S. Heinrich Himmler to 'take all security measures which he deems useful' in Austria. On this occasion Heydrich published an article on the 'new province' in the S.S. weekly, *The Black Corps*. 'The Führer's will', he wrote, 'can henceforth be performed in Austria after the happy conclusion of the fierce struggle conducted against the political, intellectual and criminal elements opposed to the unification of the German people. The former Austrian police bears the blame for the death of the excellent Germans. Its honour was nevertheless saved by its National Socialist members who did not hesitate to sacrifice their lives or liberty for the ideal of a greater Germany.' The article ended by announcing that all this police force would henceforth be 'happily subordinated to the Federal Chancellery', that is, in reality, to Heydrich himself.

The S.S. secret service had played a role, an important role, in the annexation of Austria. It would carry even greater weight in the Czechoslovak crisis.

As we have said, the S.S. had long since secured for itself, through the medium of *Vomi*, directed by Werner Lorenz, a position of strength in central Europe, in Czechoslovakia especially, and above all in the Sudeten region where nearly three million Germans gave Germany an ethnic predominance. The diplomats of Foreign Minister Joachim von Ribbentrop[4] learned this quickly, to their cost, and found themselves everywhere supplanted by the men of the Black Order.

In 1936 Heydrich had created a special Intelligence service for Czechoslovakia which was run by its own office in Berlin. This service had swiftly taken on considerable amplitude. Its chief was to exercise, by his reports and memoranda, a strong influence on Hitler's policy with regard to the Sudeten question. The S.S. espionage centre against Czechoslovakia was established at Dresden —where there already existed an Abwehr centre for the same purpose—and multiplied its activities in the course of 1937. As in Austria, the Nazi infiltration of Czechoslovakia became intensified at the beginning of 1938. The agents of the S.D. proliferated in gymnastic, nautical and equestrian clubs, veterans' organisations, universities and academic circles, cultural groups both regional and local, businesses, industries, banks, etc. Nazism spread like a drop of oil. The information flowing in from its thousands of agents became so abundant and important that the S.S. secret service had to instal at two points on the frontier special telephone lines to forward it to Berlin.

We should note that the Sudeten Germans were far from constituting a united bloc and that most of them were even opposed to the Nazis. How did it come about that within a few months they almost unanimously and totally espoused the Hitlerian theses? I admit that I found this question unanswerable for many years. What seemed especially strange to me was the rallying to the Nazis of the former gymnastics teacher Konrad Henlein. Henlein, in 1933 the founder of the 'Fatherland Front' of Sudeten Germans, had been a fierce defender of individual liberty, altogether anti-Nazi and partisan of Sudeten autonomy within the frame of the Czechoslovak state. He was opposed to the union of the Sudeten to Germany and did not conceal the fact. The post-war trials enabled me to understand the general outlines of the drama that has been enacted but large tracts remained in total obscurity. I knew that the S.S. had played a decisive role but I didn't know what it was. Like many historians I was put on the track by Wilhelm Höttl's, alias Walter Hagen's book. Certain former S.S. who had belonged to the S.D. as well as former officers of the Abwehr brought me various elucidations. Walter Schellenberg was virtually dumb on this matter. One survivor of the S.S. secret service, Brigadier-General Heinz Jost, who had directed the espionage service abroad (S.D.-Ausland) until 1941, seemed the only witness who could enlighten me. Alas, captured by the Allies in 1945, he was sentenced to life imprisonment on April 9th 1948.

In the years 1955–60, in 1958 I think, I learned from an agency despatch that Heinz Jost, whose sentence had been reduced to ten years, was free. Through different correspondents I tried to establish contact. In vain. On each of my visits to Germany I asked, 'Where is Jost?' He was as elusive as the Snark: I always heard mention of him, I never saw him. I had lost hope of one day meeting face to face this man whose past I had summarised on a filing card.

Heinz Jost, born in 1905, had pursued his studies in law and economics at the universities of Giessen and Munich. He practised law in the court of Darmstadt before enrolling in the Nazi party in February 1928 and becoming a member of the S.A., then of the S.S. In 1932 he entered the S.D. under Heydrich's orders and quickly became the head of espionage abroad. He remained as chief of this service until June 22nd 1941, when he incurred Heydrich's displeasure, in part because of the intrigues of Schellenberg, who coveted his post and obtained it. His subordinates said of Jost that he left behind the memory of a chief 'of strong personality but possessing more goodwill than technical abilities.' Some even accused him of being 'incompetent, inefficient and corrupt'. In 1941 he was sent to the Eastern Front in charge of an extermination commando (*Einsatzgruppe A*) in the area of Riga and Krasnogwardeisk. He then had the rank of Brigadier-General in the S.S. and Divisional General in the police. From various German archives, it emerged that *Einsatzgruppe A* exterminated hundreds of thousands of people and that Jost was equally responsible for the deportation to forced labour (Sauckel's service) of thousands of civilians. At his trial, which took place at Nuremburg from July 25th 1947 to April 9th 1948, he showed that he had paid visits to Heydrich and Himmler to ask to be relieved and to Rosenberg to oppose the programme of extermination.[5] Later he had been recalled by his superiors and subjected to a disciplinary penalty: the S.S. Brigadier-General was in fact sent to the front as a Sergeant in a Waffen-S.S. regiment.

Such was the man I wanted to meet, not to question him about his activity after June 22nd 1941, but about that which had preceded this date.

During a short journey to Düsseldorf in 1961 the miracle happened. I was dining with a German friend, Hilde R., whom I had known since 1953. She had worked in the S.S. secret service for eight years and had opened, since we had known each other, many doors reported to be hermetically sealed against those who had not belonged to the S.S. She suddenly asked me, 'Do you still want to meet Heinz Jost?'

'Jost? It's impossible. I don't believe in it any more. Certainly. Can you take me to him?'

'Yes, tomorrow if you're free.'

There are men who imprint their image on things. An organisation—particularly in a field as special as Intelligence—is worth what he or those are worth who constructed, animated and directed it. I knew this since I had chanced to meet Walter Schellenberg and several others. What would I get from a meeting with this Heinz Jost, an undeniable war criminal, but possessor of a certain number of secrets dating from the period when he directed the S.S. espionage? Would he agree to talk?

Next day after lunch Hilde R. drove me to a place on the Rhine forty kilometres from Düsseldorf. Heinz Jost had agreed to receive me.[6]

The handshake was nervous. The man before me was almost completely bald, short—about five feet six inches—broad of shoulder and chest. His face was rectangular, expressively wrinkled, the ears long, the nose strong and aquiline. His very blue eyes, flecked with fiery spots, often wore a hard, cruel expression. He had rectangular hands with round, almost square, fingers and hollow palms. His constitution was vigorous but marked by his time in prison: he was only fifty-six but seemed ten years older. He must have been energetic and domineering, brusque, impatient, perhaps even violent and passionate. I was to discover that he was quite hot-tempered and touchy, sometimes to extremes, thus no doubt concealing some kind of latent apprehensiveness. He was nevertheless endowed with great cold-bloodedness which enabled him to control his first excessive reflexes and inclined him towards greater deliberation. He lacked suppleness and culture but his intelligence where clear and simple ideas were involved was keen and balanced. He displayed a sense of the essential and a fairly rare sureness of judgement.

In the course of our talk which went on to dinner then late into the night I learned nothing I did not know about various 'great events' of the S.S. secret service, such as the Night of the Long Knives, the Sosnowski, Tukhachevsky, Formis affairs, etc. On the other hand I understood better the psychology of certain S.S.

chiefs like Himmler, Wolff, Kaltenbrunner, Best, Daluege, Conti, Ohlendorf and even Schellenberg, whom Jost detested (it was natural enough) and especially Heydrich whom he had feared but admired. Finally Jost was to enlighten me remarkably about several specific matters which are the object of the present and following chapters: the invasion of Czechoslovakia, the attack on the radio station at Gleiwitz, the organisation of the Reich Security Service (R.S.H.A.) and of the S.D.-Foreign Service (Amt VI of the R.S.H.A.) and the Venlo kidnapping.

Regarding the internal divisions amongst the Sudeten Germans Heinz Jost explained to me: 'It is undeniable that Hitler's assumption of power, on January 30th 1933, strengthened the opposition between the various national groups in Czechoslovakia without reconciling the objectives of the two right-wing parties of the Sudeten Germans, the National German party and the German National Socialist Workers party. When Henlein founded the Fatherland Front in collaboration with the distinguished Dr. Walter Brand, the new organisation obtained a considerable number of adherents. It was straightforwardly anti-Nazi and advocated autonomy within the Czechoslovak republic. At Berlin this Fatherland Front was regarded with distrust. When Henlein's anti-Nazi remarks were reported to Hitler, the Führer expressed himself several times in terms, to say the least, unamiable. In the loftier spheres of the S.S., it was worse; Himmler and Heydrich discharged volleys of abuse on the leader of the Sudeten Fatherland Front. I received the order to maintain a constant watch on Henlein. I must say that the task was greatly facilitated by the information sent to me by former members of the German National Socialist Workers Party and especially by their leader, Karl Hermann Frank.[7]

'The uncompromising and malignant policy of the head of the Czech Government, Dr. Edward Benes, was a decisive step in the progress towards the dismemberment of this artificial republic, born in 1919 at Saint-Germain-en-Laye and composed of a motley population—Czechs, Slovaks, Germans, Poles, Hungarians—at cross-purposes with one another.'

After a short pause to finish a cup of coffee with cream Jost went on; 'At the elections of 1935[8] the Fatherland Front declared its candidacy under the name of the Sudeten German Party. Its success was overwhelming: two-thirds of all the Sudeten German votes. It became the strongest party in the new Parliament. From then on, through hatred of Germanism, the President of the Republic,

Edward Benes,[9] never ceased to combat Henlein's party. The law of April 30th 1937 which he had passed by Parliament and which was called the Law of National Defence made him a veritable dictator and was essentially aimed against Henlein's party. The latter still tried by Parliamentary means to have his project of autonomy adopted. Benes and his circle spurned this claim and his attitude allowed the National Socialist trend, favourable to union with the Third Reich, to harden its position and gather strength. Himmler and Heydrich supported this trend by every means. Hitler's distrust of Henlein grew all the greater as Heydrich multiplied his reports on the friendly links uniting Henlein to the English Colonel Graham Christie, head of the Central European section of British Intelligence. Henlein had several times gone to London to sound out international public opinion and inform foreign governments of the situation and of the Sudeten claims. He had there made the acquaintance of various British personalities such as Duff Cooper, Duncan Sandys, Harold Nicolson and many influential journalists. The reports on these journeys concocted by Heydrich were packed with venom. When, in October 1937, Henlein again went to London under the patronage of the Intelligence Service and Sir Robert Vansittart, and met Winston Churchill, Hitler's suspicion increased. Henlein, with his idea of a "friendly compromise" with the Czechs, hampered the Führer's real and already fixed intentions. Heydrich kept going one better: "Henlein is betraying German interests," he declared. At the end of 1937 I was detailed, along with several other members of the S.S. secret service—'

I interrupted, 'Amongst them Schellenberg?'

'Yes, Schellenberg, Best and others. We were to compile a memorandum to be presented to the Führer to advise him to incite a revolt in the Sudeten German party for the purpose of getting rid of Henlein and his followers and put Karl Hermann Frank and a National Socialist team in his place. Apprised I don't know by whom, Henlein felt himself strong enough to react harshly, and expelled a number of National Socialists, amongst them the deputy Rudolf Kasper.'

Jost continued, 'The Anschluss with Austria was a terrible blow to Henlein. After this striking success attained without a shot fired, Hitler felt himself to be riding fortune. Heydrich let me know that the Führer, fortified in his idea that a "total" settlement of the Czechoslovak problem should take place as soon as possible, had decided on annexation pure and simple. There was first the summons of Henlein to Berlin. On March 29th 1938, he took part in a conference which included Ribbentrop, Minister for Foreign Affairs, the Secretary of State Hans George von Mackensen, the German minister at Prague, Ernst Eisenlohr, the Counsellor of State Ernst von Weizsäcker, several diplomats, Professor Karl Haushofer, S.S. General Werner Lorenz, head of *Vomi* and of course Karl Hermann Frank. It was by the last that Heydrich and I were informed of what was said. In a few words, Henlein, who the evening before had had a long interview with the Führer, had entirely given in to Hitler: the idea of autonomy was set aside and what henceforth mattered was to promote the integration of the Sudeten into the Third Reich.'

'What caused Henlein's sudden change of mind?'

'I think I know, having talked to him about it later, that it was not without a struggle of conscience that he sided with the Führer. After the Anschluss he saw himself faced with a heavy historic responsibility. The hesitant, passive attitude of Great Britain shook him. Benes's narrow outlook, certain to lead to war because of his obstinate resistance to legitimate Sudeten claims, made him understand that sooner or later Czechoslovakia would fly apart. What was he to do? Withdraw from the political scene and hand over to Karl Hermann Frank or remain and try to save what could still be saved? He gave in.'

'Schellenberg told me that Henlein's change of front did not impress Heydrich. Is that true?'

'Yes. In a secret note to Hitler, compiled in collaboration with the various heads of the S.S. secret service, Heydrich emphasised that they must remain distrustful of Henlein. He stressed the fact that the change of mind occurred after the Anschluss and that Henlein still maintained too many links with London to be completely sincere. The conclusion of the note could not be clearer: Heydrich proposed that Henlein be "liquidated" after the annexation of the Sudeten territories by giving him some honorific title and placing the real power in the hands of Karl Hermann Frank.'

'Which is just what Hitler did.'

'Yes, and I must say that Heydrich's influence during that period was decisive. My chief proved to everybody that he had political acumen and in foreign affairs he was altogether superior to that imbecile Ribbentrop, conceited but losing all his wits when in Hitler's presence. The prestige which Heydrich acquired in

Hitler's eyes during the Czechoslovak crisis of 1938–39 was the reason for his appointment in 1941 as Protector of Bohemia and Moravia.'

'How far would he have got if he had not been assassinated?'[10]

'It is certain that Heydrich outclassed the majority of the leaders of the Third Reich. In 1941 we in the S.S. reckoned that after a period in Prague he would become either Minister of the Interior or Minister for Foreign Affairs. More and more he looked like the Führer's heir-apparent.'

I said to Jost, 'Let's go back, if you will, to 1939. I know from Schellenberg that Henlein remained in constant contact with the British and that a meeting was arranged at Zürich with his friend Colonel Christie.'

'That's right. Heydrich had been informed by K. H. Frank and he summoned me as well as Schellenberg to order the latter to go to Zürich and let himself be seen so that Henlein should know he was under supervision.'

'According to Schellenberg, Colonel Christie was amazed to learn how far Henlein had given in to the Führer's demands. Henlein may have stated in fact that the German Sudeten party and the Führer couldn't wait any longer and the problem had if necessary to be resolved by force.'

'In fact he might have said that,' Jost answered. 'I'll tell you a secret. After the war, when I was being interrogated by the Allies, the officers of the Intelligence Service who raised this matter with me said that Colonel Christie's report on his Zurich conversations had made a strong impression on the Foreign Office. They declared that it prompted Neville Chamberlain's historic visit to Berchtesgaden, on September 15th 1938, then the German–British conference at Godesberg, and finally the Munich treaty.'

'Hitler had duped the English . . .'

'Not at all!' Jost protested. 'Hitler was looking further ahead than the Sudeten. He had determined to expunge Czechoslovakia from the map. The Munich treaty for him represented a bad compromise. He had to accept it for two reasons. The first was that the intervention of Mussolini caused him to overcome his personal feelings. He could not yet face up to the whole world alone. All the less because the second reason compelled him to consider the situation realistically: the reaction of the German people in September 1938 revealed to him that they were by no means ready, as he was, to buy an increase of power at the price of a war.'

'Yet, despite the Munich treaty, Hitler put his plan into effect.'

'Before and after Munich Hitler had decided to seize Czecho-slovakia. I must acknowledge again that Heydrich encouraged and supported him. It was Heydrich especially who had the idea of creating "action groups" of S.S. in civilian clothes who were to occupy key positions in Czechoslovakia.'

'Can you see in these "action groups" the predecessors of the sinister "intervention groups" or "extermination commandos", who operated in Poland, then in Russia, and of which you were one of the leaders?'

As I put this question Jost's face turned pale, his expression became hard. He clenched his hands on the table. I well understood that he was trying to master a violent internal anger. Would he throw me out? I questioned my friend Hilde with my eyes. She was also watching for Jost's reaction but appeared calm. She knew him well, it seemed, and ought to know how he would react. In fact Jost plainly succeeded in controlling himself. In a voice less tense but more apprehensive than angry he answered, 'I insist, as I did at my trial in Nuremberg, that I was unaware of the activity expected of the *Einsatzgruppen* when I took command of Group A. As soon as I understood I put in for a transfer.'

'I'm not accusing you, it's not my business. What I think of your acts does not concern you. It is not for me to judge you, that was done by the Nuremberg court.'

'I paid for that!'

'Once more, that's not the question. I spoke of the "inter-vention groups" planned for Czechoslovakia. Didn't you know about them?'

'No.'

'Is it true that it was Walter Schellenberg who started them?'

'It is.'

'He told me the contrary.'

'He was lying.'

'I think, in fact, that he was.'

In the documents of the International Military Tribunal at Nuremberg there exist four texts which require no commentary.[11] The first is of June 1938. It is endorsed 'very secret'. Its subject is 'The use of the S.D. in the matter of Czechoslovakia'.

There one can read, 'In case of complications between the German Reich and Czechoslovakia, the S.D. should be prepared eventually to be used . . . The S.D. will immediately follow the advancing armies. It will assume, as in Germany, all the tasks necessary to assure the security of political life as well as the security of all the enterprises of some importance to the national economy no less than for the war economy . . . The S.D. will co-operate with the Gestapo. The measures for the occupied territories will be taken under the direction of a high official of the S.D. The operational staffs will receive officers from the Gestapo. What is important is that the Gestapo shall, as far as possible, concern itself, like the S.D., with the preparation of directives for the utilisation of stores, etc.' This order was signed 'Walter Schellenberg, Chief of the Central Service I—IA of the S.D.'

The second text was earlier, of February 5th 1938. It was a departmental memorandum addressed by Heydrich to Schellenberg directing him to 'draw up a list of persons resident in Berlin capable of teaching Czech to officers of the S.S.' and to set in motion 'a scheme for the organisation of intervention groups in Czechoslovakia'.[12]

In March 1938, in a letter to Himmler, Heydrich announced that the teachers recruited by Schellenberg had been found politically reliable and that 'the training . . . of the nuclei of the "intervention Groups" could begin.' The letter ended with this sentence, 'The plan for the organisation of the "intervention groups" is ready and, in conformity with the Führer's order, comprises the formation of the two sections envisaged: first, the section of groups in civilian clothes, before the action; second, the section of groups in uniform, after the action, which will follow the units of the army.'

Finally, the fourth text is a note from Schellenberg to Heinz Jost. The heading reads, 'Berlin, September 13th 1938. State Chancellery. I/113. To the chief of service III Oberführer S.S. Jost or his substitute. Object: To make ready the *Einsatzkommandos*.' This note ended, 'In conformity with the report mentioned above will be found enclosed a photocopy of the plan for setting up the *Einsatzkommandos*. This has been ordered by C[13], in the manner indicated above.'

'The Chief of the central service I–IA. Signed: Schellenberg.'

There is no need to keep on. These documents prove, contrary to what certain S.S. men have contended, that the S.S. secret service was not only aware of the elaboration of the plans for the aggression but very actively took part in them.

On September 30th 1938 the Munich treaty was signed by Germany, France, Great Britain and Italy. On October 1st Hitler signed an order for General von Brauchitsch to occupy the territories to be ceded by Czechoslovakia. Then he named Konrad Henlein Reich Commissioner for the Sudeten territories. This was only to prove temporary. Karl Hermann Frank was to receive the reward for his services, which consisted of his unqualified obedience to Hitler's policy supported by Heydrich, and in his attitude of opposition to Henlein. After the complete liquidation of Czechoslovakia he would be the most important person in Prague, the key person, sitting beside the Reich Protector in the role of German Minister of State. He would become famous in this capacity by an extraordinary ferocity throughout the occupation.

The 'Peace of Munich' did not last long. On October 21st Hitler gave his instructions to his general staff: to prepare without delay the annihilation of what was left of Czechoslovakia.

On the morrow of Munich, on October 4th, Benes resigned as President of the Republic. On October 22nd he left Czechoslovakia for London where he lived in exile until 1945. In the *Populaire* for October 6th the French Socialist leader Léon Blum wrote, 'Edward Benes no longer represents in his country anything but defeat, mourning, the past.'

Czechoslovakia was in tumult. Simultaneously an autonomous government of Ruthenia (sub-Carpathian Ukraine) was set up at Uzhorod under the presidency of André Brody, then of Mgr. Augustine Volozin, and an autonomous government of Slovakia was proclaimed at Bratislava under the presidency of Mgr. Tiso, head of the Slovak Popular Party which had long demanded autonomy. The break-up of the Czechoslovak state accelerated.

On November 29th, Dr. Emil Hacha, President of the Council of State, was elected President of the Republic. He was sixty-seven but looked a good deal more. Politically he was at the opposite pole from his predecessor and his friends. 'I always disapproved of their policy,' he was to say, 'since I never believed it possible to make populations which hated one another to live together.'

Could Czechoslovakia with the Sudetenland amputated find its equilibrium? No. There remained in the country 175 000 Germans who had seen themselves left out of the Munich settlement. Their feeling of frustration expressed itself in a growing agitation. The Czechs, for their part, traumatised by the Munich agreement, felt a growing hostility towards the German minorities which took the form of innumerable vexations. On the other side they were exasperated by the Slovaks' and Ruthenians' wish for autonomy. They poured oil on the fire. Under the pressure of public opinion Hacha sent General Prchala into Ruthenia to 're-establish order' with virtually dictatorial powers. Mgr. Volozin protested. Hacha turned a deaf ear.

The precedent thus established, Hacha next turned against the Slovaks. To put an end to the separatist tendencies, he summoned Mgr. Tiso to an explanation in Prague. Mgr. Tiso refused. Hacha insisted. On Thursday, March 9th 1939, he dismissed Mgr. Tiso as well as three other Slovak ministers, had the capital occupied by troops, dissolved the Diet of Bratislava (formed in October 1938) and had three influential members of Parliament known for their separatist tendencies arrested: Adalbert Tuka, Cernak and Mach. He then set up a new government completely devoted to him, presided over by Sivak. But Sivak, who was in Rome, formally declined. President Hacha then perforce had to beg Mgr. Tiso to resume power. Mgr. Tiso, who on March 10th had withdrawn to the presbytery of his parish in Western Slovakia, declined. It was an impasse. Karol Sidor, who as a last resort formed a new government, knew that he was only there for a 'period of transition'.

Mgr. Tiso had good reasons for acting so. Although hoping for the maintenance of the federal state in a climate of mutual confidence, he knew that he was being discreetly backed by the Third Reich. It was not that he was favourable to it—he was fiercely opposed to the 'solution of the Jewish question' and hostile to the Nazi leanings of the Hlinka Guard—but he had been negotiating secretly with Berlin for several weeks. We should note that Hitler's entourage, and Hitler himself, entertained some distrust of this ecclesiastic of whom it was said that he conducted a policy directed by Pope Pius XI. However that may be, at the end of January 1939 Hitler assembled his associates, the Secretary of State Wilhelm Keppler, his assistant Dr. Ermund Veesenmayer and the chiefs of the secret service, amongst them Heydrich, Heinz Jost and Walter Schellenberg, to impart to them the following confidential order: 'German foreign policy requires that the Czechoslovak Republic be broken and destroyed within the next few months—by force of arms if necessary. To prepare and facilitate the measures to be taken against Czechoslovakia it seems opportune to support and encourage the efforts of the Slovaks in their claims for autonomy. After which it will be very easy to take action against the Czech portion of the Republic.'

Schellenberg and Jost assured me that on that day Hitler declared,

'This order must remain strictly secret; neither the Ministry for Foreign Affairs, the Wehrmacht nor the Party must know about it.'

From the beginning of February agents of the S.S. secret service, amongst them Wilhelm Höttl[14], met responsible Slovaks in the outskirts of Bratislava. The German agents received a friendly welcome. No exact information leaked out. It is known that there was the question of propaganda, of German financial support at the moment of launching the political movements leading to independence. Nevertheless Hitler had only limited confidence in the responsible Slovaks. 'They haven't enough influence on the people,' he said. It is true that while an overwhelming majority blindly followed Mgr. Tiso, it did nothing that would lead its chief's efforts to a successful result. So, at the suggestion of Heydrich, the Führer ordered that several 'intervention groups' be introduced into Slovakia secretly, which, by perpetrating a number of acts of terrorism would rouse the Czechs from their lethargy. Heydrich appointed his brilliant subordinate Alfred Naujocks to co-ordinate the clandestine S.S. actions in conjunction with the Waffen S.S. General Gottlob Berger.

The day after the Czech attack on Slovakia on March 10th the most extreme confusion reigned throughout the whole republic. The entire world had its eyes fixed on Prague. What was going to happen?

A current of pessimism blew in London, Paris, Washington and Moscow. Sir Neville Henderson, British Ambassador to Czechoslovakia, wrote to his Minister in London, Lord Halifax, 'The trouble with this business is that no solution can be found to the Czech problem without receiving the previous approbation of the German Government. In these circumstances one may wonder if it is not in the best interests of the Czechs themselves to leave the initiative to Berlin.'

In this chaotic situation, which naturally favoured Hitler's designs, Poland and Hungary bobbed up. The Warsaw Government demanded a common frontier with Hungary and to achieve this proposed to Roumania to divide Ruthenia with her. On its side the Budapest Government claimed the whole of Slovakia and Ruthenia.

The sky was overcast. The rattle of arms was heard on all sides. Would the guns speak? Was it war?

The Hungarian army concentrated on the Slovakian border and prepared to invade the country. Poland and Roumania hastened to reinforce their armies stationed along the Ruthenian frontiers. On Sunday, March 12th, Hitler, who was following events with sustained attention issued orders to the Wehrmacht and the Luftwaffe to hold themselves in readiness to invade Bohemia on March 15th at six o'clock in the morning. Central Europe was on the point of going up in flames.

That same Sunday, March 12th, round ten at night, a brown D.K.W. car left the Hotel Imperial in Vienna. Two men were in it, two S.S. of the secret service. One was Wilhelm Höttl. His mission was to bring Mgr. Tiso a message from Chancellor Hitler inviting him to confer with him in Berlin. His goal was Banovce nad Bebravou, a small place in Western Slovakia, in the Valley of the Bebrava at the southern point of the Fotza hills. It was there that Mgr. Tiso had, since March 10th, taken refuge in the presbytery of his parish.

The two S.S. men were with Mgr. Tiso towards one in the morning. The prelate was surprised by the visit and the invitation. 'I can't leave like this with you,' he said. 'I am ready to accept the Chancellor's invitation, but I prefer it to be official and transmitted to me through diplomatic channels.'

Wilhelm Höttl replied,[15] 'The invitation will arrive in Bratislava in a few hours. We have come to ask you to act very quickly. The fate of Slovakia is at stake.'

'I shall be in Bratislava this very morning,' Mgr. Tiso promised. The two secret agents set off again for Vienna.

At his trial after the war Mgr. Tiso, alluding to this decision, said, 'As a priest I intended to serve God, the Church and the nation into which I was born and within which I exercised my priestly calling.'

The morning of Monday, March 13th, he went to Bratislava. There he saw his colleagues and assured them that in Berlin he would give no formal promise; he would decline to take any final decision, this must be submitted to the Bratislava Diet. These points made clear, he left for Vienna accompanied by the German consul, Ernst von Druffel. He then proceeded to Berlin by air, landing at five o'clock. His first meeting was with Joachim von Ribbentrop, Minister for Foreign Affairs. The second was at the new Reich Chancellery with Hitler. It was 6.40. The conference ended at 7.15, having lasted thirty-five minutes. Hitler had stated, 'I have asked you here to know what Slovakia really wants. The question is, does Slovakia want to be free or not. If it does, I am ready to guarantee its independence. If not, I have only to let things follow their course . . . In the next hours Slovakia must declare itself, clearly and irrevocably.'

Mgr. Tiso answered, 'I have noted what you say and thank you. It is a long while that I have wanted to hear from your own lips what you think of my country and of your intentions with regard to it. I am too moved to answer you at once formally. I shall consult my friends and think over the whole matter at leisure. But you may rest easy; Slovakia will not disappoint you. Its answer will be worthy of the interest you take in it.'

Mgr. Tiso and Ferdinand Durcansky, a member of the government who accompanied him, left the Chancellery and went to the Czechoslovak legation in Berlin. Mgr. Tiso telephoned to the head of the Government in Bratislava, Karol Sidor: 'The Diet must be convoked in extraordinary session tomorrow morning, March 14th. I have a communication to make of extreme urgency, after my interview with the Chancellor of the Reich.'

After dinner Mgr. Tiso and Ferdinand Durcansky conferred with Ribbentrop. They discussed the relations between Germany and Slovakia, should the latter opt for independence, a treaty of protection, a special zone reserved on Slovak territory for German troops. The discussion lasted until one in the morning. At dawn on March 14th, Mgr. Tiso, Durcansky and their companions returned to Bratislava.[16]

The sitting of Parliament opened a few minutes before eleven. Mgr. Tiso gave his account of his visit to Berlin. At noon the sitting was suspended. It was resumed six minutes later.

'The Slovak nation proclaims itself an independent state. The Parliament of the Slovak nation is transformed into the legislative assembly of the Slovak State. Until the adoption of the constitution of the Slovak State the executive power is entrusted to the Government appointed by the presidency of the Parliament . . .'

Independence was voted unanimously. The fifty-seven deputies present of the sixty-three which composed the assembly rose and sang the patriotic hymn *Nad Tatrou sa Blytca* (Light Shines on the Tatras). Mgr. Tiso immediately sent the following telegram to Goering, 'I beg you to bring the knowledge of the following to the Führer and Reich Chancellor: "In testimony of the confidence you have shown in it, the Slovak State places itself under your protection. It asks you please to assume with respect to it the part of Protector." '

Hitler at once answered Mgr. Tiso, 'I have the honour to acknowledge the receipt of your telegram. Henceforth I assume the pro-
tectorship of the Slovak State.'

The announcement by radio of the proclamation of independence
aroused the enthusiasm of the Slovak people. In the whole country
there was joy. In Prague there was anxiety, panic. Hacha sent a
telegram to Hitler asking for an audience 'as soon as possible'.
Hitler answered. 'This very day'. At four o'clock Hacha and his
minister Chvalkosky took a special train to Berlin, where they arrived
at 10.15. At the Hotel Adlon, during a preparatory meeting with
Ribbentrop, Hacha declared, 'I have come to place the fate of
Czechoslovakia in the hands of the Führer.' Ribbentrop, who
desired always to show himself impassive, caught his breath.

At 1.15 in the morning Hacha and Chvalkovsky were introduced
into the Führer's office.[17] Hacha advanced towards Hitler with
both arms extended. With a strong Bohemian accent he said.
'Excellency, you cannot know how much I admire you. I have read
all your writings, I have arranged to hear nearly all your speeches,
and now I at least have the pleasure of making your acquaintance.'

This exuberance at so tragic an hour was shocking. All present
were amazed, Hitler the first. But the man persisted, 'Mr. Chancellor, I have asked to see you in order to dissipate the misunder-
standings which have arisen between our two countries and to place
my people's fate in your hands, convinced that it could not be in
better ones.'

Was he mad or drugged? Was it a diplomatic ruse? One doesn't
know. He spoke with tears in his voice. He implored, pleaded. He
evoked his past, told the story of his life, tried to justify himself,
called the Führer to witness. It was a circus turn. The grotesque
little old Bohemian drowned in the flood of his own words. Hitler,
surprised, listened with an impatience shown by abrupt movements
of his head. The other went on. Hitler opened his mouth but didn't
get in a word. Hacha finally fell silent.

The Chancellor of the Reich first answered in a dull voice on a
note of condolence, after which he began to fulminate against the
former Czechoslovakia. He worked himself up in talking, raised his
voice little by little and proceeded to express himself with a certain
vehemence. The tempest was let loose. The lightning struck Hacha.

'The die was cast on Sunday, Mr. President. I gave the order to
the Wehrmacht to invade what is left of Czecho-Slovakia (he separated the two words) so as to incorporate it into the Reich. Tomor-

row morning, Wednesday March 15th at six o'clock, the German army will enter Bohemia and Moravia from all sides at once and the Luftwaffe will occupy the Czech aerodromes.'

Hacha and Chvalkovsky were petrified.

'I well realise,' Hacha succeeded in saying in a choked voice, 'that all resistance is useless, but . . . it's two in the morning . . . You tell me that your troops will enter Czechoslovakia in four hours. How . . . how do you expect me in that time to prevent the Czech people from having resort to arms?'

'You've only to telephone Prague,' replied Hitler frigidly.

Hacha was exhausted. In a small sitting room adjoining the Führer's office Chvalkovsky and he tried to get in touch with Prague. The snowstorm which raged over all Central Europe had upset telephonic communications so that it was difficult to get the Czech capital. Finally contact became possible. Hacha took the instrument but he had hardly exchanged a few words when the line was cut. They tried again. At that moment Hacha fainted. Goering exclaimed, 'If Hacha dies here before being able to talk to Prague, the whole world will say tomorrow that we murdered him.'

The Führer's personal doctor, Morell, gave the President an injection which revived him. Communication with Prague was established. Hacha succeeded in convincing the commanding general, Sirovy, to issue an order to the army and the people not to oppose the German troops. With death in his soul Sirovy, a hard yet disciplined man, resigned himself to obey. It was 3.45 in the morning. At 3.55 Hitler, Hacha, Ribbentrop and Chvalkovsky signed a common declaration which was for Hacha unconditional surrender.

Two hours and five minutes later the German troops started to march in swirling snow and crossed the frontier. Czechoslovakia was dead.

Five and a half months later it would be the turn of Poland.

NOTES TO CHAPTER 12

1. Speech of November 8th 1937 at Munich.
2. It was resumed on March 17th. Von Fritsch was acquitted next day but, though rehabilitated, was not restored to his post. In June he was appointed commander of the Twelfth Regiment of Artillery. It was at the head of this regiment that he was killed before Warsaw at 9.40 a.m. on September 22nd 1939.

3. Dr. Ernst Kaltenbrunner, who was hanged by the Allies on October 16th 1946 at Nuremberg, succeeded Heydrich in January 1943 as head of the R.S.H.A., but Schellenberg, appointed head of the S.S. secret service (Amt VI. SD-Ausland), was only in theory subordinate to him; in fact Schellenberg was responsible direct to Himmler. In 1933 Odilo Globocnik took refuge in Germany after having murdered a Viennese jeweller during a robbery. He entered the S.S. in 1934. Five years later he was dismissed from his post as Vice-Gauleiter for foreign exchange dealings but was pardoned by Himmler. He became an S.S. General and notable exterminator of the Jews in the East. He committed suicide in April 1945.

4. Joachim von Ribbentrop, who was hanged by the Allies at Nuremberg on October 16th 1946, was appointed head of the Ministry of Foreign Affairs in February 1938. Until that date he was in charge of questions of foreign policy on the staff of the Führer's personal representative, Rudolf Hess. His department was known as 'the Ribbentrop Office'.

5. The trial in question was the Ninth Nuremberg trial, called the 'Trial of the Einsatzgruppen', which took place between July 25th 1947 and April 9th 1948.

6. I must state here that I was unaware at this time of Heinz Jost's belonging to the espionage and counter-espionage organisation of the German Federal Republic directed by Gehlen. Jost had a 'cover' as industrial representative and administrator of a building society, in contact with the Mannesmann group of ex-S.S. General Franz A. Six. The latter, with whom I communicated at various times, always refused to receive me.

7. Karl Hermann Frank is not to be confused with Dr. Hans Frank, German jurist, Hitler's lawyer and intimate, who became Governor-general of Poland and was hanged by the Allies at Nuremberg on October 16th 1946. Karl Hermann Frank was also hanged, at Prague by the Czechs, in 1946.

8. May 26th 1935.

9. Elected December 18th 1935, after the retirement of the founder and first President of the Republic, Thomas Masaryk.

10. Heydrich perished on June 4th 1942 as the result of an attack on him in Prague on May 27th by two Czech parachutists sent from London.

11. *T.M.I.*, Vols. I (324); IV (319, 320, 350, 387, 389, 396); VI (483); XV (423); XX (620, 622, 678); XXI (23, 408, 409); XXII (91–92, 166, 281, 373, 382) and Doc. PS. 3710.

12. The preparation of the groups for intervention in Czechoslovakia was entrusted to S.S. General Gottlob Berger.

13. Within the secret service the letter C designated Reinhard Heydrich.

14. Austrian by origin, Wilhelm Höttl, alias Walter Hagen, born in 1915, doctor of philosophy, graduate in history at the University of Vienna, in October 1938 entered the S.S. secret service under Heinz Jost, and was considered one of the experts on central European and Balkan questions. His office was then quartered in the Rothschild palace,

Auf der Wieden, in Vienna. In 1941 he underwent the same fate as Jost and Naujocks, being sent as a private to the Eastern front. Restored to Himmler's favour in 1943, Dr. Höttl occupied important posts in the S.S. secret service (Amt VI of the R.S.H.A.): assistant chief of Amt VI-B, (German and Italian spheres of influence in Europe, Africa and the Near East), chief of *VI-B6* and *VI-B7* (Balkans and the Vatican), assistant chief of *VI-E* (hunting ideological opponents abroad), the successive chiefs of which had been Helmuth Knochen, Dr. Hammer and *Obersturmführer S.S*.Wanck. He lived in Rome from February to September 1943 and played a part in the dramatic and bloody end of Count Galeazzo Ciano, Mussolini's son-in-law. (Cf. André Brissaud, *La Tragédie de Vérone*.) After the war Wilhelm Höttl worked for a while under Gehlen, then founded a school in Aussee, Austria. Under the pseudonym of Walter Hagen he wrote a book entitled *Le Front Secret*, (*The Secret Front*) op. cit.

15. In his book *The Secret Front*, Höttl does not mention that he was writing of himself. The truth was made known at the trial of Mgr. Tiso in 1946 at Bratislava.

16. Testimony of Mgr. Tiso (at his trial), of Joachim von Ribbentrop (*T.M.I.*), of the German consul Ernst von Druffel (Wilhelmstrasse Archives) and *T.M.I.* Doc. PS. 2802.

17. Paul Schmidt, *Ma Figuration auprès de Hitler*. It should be noted that Schmidt was not present. The conversation was reported by Ribbentrop to Schmidt.

13

At Gleiwitz
the Corpse Was on Time

On Friday, August 4th 1939, Heydrich was in his Berlin office in Prinz-Albrechtstrasse. His bad humour was evident. Was it because it was raining?—and what rain! For forty-eight hours cloudbursts had been causing the gutters of Berlin to overflow. A godforsaken summer. Clouds and still more clouds . . . since the end of June. How was one to start a war in weather like this? For that was the problem. Heydrich knew that before autumn Hitler would launch his armoured divisions and his air squadrons against Poland. It was up to him, Heydrich, to lead the initial phase of the aggression in such a way that the German attack could be presented to international opinion as a 'riposte' to 'bloody Polish provocations'. This was why he had summoned to his office a man he didn't like much but whose great abilities he appreciated: S.S. General Herbert Mehlhorn.

When the two men were together Heydrich told the other without preamble that the Führer had decided to settle accounts with Poland. He had no intention of undertaking a winter campaign in the Polish plains, 'he counted on carrying through a lightning war that would last at most a few weeks'. The generals' draft plan was ready. Hitler had instructed the S.S. secret service and Canaris's Abwehr to carry out various auxiliary operations. The destruction of the big bridge over the Vistula at Dirschau must specially be prevented in order to keep a vital link with East Prussia. The mines and industries of Polish Upper Silesia must so far as possible be saved.

It was the Abwehr which would be responsible for this task together with the Luftwaffe. Then Heydrich elaborated his ideas: 'There is a village called Kreuzburg near the German–Polish frontier to the east of Breslau. On the eve of the outbreak of war a company of men, looking as Slavic as possible and wearing Polish uniforms, will theoretically come into collision with some German troops east of Kreuzburg. They will loot the frontier post of Pitschen, where photographers will be in readiness. Furthermore, a violent combat will be simulated near the frontier post of Hochlinden. It is you who will organise this last incident.'

As Mehlhorn expressed his surprise, his hesitation, his doubts, Heydrich cut him short with a sharp, 'It's the Führer's orders.'

Mehlhorn had no choice but to obey or find himself—at best—in a concentration camp. He bowed his head in sign of acceptance. Heydrich said in conclusion, 'There will be a third incident, but this has not yet been finally arranged. You will later be kept informed. *Heil Hitler!*'

'*Heil Hitler!*' responded Mehlhorn.

When he reached the door Heydrich flung after him, 'There is no need to remind you that what I have just told you is a state secret.'

Mehlhorn's gaze met Heydrich's, which was harsh and aggressive. It signified 'Talk and you die.' Standing at attention, Mehlhorn said in a firm voice, '*Ja, mein Gruppenführer.*'

'*Gut, Oberführer.*'

The third 'incident' referred to by Heydrich was to be instigated by the chief of the S.S. 'thugs', Alfred Naujocks. Heydrich summoned him on Saturday, August 5th.

To Heydrich's smile that morning Naujocks responded with another smile faintly shadowed by distrust. It was not in the character of his chief to show cordiality. His distrust grew as Heydrich said, 'Alfred [calling him by his first name was also unusual], I've got something here that seems expressly designed for you.' He paused, still smiling, and fixed his gaze firmly on Naujocks, who did not conceal his anxiety.

'This time,' Heydrich went on, 'no insurance company would issue you a policy, whatever the premium, but I know that you are the man who will carry through this operation successfully. The matter is called. . . .'

He drew a dossier from a drawer and leafed through it with his slender fingers. There was a contemptuous twist to his large mouth when he continued, 'Operation Himmler. Don't ask me why this name was chosen. It was not his idea, you will suspect. The order came directly from on high, from the Führer himself.'

His face stiffened: he was no longer smiling. His look grew harder: 'The importance of this mission exceeds anything the S.S. secret service has undertaken until now, although at bottom it is merely a matter of a commando raid. So many political and military interests depend on the result that failure is entirely out of the question.'

Naujocks sat down, his legs a bit weak. His hands trembled. He knew that the conversation would be long. The business must be of considerable importance.

'The risk of being discovered is great and that, of course, would be the worst crime we could commit,' Heydrich continued. 'In any case, the Führer has given this matter top priority and will not permit any discussion or modification of the plan. I'm in your hands and I can't deny that I hate that.'

He regarded Naujocks with his crafty eyes which possessed a strange power of fascination. To the other's silent question he answered drily, 'It concerns Poland. We shall be at war next week. But first we must have a motive, an excuse, for opening hostilities. That's where you come in. You know that there have been, during these past months, dozens of annoying incidents along the border . . . Nothing serious, a shot here and there, the usual diplomatic protests. In short, nothing that can spark off the gunpowder. Well, we are going to try ourselves to light the fuse.'

'And it's me who . . . will have to strike the match?'

Heydrich rose, went to a large wall map and put his pencil at a point on the frontier. In an excited, jerky voice he explained, 'Here there is a small locality called Gleiwitz. Gleiwitz is in Germany, of course, but exactly on the Polish border. Good. Now suppose that Polish troops attack the radio station at Gleiwitz and occupy it for just enough time to broadcast a message denouncing Hitler as a warmonger. That would be a serious, a very serious provocation, wouldn't it? It would become perfectly clear that the Poles were looking for a quarrel, especially if afterwards one or two corpses were found at the place, and more especially if by chance the German radio network relayed the Polish message and transmitted to the whole country.'

Heydrich asked deliberately, 'Do you think you could arrange such an incident?'

This time Naujocks was petrified. He did not know what to answer.

'Well?' demanded Heydrich coldly.

'Well,' said Naujocks, choosing his words with care, 'I should like to guarantee you success but before examining the project more closely I can tell you straightaway that the risks of failure are considerable. If you put your confidence in me I'll of course do my best.'

'Your best will be far from enough. A failure would destroy the plans and efforts of thousands of people over many months. Moreover it would be a disgrace for Germany. I take it that you have no moral objections?'

Naujocks slowly shook his head. Heydrich would be too pleased to uncover in him a trace of 'flabbiness'.

'No, of course not,' said Naujocks with a small grimace. He felt a terrible weight on his stomach.

'You see that I've been absolutely frank with you. I think you understand the problem. There's no question of your refusing. You must see it through to the end. Now let's settle the details.'

Naujocks had embarked on Operation Himmler.

The following week Naujocks, deep in his preparations, gradually forgot his anxieties. He studied the maps and aerial photographs of the frontier, read the report on the station at Gleiwitz. Heydrich asked an odd character, Otto Ulitz, to see him.[1] Since 1921 Ulitz had been responsible for the 'German Popular League for Polish Upper Silesia'. He had worked for the S.D. in Poland since 1933 and ran many centres of agitation for the absorption of Upper Silesia into the Reich. He explained to Naujocks that he knew the Gleiwitz region perfectly and even the installations at the radio station. Heydrich had directed him to advise Naujocks, to familiarise him with the future 'theatre of operations', and to bring him two specialists: one, Karl Berger, an expert in radio transmission, the other, Heinrich Neumann, who spoke Polish fluently. These three 'recruits' inspired Naujocks with little confidence. He knew that Heydrich's choices were often made in defiance of good sense. On the other hand Naujocks himself carefully chose the four members of the S.D. who were to assist him. One was a youth of high worth, solid, cold, efficient and entirely devoted to Naujocks: Helmut Kordts.[2]

Naujocks learned a little later that there would be other 'incidents' simultaneously organised along the frontier. His mission was, however, by far the most important since his incident was to be broadcast. If all went well the whole of Germany with access to a radio would be able to hear the 'proof' of the 'Polish aggression'.

The Abwehr had one hundred and fifty Polish uniforms sent to the S.D. Heinz Jost and Naujocks examined them. They were hung in cupboards and from carefully labelled boxes the two S.S. leaders removed opened packets of cigarettes and Polish matches, letters, photographs, notebooks and various papers written in Polish, destined to be put into the pockets of the uniforms. Colonel Lahousen's department at the Abwehr did its work to perfection.

Thursday, August 10th, two black V8 Fords entered Gleiwitz late in the afternoon and stopped in front of the town's best hotel, the Oberschlesischer Hof. Seven men carrying suitcases got out and entered the newly constructed white edifice.

Naujocks explained to the clerk at the reception desk that his companions were mining engineers who had booked their rooms two days earlier. The forms were carefully filled in with fictitious names, occupations and places of birth. They stayed there two days, two days in which, accompanied by Otto Ulitz who had joined them, they ostensibly collected rocks and specimens of earth.

In the O.K.W.'s conference room Naujocks's success was taken for granted. The two chief engineers of the Breslau radio station took an oath and received the order to be ready to relay a broadcast which would be sensational. They were personally to see to it that this broadcast should be re-transmitted on the German national network.

Back in Berlin on Monday, August 14th, Naujocks studied the new photographs he had taken of the station and the personal report each man had written of his own observations. Barring the unexpected the matter should not present any difficulty, Naujocks thought. The biggest unknown factor was the local police force—probably not very numerous—and it could be assumed that it too would be taken by surprise.

By Sunday, August 20th, everything was ready. Before leaving, on Monday morning the 21st, Naujocks went to Heydrich's office. Solemnly he swore an oath to keep silent about Operation Himmler. About thirty persons had been told of the project. From all the same oath was required.

Heydrich gave him a copy of the message to be broadcast by the commando, but Naujocks did not even glance at it. He was more interested in a detail he had only once mentioned, at the first conference. 'And the bodies?' he asked.

'They're seeing to them,' replied Heydrich drily. 'One will do and it will be supplied to you at the site when wanted, by Heinrich Müller.'

Müller, head of the Gestapo!

A message awaited Naujocks on his return from Heydrich's office. It came from Oppeln, some seventy kilometres distant, signed Müller. Naujocks at once went to the place by car.

The Gestapo chief greeted him with the warmest cordiality. 'My dear Naujocks,' he said, taking him by the arm. 'I've heard many praises of your plan. I must say they have chosen the right man for this mission.' He sank into a leather chair behind his desk and invited Naujocks to be seated. 'I have borrowed this office temporarily to keep up with the night's work. My co-operation is limited to supplying you with the *corpus delicti*.'

He laughed. 'People would have a poor opinion of our police if the Poles could execute an attack like this without a single victim. I'll tell you what I'm going to do for you. Two minutes after the start of the operation at 7.30 on the evening of August 25th, I shall pass in front of the radio station in a black Opel and deposit at the entrance a newly killed corpse, dressed of course in a Polish Army uniform. I understand that you will be waiting for a radio signal before launching your operation. The signal will be given as soon as I have announced that the body is available. I wish you good luck, Naujocks, but I'm convinced you won't need it. Everything seems to have been meticulously organised. A propos, don't worry about the victim. He has already been chosen in a camp, a Jew . . .'

It was not only Heinrich Müller whom Naujocks encountered at Oppeln. There were also the leaders of the two other commandos, Herbert Mehlhorn and Otto Rasch.[3] With Naujocks the three men studied the plans for the other 'frontier incidents'.

During the trial of the chief war criminals, Naujocks, testifying as a witness, said, 'The chief of the Gestapo, Heinrich Müller, told us that he had available twelve or thirteen common criminals whom he would dress either as Polish soldiers or as German frontier guards, whose bodies they would leave at the scene of action to make it look as if they had been killed in the course of it. A doctor in the pay of the Gestapo would previously give them fatal injections while it was being arranged that they should bear the marks of rifle bullets. After the incident journalists and others would be brought to the place. Müller informed me that he had received the order from Heydrich to supply me for the Gleiwitz operation one of these criminals who would have the code name of 'tinned goods'.[4]

Other 'tinned goods' were to be supplied to S.S. General Otto Rasch, in command of the operation at Pitschen, and to S.S. General Herbert Mehlhorn for the pretended combat at Hochlinden.

This same Monday, August 21st, Hitler was at the Berghof. He was awaiting with growing nervousness Stalin's reaction to the message he had sent him the evening before in which he said, 'I regard it as of the highest urgency to elucidate as soon as possible the questions arising out of our pact of non-aggression . . . it is desirable to lose no time . . . the tension between Germany and Poland has become insupportable . . . I propose that you receive my Minister for Foreign Affairs on Tuesday August 22nd or at the latest Wednesday the 23rd; he will have full powers to define and sign both the pact of non-aggression and the protocol. I shall be pleased to receive your answer promptly.'

The hours passed. Hitler walked up and down the enormous drawing room of the Berghof. His intimates and the servants changed themselves into ghosts, even Eva Braun avoided his presence as far as possible. Hitler was wrong to worry, Stalin was as eager as he, if not more so, for this pact.

Finally, at 10.50, Stalin's affirmative answer arrived. Hitler's explosion of joy was unique. His eyes sparkled, he raised his arms crying 'Ho! Ho!' and adding with passion, 'We've won! Now I've got the world in my pocket. We can spit in anybody's face, no matter whose.'

A little before midnight the whole world heard the astounding news. Hitler summoned for the late morning of the next day the general officers of highest rank in the army, air force and navy. There were nearly a hundred of them. The meeting was not kept secret, but the proceedings were.

This exceptional military conference ended with these words from Hitler, 'Our armies must strike like lightning. The aim, I repeat, is the annihilation of Poland . . . I shall probably give orders to begin operations Saturday morning.' The war was thus to begin on Saturday, August 26th 1939.

On Wednesday the 23rd[5] Herbert Mehlhorn telephoned his friend Schellenberg to ask if he had the evening free. He wanted urgently to discuss a personal problem with him and didn't think it prudent to come to his office. Schellenberg answered that he would make himself free and told him to come at eight to a discreet little restaurant. In fact it was a meeting-place used by the S.S. secret service, where from cook to headwaiter the whole staff had been chosen from amongst S.D. agents.

Schellenberg noticed at once that Mehlhorn was deeply troubled and depressed. Without pressing questions on him Schellenberg let him take his time. Mehlhorn spoke of nothing during dinner. Afterwards, to escape the oppressive heat weighing on Berlin they went by car to the Wannsee, a lake situated between Berlin and

Potsdam. Schellenberg long remembered thus crossing the city in the last hours of peace: 'At that time,' he writes, 'Berlin was a magnificent city, at the peak of its power and wealth, the elegant show-windows flooded with light, the flashing of the multi-coloured electric signs, the continuous flow of cars, the bustling crowd, in a word the gay life of peacetime.'

He was about to take Mehlhorn to a little bar and was looking for a place to park when his passenger asked him to drive on. 'I need fresh air,' he said, 'and want to get away from the crowd.' They followed the lake, then, after a minute, stopped, got out and began to walk. Schellenberg writes, 'Mehlhorn, more relaxed, began to talk, but rather as if talking to himself. From time to time a puff of fresh air came from the lake and rustled the tall trees. Then, apart from my companion's voice, silence again reigned. Mehlhorn spoke in short, quick sentences, jerky and almost without a pause.

' "There's going to be a war," he said. "It can't be avoided. Hitler took his decision long ago, you must know that. Everything's ready. Even if the Western Powers or Poland make an attempt at conciliation at the last moment, even if Italy intervenes, that will not change Hitler's basic plans. At the most there might be a short delay—that's all."

'In a voice still more perturbed, he next told me that Heydrich had summoned him to confide—to his great surprise—Hitler's secret orders. "Before September 1st," said Mehlhorn, "an absolutely flawless *casus belli* must be created, one of those cases which in the eyes of history constitute a complete justification and which in the eyes of the world will brand Poland as the aggressor against Germany. For this purpose he proposes to dress troops in Polish uniform and launch them in an attack on the German radio transmitter at Gleiwitz, to simulate a violent combat near the frontier post of Hochlinden between German and Polish troops, and to sack the German frontier post of Pitschen, north of Kreuzburg. Hitler has instructed Heydrich and Admiral Canaris to carry out these operations. This order so displeased Canaris that he managed to get out of it. He only supplied the Polish uniforms and papers. Heydrich is in sole charge of the operations." '

Schellenberg asked Mehlhorn where Heydrich would get the Poles who were to wear the uniforms.

'That's the problem,' Mehlhorn answered. 'It's the diabolic feature of the plan: the "Poles" will be prisoners from the concentration camps. They will be furnished with genuine Polish arms.

Those of them who come out of it have been promised their immediate release. But who will believe such a promise! Müller has given me to understand that these prisoners from the camps will be delivered "tinned", that is to say dead. A fatal injection, a few shots fired into the bodies dressed in Polish uniforms and they will be ready to play their part as aggressors on German soil.'

'It's insane!' Schellenberg exclaimed.

'Heydrich has put me in charge of the Hochlinden commando.'

Mehlhorn paused. He squeezed his friend's arm hard and went on, 'Heydrich wants my skin. He's given me this mission in order to get rid of me, I know. What can I do?'

Schellenberg returned roughly, 'This whole affair is mad. You don't make world history by methods of this sort. The business can never be kept secret. Not for long, anyway. Somewhere, some way or other, it will be exposed. You must absolutely get out of it. Invent an excuse. Say you're ill. Or just refuse. Whatever comes of it, a refusal will be preferable to the results of accepting. Let Naujocks, who's a thug, do it. But not you.'

Wednesday the 23rd, Thursday the 24th, Friday the 25th, the fever still soared in Europe. They were days charged with electricity and filled with menace. In Danzig the air was unbreathable. In Germany the motorised columns ploughed their way to the east. In France the reservists recalled to service made for their depots. In Belgium and Poland a partial mobilisation was ordered. In Holland mines were laid between Nijmegen and Maestricht. Roosevelt and the Pope issued appeals for peace. In London and Paris they discussed resistance.

On the 24th the three S.S. commandos reached their starting point. The tension on the German–Polish border reached breaking point. On the night of the 23rd/24th a score of armed German customs officers broke into the Polish post of Makoszow, near Kattowice, firing a hundred or so shots. There were no victims but this time, despite the counsels of prudence from Léon Noël, the French Ambassador in Warsaw, the Polish Government, via their ambassador in Berlin, lodged a protest with the German Ministry of Foreign Affairs.

During the morning of the 25th the information coming from the frontier reported many incidents more or less grave. At Bielitz in particular a collision had caused eight deaths and several injuries on the German side. Hitler was mad with rage: 'This time my patience is exhausted,' he exclaimed. 'It's impossible to let this situation go on.' He at once dictated a letter to his friend Mussolini in which he warned him that he would probably be obliged shortly (he gave no date) to begin hostilities against Poland. However the news from Moscow (Stalin would stand aloof from the conflict) and from London (the English forcibly re-affirmed their solidarity with the Poles) calmed his belligerence.

At noon he called Keitel, chief of the O.K.W. and said, 'I need time. Can we halt the march of the troops?'

'I think we can, on the condition that the order be sent at once. We've only just got the time.'

'What is the latest that you must have orders to attack tomorrow at 4.45?'

'Three o'clock this afternoon.'

'Will you postpone all movement of the troops till then? I will give you my final instructions in time.'

The meeting he had, at the beginning of the afternoon, with the British Ambassador, Sir Neville Henderson, was disappointing for Hitler, who learned of the signature of an Anglo-Polish treaty of alliance. The clauses of the treaty left no doubt: if Germany fired a single cannon shot against Poland, England—like France in virtue of the Franco-Polish pact—would declare war on the aggressor. It was three o'clock. At 3.02, Hitler rose from his office chair, went to the door, opened it and uttered two words to General von Vormann, who was waiting in a small room: 'White plan.'

The general immediately understood: the attack on Poland would begin next morning at dawn. He leapt to the telephone and transmitted the Führer's order to the O.K.W.

The German war machine resumed its march after a three hours' halt.

From Prinz-Albrechtstrasse Heydrich telephoned to Oppeln, where was based S.S. Lieutenant-Colonel Ottfried Hellwig who had been appointed to co-ordinate the activities of Operation Himmler. He told him to be ready for action at the frontier during the next hours.

The three commando leaders took up their positions. Naujocks was at Gleiwitz, Mehlhorn two kilometres from the frontier post of Hochlinden, Rasch in a farmhouse on the edge of the forest of Pitschen.

The Gestapo chief, Heinrich Müller, was at Oppeln. The prisoners from the concentration camp were cooped up in two huts. In the first, ten had exchanged their striped pyjamas and clogs for uniforms of the German frontier guards. In the second, five others had put on Polish uniforms. Three lorries were waiting to transport to the site of the 'combats' the 'tinned goods' to whom the fatal injections would be administered at the moment of departure.

Berlin sweltered in sultry stifling weather. At 5.30 p.m., in the Reich Chancellery, Hitler received the French Ambassador, François Coulondre. He said to him, 'I don't want a conflict with your country. The thought that I might have to fight France because of Poland is infinitely painful to me . . . I shall not attack France. But if she enters the war I will see it through to the end.'

Half an hour later the Italian Ambassador, Bernardo Attolico, arrived at the Chancellery in his turn to give Hitler Mussolini's answer. 'At last,' said the Führer, who had for hours been impatiently waiting for it. He first read the Duce's personal note then the official answer. They were two hammer blows. Mussolini was categoric: 'Italy is not ready for war. . . .' In this answer there was approval of the German–Soviet pact but also a warning against a rupture with Japan. Mussolini evinced a 'complete understanding' of Germany's attitude towards Poland, then went on to Italy's position: if the conflict remained localised, she would give Germany all political and economic help; if it became general 'Italy will take no initiative of a military nature.' Then came a request for massive deliveries of war material, and raw materials, then a reminder of the Pact of Steel according to which the eventuality of a conflict had been explicitly deferred until after 1942.

Hitler took leave of Attolico with obvious coolness. He who admired the beautiful and intelligent Donna Eleanora Attolico—'the loveliest gift from the South', he called her—did not, contrary to custom—even ask the Ambassador to present his respects to the Countess. Hitler was 'groggy', as they say of a boxer.

A few minutes later General Halder, who had just come in, heard him say in a low voice to Ribbentrop, 'The Italians are acting exactly as in 1914.'

Halder, who did not know of the Duce's reply, found the Führer 'very depressed'. He had come to receive orders from Hitler, but the latter hardly seemed to see him. His brow was careworn, his mouth bitter, his colour pallid. His anxiety was understandable. Stalin turned a deaf ear and delayed the despatch of a military mission to Berlin; Japan refused to follow up the conversations intended to bring about a tripartite pact; London had just solemnly confirmed its guarantee to Warsaw; the French were doing the same.

And now Italy was balking! Hitler was, however, the last who could complain of Italy's conduct. It was only the rejoinder to the Führer's facing his friend and partner the Duce with a *fait accompli*. Germany was not observing the letter of the Pact of Steel, and Italy was disregarding its spirit. Count Galeazzo Ciano's bitter remark after the signing of the Pact of Steel—of which he nevertheless had been the artisan—now revealed its full meaning: 'Pact of Steel, Pact of Blood!'

Hitler, sunk into an armchair, was silent. Halder, Ribbentrop and Bormann, sitting apart, held their breaths. Painful minutes passed.

At seven Hitler suddenly seemed to pull himself together. He called General von Vormann and asked him to summon immediately Generals Keitel and Brauchitsch. When the two arrived at 7.30, he said to them in a tired voice, 'Have the orders for the attack countermanded . . . I must reconsider the situation . . . I have to look over the international scene as a whole . . . I must have time to negotiate. . . . I must see if I cannot avert British intervention.'

At General Headquarters of the land forces in Zossen it was 7.35 when the Chief of Operations was called to the telephone by General Jodl, Chief of Staff of the Wehrmacht. He asked, 'What's happening, General?'

'The Führer', said Jodl, 'wants to know if the troop movements can still be stopped and the troops brought back to their starting points before dawn.'

'But what's happening?'

'The English have interfered again.'

'I can't say at once if it's possible. It's a matter of communications. I must first talk to Fellgiebel.'

'Right. Call me back.'

The Chief of Operations called General Fellgiebel and said, 'General, don't be alarmed. A question from the Führer. Can the movements still be stopped?'

'Have you gone mad?' exclaimed Fellgiebel. 'There's no need to push a joke too far. You can't command a front like a battalion. I can guarantee nothing about the extreme wings in Slovakia and East Prussia. I don't know if the links with them are fast enough. As for the rest of the front, it ought to be all right.'

'Thanks very much. I'll shortly give you definite orders.'

The Chief of Operations again rang General Jodl and said, 'It's possible except for the extreme wings.'

'The Führer has instructed me to stop everything. Give the orders! Fellgiebel must do all he can.'

At the S.S. secret service headquarters Heydrich learned of the Führer's new orders at 7.40. He at once telephoned to Ottfried Hellwig, 'Stop everything!'

Hellwig exclaimed, 'It's insanity. I can reach Naujocks, who is waiting for the radio signal to go ahead, and maybe Rasch at Pitschen, but it will be very difficult for me to teach Mehlhorn, who has been moving towards Hochlinden for twenty minutes.'

'Everything must be stopped. Do you hear? It's the Führer's order.'

As Hellwig had foreseen, he was able to reach Naujocks and Rasch immediately, but not Mehlhorn. It was by pure chance that the last-named established radio contact with Hellwig at eight. The advance party of his commando was in contact with the Polish frontier guards. The S.S. had crossed the frontier without realising it. Mehlhorn asked, 'We were to simulate a combat. Here's a real one. What should I do? We can easily clean up the Poles, there are only ten of them, but it's happening on their soil! Furthermore Müller's "tinned goods" dressed in German uniforms haven't arrived. What are the orders?'

Hellwig was furious. He had not been able to say a word since he had been in radio communication with Mehlhorn. He retorted with rage, 'First shut your trap! There's no question of playing with fire. I had Heydrich on the 'phone more than twenty minutes ago, he passed on an order from the Führer: everything must be stopped at once. Do you understand?'

'Yes, I understand, but. . . .'

'There aren't any "buts". It's an order from the Führer: draw back immediately.'

'What bloody. . . .'

'Good luck all the same. Call me back when you're again at your starting point.'

'Right.'

Three hours later, at the Polish frontier in East Prussia to the south of Johannisburg. The commander of a cavalry regiment was in a small inn with his staff. The regiment was ready to go. The telephone rang, Brigade calling the Colonel.

'Hello, who's there?'

'The Chief of Staff.'

'Oh, it's you. What's happening? I was about to start.'

'We've received the order to drop it. The regiment is to return to its billets before dawn if possible. If patrols have already crossed the border, they must be recalled at once.'

'What does it mean? We're going to make fools of ourselves.'

'I can't do anything about it. I don't know the reasons. Have the patrols already left?'

'Of course. I don't know if I can get them back. Order, counter-order, disorder.'

An hour later the Colonel's Chief of Staff entered the inn and said, 'At your orders, Colonel. We can leave, the regiment is marching back to barracks.'

'And the patrols?'

'We were able to reach the one at Kolno, but not the one at Grabowo. We heard firing.'

At this moment a subaltern entered and announced, 'Colonel, the Grabowo patrol has just returned. A sergeant is missing.'

The colonel growled, 'Done it this once! One push forward, one back!'

The immense German war machine had stopped, not without creakings. Was peace saved?

Alfred Naujocks, Rasch and Mehlhorn returned to Berlin with their men. Mehlhorn went to Heydrich to tell him that a sudden stomach attack rendered him incapable of strenuous action. 'Was it a diplomatic illness?' It is what Heydrich thought, and would not at first accept the excuse. But Mehlhorn persisted in spite of his chief's threats. Luckily the latter was overloaded with work and ended by allowing the evasion. Nevertheless ten minutes after the interview he replaced Mehlhorn by S.S. Colonel Hans Trummler and the 'invalid' found himself assigned to an inferior and very difficult post in the East. Mehlhorn's stomach recovered quickly and he ignobly distinguished himself by the terror he instituted in Poland.

It was a weekend of peace. Was the movement towards war irreversible? A few men, Birger Dahlerus, Georges Bonnet, Sir Neville Henderson, even Mussolini, attempted the impossible. The last flicker of hope was not extinguished.

History marked time. Hitler, the man of lightning decisions, temporised. His army, 1 500 000 helmeted men, waited. The northern group of armies under General von Bock and the southern group under General von Rundstedt were ready to swoop on Poland. In the West there was not the slightest military cover; only a few divisions were deployed behind the Siegfried line. If the French and English had started an offensive, had attacked during the operations in Poland, it would have been a catastrophe for Hitler. He knew it. This was why he did not want a general conflict. His indecision did not last. He evolved another idea. To free his hands in Poland? To avoid the conflict? No one knows. He proposed to the English an alliance joined to a solution of the Polish business on the hypothesis that Great Britain would accept a settlement of the Danzig problem in Germany's favour.

The British answer was qualified, Hitler became irritated. If on Monday the 28th the scales tilted towards peace, the next day they tilted towards war. Almost everywhere in Europe, in France, Belgium, Italy, Hungary, Bulgaria, Roumania and even in Turkey, measures for partial mobilisation were taken.

The Poles persisted in believing that Hitler was bluffing and that if he wasn't they were perfectly capable of defeating him militarily: war would start a revolution in Germany and Marshal Rydz-Smigly's troops would march on Berlin. On this Tuesday the 29th Poland took the final step and ordered general mobilisation.

Hitler was wild with rage. Was he manoeuvring for a diplomatic advantage when agreeing to receive a Polish envoy the next day, Wednesday August 30th, or was it duplicity to keep Great Britain out of the conflict? Only Hitler knew the exact truth. Europe already felt the hot and terrifying breath of war.

Tuesday, August 29th, the S.S. commandos for Operation Himmler returned to their several starting points. On Wednesday, August 30th, Birger Dahlerus tried to persuade the English and the Germans that peace could still be preserved. However, no Polish emissary had come to Berlin, and Ribbentrop gave Dahlerus to understand that the iron dice had already been cast. War was on the way, very near.

On Thursday, August 31st, the positions were, alas, very plain. Beck in Warsaw was inflexible, Chamberlain in London was resigned; Bonnet in Paris was as powerless as Mussolini in Rome. In Berlin Hitler was at the moment absolutely decided. At 12.40 he called in Keitel and handed him the 'Directive No. 1 for the conduct of the war', which contained the words: 'Day of attack: September 1st 1939; hour of attack 4.45 a.m.'

At 1.30 p.m. Heydrich gave his three commandos the alert: 'Proceed with Operation Himmler.' At four Naujocks summoned his men to a conference in Room 7 of the Oberschlesicher Hof. His nerves felt tense. It was the day he was to 'strike the match'. He was obsessed with the idea that after this night he would be a marked man: the man who had sparked off the war. He would know too much, much too much. The bearers of State secrets do not die old. Would he and his six companions still be alive the next day, September 1st, at the same hour? Would success be as fatal to them as failure?

The six men entered and distributed themselves round the room: two on the bed, three on chairs and the last, Helmut Kordts, leaned against the mantelpiece. Naujocks sat on the window sill and began, 'Here we are. The two trunks are in my car. The first contains seven Polish army uniforms. This evening at seven we'll be in Ratibor Woods, a few kilometres from our objective, and there we'll change.'

He turned to the radio expert appointed by Heydrich. 'Karl, you will start the set which is in the other trunk working and wait for the signal a little before 7.30 which will send us into action. At exactly 7.30, leaving our clothes, and all signs of our identity behind, we'll go to the station and overpower its personnel—there won't be more than five or six on duty. You will not say a word and let them think we are Poles. Once inside, Karl and Heinrich will stay with me.' Heinrich was the speaker of Polish, likewise appointed by Heydrich.

Naujocks continued, 'You should connect up with the Breslau line, you know it. Heinrich, I've got the text of a little speech for you which you will broadcast. At the same time I'll fire a shot in the air; I'm warning you so that you won't be alarmed. A black Opel will arrive in front of the principal entrance to the station a few minutes later than us and a corpse will be thrown on the steps. Don't get involved in this; another department is seeing to it. We shouldn't stay more than five minutes at most, and I don't expect to meet with any opposition. But if the police turn up, don't hesitate to fire. Whatever happens, we must get away. If one of you is captured, he must claim he is Polish. Headquarters in Berlin has foreseen such an eventuality and will demand that the prisoner be handed over. Remember: at 7.30 this evening you become Poles and shoot at anybody who tries to bar your way. Even if you kill somebody there won't be any prosecution or enquiry. These are your orders.'

To break the silence that followed, Naujocks put a hand in his pocket, drew out the envelope containing the speech and handed it to Heinrich, who read it impassively without comment. A few questions were asked and the meeting ended.

Naujocks had not the least idea what his companions thought of the operation. He felt slightly nervous, and after telling his men to meet him at the hotel at 6.30 he went down to the bar for a drink.

When they assembled again they all seemed to feel better. Far from being silent, they talked a good deal. The prospect of action soon, which would break the tension, comforted them. The afternoon had been endless for them all and Naujocks checked that none of his companions had been drinking. He himself had taken two glasses and regretted them. 'Let's go,' he said.

They descended the stairs and got into the two black Fords with an air as natural as possible. Naujocks was in the first with Karl and Heinrich. The others, driven by Helmut Kordts, followed at a few metres. The two cars sped rapidly to the frontier. The Gleiwitz station was on their left and slightly to the rear when they entered the Ratibor Woods by a narrow path. The cars stopped at the first clearing, quite invisible from the road. Naujocks got out and motioned to his companions to keep quiet. He had the two trunks removed from the boots. The first contained seven new Lugers whose barrels still bore traces of grease, lying on a pile of seven Polish army uniforms. Each man changed quickly, still silent. While they examined their pistols, Karl twiddled the wireless taken from the other trunk, and, wearing the ear-phones, awaited the signal from Berlin. It came at 7.27.

Naujocks at once got into the car, shutting the door silently. The others followed except for Karl, who did not know what to do with the wireless. They had forgotten to give him instructions, but it was not the moment to bother with details. He abandoned it and in his turn got into the back seat. They returned to the main road as quietly as possible. The two Fords stopped with a sharp squeal of tyres in front of the station.

Night was falling. When ascending the six steps to the large glass door Naujocks noticed a light in a window on his right. Good. It indicated where at least one of the personnel was to be found.

He opened the door, his two companions at his heels. A man wearing a navy-blue uniform appeared in the little hall and stopped short on seeing them. Before he could utter a cry Heinrich seized him and banged his head twice against the wall. It proved effective.

Turning into the corridor at his right in search of the employee whose light he had seen, he found him in the second room bending

over a filing cabinet. Before he could turn Naujocks knocked him
out with a blow from the pistol-butt. He collapsed, bringing down
with him a chair and coat-stand which broke in two on the edge of
a metal cupboard. Cries and the sound of footsteps came from the
end of the corridor on the other side of the hall. These were from
the other members of the commandos who were dealing with the
other employees of the station.

Issuing precipitately from the room, Naujocks bumped into Karl.
He heard him say, 'Quickly, this way.' Both ran towards a green
door to which was affixed a notice in red: 'Silence'.

Heinrich was already inside the studio, a small room with light-
grey furniture including, in the centre, a desk on which stood a
microphone. In the wall facing the door two rectangular openings
covered with thick glass gave on to an even smaller room filled with
apparatus which enabled transmission to be effected to Radio
Breslau and thence to all Germany. Heinrich was bent over the desk
holding the microphone in one hand and in the other a crumpled
paper with the text of his speech. He was waiting for an order.

Through the glass-covered openings giving on the transmitting
room, Naujocks and Heinrich saw Karl moving about lowering and
raising all the switches one after another. He looked completely
bewildered. Naujocks joined him and asked, 'What's the matter?'

'I can't find the switch for the connection with Breslau.'

'You great oaf, you've got to find it! I thought you knew your
business.'

In a choked voice Karl returned, 'How do you expect me to know
where it is? I can work it but I've still got to find it.'

It was a disaster. The transmission had to be made, one way or
another. On the other side of the glass Heinrich was fidgeting and
waving his text. He also had lost his calm and looked terrified. 'Can
you at least make a local transmission?' asked Naujocks, in a state of
near-collapse.

'Yes, but only on the local wave-length. It's not enough. You
could only hear within a radius of forty kilometres.'

'Well, do it. Do something. This bloody text has to be read to
somebody.' He quickly returned to the studio, leaving Karl to
manipulate his switches again. 'At his signal begin to read,' he said
to Heinrich, 'Shout it because I'm going to make a noise and fire
shots.'

During the two or three seconds before Karl's signal Naujocks
thought, 'Still, it's lucky there's been no intervention from outside.'

Heinrich recited his text at speed, almost yelling. Naujocks didn't even listen. He had read the speech a dozen times: 'Germany's leaders are hurrying Europe into war. . . . Peaceful Poland is being constantly threatened and bullied by Hitler, who must be crushed at all costs. . . . Danzig is Polish . . .' Naujocks wondered who could have written the speech; probably Heydrich.

He fired three shots in the air and began to roar. Heinrich was expecting it, but nevertheless dropped the microphone at the first shot and went astray in his reading. He recovered himself, restored the microphone to its place at an imperious gesture from Naujocks, who fired another shot at a wall and motioned to Karl, hypnotised behind the glass, to stop transmission.

A few seconds later the three men left the studio from which drifted the smell of powder, and ran to the main door. They met two of the four others, revolvers in hand, and the group left the building.

Naujocks could imagine the consternation of his superiors at this precise moment; they must be gathered round their radios, waiting impatiently to be witnesses of their Führer's diabolic machinations. He thought of the two engineers at Radio Breslau desperately manipulating switches in their control room. And Hitler, at the Chancellery, foaming . . . Naujocks felt an icy sweat on his back. He already saw himself with a rope round his neck, hanged like a 'dirty dog of a Jew' with his six companions. As he went down the steps he nearly stumbled over his eighth, and involuntary, helper who had arrived a few minutes earlier in Müller's car and 'lay in a grotesque posture' on the steps, dead. Müller must have killed him himself. The corpse was on time. As were all the other corpses which Müller had had planted at Pitschen and Hochlinden. Naujocks only paused for a glance at the body, that of a tall blond man who looked to be about thirty.

At Nuremberg Naujocks stated, 'He was alive but already unconscious, his breathing that of one dying. I didn't see any bullet mark, but his face was covered with blood.'

The door of the car was left open for Naujocks. The engine was running, and the other car just behind. He sprang into his seat and the Fords made off. In the rear-view mirror Naujocks could see that there was no sign of excitement in front of the station. He reflected gloomily that no one, perhaps, had heard the broadcast from Gleiwitz, any more than the infernal din they had made. He kept a look-out for the turning that led to the clearing they had left . . . When? Fifteen minutes before. It seemed improbable. The actual operation had taken only four minutes.

At dawn on Friday, September 1st, the telephone rang everywhere: Hitler had launched his troops against Poland. In Warsaw it was not the telephone but the bombs that woke the population at six in the morning. Houses collapsed under the hellish deluge signed Goering. Colonel Beck was in communication with Army Headquarters. He was appalled. The German offensive was general from the Baltic to the Carpathians. The sky over Poland was already dominated by the Luftwaffe and the cavalry charges were being shattered by Rundstedt and Bock's armour. The German advance was irresistible. The 'march on Berlin' would not take place.

At 4.45 a.m., H hour for the start of hostilities, the *Schleswig-Holstein*, an armoured cruiser arrived the day before in territorial waters, opened fire on the Polish enclave of Westerplatte. At eight, before a Senate vibrant with enthusiasm, Forster proclaimed that Danzig and its territory were an integral part of the Reich. At once those present rose and sang *Deutschland über Alles*. The city of Danzig draped itself in swastikas.

At the end of the ceremony in the Senate, Gauleiter Forster led a small group to the seat of the League of Nations delegation and asked to speak to Carl Burckhardt. 'Mr. High Commissioner,' Forster said to him, 'you here represent the Treaty of Versailles. But the Treaty of Versailles no longer exists. The Führer tore it up this morning. I give you two hours to leave the territory.' A few minutes later the German Consul-general in Danzig telephoned to the Wilhelmstrasse in Berlin, 'The High Commissioner, accompanied by his secretary, has left Danzig by car for East Prussia.'

In Rome, Mussolini was in his office in the Palazzo Venezia maintaining communication with his Ambassador in Berlin, Attolico. The Duce was furious, uneasy and perplexed. Furious because his Axis partner had not thought it necessary to inform him of the attack. Uneasy because he had not decided to follow in this matter and wanted the Western powers to be fully aware of his neutrality. Perplexed because he was wondering how Hitler would react when he, the Duce of Fascism, offered himself as ultimate mediator before the whole world . . . The Ambassador, Attolico, understood perfectly Mussolini's state of mind. Hitler also understood it. He had a telegram telephoned by way of the German embassy in Rome addressed to the Duce and signed Adolf Hitler: 'I do not think I shall need military help from Italy.'

The chief of the French Deuxième Bureau, Colonel Rivet, who then lived in the Square de Latour-Maubourg in Paris, remembers that his face was lathered for shaving when the telephone rang. He put the receiver to his ear cursing the caller. It was the generalissimo, Gamelin, who asked, 'Have you heard the wireless?'

'No, General, not yet. . . .'

'Ah,' said Gamelin.

'Why?'

'Hitler has attacked Poland.' And he hung up.

At the Quai d'Orsay it was Georges Bonnet who was awakened by the telephone. The director of the Havas agency personally gave the minister the news. He who had done so much to save the peace, who until late at night had tried to give concrete form to the idea that Mussolini should urgently convoke a four-power conference, could not believe it. He wanted to hear the few words again which ruined all his hopes. He heard, 'At dawn German troops crossed the Polish frontier.'

'Have you any details?'

'I don't know anything more.'

Dismayed, he hung up. He took several steps round his room then again picked up the telephone and called Daladier. The President of the Council was also not yet informed, and at first failed to grasp it. Bonnet repeated, 'At dawn German troops crossed the Polish frontier without a declaration of war.'

Daladier went immediately to the Ministry of War in the Rue St. Dominique, where Georges Bonnet found him a few minutes later. The two men quickly reached agreement on the measures to be taken.

In London the functionary at the Foreign Office who received the urgent message from Berlin could not conceal his astonishment. Had Dahlerus, the unofficial Swedish diplomat, gone mad? The news seemed to him all the more absurd in that his informant passed on faithfully the version given him by his friend Hermann Goering: it was the Poles who had attacked.

One had to accept the evidence: it was war. In London as in Paris the Polish ambassadors, Raczynski and Lukasiewics, forcibly pressed open those responsible for foreign affairs, Halifax and Bonnet, the recollection of the treaties of alliance which stipulated that in case of aggression immediate help would be given.

The hours passed in the most disagreeable confusion. England

and France did not, after hesitation, decide on a declaration of war against Hitler until the evening of September 2nd.

In Berlin, September 1st 1939, it was seven in the morning when Naujocks arrived in Heydrich's office. He hadn't taken the trouble to shave, felt dirty and had a terrible migraine. Fear gnawed at his entrails since leaving Gleiwitz.

Heydrich, elegantly dressed as always, looked at him calmly. Naujocks stared at the carpet and awaited the outburst. He raised his head, astonished, when he heard his chief say, 'Congratulations!' Heydrich went on, 'Pity about the mix-up, but I suppose nothing could be done. I must admit that I was disturbed yesterday evening when I didn't hear anything at 7.30. But you needn't worry about it. The main thing is that the broadcast took place and no one was captured.'

Naujocks' surprise gave way to distrust. He had never before been congratulated by his chief. No one ever had, in fact. Naujocks did not answer but drew from his pocket a report which he had only completed at three that morning and flung it on the desk. 'It's all there. We had no troubles. There were only five men in the building: after six Gleiwitz, except for news bulletins and weather reports, merely re-transmits broadcasts from elsewhere. We took care of them before anyone could give the alarm or telephone. It was easy, but I was furious not to be able to relay to Breslau.'

'It happens,' said Heydrich, 'that I had foreseen the possibility. Have you read the morning papers? Well, have a look at the *Völkischer Beobachter*. You will find a very interesting article on the first page.'

It was in fact interesting. The official organ of the Party had an exclusive story: Heinrich's little speech reproduced under the headline, 'Aggressors Attack Gleiwitz Radio.' The article read: 'A group of Polish soldiers seized the Gleiwitz Radio building last night a little before eight. Only a few of the staff were on duty at that hour. It is obvious that the Polish assailants knew the ground perfectly. They attacked the personnel and broke into the studio, knocking out those they encountered on the way.

'The aggressors cut the relay line to Breslau and read out at the microphone a propaganda speech prepared in advance, in Polish and German. They stated that the town and the radio station were in the hands of the Poles and insulted Germany, alluding to "Polish Breslau" and "Polish Danzig".

'The listeners, at first taken by surprise, notified the police, who arrived a few minutes later. The aggressors opened fire on the forces of order but at the end of a few minutes they were all taken prisoner. During the battle a Pole was killed.'

In his high-pitched voice Heydrich remarked, 'The Führer is very pleased. He called me at five o'clock this morning to congratulate me.'

Hence the reason for Heydrich's satisfaction. Hitler was pleased. Therefore Heydrich was also pleased. Naujocks began to relax. He breathed easier.

The Gleiwitz affair had been for the Führer the first good news of the day. He had passed an excellent night: 'Führer calm and slept well . . .' one can read in General Halder's Journal. 'Opposed to evacuation . . . proof that he hopes Great Britain and France will remain at peace.'

At ten Hitler went to the Reichstag to deliver an important speech. He had changed his brown jacket of head of the Party for the field-grey tunic of the soldiers of the Wehrmacht. After a historical survey of the Danzig question and German–Polish tension, Hitler evoked the surprise attacks at Pitschen, Hochlinden and Gleiwitz. He declared, 'While recently twenty-one border incidents have been recorded in a single night there were fourteen last night, *three of them very serious,* so I have decided to speak to the Poles in the language they have used to us for months . . . Last night, for the first time Poland has opened fire on our national territory, with *soldiers of her regular army.* Since 4.45 we have been answering their fire. As from now we answer bomb with bomb . . . I shall conduct this struggle against whomsoever until the safety of the Reich and its rights are secured . . . More than ever my life belongs to the German people. I want nothing more than to be the first soldier of the Reich.

'I have resumed the dress that is to me dearest and most sacred. I shall not discard it until victory is won or else an end reached which I shall not see . . . I enter upon this struggle with an indomitable heart. My entire life has been but a single unique combat for my people, for their restoration, and this struggle is being inspired by one sentiment alone: my faith in the German people. There is only one word which I have never known; that word is surrender. There will be no repetition of November 1918 in German history! . . .'

The sinister 'Operation Himmler' had attained its object. Hitler needed an alibi and he had it. His Minister for Foreign Affairs Joachim von Ribbentrop told the French Ambassador, 'The Poles have crossed the German frontier at three separate points.'

On the shore of Lake Maggiore Walter Schellenberg explained to me that at a pseudo 'commission' headed by the chief of the Gestapo, Heinrich Müller, the same as had delivered on time the 'tinned goods', conducted an 'enquiry on the spot into the crimes committed by the Polish aggressors'. Schellenberg added, 'These are the very words of the official communiqué.'

The chief of the criminal police, Arthur Nebe, had had installed for the benefit of visitors from neutral countries an electric table showing the different phases of 'Polish aggression'. When a key was pressed, electric bulbs affixed to a map of the frontier zone lit up and enabled the beholder to see at a glance the series of recent events on the frontier. Heydrich freely commented on these demonstrations, saying, 'Ah, yes! That's why war began.' No one was fooled.

NOTES TO CHAPTER 13

1. Otto Ulitz was appointed ministerial councillor to the chief of the administration service of Kattowitz in October 1939; decorated on October 18th with the gold badge of honour of the National Socialist Party. After the war, secretary of the Refugees Association of Upper Silesia, in West Germany.

2. Helmut Kordts, N.S.D.A.P. card No. 4 040 308 and S.S. card No. 174 902.

3. Born in 1891, Otto Rasch was a Sub-Lieutenant in the Navy during the First World War. He pursued his studies in law, philosophy and political economy (Doctor of Law and of Political Economy) and became a lawyer in Leipzig. Member of the N.S.D.A.P. in 1932 he entered the S.S. and the S.D. in 1933. Councillor to Ministry of the Interior, he became chief of the Gestapo at Frankfurt-am-Main, then in Upper Austria, in Prague and at Koenigsberg. From May to October 1941 he commanded an extermination group in the East (*Einsatzgruppe C*) but had a terrible clash with Himmler. Until the end of the war he directed the *Kontinentale Oel AG* in Berlin. Captured by the Allies and sent to Nuremberg to be tried as a war criminal, he fell gravely ill of Parkinson's disease and was not sentenced.

4. *T.M.I.* Vol. IV (249–251) and Doc. PS. 2751 (U.S.A.–482). Cf. also *T.M.I.* Vols I (541–543), II (447), III (17, 138, 246), X (534).

5. Not the 26th, as Schellenberg writes in his Memoirs.

14

The Intelligence Service Foiled

The Blitzkrieg conducted by Hitler and his generals against Poland was a masterpiece of strategy and tactics. The White Plan was systematically applied. Every day the German wireless broadcast victory bulletins.

All the leaders of the Third Reich, Hitler the first of them, followed in the wake of the triumphant Wehrmacht in its irresistible advance. Only Heydrich stayed in Berlin. His presence on the Polish front was not indispensable: he had attached Walter Schellenberg to Himmler and so was in constant touch with the Reichsführer S.S.'s special train. In the capital Heydrich, with Professor Franz A. Six, was preparing the realisation of his vast project: to gather in his own hands the personal control of all departments of the police, of security and Intelligence, except for the Abwehr. Himmler had raised no objections. He only saw in it an enlargement of his powers as head of the S.S. for the Reich and of the German police. In reality the new project would give Heydrich, and Heydrich alone, a power comparable to no other.

During September 1939 Heydrich and Six settled various administrative problems, still pending, and for which it would be necessary to gain Hitler's approval. It took three weeks. Finally on September 27th the Führer signed the decree creating a Directorate General of Security for the Reich (*Reichssicherheitshauptamt. R.S.H.A.*) and placing Reinhard Heydrich at its head under the authority of Reichsführer S.S. Heinrich Himmler. The central office of the R.S.H.A. was installed in Berlin, at 8 Prinz Albrechtstrasse, the premises occupied hitherto by the Gestapo alone.[1] For the first time Heydrich appeared in the eyes of the German public as one of the leaders of the Third Reich.

Within the framework of this organisation, as part of the Gestapo (Amt IV), a counter-espionage section was created (IV E). The direction of it was given to Walter Schellenberg, raised to Colonel

S.S. In collaboration with Dr. Best he was to centralise the work of counter-espionage, political as well as military. What did it matter to Heydrich that the field of military counter-espionage was reserved to the Abwehr? Schellenberg explained to me how his chief set out the position for him: 'Let's have a clear understanding. Your work of counter-espionage must not be limited to the civilian field. We're at war. We're making total war. There is no longer a frontier between civil and military. Everything is everything. If necessary don't hesitate to confront, to compete with these gentlemen of the Abwehr. Don't worry, sooner or later we'll have their skins and occupy the house opposite.'

Theoretically Schellenberg was subordinate to Heinrich Müller. In reality he was independent of him. His chief was Dr. Best, direct assistant to Heydrich. There is no need to stress that this situation scarcely pleased 'Müller-Gestapo'. But he had to put up with it as best he could. Not only was Schellenberg now his equal in rank—they were both S.S. Colonels—but particularly because within the R.S.H.A. he passed for 'Heydrich's factotum': everyone knew that in the upper regions of the S.S. he enjoyed the open approval of Himmler, who called him 'my Benjamin'. If Müller hid his feelings so as not to offend either Heydrich or Himmler, he never failed to 'strew banana skins' in the way of his so-called subordinate.

So Schellenberg assumed charge of counter-espionage, but it was not his only task. He told me, 'I constantly received orders directly from Heydrich or Himmler. They entrusted me with special missions both in the field of counter-espionage and of espionage abroad. It often happened that I worked fifteen or seventeen hours a day.'

In mid-October, 1939, he was given a really special mission.

On the 17th he returned to Berlin. He had just completed a tour of inspection in the Ruhr, and at Dortmund had unmasked several spies working for England. He reported to Heydrich, emphasising how incompetent were the various agents of S.S. counter-espionage installed in an area of such vital importance to the Third Reich.

'You will have the chance to change all that,' said Heydrich, 'but before you get busy on it I've another job for you. For several months one of our agents in the Low Countries, a deserter from the Czech Intelligence which took refuge in London, has been in contact with the British secret service to which he has supplied false information impossible to check and other authentic intelligence, which could be. By transmitting the good political *Spielmaterial* he has patiently, painfully, won the confidence of the Intelligence Service.

At the same time he has created a network of personal informers and even several contacts with the French Deuxième Bureau, always thanks to his former Czech employers.'

'Is this agent a Czech?'

'No. He is a former German policeman from Hamburg by the name of Mörz who sometimes calls himself "Michelson", sometimes "Fischer". He has been a member of the Strasser brothers' Black Front. Escaping to Switzerland after the Night of the Long Knives, Mörz–Michelson showed great activity and rendered numerous services to the Czechs.'

'But how did he come to the S.D.?'

'The automobile racing champion Mahr, a former Czechoslovak officer cashiered for fraud, recruited by the S.D. under the name of Geullert, was sent to find Mörz–Michelson after the entry of our troops into Prague. We knew that Mörz–Michelson knew the fate waiting for him: a court and a firing squad. He loved life and his wife too much not to offer us his services, which he did. I saw him personally. Agreement was quickly reached. In the S.D. he is registered as F.479. At the beginning of the summer I sent him to the Netherlands to renew contact with his former Czech employers.'

'Does the old Czech Deuxième Bureau operate in the Netherlands?'

'Yes, in connection with the Intelligence Service.'

'And F.479 has renewed contact with his old employers?'

'Not exactly. He has made contact with two important agents of the English secret service in the Netherlands, Major Stevens and Captain Best. They have allowed themselves to become rapidly convinced of Mörz–Michelson's desire again to work against Germany. They informed the office of the Czech Intelligence Service in London without delay. The Czech Major Bartik came to Holland expressly at the beginning of September to meet Mörz–Michelson. The interview took place near the Hague, at Scheveningen. Bartik, while acknowledging the past services of our F.479, seemed markedly distrustful. He sensed a trap and broke off contact. Best and Stevens didn't understand. F.479 had already supplied them with very good and interesting information and they had complete confidence in him. They went him to London about three weeks ago for another meeting with Major Bartik. The latter had not overcome his distrust and the interview proved abortive.'[2]

After a short silence Heydrich continued, 'Meantime one of our young agents whom you know, Dr. Helmut Knochen,[3] was likewise in contact with Best and Stevens. He claimed to have links with a powerful group opposed to National Socialism within the Wehrmacht. This information, as you may well imagine, greatly interested the two Englishmen.'

'Were Knochen and Mörz–Michelson in contact?'

'Yes, and the Englishmen knew it. Mörz–Michelson returned from London to the Netherlands, then made a short stay in Germany last week. Back in The Hague, he told Best and Stevens that he was the bearer of important news. Captain Schämmel, of the O.K.W. Transport Service, representing a group of high officers of the Wehrmacht who wanted to get rid of Adolf Hitler and take over the government of Germany, wanted to get in touch with the English Government.'

'It's a fantastic story!' exclaimed Schellenberg.

'No doubt. But what's important is that Best and Stevens swallowed the bait. They indicated to F.479 their desire to know who the leaders of the opposition were and if they were sufficiently strong to succeed. Captain Schämmel is due to meet them shortly in the Netherlands.'

Schellenberg took the liberty of interrupting his chief. 'But who is this Captain Schämmel? Does he work for us?'

Heydrich fixed a cold stare on his interlocutor. 'Captain Schämmel is no other than S.S. Colonel Walter Schellenberg.'

Now a glimmer of joy lit Heydrich's peculiar gaze. Schellenberg opened his mouth, then shut it again. His eyes were round with surprise. He was used to the bizarre ideas of the head of the S.S. secret service, but this time he was speechless. Heydrich plainly enjoyed his effect. Then, after a period of silence he resumed, 'The moment has come for us to decide whether to continue this game or stop it and be satisfied with what we have already learned through Knochen and Mörz. I won't hide from you that I suspect a real conspiracy by the Wehrmacht generals. They must be more or less in contact with the British. I think that through Best and Stevens we can take advantage of it. Finally, I have the feeling that you are the man best fitted for this important and delicate matter. I want you to examine all the documents at once; you will thus be able to form an opinion and submit your suggestions to me.'[4]

What historians call 'The Venlo Affair' began. It would cause much ink to flow. The story would often be told. It would always be the same, based on the memoirs of the three principal protagonists, Stevens, Schellenberg and Naujocks, without fear of contradiction, however flagrant, omissions deliberate or not, and, particularly, without illuminating the deeper motives. I should have fallen into the same trap had I not had the luck to receive from Schellenberg a version which is not exactly that given in his Memoirs. We have seen in other matters that it was quite often the case. This version engaged my attention and awoke my distrust several years after Schellenberg's death. An American researcher, a friend of mine, discovered at Coblenz, Schellenberg's written reports to Heydrich and a note on the whole affair addressed by the latter to Himmler. He communicated them to me. The story Schellenberg told me was confirmed. It is this version, with a few corrections of details, that I give here. I hasten to add, at the risk of disappointing, that nevertheless in my view all the light has not yet been cast. In this astonishing story many mysteries remain.

To return to October 17th 1939. After his meeting with Heydrich, Schellenberg set to work at once. For two days he studied documents. He was quickly gripped. To the young S.S. leader of twenty-nine the 'game' was fascinating. On entering the S.D. five years earlier he had not anticipated that he would one day participate in so thrilling an adventure, in the tradition of the great affairs of the world of espionage. The 'game' obviously entailed a large element of risk, but this was inevitable in secret service activity. Schellenberg soaked himself in the dossier to obtain a perfect acquaintance with the business, remembering all the details of the fictitious conspiracy, everybody's name and his relations with the rest of the world, all the information the S.D. possessed about the British agents he was to meet. In the dossier passed to him by Heydrich there was also a precise and detailed report on the real Captain Schämmel—envoy on a protracted mission to Poland—his antecedents, his manner of life, his appearance and comportment. He wore a monocle and Schellenberg had to do likewise, 'which was not without difficulties, since I am near-sighted in the right eye' he told me. The more he fitted himself exactly into the part, the greater was his knowledge of the opposition group, the more he had a chance to win the confidence of the Englishmen, since the smallest error would at once arouse their suspicions. But Schellenberg was a great actor. He felt himself up to sustaining the part.

On October 19th, accompanied by S.S. Lieutenant-Colonel Bernhard Christensen who took the name of Second Lieutenant Grosch, Schellenberg arrived in Düsseldorf where the S.D. had a house equipped with everything necessary for the headquarters of a secret service. It was outwardly a *pension* with several bedrooms, a kitchen, a sitting room, a large dining room, offices comfortably furnished, a wireless—studio, tape recorders concealed almost everywhere, photographic material, a small laboratory and a direct telephone line to the headquarters of the S.D. in Berlin. A teleprinter was in course of being installed.

On October 20th at 6 p.m. a message reached him. 'Meeting arranged for the 21st at Zutphen, Netherlands. A black Buick will await you on the Issel bridge along the Emmerich–Zutphen road.' In the evening to his great surprise he received a telegram from Berlin. It was from Heydrich and read: 'I have received full authorisation from the Führer to let you conduct the negotiation in your own way. You have complete liberty of movement. I advise you to be very prudent. It would be too stupid if anything happened to you. But in case of the business going wrong I have alerted all the frontier posts. Call me immediately on your return.'

This mark of solicitude surprised Schellenberg a little. At the same time he realised that it was not so much humanity on Heydrich's part as purely practical considerations.

In his Memoirs Schellenberg describes this first journey exactly as he described it to me in Italy. 'With S.S. Lieutenant-Colonel Bernhard Christensen I checked our passports and car papers for the last time (the German customs officers and police at the frontier had orders not to ask us indiscreet questions). We had very little luggage, and took particular care that our clothes and linen bore no marks which could betray our identity. Neglect of such details sometimes leads to the failure of the best laid plans.

'Early on the morning of October 21st we drove towards the Dutch frontier. It was dark and rainy. My companion did the driving whilst I sat next to him lost in my thoughts. I could not keep myself from feeling uneasy, especially because I had had no chance to talk with F.479, and the feeling grew in proportion as we drew nearer the frontier.

'The German formalities were quickly completed. The Dutch, on the other hand, were more tiresome, insisting on a thorough inspection. However we passed without too much trouble.

'When we arrived at Zutphen a large Buick was waiting for us as arranged. The man at the wheel introduced himself as Captain Best of the Intelligence Service. After a brief exchange of courtesies I sat down next to him and we started. My companion followed in my car.

'Captain Best, who incidentally also wore a monocle, spoke

excellent German and friendly relations were quickly established between us. The interest we both took in music—Captain Best seems to have been a very good violinist—helped break the ice. After a short time I told myself that I was forgetting the object of my journey. But, though affecting the greatest calm, it was with a terrible inward flutter that I awaited the Captain's overtures on the subject we were to discuss. He did not seem in the least desirous of broaching the matter before our arrival at Arnhem, where his colleagues, Major Stevens and Lieutenant Coppens, were to join us. When we arrived they got into our car which at once set off again. The discussion was pursued while the Buick travelled through the Dutch countryside.

'They regarded me, without apparent reservations, as the representative of an opposition group within the highest circles of the German army. I told them that the head of this group was a German general whose name I could not divulge at this stage of the negotiations. Our aim was to overthrow Hitler by force and instal a new regime. I intended during this conversation to find out what would be the attitude of the British Government to a government controlled by the German army and to know if it would be disposed to conclude a secret treaty with our group, which would lead to a treaty of peace once we were in power.

'The British officers declared that His Majesty's Government took a great interest in our attempt which would contribute powerfully to prevent the spread of the War. It would look with favour on the overthrow of Hitler and his whole regime. Furthermore these gentlemen offered us their aid and support. As for engagements and political agreements, they were not for the moment authorised to discuss them. Nevertheless, if it were possible for the head of our group or another general to take part in our next meeting they thought they would be in a position to make a statement binding the British Government further. They assured me that they were in direct contact with the Foreign Office and Downing Street.

'It was certain that I had won their confidence. We agreed to resume our conversations on October 30th at the central office of the Intelligence Service in The Hague. After lunching together we parted on the best of terms. The return journey passed without incident.'

On his arrival in Düsseldorf, Schellenberg telephoned Berlin to announce his return. Heydrich ordered him to come at once to make his report. The two S.S. chiefs had a conversation which lasted late into the night. Schellenberg received *carte blanche* for the future conduct of the negotiations as well as the choice of suitable collaborators. Heydrich said to him, 'Our game is more credible than would appear. The Führer considers the only way of overcoming the French and the English, if hostilities must be carried on, is to attack, not to rest on the defensive behind the Siegfried line. By means of a lightning offensive with overwhelming force, our troops will launch an attack across Holland, Belgium and Luxembourg on a front so wide that the French and the English will never succeed in forming a sufficient line of defence, and will be annihilated. "Any offensive", says the Führer, "which does not aim primarily at the destruction of the enemy forces makes no sense and only ends in a useless waste of lives". That seems obvious to me. But it's not the opinion of those gentlemen on the General Staff. They are pessimistic and put the maximum restraint on the Führer's decisions. They say that the Wehrmacht is not yet up to confronting the British and French armies. Guderian, Hoepner and von Reichenau think that a motorised attack at this time of the year will be bogged down in the mud on the roads and in the fields. Kesselring, Student and Sperrle reckon that the November fogs will greatly impede the air protection indispensable for an operation on such a scale. These gentlemen grumble, pare down. Their defeatism is plain. I am having their remarks recorded. One never knows. However none of this merits even remotely a charge of high treason. We can congratulate ourselves. This defeatist atmosphere must be perceptible to the enemy's agents. I am convinced that in London they must think that all the dissatisfied are conspiring. It's grist to our . . . Dutch mill, dust in the eyes of those gentlemen Best and Stevens.'

Heydrich's analysis was nearer the truth than he himself suspected. Best and Stevens's reports regarding 'Captain Schämmels' approaches' reached London the evening of October 21st, only a few days after Philip Conwell-Evans sent Theodore Kordt in Berne extracts from Chamberlain's speech of October 12th, adding that his words should be taken as a solemn promise to any regime which should succeed in overthrowing Hitler. What more natural, then, than this prompt response by Schämmel, 'spokesman for the conspiracy', to Chamberlain's undertaking, than this desire on the part of the conspirators to know in detail the intentions of the British Prime Minister? It was the most natural thing in the world. The English were perhaps guilty of a little haste and naïveté but, after all, was not the 'Zossen Putsch' with Halder, Beck, Canaris and the civilian conspirators, actually being prepared? Had it not been decided on in principle for November 11th?

There was in this whole affair an extraordinary combination of circumstances founded uniquely on deductions and outside any knowledge of the real concordance of the two actions. Schellenberg agreed about this with a smile during our talks.

During the following days Schellenberg perfected his plans. At that period he had the habit of spending most of his free time with his best friend, Professor Max von Crinis of the University of Berlin, director of the psychiatric department of the Charité hospital. An Austrian, born in Graz, he was a man of refinement and dignity, extremely intelligent and cultured, a colonel in the Medical Corps of the Wehrmacht and in the S.S. One morning Schellenberg and von Crinis went for a ride on horseback. Fresh air clears the mind. Schellenberg had a sudden inspiration. He spoke to his friend of the operation in Holland and asked him if he would like to come along to the Hague. He would present him to the Englishmen as the right hand of the head of our opposition group to Hitler. Von Crinis was amused, then persuaded. He accepted. The same evening Heydrich gave his consent.

On October 29th, Schellenberg, Christensen and von Crinis left Berlin for Düsseldorf, where they spent the night. The new 'conspirator' assumed the identity of a certain 'Colonel Martini'.

'Von Crinis and I,' wrote Schellenberg in his memoirs, 'agreed on a system of signs whereby we could communicate with each other during the discussion with the Englishmen. If I removed my monocle with my left hand, that meant that he would immediately stop talking and leave me to pursue the conversation. If with the right hand, that I needed his support. The sign of an immediate breaking off of the conversation would be my having a migraine.

'Before leaving I carefully checked my friend's luggage. This time we passed the frontier without the slightest difficulty. At Arnhem we went to the crossroads where we were to meet the Englishmen. When we arrived they were not there. We waited in vain for half an hour, then three-quarters. Nervously we paced the street. Von Crinis, who was not used to such hitches, was obviously the most nervous of the three of us and I tried to calm him.

'Suddenly we saw two Dutch policemen slowly approaching our car. One asked in Dutch what we were doing there.

'"Waiting for friends," answered Christensen. The policeman shook his head, got into our car and ordered us to drive him to the police station. To all appearances we had fallen into a trap. The important thing was to keep calm and in control of ourselves. At the station we were treated very politely. The policemen searched us from top to toe. Von Crinis's toilet-case, for instance, was examined with greatest care. Whilst they were thus engaged I quickly inspected our luggage since I had just remembered that, being very busy in Düsseldorf, I had not checked Christensen's. His toilet case was open on a table beside me and I noticed with apprehension that it contained a tube of aspirin in the current wrapping used by *S.S. Sanitas Hauptamt.* (S.S. Medical Service). I pushed my own luggage nearer the toilet-case and succeeded in hiding from sight the dangerous wrapping. A long interrogation followed. I said that we refused to answer anything whatever before we had seen a lawyer. The discussion lasted an hour and a half. At that moment Lieutenant Coppens came in. He showed the policeman several papers and their attitude at once changed. They let us go with apologies.

'On leaving the station we saw Best and Stevens in their Buick. They explained that it all arose out of an unfortunate mistake. They had waited for us at another crossroads, they claimed, and subsequently lost a good deal of time in looking for us. They apologised several times, but of course I understood that the whole scene had been staged by them, using our arrest, search and interrogation the better to verify our identities and obtain satisfactory reassurances about us. I foresaw that we were not at the end of our troubles.

'We reached The Hague at a good speed and entered a large room, Major Stevens's office. The conversation began and Captain Best did most of the talking. After a detailed discussion in depth we reached agreement on the following points:

'The political overthrow of Hitler and his chief colleagues to be followed by the immediate conclusion of peace with the Western Powers. It would provide for the restoration of Austria, Czechoslovakia and Poland to their previous status, Germany's abandonment of her economic policy and her return to the gold standard. The return to Germany of the Colonies she possessed before the First World War was one of the most important topics of our discussions. This point had always interested me and I returned to it over and over again. I emphasised the importance to the whole world of this safety valve for Germany's surplus population: without it German compression between her eastern and western frontiers would inevitably continue to constitute an element of danger in central Europe.

'In the end we set down the results attained in the form of an aide-mémoire. Major Stevens went to the telephone to inform London of the conclusions we had reached. He returned after half an hour to say that London's reaction had been favourable but that the accord had still to be discussed with Lord Halifax, the Foreign Minister. It would be seen to at once and we could count on a categorical decision in the course of the evening. Simultaneously a formal agreement from us was indispensable, it would represent a final and absolute decision of the German opposition and would likewise include a time-limit.

'These discussions had lasted nearly three and a half hours. At the end I had a migraine, mainly because I had smoked too many strong English cigarettes. While Major Stevens was talking to London, I went to freshen my face in the washroom. Absently I ran the water over my wrists when suddenly Captain Best came in without my noticing and murmured in a low voice behind me, "Tell me, do you always wear a monocle?"

'Luckily he could not see my face, for I felt myself blushing. After a second or two I collected myself and answered calmly, "Odd, I was going to put the same question to you."

'We then went by car to the villa of a Dutchman, an associate of Best's, where three comfortable rooms were ready for us. After a short rest we changed since we were invited to dine at Best's.

'Best's wife, daughter of the Dutch General van Rees, was a painter. She was a most agreeable conversationalist. Stevens arrived late. He took me aside to tell me that he had received an affirmative answer from London: it was a success!

'Our agent F.479 was also invited and I was able to have a few minutes' conversation with him apart. He was very nervous, enduring the tension with difficulty. I tried to reassure him and told him that if he found a pretext to return to Germany I would do my best to facilitate things with the authorities in Berlin.

'The meal was excellent. Never had I tasted such succulent oysters. Best, at dessert, made a short speech full of humour. Von Crinis responded with all his Viennese charm. After dinner the general conversation became very interesting, and gave me a clearer insight into the English attitude to the War. They had not gone into it lightly and would fight to the end. If the Wehrmacht succeeded in invading their island they would continue the struggle from Canada. We also talked about music and painting, and it was very late when we returned to our villa.

'In the morning I saw von Crinis for a few moments in the bath-room. He was radiant and said to me in his purest Viennese dialect, "Well, well, the chaps are rather eager to press on, aren't they?"

'They served us a copious Dutch breakfast; at nine a car came to take us to a short final meeting at the offices of a Dutch firm which served as a cover for the British secret service (the *N.V. Handels Dienst Veer Het Continent*, Bank of Continental Commerce) at Nieuw Vitleg 15. They gave us an English transmitting and receiving set, also a special code with which we could maintain contact with the offices of the English secret service at The Hague; the call number was O-N-4. Lieutenant Coppens handed us credentials asking the Dutch authorities to facilitate any call from us to a secret telephone number at The Hague; 556.331. After having agreed to set by radio the date and place of our next meeting, Captain Best accompanied us to the frontier, which we passed without difficulty.'

The three S.S. men did not stop at Düsseldorf. From Emmerich they reached Duisburg, then the motorway leading to Berlin. The next day Schellenberg made his report to Heydrich, suggesting to him that they follow up the negotiations with the object of getting to London. The answer was not encouraging. 'All this seems to me a little too good to be true. I find it hard to believe that it's not a trap. Be very careful going to London. Before making a decision I shall have to talk not only with the Reichsführer but more particularly with the Führer. Wait for my orders before proceeding.'

Schellenberg's twenty-nine years accommodated themselves with difficulty to such prudence. He returned to Düsseldorf with von Crinis and Christensen. They were in daily contact with the Englishmen by means of O-N-4 which functioned perfectly. Three times in the course of the week the Englishmen asked to fix the date for the next meeting.

On November 6th, Schellenberg had not yet received any directive from Berlin. He began to believe that contact with the Englishmen might be lost. He decided to go ahead. On his own initiative he agreed to a meeting on November 7th and fixed the meeting place at a café—the Café Backhus near the frontier, between Kaldenkirchen and Venlo on the Meuse.

If Heydrich showed a certain distrust, Colonel Alois Frank, of the Czech Deuxième Bureau, who divided his time between Holland and England, was also mistrustful. Speaking of his recollections, he said, 'The officers of the Intelligence Service, Major Stevens and Captain

Best, had an excellent network in Holland and good agents working for them. From time to time I met Stevens; at the beginning of my stay in Holland he helped me a good deal. At the beginning of November he telephoned me to make an appointment. We agreed to meet at a café in Leyden. He told me that he had a tremendous "job" in hand with the Germans from which he expected a great deal. He couldn't say more, but suggested seeing me again in two or three days to give me the details. The third day he telephoned me. We met in an old café in Utrecht. After a few minutes he said, "I have received an extraordinary offer from Germany. We have arranged by agreement a place for a meeting between high German officers and official British representatives. The meeting will take place tomorrow evening, at the frontier near Venlo. It's a matter of an actual cessation of hostilities between Germany and England. What do you think of it, Frank?" he asked me, his face lighting up with pleasure. What he had confided to me made me realise that it was not a problem entirely within the competence of a secret service. I remember answering him, "Major, I don't like this business at all. It seems to me that you have made a big mistake in fixing your rendezvous at the frontier. You yourself, being the responsible head here, could have personally determined the place. I think that for such talks a suitable spot would have been a commercial city like Utrecht. So send your men to the frontier to bring your opposite numbers back here. If it is still possible to change your instructions, don't go to Venlo, nor Best either. Wait for your company here in Utrecht." Stevens seemed a little embarrassed, but soon recovered his serenity when telling me the whole operation was well laid on from the Intelligence point of view. Security would be assured by a Lieutenant in the Dutch army, an officer in their Intelligence service.'

We have to admit that Colonel Frank was right. Major Stevens gave proof of an astonishing naïveté which augured badly for what was to follow. One need not be surprised at the 'levity' of the man who at this time was the 'big boss' of the Intelligence Service in Holland, a vital post in its secret war with Germany. There was an effort to make us believe, before and after the Second World War, that the Intelligence Service had always been the ablest organism by far in penetrating, infecting and blinding the different German secret services and to counter Hitler's formidable policy of subversion. It is a myth. In reality we could demonstrate it by numerous examples but that would take us too far. The Intelligence Service in 1939 was in a bad way. It was no longer the great service it had been.

It reflected English political weakness (which was perhaps worse than the French). The drop in national sentiment was general and the recruitment for the Service was not up to the demands of the situation. Churchill's cracks of the whip to engage England in the war fortunately transformed this deplorable condition. Chiefs like Major Felix Cawgill, Brigadier Dudley Clarke and Sir Claude Dansey, called Uncle Claude, would do magnificent work from 1940 to 1945.

We return to Major R. H. Stevens, who was to let himself be hoodwinked like a child fallen into the hands of brigands. After the war he tried to justify himself when writing his memoirs, but passed over in silence the friendly warning of Alois Frank.[5] When the latter gave testimony in his turn Stevens disputed it. He declared that he had never met nor had dealings of any kind with anybody answering to the name of Major Bartik. 'Such persons', he said, 'were absolutely unknown to me'. He swore, on the other hand, that he never divulged to anybody whatsoever any detail concerning the Venlo negotiations except to his superiors in London and to the Dutch authorities. Strange behaviour. We leave it at that.

On November 7th, Schellenberg again met Best and Stevens in the Café Backhus near Venlo. Since he had not yet received any directive from Berlin he explained that the 'opposition general' could not yet, unfortunately, disengage himself from his duties in Berlin. The three men decided that Schellenberg should make every effort to bring the head of the German opposition to a meeting on November 8th, that is, the next day, in the same cafe.

Schellenberg returned to Düsseldorf and addressed an urgent appeal to Heydrich, observing that without a decision one way or the other his position would become precarious. Heydrich answered that the Führer still hesitated to send a bogus general 'of the opposition' to London, and he would even 'be more inclined to break off the negotiations'. Heydrich added, 'He thinks that we have already gone far enough. He plainly dislikes any allusion to the subject of his overthrow, even a fictitious one. The Führer is leaving for Munich for the anniversary of the putsch of 1923 and asked me to await his return, on November 9th, before making a decision. Manage as best you can till then, my dear Schellenberg, but no imprudence.'

That same November 7th, in Berlin. Ten weeks had elapsed since Operation Himmler and the attack on Gleiwitz radio station. Alfred

Naujocks had two weeks' leave, passed two weeks in Dellbrück-strasse where the S.D. continued to fabricate forgeries of every description, then a week in a school of espionage near Hanover to discuss current technical problems. He had just returned to the capital. Once more he was summoned by Heydrich. Once more Naujocks augured nothing good from this new interview. He was only half wrong. Heydrich brought him up to date on an incredible story: the one that Schellenberg was now directing.

Heydrich did not hide his uneasiness: 'Schellenberg telephoned me a little while ago from Düsseldorf to tell me that his English interlocutors proposed that he accompany his "general" to London, where final discussions at the highest level would take place with the British Government. A special 'plane would be chartered which would bring them on the 8th or 9th from the Dutch airport of Schiphol. I was afraid lest Schellenberg should be carried away too soon by his enthusiasm. If he were arrested in London we should all pass for imbeciles, and the price to be paid would be high. However, he is responsible for this business and has a free hand. I want above all to be sure that nothing happens to him in Holland at the next meeting. It is important and I have the feeling that if anything goes wrong it will be then. I want you to protect him. Take a dozen men, whom you will of course choose yourself and post them at the frontier where they will serve any useful purpose. I advise you to "retrieve" F.479 and Dr. Helmut Knochen, who are in danger of soon being "grilled" in the Netherlands; they can be useful to you. You will act as circumstances dictate. If you feel that something isn't right, take the necessary steps at once. The meeting with the Englishmen will take place in a café near Venlo on the Meuse. Settle the details with Schellenberg.'

I have several good reasons for thinking that Heydrich's fears were not only of this sort. Distrustful by nature, he must have suspected Schellenberg of playing a quite personal game. He must have been puzzled by the desire the latter had shown to accompany the 'opposition' general to London. What was he hatching? That November 7th, in instructing Naujocks to go and 'protect' Schellenberg—we notice that the latter was running exactly the same risks as at the earlier meetings—Heydrich was in fact sending a supervisor, a strong-arm man who could if necessary bring his S.D. colleague to order. Schellenberg was not deceived and received Naujocks very coolly. That being so, Heydrich's suspicions were not, perhaps, baseless. I have the conviction that Schellenberg had not told the whole truth about his meetings with Best and Stevens: neither in his reports to Heydrich nor in his Memoirs nor during my talks with him in Italy. The way in which he was treated by the English from 1945 on gives me to suppose that it was a kind of compensation for some important service rendered in October–November 1939. But I may be wrong.

Schellenberg in Düsseldorf felt powerless and frustrated. The game excited him more and more, so much so that he decided to go ahead with it without waiting for the green light from Berlin. He got in contact with The Hague by radio and confirmed the appointment for the next day. He still had no idea what he would say to the Englishmen and realised that he might put himself into a tricky position. If he again aroused their suspicions he risked being arrested by the Dutch, and the whole affair ending in a most unpleasant way for him. But he decided to go ahead. He was furious with his superiors while knowing that they did not lack good reasons to justify their hesitations.

Schellenberg relates in his Memoirs: 'I passed a sleepless night, all sorts of thoughts and projects turning round confusedly in my mind. While having my breakfast I glanced at the morning papers. Large headlines announced that the King of the Belgians and the Queen of Holland had made a joint offer of intercession with a view to bringing the belligerents to negotiate. I heaved a sigh of relief; it was a solution to the immediate problem before me, I would merely say to the English agents that the German opposition had decided to await the Führer's reaction to the Dutch–Belgian proposals. I would add that illness prevented the leader of the opposition from being present at today's meeting but that he would probably come the next day, November 9th, and would probably wish to go to London just the same.

'In the morning I had a talk with the man I had chosen for the role of general, head of our opposition group. He was an industrialist holding, as officer of the reserve, a high rank in the army, a leader of the S.S. admirably adapted to the part.

'In the afternoon I again crossed the frontier. This time I waited nearly three-quarters of an hour at the café. I noticed that I was closely observed by several persons who sought to pass themselves off as harmless civilians. It was clear that the Englishmen were again distrustful.

'They finally arrived. The meeting was short and I was spared the trouble of presenting the situation to them as I had planned that

morning. Their suspicions seemed entirely dispersed and we parted
with renewed cordiality.'

In the evening, at Düsseldorf, Naujocks presented himself and
explained to Schellenberg the task Heydrich had assigned him.
Schellenberg didn't like it and exclaimed (he told me): 'I don't need
a nurse. I've told Heydrich many times that the Englishmen have
swallowed the bait whole. You and your men can only complicate
things.'

Naujocks improved matters by stating that Heydrich was thinking
of the improbable, that the S.S. secret service could not run the
shadow of a risk of losing (he allowed it be understood) so important
a personage. His colleague retained a feeling of unease but was
softened. After all, it wasn't given to everybody, in fact, to have a
dozen picked men from the S.S. as a bodyguard. The two then
discussed what measures to take if the Dutch tried anything.

Schellenberg had dinner with von Crinis, Christensen and the
industrialist who was to play the part of the head of the opposition.
They went over the whole project down to the smallest details and
retired late. Schellenberg took a sleeping pill to avoid another
sleepless night.

At 3.30 on the night of November 8th/9th the distant ringing of
the telephone awoke Schellenberg. It was Berlin on the direct line.
Here is Schellenberg's account: 'Heavy with sleep I picked up the
receiver and with bad grace growled, "Hello". At the other end of
the wire I heard a sober voice in which a quiver was discernible ask
"What's that you say?"

'"Nothing for the moment," I answered. "Who's speaking?"

'The reply came, cutting, "This is Reichsführer S.S. Heinrich
Himmler. Is that you at last?"

'Caught between my emotion and my sleepiness, I stammered the
customary "Yes, sir."

'"Then listen," Himmler went on. "Do you know what's
happened?"

'"No, sir."

'"Well, this evening, just after the Führer's speech in the beer
hall, an attempt was made to kill him. A bomb exploded. Luckily he
had just left. Several old Party comrades were killed and the damage
is considerable. There is no doubt that the British secret service
instigated the attempt. The Führer was already in his train when the
news arrived. He now says—and it's an order—that tomorrow, when
you meet the British agents, you are to arrest them immediately and

bring them to Germany. That may mean a violation of the Dutch frontier but the Führer says that is of no consequence. The S.S. detachment appointed for your protection—which, parenthetically, you certainly didn't deserve after the arbitrary and obstinate way you've been behaving—this detachment will help you accomplish your mission. Do you understand?"

'"Yes, Reichsführer, but—"

'"There aren't any buts," Himmler cut in drily, "You are simply carrying out an order from the Führer. Do you understand now?"

'"Yes, sir," I replied, realising it would be futile to try to discuss it.

'So I found myself in an entirely new situation. There was nothing left but to forget all my plans.

'I immediately awoke the leader of the S.S. special detachment [Naujocks] and told him of the Führer's orders. He and his second in command [Baer] received them with a certain scepticism, saying this plan seemed very difficult to carry out. The ground was certainly not favourable for such an operation, and for several days the frontier in the Venlo sector had been so crammed with Dutch frontier guards and agents of the secret police that it would be hardly possible to escape without a fusillade. And when gunpowder began to speak no one could know how and when it would stop. Only the element of surprise might weigh in our favour. If we waited for the British agents to join me in the café it would be too late. The moment to act would be that of the Buick's arrival. Our agents [Naujocks and Baer] had carefully studied the Buick the evening before and were sure to recognise it at once. At the Englishmen's arrival the S.S. men would dash full speed over the frontier, nab the Englishmen in the street and push them quickly into one of our cars. The driver of the S.S. car was an expert at driving in reverse; he would therefore not have to make a U-turn, which would give the S.S. a wider field of fire. At the same time men would advance from both sides of the street to cover the flanks during withdrawal.

'The S.S. men thought it preferable that I should personally not take part in the affair but only wait for the Englishmen in the café. When I saw their Buick approaching I would go out as if to greet them. Then I would get into my own car and make off at once.

'This plan seemed good and I agreed to it. However, I asked to be introduced to the dozen members of the special detachment so that they should be able to recognise me. Captain Best, though slightly taller, had practically the same figure as mine, a similar coat and also wore a monocle. I wanted to be sure that no mistake should occur.'

November 9th was cold and misty. Clouds loaded with an icy rain which would only fall in the late afternoon darkened the sky. When his alarm clock rang at 7.30 Naujocks got up with reluctance. After his nocturnal talk with Schellenberg he had only slept three hours. He rang and ordered coffee. To complete the make-up of the S.D. 'pension' at Düsseldorf two maids and a cook had been installed by the S.S. The girl who brought him his breakfast was very sprightly. This cheered him up a bit but he soon recovered his ill-humour: the beverage was cold. He then remembered his conversation of the night with Schellenberg and his fears returned. 'I bet something will go wrong,' he thought bitterly. Going to the wash-basin he banged his toe against a leg of the bed. While shaving, he nicked his chin. 'It's starting well,' he said aloud. When giving his instructions curtly and sharply to his dozen men, his bad temper was not allayed. No one dared address a word to him.

Before lunch Schellenberg had the twelve introduced to him and spoke with each of them 'so that they would easily recognise him'. A little before 1 p.m. he left Düsseldorf with Christensen and the 'general of the conspiracy'. Thirty-five minutes later they traversed Kaldenkirchen and reached the German customs office where the 'general' remained under cover to await events. Schellenberg and Christensen proceeded to the Café Backhus. We allow Schellenberg to testify again: 'At the café we ordered aperitifs. The room was crowded and the traffic in the street abnormal, many cyclists and people of strange aspect wearing civilian clothes and accompanied by police dogs. This time, it seemed, our English friends had taken special security precautions in honour of this reunion.

'I must acknowledge that I was very nervous, especially as time passed without our partners turning up. I began to wonder if they were keeping a trick up their sleeves as they had at Arnhem. It was after three, we had been waiting more than an hour. Suddenly I started; a grey car was approaching at speed. I wanted to go out but my companion held me by the sleeve: "It's not the car," he said. I was afraid for an instant lest Naujocks make the same mistake, but all remained quiet.

'I had hardly taken the first sip of a very strong coffee I had ordered—it was 3.20—when Christensen said, "Here they are". We got up. I told the barman that our friends had arrived . . . and we went out, leaving our overcoats in the café.'

Above Heydrich and Naujocks. (*Bundesarchiv Koblenz—Ullstein*)
Below Gleiwitz radio station.

Above left Major Best. *Above right* Major Stevens.
Below Venlo frontier post today.

Naujocks and his S.S. men left Düsseldorf in two cars about three-quarters of an hour after Schellenberg and his friends. At something like fifty metres from the German frontier post Naujocks had the cars stop and went along to the concrete building astride the roadway. He showed his mission order to the old customs officer and gave him his instructions. The barrier was slowly raised while Naujocks had his two cars drawn up behind the building out of sight of the Dutch. The S.S. men and their leader began their wait, keeping their eyes fixed on Dutch territory, on the Café Backhus.

All was peaceful. A little girl, her head enveloped in a black scarf, crossed the road. A shopkeeper was smoking a pipe before his door. An old Renault with French plates stopped a moment at the Dutch frontier post, its occupants looking towards Germany but at a sign from the guard at once left. Here and there, however, various signs worried Naujocks. Many questionable-looking people, groups of policemen near a concrete casemate encircled by coils of rusty barbed wire. Not far from there teams of workmen and soldiers were constructing anti-tank barriers. The sentries all carried sub-machine guns on their shoulders.

Naujocks glanced at the clouds: it was not yet raining. He must lower the hood of the car which was to cross the frontier and it would be disagreeable if the sky were to open its sluice-gates at that precise moment. With the help of one of his men he drew up the hood, which was rolled back. He looked at his watch—3.10. He gave a signal. The six S.S. men in the second car came to rejoin the others on the seats, their legs pressed together so that sub-machine guns should be ready to be grasped when the moment came. The six new S.S. men grouped themselves three on each side of the car, each with a foot on the footboard. Like this they resembled a sequence from a gangster film shot in Chicago.

The minutes passed slowly. Best and Stevens should already have been there some while. Suddenly a large grey car arrived making for the café. Naujocks took his seat next to his driver, Jansch. The engine was started. But it was not the expected Buick. Naujocks relaxed and glanced at his watch—3.17. What were they doing?

Naujocks had reckoned that he would need less than a minute to reach the café. The two Englishmen's car had to take a curve before arriving and, its occupants would be unable to see the 'reception committee' waiting for them on the German side before they were directly in front of the café's door.

It was 3.20. A long, low Buick came round the bend at high speed. It was they. Naujocks shouted savagely, 'Let's go!'

The car leaped forward—Jansch, the driver, had let in the clutch roughly. The six S.S. men who embellished the footboards had to hang on with all their might. The Dutch barrier was broken to bits. The petrified guards did not react. One of the S.S. men on the footboard fired a shot in the air. Naujocks discharged a volley of oaths at him. The Englishmen's Buick had reached the parking space near the café. Jansch's foot shifted from the accelerator to the brake. He had calculated the distance well and the big Ford was swallowed up in the parking lot, jammed in just behind the Buick.

Even before the car stopped the S.S. men were out. At the exact moment when Naujocks leaped to the ground the windscreen flew into splinters. It was Coppens who, realising the danger, had fired. He had a large military revolver in his hand and now aimed at Schellenberg. Entirely unarmed the latter jumped aside, trying to present a target as small as possible. He was to write, 'An eternity seemed to pass before anything happened. Suddenly I saw the form of the S.S. leader get out of the car. He also had drawn his revolver and a veritable duel began between Coppens and him. Having had no time to move I found myself between them. Both fired calmly, taking careful aim. Then Coppens slowly lowered his weapon and sagged to his knees. I heard Naujocks call to me, "Get out of there, dammit! I wonder you weren't hit."

'I ran round the corner of the house. Looking back, I saw Best and Stevens pulled out of the Buick by the S.S. like trusses of hay.

'Hardly had I turned the corner when I found myself face to face with a gigantic S.S. subaltern who, not having seen me before, grabbed me by the arm and shoved a huge revolver under my nose. Plainly he took me for Best. I later learned that, against my express orders, a detachment had been added at the last minute. I pushed him violently away, crying, "Don't be an idiot. Put that pistol away."

'Nervous and excited, he wouldn't listen. I struggled with him, trying to push him aside, while he continued to threaten me with his revolver. But in the same second as he pressed the trigger a blow on his right hand deflected the weapon. The bullet missed my head by barely two inches. I owed my life to the S.S. second in command who, realising what was happening, had intervened just in time.

'I did not wait for other explanations but leaped into my car, where Christensen was waiting for me, leaving the S.S. detachment to terminate the operation. Each was to return to Düsseldorf on his own as quickly as possible.'

Whilst Schellenberg and Christensen made off, Best, Stevens and their Dutch driver, Jan Lemmens, were pushed into the S.S. Ford. Coppens, who was lying in his own blood, was picked up and also taken away: the lightning raid was over.

The car made for Germany. Jansch, the driver, had the accelerator pressed to the floor. The road was black with people: civilians, soldiers, policemen. It was a strangely silent crowd. Cries were raised of 'Brigands! Murderers!' but the car had already reached the German frontier post. The old officer said to Naujocks in a low voice, 'It seems to me there's going to be trouble. Couldn't you relieve us of your men, I beg of you? We're in a rather vulnerable position, you see.'

Naujocks agreed. When leaving he was joined by his second in command, Baer, who said, 'We've made another prisoner. His name is Jan Lemmens. He's Dutch and drove the Englishmen's car.'

'Good. Get everybody in the cars. We're leaving for Düsseldorf.'

Naujocks and Baer made their report to Schellenberg after having taken the wounded man to the Düsseldorf prison hospital. Baer said, 'It appears from Lieutenant Coppens's papers that he's not English but an officer of the Dutch General Staff and that his real name is Dirk Klop. He is, unfortunately, seriously wounded. The doctors are seeing to him.'

Naujocks added, 'I'm sorry to have had to fire at Coppens–Klop, but he fired first. It was a question of his life or mine. It turns out that I'm the better shot.'

Lieutenant Dirk Klop died in the night of his wounds. Best, Stevens and their driver, Lemmens, were taken to Berlin by the S.S. men commanded by Baer.

Schellenberg, Naujocks, Christensen and von Crinis remained in Düsseldorf for the night. Before dinner, having changed, they had a drink at the Grand Hotel and attentively read the newspapers, all of which carried the headline: 'Attempt on Führer's Life in Munich.'

On November 10th the four S.S. chiefs returned to Berlin. Schellenberg was dissatisfied with the outcome of the Venlo incident and had the feeling that it would have been infinitely preferable to pursue the conversations as he had desired. He said so to Heydrich who didn't listen. What interested Heydrich was to prove that Best and Stevens were involved in the attempt on Hitler. The central office of the Security Service (R.S.H.A.) resembled a hornet's nest into which a fork has been thrust. The entire machinery of the Gestapo and Criminal Police had been set in motion; all telegraph and telephone communications for any other matters than those connected with the attempt were blocked. Hitler wanted to know who had caused the carnage in the Munich beer cellar. It was an 'order from the Führer'.

NOTES TO CHAPTER 14

1. See Appendix I, *The Structure of the R.S.H.A.*, with explanatory diagrams.
2. After the war R. H. Stevens always denied having contact in the Netherlands with an individual (F.479) claiming to be a former Czech agent. Major Bartik (today a General) has on the contrary supported the Heydrich–Schellenberg version in his memoirs.
3. From 1940 to 1944 Dr. Helmut Knochen was supreme head of the S.D. in France and assistant to S.S. General Karl Oberg.
4. Personal testimony of Walter Schellenberg. The day of England's entry into war, September 3rd 1939, three special trains left Berlin for the Polish territories conquered in some sixty hours. The first train was Hitler's, with him Generals Keitel and Jodl and the whole General Staff of the Wehrmacht. The second was Marshal Goering's and his staff's. The third was Himmler's, which carried, in addition to the Reichsführer S.S.'s staff, the Minister for Foreign Affairs Ribbentrop, and the Secretary of the Reich Chancellery Dr. Lammers. Walter Schellenberg, detached by Heydrich for service with Himmler was in the third train. He was to settle urgent questions relating to the S.S. secret service, see to couriers and assure the most rapid communication by messenger, radio and telegraph between the special trains as well as with Heydrich in Berlin. He remained in the train a month and definitely won Himmler's confidence and sympathy.
5. Payne Best, *The Venlo Incident*. There has since been found a report addressed to Heydrich on March 27th 1942, under the number 432–41 gRs. III, by Otto Geschke, Gestapo chief in Prague, citing the *Komplex Stevens–Best* to establish the presence in the Low Countries in October 1939 of agents of the Czechoslovak secret service in exile, amongst them Alois Frank, Major Bartik and Paul Thümmel (agent A-54), all of them in permanent contact with Best and Stevens. The latter explicitly denied these allegations, it is hard to say why. Captain Best could not be questioned since he died before the discovery of these documents.

15

Carnage in the Beer Hall:
The Attempt Against Hitler

It was nearly ten at night. In his house at Zehlendorf in Berlin, the chief of the Criminal Police, Arthur Nebe, finished his dinner. This Wednesday, November 8th 1939, had been a full day for him. Once again he returned late and felt tired. Suddenly the telephone ringing startled him. At the end of the wire he heard the distracted voice of Reinhard Heydrich bluntly announcing that an attempt on the Führer's life had just been made in Munich, at the *Bürgerbräu* beer hall. There were many dead and wounded lying under the debris, but Hitler was safe and sound: he had left the room fifteen minutes before the explosion. Nebe was surprised for he had never heard so much emotion in his superior's voice. Heydrich explained that he had not yet been able to contact Himmler but had alerted the railway station at Nuremberg. It was the first stop of the Munich–Berlin train in which Himmler was travelling with Hitler and his suite. Heydrich expected thus to be in communication with the Reichs-führer S.S. in a few minutes. Meantime he ordered Nebe to set up a special commission of enquiry that very night and to leave for Munich by air at dawn.

To return to 'the distraught voice of Heydrich'. It was H. B. Gisevius who produced the vital testimony of Nebe. One of the keys to the strange affair of the carnage in the Munich beer hall is perhaps to be found there.

In the 'plane which on the morning of November 9th flew to Munich, Heydrich, 'his expression malicious', congratulated Nebe: by order of the Führer the enquiry had been entrusted to the head of the Criminal Police and not to the chief of the Gestapo, Heinrich Müller.

Nebe himself did not altogether appreciate this confidential mission. He was not displeased to show off his Criminal Police and demonstrate the inefficiency of the Gestapo's barbarous methods but he knew only too well that Heydrich and Müller would seek means to take revenge. Why had the Führer designated him, Nebe? It concerned a political matter which thus fell within the competence of the Gestapo. Did Hitler distrust it? The situation seemed highly dangerous. However, Nebe consoled himself. If Hitler demanded an objective enquiry, it tended to prove that, this time at least, it was not a matter of a radio-controlled machinations, and the enquiry could be carried out on solid ground. This mood of Nebe's did not last long. Through a window he watched the clouds which hid the earth. His habitual pessimism regained the upper hand. Might it not all the same be a clever propaganda move, organised by the Nazis themselves, as he had suspected since Heydrich's telephone call? No, Heydrich's voice had been 'distraught'. Yet might not a search for the guilty within the Party itself be indicated? Amongst the S.A. for instance? For some time unverified rumours had suggested that the veterans of the Party were not happy about the German–Soviet pact. But no, it was impossible. Hitler assassinated by his own Household Guard? Come on! The year 1939 had been an unbroken series of successes for Hitler: Czechoslovakia wiped off the map without a shot fired; the Pact of Steel with Italy; the pact with Stalin which assured peace in the East; the liquidation of Poland in less than a month . . .

The draconian measures enacted by the regime rendered a terrorist action organised by the Communists more than improbable; it would be logical to seek the authors of the crime in opposition circles within the army. Nebe was kept informed by Gisevius of the friction that existed in headquarters at Zossen between the partisans of a putsch, those favouring assassination and the simple 'wait and see' men. Perhaps this attempt should be attributed to a group of young officers of the General Staff who, tired of the hesitations of their argumentative superiors, had taken the initiative. Nebe's confusion was great. He believed in the possibility of a terrorist action by an isolated group. And what if his enquiry should lead sooner or later, directly or indirectly, to the people closest to Admiral Canaris—the circle whose most representative element, its most active and anti-Nazi, was no other than Nebe's friend Colonel Oster? This time anguish gripped the chief of the Criminal Police: he was much better informed about various subversive machinations than he liked. He saw again the malignant expression on Heydrich's face before the take-off. He would not miss any chance. His reflections veered towards certainty: sooner or later the enquiry would uncover a military conspiracy, the links with Canaris's Abwehr and those of Nebe with the Abwehr. The pessimist already saw himself and all his friends in the cellars of the Gestapo.

On arrival in Munich Nebe's first care was to consolidate his role in the enquiry so that he could not be dislodged from it. He was entrusted with it 'by order of the Führer', he acted 'by order of the Führer'. He organised two groups of investigators despite the unforthcoming attitude of Heydrich. He led the first, which was to determine the circumstances of the crime. The most important thing, it seemed to him, was to find the trails and, if that were necessary and possible, to muddy them. The head of the Gestapo, Heinrich Müller, was to discover the author or authors of the crime, following the results of the investigation by Nebe's group, and by means of denunciations, anonymous or otherwise. A reward of six hundred thousand marks would recompense anyone responsible for the criminals' arrest.

When Nebe entered the beer hall he was astonished at the bomb's ravages. There was nothing but broken beams, ceilings fallen in, walls burst open, tables and chairs splintered, windows and doors torn out. There was blood everywhere. If Hitler had still been there, thought Nebe, they wouldn't even have found his moustache. It was a massacre: seven dead and sixty-three injured.

The chief of the Criminal Police knew that the security of the reunion had been assigned to the S.S. under the direction of Christian Weber, and not to the Munich prefecture of police.

We have the testimony of the Prefect of Police of the period, Friedrich Karl, Baron von Eberstein, who after the war told Lucien Corosi:[1] 'On November 8th I went in person to the *Bürgerbräu* to check whether any security measure had been overlooked. I was stopped by an S.S. man of Hitler's bodyguard who refused to let me in. "I am the Prefect of Police," I said. He answered, "That's no concern of mine. The supervision of the *Bürgerbräukeller* for to-morrow's meeting is in the hands of the *Leibstandarte S.S. Adolf Hitler*. Apply to Lieutenant-Colonel S.S. Christian Weber." The latter confirmed that I had no business there. I exclaimed, "Do you realise the responsibility you're assuming? I shall refer the matter to Reichsführer S.S. Himmler." Weber said with a snicker, "You can refer to God himself. It's a matter between the Führer and me." I saw Himmler who said, "Mind your own business. Christian Weber has full powers." I went home and drew up a memorandum of these conversations of which I sent a copy to Himmler, another to Weber and kept one for myself.'

The precaution was not useless. Baron von Eberstein in fact said, 'The Gestapo's first care on the morrow of the explosion was to come and arrest me. Was I not the Prefect of Police of Munich, responsible for the safety of persons of note in my city? To the man allotted this duty I handed the copy of my letters to Himmler and Weber. Perplexed, he asked for instructions from his superiors, Himmler, particularly, who could only exonerate me completely. Christian Weber rendered me a great service in claiming the supervision of the *Bürgerbräukeller*, since if I had had undertaken the safety of the meeting (which would have been normal) there is every reason to believe that my men would not have discovered the presence of the infernal machine in the hall either . . . The result would have been my being sent straight into a concentration camp.'

In the beer hall Arthur Nebe had the S.S. chief Christian Weber explain to him what had happened.

On the evening of November 8th, the anniversary of the Munich putsch of 1923, the arrest of the future Führer and the death of the first National Socialist 'martyrs', three thousand Nazi enthusiasts filled the large hall of the *Bürgerbräukeller*, where in the 'heroic' period the first meetings of the faithful were held. Invariably each year it was Hitler who pronounced the customary discourse, generally long—an hour and a half to two hours—and violent, both to pay homage to the victims and to threaten with his thunderbolts the internal and external enemies of the regime. Since 1933 the commemoration had become official; to attend it was no longer a duty but a privilege, an honour.

A little before eight the Führer's arrival was greeted by frenzied applause and a prolonged ovation. The enthusiasm showed on all faces. Only Hitler seemed preoccupied, nervous and tired. He went up to the rostrum. Silence fell. It was exactly eight minutes past eight when he began to speak.[2]

'I have come to pass a few hours amongst you,' he said, 'to revive in your company the memory of a day which for us, for the movement, and in consequence for the whole German people has been of the highest importance. It was a grave decision I then had to take and put into execution. Its apparent failure in reality ended in the birth of the great National-Socialist movement. In fact it was from the development resulting from this failure that sprang the marvellous evolution which allowed us to enter the lists in the full blaze of publicity for the defence of our ideas and aims, to assume responsibility for them and so to initiate the great mass of our people into harmony with them . . .'

It was 8.45. Hitler had been speaking for thirty-seven minutes when an S.S. man put a note on the speaker's table as he was saying '. . . Today I confine myself to giving you the assurance that our adversaries will be utterly unable to subjugate us either militarily or economically. There can be only one victor, namely ourselves.'

Whilst the hall was showing approval of this tirade by resounding applause Hitler read the message.[3] He resumed, 'We are perfectly aware of the support Providence has given us. Without it this work could not have been accomplished in so short a time. Also we believe that Providence willed what has occurred . . . In the course of countless centuries and even millennia [sic] millions and millions of Germans have given their lives for their people. Millions of others have spilled their blood. And none of us knows if this may not one day be our destiny. . . .'

It was 8.57. Hitler quickly ended his speech: 'I cannot close this evening without thanking you, as always, for your faithful devotion during these long years nor without promising that we shall continue to exalt in the future our traditional ideas, to vow ourselves to them and not hesitate, if circumstances so require, to sacrifice our lives for the realisation of the programme of our Movement, which only aims to assure in this world the life and existence of our people. It is the first article of our profession of National Socialist faith and will also be the last, the one that will be engraved on the memory of every National Socialist when, having fulfilled this task, he quits this world.

'Comrades of the Party! Long live our National Socialist movement, long live our German people and, now especially, long live our victorious army!'

It was 8.58. Hitler had only spoken for fifty minutes. Contrary to his habit, he did not tarry to chat with his old friends, with the families of the victims of 1923. He said short goodbyes while shaking a few hands and left the hall at nine minutes past nine. At that precise moment the waitress Maria Strobl looked at the clock and went to clear the table of the 'old friends' Hess, Lutze, Lammers and Schaub.

Hitler and his suite reached the station at 9.24. They were in the train's lounge-car three minutes later. The regular train 71 left for Berlin at 9.31. In the *Bürgerbräukeller* most of those present, a little disappointed, hurried to the cloakroom. The hall practically emptied in a few minutes. A few Party members remained chatting amongst themselves, the employees, waiters and waitresses, about ten S.S. men and policemen.

At 9.20 a terrific explosion shook the beer hall. The room was ravaged. The infernal machine, extraordinarily powerful, had burst within a few metres of where Hitler had been standing for his speech. Eleven minutes earlier it would have mangled the Führer and some fifty high Nazi dignitaries. In the stupor, horror and confusion no one thought of informing Hitler at the station before the train's departure.

One of Hitler's secretaries testified, 'I was with the Führer in the train which took us back to Berlin on the evening in question. He was witty and very animated, as always after a successful meeting. With us was also Goebbels who enlivened the conversation with his caustic wit. At this time the Führer's entourage was still allowed to drink alcohol, with the result that the whole carriage was suffused with an atmosphere of gaiety. The train stopped at Nuremberg for a few minutes to permit the receiving and sending of some urgent messages. This task was allotted to Goebbels. When he returned to the Führer's saloon car he told the latter what had happened at Munich after their departure. Hitler, incredulous, did not take it in at first but finally, at sight of Goebbels's haggard look, took it seriously. When there was no further doubt about the authenticity of the news, the Führer's expression froze into a hard, stubborn mask. In his look flickered the mystical flame which I knew at the moment of great decisions. In a peremptory voice harsh with emotion he exclaimed, "Now I am completely reassured; the fact of having left the *Bürgerbräukeller* sooner than usual is the confirmation that Providence wants my destiny to be fulfilled." We were nailed to our seats by emotion. These words acted on us like the culmination of a hallucinating drama. But Hitler quickly recovered his spirits and passed on to action. He asked for news of the injured and instructed Schaub, his aide-de-camp, to see to the victims. Then Hitler expressed certain hypotheses on the possible origins of the conspiracy. Schaub, who had drunk a good deal, drew the Führer's thunderbolts on himself by an unseemly remark he made during the discussion. Hitler simply ordered him out. It is needless to add that till Berlin the atmosphere in the carriage remained stormy.'

Hitler later explained to this secretary the reason for his leaving the *Bürgerbräukeller* earlier than expected: 'Suddenly I felt within me an imperative need to cut this meeting short, to return to Berlin the same evening. At bottom there was no urgent reason, there being nothing of importance waiting for me there; but I hearkened to the inner voice that was to save me. If I had, as usual, greeted my early comrades, as I had at first meant to do, my enemies would undoubtedly have succeeded in doing away with me.'

This was the official version circulated by Goebbels: 'The inner voice . . . Providence. . . .' Only, Hitler lied.

We have three important witnesses. First, General Hans Baur, pilot of Hitler's personal 'plane. 'On November 8th 1939, we left for Munich for the traditional celebration of the anniversary of the events of 1923. A little after landing, the Führer asked me if it was possible to be back in Berlin on the 9th by ten in the morning, since he had an important appointment he could not put off. I couldn't give him an absolute assurance because of the fog, frequent in November, which might prevent our landing for several hours. Hitler then decided to return to Berlin by train.'

The second witness is Doris Mehner, attached to Himmler's secretariat:[4] 'The Reichsführer told me on November 8th round three in the afternoon that the meeting at the *Bürgerbräukeller* had been moved forward and would be shorter than expected. The Führer would not be returning to Berlin by 'plane but by train. A private carriage would be attached at eight in the evening to the regular train 71 for Berlin which left Munich at 9.31. The Führer desired that the train should leave at the scheduled time. Consequently I had to have Himmler's luggage and that of S.S. chiefs present transported at the hour stated. The Reichsführer S.S. added, "I prefer this solution. By train we are sure to arrive. By 'plane, with the November fogs. . . ."'

The third witness is Emmy Goering, who on that evening was in Berlin with her husband: 'The evening of November 8th 1939 my husband told me that a German living abroad under a false name had come to bring him sensational news. The man had to leave by train on the following morning and had to see Adolf Hitler before then. At that moment an aide-de-camp burst into the room to announce that a bomb had just exploded in the *Bürgerbräukeller*. There were dead and injured. I was astonished at my husband's calm when the aide-de-camp added, "What can have happened to the Führer?"

'"Nothing at all," answered Hermann. "He is at present on his way to Berlin."

'We looked at him, bewildered. My husband then explained that he had telephoned to the *Bürgerbräukeller* while the Führer was making his speech to order a note to be put on the table in front of him which said, "Hermann Goering asks the Führer to shorten his speech and to return to Berlin as anticipated by the quickest means possible. It is a matter of real importance."'

The mysterious German—not identified—did in fact leave Berlin by air at noon, after having talked with Hitler for more than an hour in Goering's presence.

While Nebe was listening to Weber's explanations in the beer hall his investigators set to work. In less than an hour of searching they found the elements of the infernal machine in the ruins. Nebe at once felt relieved. The bits of twisted brass, which were without doubt pieces of a detonator, as well as traces of powder at the point of the explosion, left no doubt of their origin: none of it came from a military arsenal. It was a primitive work, a tinkering, although correctly executed, by artisans using explosives employed in mines.

It remained for Nebe to reconstruct the machine, to analyse its elements minutely, to determine their origin and the place where the machines had been bought. It was only then that one could find the trail of the author or authors of the crime. It was only then that Müller could unleash his Gestapo bloodhounds.

Nebe's criminologists worked rapidly. By the afternoon they had collected a certain number of corroborative clues of the highest interest. They had succeeded in identifying the clockmaker who sold the alarm clock mechanism. The man had given a description of the buyer: a young man with a triangular face, wavy brown hair and thick eyebrows who spoke with a strong Swabian accent. A second clue: it was established that a young Swabian workman, of about thirty, had bought in Munich squares of cork of an uncommon type which had been used to affix the bomb and detonator to the interior of the pillar in the beer hall. A third clue: a locksmith by the name of Solleder had lent his workshop to a young Swabian so that he might perform various tasks concerning, he had said, an 'invention of the greatest interest'. A fourth clue: a young man, speaking in Swabian dialect, whose description corresponded with that given by the clockmaker, had for weeks been an habitué of the *Bürgerbräu*. He had been the lover of one of the waitresses killed in the explosion. She had even spoken for him when he had been surprised one night in October by a caretaker and the proprietor of the beer hall, Anton Payerl, in a washroom in the corridor. He had claimed he was there to dress a wound in his leg (he had in fact a large carbuncle) and had been shut in by an oversight.

All the clues were perfectly consistent and the police of Nebe's group began to make discreet enquiries of their colleagues of the Müller group. They wanted to know if a young man of Swabian origin was amongst the several hundred suspected persons under preventive arrest: employees of the beer hall, waiters and masons working nearby, to whom had to be added some forty Bavarian monarchists whom Heydrich had had imprisoned 'on the off-chance'. They did not have to look long. The Munich Criminal Counsellor, Franz Joseph Huber, learned from the Gestapo that a radio message had arrived in the morning sent from the frontier post of Lörrach. The message announced that a certain Georg Elser, aged thirty-six (he was born in 1903 at Hermaringen, in Württemberg, the heart of the Swabian country), a carpenter-cabinetmaker by trade, had been arrested on November 8th at 8.45 p.m. while trying to cross secretly into Switzerland. When, not an hour later, news of the explosion was received, Elser was suspected of having participated in the attempt because on arrest he was wearing, pinned to the back of his lapel, the badge of the former 'League of Red Front Fighters', and in one of his pockets had been found a fragment of a detonator for explosives as well as a post-card depicting the *Bürgerbräu* beer hall, on one of the pillars of which a red pencil had marked a cross.

Huber's first reaction, like Nebe's, was that, even for the Gestapo, all this was too lovely, too easy and too stupid. Elser's behaviour allowed only one interpretation: he wanted at all costs to be arrested. Again, doubt assailed Nebe: whether this Elser had fulfilled a role planned beforehand. Unless . . . Elser might be a sick man suffering from a mania for celebrity, a mania he had to satisfy at any price, even that of his life; the meaning of his strange conduct at the frontier would then have been to compel his arrest. The childish 'exhibits' he carried on him must constrain the police to accuse him of the attempt in Munich, which he had not committed but was usurping, in short, in order to be 'celebrated' . . . No! It was unthinkable. All the clues and testimonies showed that Elser was the author of the attempt. Then Nebe found himself before the twofold dilemma: had he acted alone or with accomplices? If there were accomplices were they anti-Nazis or were they on the contrary, Nazis?

The order to transfer Elser to Munich having been given, he arrived late in the afternoon of Friday, November 10th. Arthur Nebe at once proceeded to interrogate him. The chief of the Criminal Police, face to face with Elser, was much surprised. With his thin face, his wavy hair brushed back, his open, intelligent and alert expression, his delicate, nervous hands he did not at all give the impression of being a fanatic, still less that of a 'radio controlled' agent. From the fact that at the time of the explosion Elser was not in Munich, but in Constance, his alibi might appear valid. He claimed that he wanted to avoid military service. In any event, Nebe reflected, he totted up well: refusal to do military service, effort at an illicit crossing of the frontier, it was more than enough. At this first interrogation Nebe extracted no more from Elser. The latter denied all participation in the attempt. Nebe was puzzled. The exact reconstruction of the complicated crime had been accomplished. It showed that its author, or authors, needed intelligence, manual dexterity and at the same time political fanaticism. This did not seem to fit in with the personality of Georg Elser.

On Saturday, November 11th, Hitler came to Munich for the funeral of the victims and to visit the injured in hospital. He also went, with Himmler and Nebe, to the *Bürgerbräukeller* where he had Nebe explain all the details to him. The latter told Gisevius, 'The Führer seemed impressed by the minuteness and precision with which the rubble had been sorted and the fragments of the bomb laid out on a plan of the beer hall in order to determine the power of the infernal machine on the basis of the distance which separated them from the point of explosion. The twisted elements of the clockwork movement were attached to a cardboard with linen threads.

'Hitler examined with the keenest interest the pillar in which the machine had been installed. The pillars were split open, the beams which held the masonry broken. I watched my visitor. I said, "It is here that the largest part of the wreckage occurred, where you were standing eleven minutes before. Whoever was there was in danger of death." Nothing in the Führer's face suggested a premeditated attitude. On the contrary, he seemed upset and frightened and, while the members of his suite kept at a distance from the threatening pillars, Hitler came close up to them. Since that day I no longer share the opinion of those who think the Führer was a hysterical coward. Don't be under any illusion, that man was no poltroon, he merely didn't want to be assassinated. He might take cover like a ferocious animal, but he wasn't afraid and was always ready to hurl himself on his enemies.

'He questioned me. He wanted to know how much time would have been needed to place the bomb in the pillar—it really was a perfectly executed job. I answered that at least two hundred hours would have been necessary. Such preparations could not have been undertaken, Hitler judged, except by a very considerable group of conspirators. And he at once mentioned the followers of Otto Strasser, those of the Black Front who had gone abroad. He added that the operation had been financed by the English secret service.'

In answer to this last affirmation Nebe did not hide his scepticism: 'Would a secret service with vast resources at its disposal have used so primitive a device?'

Himmler was exasperated at this spirit of contradiction in his subordinates, while the Führer seemed to pay attention to the chief of the Criminal Police's arguments.

In Himmler's tortuous mind an idea was born. To disparage the criminologist Nebe's deductions he summoned to Munich an extra-lucid medium much in vogue in Vienna. He arrived during the night. At nine in the morning, in the office of the Munich prefect of police, Himmler assembled round the medium the principal investigators and their chiefs, Heinrich Müller and Arthur Nebe. The latter described the grotesque scene to his friend Gisevius. 'Going into a trance the medium writhed on the Prefect's sofa and promptly stammering and rolling his eyes, called out the name of "Otto" . . . He saw him . . . he spoke a foreign language with three smartly-dressed men . . . on the shore of a lake . . . He receives papers . . . there is a false passport . . . A false identity card . . . and also a plan . . . a plan marked with a cross . . .'

Himmler was deeply moved. He listened religiously while watching Nebe out of the corner of his eye. The latter suppressed as best he could his strong desire to laugh.

To make better contact with 'Otto' the medium suddenly asked for an object from the ruins of the beer hall. Nebe went out and quickly returned with a piece of metal. It was only a tool borrowed from a neighbouring room and not a bit of debris from the beer hall. The sight of the object released a torrent of words from the medium: 'Otto takes a train. . . . In the station he receives a bulky chest containing a mysterious object . . . two well-dressed men give it to him. . . .' The medium then claimed that the image had become blurred.

Himmler was disappointed, it showed in his face. The medium noticed it. At once he resumed his recital: he again saw 'Otto' on the night of November 7th/8th . . . this time he was in Munich . . . He recognised the streets, the avenues . . . 'Helped by two men, "Otto" climbs through a window of the *Bürgerbräu* beer hall . . .' The medium hears the sound of broken glass . . . then another noise of falling stones . . . suddenly the chest disappears into a wall . . . No, it's not a wall but a pillar of the beer hall. . . .'

Nebe pinched his lips to stop himself from remarking that on that night, the one before the crime, the beer hall was guarded by Weber's S.S. men who were patrolling inside and outside the beer hall.

Himmler was satisfied. He beamed. He fixed his eyes on Nebe as he commented on the extraordinary 'clairvoyance' which was 'so near the truth'. Despite what he thought Nebe declared himself in agreement with his superior, Heinrich Himmler, 'There are more things in heaven and earth than are dreamt of in your philosophy.'

What Nebe perfectly understood was that his chief, the Reichsführer, was either incurably credulous or unimaginably deceitful; that the 'medium' was a crook or an imbecile; that it was all utterly absurd and he had lost three hours of valuable time listening to twaddle.

The time was not lost for everybody. Himmler with his usual hypocrisy had ordered that during the séance Elser should be questioned by three officials of the Gestapo. Nebe only learned this in the evening when, having Heydrich on the telephone, he had to accept the ironical congratulations of his chief for 'having so quickly placed the author of the attempt at the disposition of the Gestapo'. In a few hours, in fact, the technicians of torture had obtained a complete confession from Elser.

This first confession and all the other interrogations of Elser as well as the details of the investigation conducted jointly by the Criminal Police and the Gestapo have been preserved. The reading of them is fascinating and enables a reconstruction to be made of the attempt.

Georg Elser confessed to the Gestapo officials that he had acted alone, to be revenged on Hitler for the arrest of his brother, a member of the Communist Party. His preparations had taken eighteen months. The Führer, he reasoned, was each year at the same time, November 8th, and for the same length of time, at the same place, the *Bürgerbräukeller*, to make a speech to his 'old comrades'. Elser therefore decided to place a bomb in the pillar nearest the spot where Hitler always spoke.

He first obtained employment as a labourer in a gunpowder

factory, the firm of Waldenmater, in Württemberg, where he stole a quantity of explosive and some shell-cases. Then he worked, still as a labourer, for the firm of Volmer, where he contrived to lay hands on a large number of cartridges of dynamite and detonators. At Easter 1939 he went to Munich and paid a visit to the *Bürgerbräu* several days in a row to familiarise himself with the place, the means of access and the habits of the personnel. Back in Württemberg he designed the plans for his infernal machine. At the beginning of summer, according to the testimony of his uncle Eugene, a violent explosion occurred in the latter's orchard. Georg Elser had been testing his explosives. When the uncle expressed surprise, the nephew explained that he was working on an invention.

On August 5th 1939, Georg Elser went to Munich carrying the powder, the dynamite and the detonators in a large valise. His first purchase consisted of two clocks of which he planned to use the movements for the mechanism of his delayed-action fuse. During the day he constructed his infernal machine. He used the workshop of a locksmith named Solleder; of a mechanic, Dreschsler, of a tool-maker, Niederhofer, and finally that of a carpenter named Brög. To all these artisans he repeated the same story: he was working on an invention. All testified that he was not talkative, gentle, a hard worker and very capable. His successive landladies, four in three months, congratulated themselves on a lodger so quiet that he never received a single visit. However, his two last landladies said they were surprised: he often came home late at night, sometimes even at dawn.

Georg Elser passed, in fact, laborious nights. According to the evidence of a waiter in the beer hall, Jakob Mayer, 'The young Swabian arrived at the *Bürgerbräukeller* between eight and ten for thirty-five consecutive evenings. He always carried a cheap black valise. Sometimes he ate a sauerkraut. Most often he took two sausages with a little cabbage. He always drank a small dark beer.'

Jakob Mayer took turns with a young waitress who came from Württemberg like Elser. According to Mayer the young customer and the waitress were quickly drawn to each other because both spoke the Swabian dialect. How far did their relationship go? Mayer didn't know. On this point Elser maintained a fierce silence. However that may be, each evening when closing time came Elser paid his bill and went to the toilets. There he waited till the lights were out. When silence prevailed in the beer hall he came out and went to the gallery which overlooked the hall to work on boring through the pillar in which he expected to place his bomb. He worked with extreme care to hollow out a cavity about eighty centimetres square. He wet his mortar in the washrooms and packed his debris in his old valise, then he left at night or sometimes at dawn, went to the Isar, crossed the bridge that straddled the river, turned right and after some fifty metres dumped the debris into the water.

Night after night he pursued his task. He was only surprised once, as we have said, by a caretaker and the proprietor of the beer hall, Anton Payerl. His story of the carbuncle on his leg aroused no suspicion in the two men.

On Friday, November 3rd, Elser installed his infernal machine. The next day he filled it with explosives and affixed his detonators. On the night between Sunday the 5th and Monday the 6th, he started the movement and adjusted the timing—the explosion was to take place on November 8th between 9.15 and 9.30—then he put back the wooden panel which concealed the cavity. He left the *Bürgerbräukeller* at six in the morning.

In the employment of his time between Monday, November 6th at 6 a.m. and Wednesday, November 8th at 8.45 p.m., the time of his arrest at the Swiss frontier, discrepancies are to be found in Elser's account. There are in fact two versions. According to the first he went to his native city, Hermaringen 'to pay a visit to a relative' or to see his Uncle Eugene, then on November 7th returned to Munich, to the *Bürgerbräukeller*, to 'check if the movement was functioning properly'. According to the second version he went directly to Constance with the intention of making a clandestine crossing of the frontier on the evening of November 6th but, anxious to know if his machine was functioning well, he returned to Munich on the 7th. In both versions he stated that he had left Munich on the morning of the 8th and gone directly to Constance by train.

He explained he had lived in Constance several years before and that he knew well a place where it was possible to reach Swiss soil without being noticed by the customs officers. 'What ruined me', he said, 'is that, passing not far from the German customs, I heard the voice of the Führer over the radio. It was a little later than 8.20. I knew that my bomb would only explode in about three-quarters of an hour and I wanted to hear what Hitler was saying. I went close up to the customs office, hiding in the shadow of some trees. I didn't see a customs officer who was walking silently in the night and took me by surprise.'

It was 8.45 when he entered the customs office. He was then taken to the office of the frontier police to have his identity checked and to explain the reason for the Communist badge on his coat-lapel. It was then that to his surprise he heard the end of Hitler's speech. It was only 8.58 on the clock in the police office. He then realised that his attempt had failed and shut himself into a stubborn silence.

Georg Elser further declared that he had intended to ask for political asylum in Switzerland. In order that his responsibility for the attempt should not be challenged he carried a badge of the former 'League of Combatants of the Red Front', some detonators similar to those he had used and a post-card of the *Bürgerbräu* beer hall on which he had marked a cross with a red pencil on the pillar where he had lodged his infernal machine.

In one of his interrogations Elser claimed that he had received the explosives from 'two anonymous visitors, a man and a woman', but no pressure could persuade him to give further details.

The enquiry proved that Georg Elser had never belonged to the Communist Party. In his youth he had played for his own pleasure in an orchestra formed of veterans of the Red Front, but already in 1933 he was no longer a member of it. He was neither Communist nor socialist nor anarchist. His political convictions are hard to define. According to Arthur Nebe, Elser, sprung from the people, quite simply loved mankind. He said with passion that war signified for the masses of all countries famine, misery and the death of millions of human beings. Elser was not a pacifist in the accepted sense. For him, more simply, Hitler signified war and he thought that after his disappearance peace would return.

When Nebe learned of Elser's confessions he still felt some doubts about the latter's personality. Nebe neither would nor could yet exclude the possibility of Elser's collaboration with a group of accomplices. The time so well chosen, the cavity so well concealed in the pillar, in the pillar of the gallery behind the Orator's table, the time needed to excavate a hole eighty centimetres square, the mechanism which was a veritable masterpiece and regulated with absolute precision to coincide with the customary duration of Hitler's speeches . . . No, so much intelligence, manual dexterity and at the same time political fanaticism seemed improbable to Nebe. He questioned Elser and believed the man incapable of acting alone.

It was in this state of mind that in response to a summons from Hitler, he presented himself at the Reich chancellery on November 14th. With surprise he heard Hitler declare that he himself would direct 'the co-ordination of the verifications of Elser's confessions', verifications which should have been effected by Nebe. The Chief of the Criminal Police stared at Hitler in surprise and exclaimed, 'But "co-ordinate" with what, with whom?'

Hitler smiled. Nebe no longer knew what to think, but he quickly learned what had been 'brewing' with the S.S.: the affair at Venlo, the kidnapping of the two officers of the Intelligence Service, Best and Stevens. This episode in the war of the secret services had taken on the character of a crime novel, and amazed and irritated Arthur Nebe. On the one hand he admitted the possibility of complicity between Elser and the Intelligence Service, but on the other he smelled a dark scheme entirely got up by the perfidious Heydrich. In the second case Nebe was not at all convinced that the relation be-tween the kidnapping of the English officers and the explosion in Munich could ever be proved. Nevertheless Nebe did not consider the search for possible accomplices as ended. He said so to Hitler, who agreed and conceded Nebe a week during which Elser would remain exclusively at his disposition. Nebe, on the other hand, did not obtain authorisation to interrogate the two English officers. 'The preliminary enquiry into the Best and Stevens affair is exclusively the business of the S.S. secret service,' said Hitler. Which was in part untrue.

The enquiry into the Venlo affair began on November 12th. Schellenberg had specially recommended that the two prisoners be subjected to interrogation by experts in counter-espionage 'with absolute correctness and humanity'. This was done. Unluckily Hitler had ordered that the reports on the day's interrogations be submitted to him every evening. From the first he became irritated. The two Englishmen denied any connection with Elser. They and Otto Strasser were the real organisers of the crime! They had to be made to speak. He summoned Heydrich and ordered him to include with the experts in counter-espionage 'Gestapo experts capable of making these mulish Englishmen talk'.

The results were nil. Hitler might multiply his instructions on 'the manner of conducting these interrogations' and give detailed orders on 'the way to handle the case', but nothing came of it. The two Englishmen refused to admit that the plot had been woven, by the Intelligence Service in collaboration with the chief of the Black Front, Otto Strasser. What did it matter! 'A great public trial which exposed the collusion', Hitler decided, 'would have the best effect.'

The exhaustive questioning of Best and Stevens had not yet

yielded the results looked for by Hitler, but the Venlo kidnapping nevertheless constituted in his eyes an important success for the S.S. secret service. And he decided to reward the authors. Walter Schellenberg was promoted to be a general (Brigadeführer S.S.). He was summoned to the Chancellery along with the special S.S. detachment commanded by Alfred Naujocks.

Schellenberg wrote: 'We entered the great courtyard of honour in military formation and remained at attention while an S.S. guard of honour fell into line in front of us. All this with the most solemn ceremony. We next entered the Chancellery. It was the first time I had been there. The furnishings were splendid, but I was even more impressed by the size of the rooms. We were conducted into Hitler's office: a large portrait of Bismarck hung over a door. Hitler came in, assuming a firm, imperious gait, and stood facing us as if to give us orders.

'He was at first content to look at us fixedly in silence, then he spoke: he was, he said, grateful for what we had done, both individually, and as a group. He was most particularly satisfied with our resolution, our initiative and our courage. The British secret services had a great tradition. Germany possessed nothing comparable, so each success signified a step towards the creation of a similar tradition. The traitors who were seeking to stab Germany in the back during the most decisive struggle in her history must be suppressed without pity. The deceit and perfidy of the British secret services were well known, but they would achieve nothing unless the Germans themselves were ready to betray the country.

'Recognising what we had achieved and starting with the premise that the secret front was as important as the struggle on the battlefield, he was going for the first time in its history to bestow decorations on members of the S.S. secret service.'

Four of the men from the special detachment, including Naujocks, Baer and Christensen, received the Iron Cross first class, all the others second class. Hitler presented them in person, shaking each man's hand and adding several words of congratulation. Then he moved away, again faced the group in a military attitude, raising his right arm. The ceremony was over. Schellenberg said later 'I admit that at the moment I was very impressed.'

The next morning, Monday November 20th, Nebe had to admit that he had failed in his search for Elser's possible accomplices. The period Hitler had allowed him was over. He had to pass the dossier over to his colleague Heinrich Müller. The Gestapo, which disposed of more 'effective' means than those of the bourgeois Criminal Police, rejoiced. Müller appeared triumphant. He even had Nebe sign a document affirming that he had not held back any exhibit or any record. Nebe complied while flinging at his colleague, 'If you think that you're sharper than I am and will discover a link between Elser and your two English officers, I'm willing to be hanged . . . In any case I wish you good hunting and good luck.'

A few hours later Schellenberg was in Müller's office. He was that same evening at nine to deliver a verbal report to Hitler on the Venlo affair. Heydrich asked him to go and talk to Müller first and obtain exact information on the results of the investigation of Elser so that he would be able to answer any questions Hitler put to him on the subject.

According to Schellenberg, 'Müller was very pale and seemed exhausted with overwork.' He only opposed feeble arguments when Schellenberg tried to convince him that to seek to establish a link between the two English officers and Elser was a great mistake. Finally he declared himself in agreement but added 'with a hopeless shrug of the shoulders: "After all, if Himmler and Heydrich don't succeed in changing the Führer's opinion on this point, you can hardly hope to have better success. You'll only burn your fingers."'

Schellenberg then asked, 'Who, according to you, is behind Elser?'

'I haven't been able to get anything out of him on that subject,' Müller replied. 'Sometimes he refuses to talk, sometimes he talks nonsense. And in the end he always comes back to what he said in the beginning, that he is the sole author of the attempt, although two unknown persons gave him the explosives.'

Müller remained in thought for a moment, then added, 'It is very likely that Otto Strasser and his Black Front are involved in it.'

With his left hand Müller massaged the red and swollen knuckles of his right. His lips were compressed and his small eyes had a wicked look in them. Then he said quietly but forcibly, 'No one has ever stood up to me but that I ended by breaking him.'

At nine Schellenberg was at the Chancellery. There he found Himmler and Heydrich, to whom he gave a brief synopsis of the report he had prepared for the Führer as well as of his conversation with Müller. He went over all the arguments against a propaganda trial involving at the same time Best, Stevens and Elser. Himmler and Heydrich's faces lengthened. They recognised that he was right, but did not know how to explain to the Führer. They plainly desired that Schellenberg go first and take his chance.

During the dinner, at which Rudolf Hess, Martin Bormann, Generals Keitel and Schmundt and several other important Nazis were also present, Hitler said to Himmler, 'Schellenberg doesn't think that the two British agents had anything to do with Elser.'

'Yes,' replied Himmler, 'there is no possibility of a link between them and Elser. But it could be that the Intelligence Service made contact with Elser through other channels. They could have used Germans, members of Otto Strasser's Black Front, for instance, but for the moment we're groping amongst hypotheses. Elser admits having been in contact with two unknown persons but we're totally ignorant if he had relations with any political group. It might have been Communists, British Intelligence agents or members of the Black Front. There is only one clue: our technicians are practically certain that the explosives and the apparatus for igniting the bomb are of foreign make.' [5]

Hitler remained silent a moment and finished his buttered corn-on-the-cob. Then he turned to Heydrich: 'That seems quite possible. But what I'd like to know is the type of criminal psychology we have to do with. I want you to have recourse to all possible means of making that man talk. Try hypnotism, give him drugs, use all that modern science has discovered in this field. I must know who were the instigators of this business.'

He was brought an enormous dish of Kaiserschmarren—a kind of Viennese pudding with raisins soaked in a very sweet sauce. 'Hitler ate hurriedly and without refinement,' Schellenberg remarked. 'He remained silent when eating.'

Towards the end of the meal Hitler suddenly asked Schellenberg, 'What was your general impression during the conversation you had with these Englishmen in Holland—I mean before their kidnapping and questioning?'

'My impression', said Schellenberg with all the conviction of his thirty years, 'was that Great Britain will fight this war with all the fury and tenacity of which she has given proof in all wars in which she was thoroughly engaged. Even if we succeeded in occupying England the Government and the leaders would conduct the war from Canada. It will be a life and death struggle between countries of the same stock—and Stalin will look on with interest and amusement.'

At this, Himmler, who was sitting between Hitler and Schellenberg, gave the latter such a kick on the shin that it stopped his breath. Across the table he shot him a withering look. But Schellenberg was launched and went on, 'I don't know, my Führer, if it was really necessary to change your policy towards Great Britain after the Godesberg agreement in September 1938.'

All the guests exchanged terrified looks. Heydrich paled to the roots of his hair while Himmler lowered his eyes, very embarrassed, playing nervously with his bread. Hitler regarded Schellenberg attentively for a few moments and waited a long while without speaking. It seemed interminable. Finally he said, 'I hope that you realise that it is necessary to consider Germany's position as a whole. At the beginning I wanted to collaborate with Great Britain. But she rejected all my advances. It is true that there is nothing worse than a family quarrel and, from a racial point of view, the English are in a way our relatives. So far you may be right. It is extremely regrettable that we are engaged in this struggle to the death whilst our real enemies, to the east, wait tranquilly for Europe to be exhausted. It is for that reason that I don't want to destroy England and will never destroy her. But they must be brought to understand, and Churchill first of all, that Germany has also the right to live. And I shall fight England till she gets off her pedestal. The day will come when she will show herself disposed to envisage an accord between us. That is my real aim. Do you understand?'

'Yes, my Führer,' replied Schellenberg, 'I follow your thought. But a war like this is comparable to an avalanche. And who would venture to plot the course of an avalanche?'

'My dear boy,' returned Hitler, 'those are my worries, leave them to me.'

After dinner, before going into the next room where large comfortable chairs were drawn up round the fireplace Himmler whispered to Schellenberg, 'You pig-headed fool! But the Führer took it well. He seemed amused.'

And Heydrich added, 'My dear fellow, I hadn't realised you were such an Anglophile. Is it the result of your contacts with Best and Stevens?'

Schellenberg felt that it was wiser not to answer. He had already gone as far as it was possible to go.

The next day, Tuesday November 21st, all the German papers published the results of the enquiry into the explosion on their first page. The Party daily, the *Völkischer Beobachter*, explained how the bomb had been placed and printed a photograph of Elser. In the next column the arrest of the British secret service agents was announced, and their photographs published. It was not stated that the two events were related, but to the uninformed reader that seemed to be implied. Best and Stevens appeared to be Elser's accomplices. The instigation of the Intelligence Service seemed most likely. German public opinion did not enquire too closely what extraordinary sources of information could have led the Intelligence Service to become involved in discussions as hazardous as those with the alleged rebel generals. Hence it was not too surprised when on Thursday, November 23rd, the newspapers splashed on their first page, 'Otto Strasser was the organiser of the odious crime in Munich'. The articles accused Strasser of having wanted earlier to divide the Party by his theories and then by founding the Black Front and setting up the black radio. They denounced his collusion with the Czechoslovak government of Benes and the Intelligence Service. They charged him with having already three times fomented plots on Hitler's life, in 1936, 1937 and 1938. The journalists went into details: 'His patrons in London urged him to resume his efforts. This time he sent into German territory the "criminal Elser". The night of November 8th/9th the latter was arrested trying to cross the Swiss frontier at Constance. Otto Strasser was waiting for him on the other side. He waited in vain until next day for the arrival of his accomplice. The latter has made a complete confession. Strasser returned to London empty-handed.'

Otto Strasser later said, 'It was a good serial story and nothing in it was true except that we really did try three times between 1936 and 1939 to get rid of the tyrant, but not in the circumstances described. So far as Elser's attempt is concerned we were unluckily in no way connected with it. But what surprised me the most at the time was the enormous free publicity given for over a week to the Black Front in the whole German press. All the details about my life and our work made us better known in a few days than all our underground activity of the years before.'

Georg Elser still did not talk of his relations with the Intelligence Service or Otto Strasser. The night of the 20th/21st and the morning of the 21st in conformity with the orders given by Hitler to Heydrich, three specialists in psychiatry worked on Elser. They gave him strong injections of pervertine but he did not change his testimony under the influence of drugs.

At the end of the morning of Tuesday, November 21st, Heydrich,

Müller and Schellenberg met in the offices of the Gestapo. Müller described the failure of the psychiatrists. He added, 'I have placed all the equipment of a carpenter's shop at Elser's disposal. He has already been at work and almost finished a reconstruction of his infernal machine. He has also made a wooden pillar identical with the one in which he hid his bomb.'

Heydrich showed interest and decided to pay Elser a visit. All three went up to the room where the young Swabian was being held. Schellenberg describes the scene: 'I saw the man for the first time . . . He was the type of highly qualified artisan and the work he was doing was in its way masterly. In the beginning he showed himself timid and reserved, rather fearful. He answered reluctantly, speaking with a strong Swabian accent and using the fewest possible words. It was only when we began to put questions to him about his work, praising its ingenuity and precision, that he emerged from his silence. Becoming animated, he described for us at length and with enthusiasm the problems involved in the construction of a bomb and how he had resolved them. He became so interesting that I nearly forgot the sinister purpose to which all this skill was applied. Questioned on the subject of his two "anonymous accomplices" he gave the same answers as before. He had never known with whom he had had to do. Heydrich remarked to him that conversations with strangers about explosives and firing mechanisms seemed really imprudent—hadn't he realised that? Without displaying the slightest anxiety Elser answered that there certainly had been a danger which he did not conceal from himself. From the day he had made up his mind to kill Hitler, he knew that it meant losing his life. He had felt certain of succeeding in his attempt by reason of the technical perfection of his preparations, which had taken him a year and a half.

'We exchanged looks, Müller was very excited, but a slight ironic smile hovered on Heydrich's lips. We left the room.'

On Wednesday, November 22nd, four of the best hypnotists in Germany tried to exercise their power on Elser. Only one succeeded. But even in a state of hypnosis he maintained his version of the facts.

Himmler showed his discontent with the results obtained. Before going to make his report to Hitler he said to Schellenberg in a tone which seemed to implore his help, 'This is not really the problem we are confronted with. Our job is to find the people at the back of this affair. The Führer will never believe that Elser was acting alone, and constantly insists on the need for a big propaganda trial.'

There never was a trial. Best, Stevens and Elser were sent to concentration camps. The two English officers were liberated in 1945 by the Allied armies. As for Elser . . . he continued to intrigue all those who studied his case.

In Admiral Canaris's Abwehr no one believed it to be the work of a lone individual: it was a plot hatched by the Nazis, doubtless by Heydrich, in which Elser had been the dupe. Some, without adducing proof, even declared that the infernal machine had been tested by the technicians of the Gestapo and that its system of igniting the charge ran no risk of going off unexpectedly for it was under 'remote control'.[6] It was explained that Hitler, 'more or less in the secret', cut his speech short through prudence or mistrust, which also explained his nervousness during the evening. A former member of the Abwehr told me that Colonel Oster, Canaris's right hand, said at this time, 'Emil [a nickname he had given Hitler] probably did not know that the whole thing had been prefabricated, simply that an attempt was made on his life and that the Gestapo would nip the plot at the last minute.' Certain former officers of the Abwehr whom I met during these last years thought the same.

It should be noted that this opinion is supported by a number of historians. These bring out that the 'miracle' enabled Hitler and Goebbels to rekindle the patriotic ardour of the Germans at a time when the hope of a compromise peace with England and France was shared by the majority of the people. The proof is insufficient. According to this hypothesis, can one imagine Hitler deliberately taking his place near the bomb, already triggered, which might very well explode ten or fifteen minutes too soon? On the other hand, without having 'engineered' the explosion Hitler and Goebbels had known very well how to 'take the ball on the bounce' and exploit the criminal attempt with their usual diabolic skill. But the proponents of the theory of a Nazi plot base their proofs on two testimonies, one that of Elser himself, the other that of a certain Kopnikov, former chief of section 1A of the Gestapo.

Elser's evidence has been assembled by several of his fellow-prisoners at Sachsenhausen (the English officer, Payne Best and the Czech journalist Nicolas Koyetski) as well as at Dachau (Pastor Niemöller and the S.S. guard Franz Lechner). According to this new version Elser affirmed that he had been manipulated despite himself by the S.S. secret service. According to his statements which are, it should be noticed, in flat contradiction not only with his first ones but especially with the evidence collected by Arthur Nebe and that produced since the war, Elser was arrested by Heydrich's men in a Communist round-up and sent to Dachau in the spring of 1939, where his talents as a craftsman were discovered.[7] Mysterious civilians offered him his liberty if he would perform certain work for them. Twice they took him to the *Bürgerbräu* in Munich by night when it was empty and ordered him to instal an explosive charge in one of the pillars of the big hall. The detonator was not activated by clockwork but by an electric circuit controlled from outside. The night of November 8th/9th they brought him near the Swiss frontier, where they gave him some money in Swiss and German currency and a postcard representing the Munich beer hall on which the pillar was marked by a cross. They explained to him that he would only have to show the card to the frontier police and they would let him pass. Things didn't go like that and he soon found himself in the grip of the Gestapo. This time they taught him a new role he must play: the version of a conspiracy with Best, Stevens and Otto Strasser. They explained to him that England would soon be defeated, as Poland had been, and when that time came he would be called to testify at the trial of the heads of the Intelligence Service, who were only a band of murderers and blackguards, as everyone knew. For his trouble he would after the war receive the sum of 50,000 marks.[8]

Kopnikov's testimony confirms that of Elser in the sense that this ex-director of the Gestapo told the British investigators after the war that the details of the crime had been prepared by Heydrich, Müller and himself.[9] He added 'Unknown to Hitler'. Kopnikov may have drawn Heydrich's attention to the fact that Hitler might be in danger if everything did not go off as planned. But Heydrich seemed in no way moved by the risk being run. I only record here the testimonies of Elser and Kopnikov because of the importance they have assumed in the eyes of many historians. But the dossier of the enquiry conducted at the same time by Nebe and Müller has since been found and, likewise since then, some evidence I have cited has been produced. Nor let us forget Heydrich's 'distraught voice' when telephoning to Nebe on November 8th a little before ten. These two last versions do not stand up to the most elementary examination, even at first sight. For different reasons Elser and Kopnikov lied, invented. They had excuses; Elser wanted to pass in the eyes of his fellow-prisoners for a victim of Heydrich's machinations and, particularly, for a Communist arrested by the Gestapo whom he tried to mystify. In a concentration camp to be classified as a Communist might very often save one's life. As for Kopnikov, a prisoner of the British, he wanted to concentrate the attention of the interrogators and make them forget some others of his criminal doings little or not at all known, which might bring him to the gallows.

Almost everything is now known of the material facts: there was no link between Elser and the men kidnapped at Venlo or even with Otto Strasser; Elser placed the bomb alone; it seems improbable that he was 'manipulated' by the S.S.; if machination there was it occurred *after* and not *before* the attempt had been organised. Elser really was 'a genius at tinkering' as described by Arthur Nebe and Walter Schellenberg. Nevertheless a mystery remains: the extraordinary fate of Elser.

Until 1941 Elser was kept prisoner in the Gestapo's gaols in Berlin. If Nebe's confidences to Gisevius are to be believed, the chief of the Criminal Police saw Elser at the beginning of 1941 in the courtyard of the Gestapo building. 'A prisoner', writes Gisevius, 'ran towards Nebe followed by a guard who did not succeed in catching him. Nebe could not believe his eyes. It was the author of the Munich crime of whom he had not heard mention for a long time and whom he believed to be dead. Nebe had tears in his eyes when he told me of this haunting encounter with a ghost. Elser was only the shadow of himself, since he had been shut into an overheated cell, fed with salted herrings and denied anything to drink. They wanted in this way to extract a confession from him about his relations with Otto Strasser. But Elser stood firm. Nebe compared him to one of those guileless, almost childlike men to be found amongst the members of certain sects, for Elser spoke of his sufferings without asking for pity or even complaining. He was simply happy to see again the one man who after his arrest had treated him humanely. I still hear Nebe sighing deeply as he ended his story . . . He felt it like a torture inflicted on him personally not to be able to speak man to man, I almost said brother to brother, to those condemned to death who could no longer be wrested from the clutches of the executioner. Nebe did not like to dramatise. He spoke of all this without any emphasis.'

A few days after Hitler's attack on the U.S.S.R. Elser was transferred to the concentration camp at Sachsenhausen–Oranienburg. His regime changed completely. No longer salt herrings and the overheated cell. He did not go to cut stones near the port on the Hohenzollern canal, nor make latches, nor even do ordinary fatigue duties. From his arrival Elser was not dressed in the sinister striped pyjamas (*Drillich*), he was given a well-cut civilian suit. He did not join the *Zebras* in the overcrowded barracks but was lodged, alone, in the *Zellenbau*, a part of the camp reserved for distinguished prisoners where a solid hut was divided into cells (zellen). There were kept notables like Martin Luther, ex-Secretary of State in the Foreign Ministry, and many political and ecclesiastical personages. Not far from there four wooden cottages, one storey villas, sheltered or would shelter prisoners of note like Leon Blum, Edouard Herriot, Paul Reynaud, the former Austrian chancellor Schuschnigg, and the hereditary prince of Bavaria. Elser was entitled to a servant, a Jehovah's Witness who wore the violet triangle on his striped pyjamas, an intelligent man who sympathised with him. Elser had access to a small carpenter's shop where he could do as he liked. It was there that he made a zither on which he played till his death and which gained him the nickname of 'the zither man'.

In 1944 Elser was transferred to Dachau. There too he was treated as a prisoner of distinction. They again gave him a carpenter's workshop, for himself alone, and he could continue to play the zither when he felt inclined.

How is one to explain the special treatment of Elser? Why was he not quickly 'liquidated'. Why this privileged position both at the Sachsenhausen–Oranienburg concentration camp and at Dachau?

Was it because Elser placed his bomb, as he told several of his fellow inmates of the camps, at the instigation of Himmler and Heydrich or one of them? This would be a misconception of the two S.S. chiefs. They would never have allowed anyone to live whom they could accuse of an attempt—even sham—on the life of the Führer.

The only explanation of Elser's survival for five years is probably that the Führer, superstitious as he was, felt his own life to be linked with that of 'his' murderer and feared to cut this earthly tie prematurely. It is the theory of H. B. Gisevius, who asserts, 'The special treatment accorded Elser during the last days of the Third Reich cannot be explained otherwise.' Gisevius adds, 'A secret order was later discovered at Dachau emanating "from the Head of State and by direction of Reichsführer S.S. Heinrich Himmler" recommending that Elser be assassinated and declared dead during an air-raid.' When the Gestapo killed it was not its custom to do so in such a roundabout way. Nor were Hitler's orders for liquidations drawn up with such tact. The great mystery of the zither player thus resides in the fact that at the moment when the final strains of the

Twilight of the Gods were sounding and the set for the brown millennium was already collapsing with such an uproar, Hitler remembered him and the murderer guilty of millions of crimes felt a sort of mysterious fear to add to them the disappearance from the revolutionary scene of the author of a crime long since forgotten by the world.

On the morning of April 5th 1945 the commandant of the Dachau camp, Eduard Weiter, received instructions from Himmler 'by order of the Führer' that Georg Elser was to be made away with.[10] S.S. Sergeant-Major Fritz and S.S. Sergeant Franz Lechner were detailed to take Elser to the place of execution—the crematorium. They were two of the guards of the Bunker of Honour where prisoners considered notable (*Prominente*) were kept, amongst them, beside Elser, General Delestraint, the Bishop of Clermont-Ferrand, Mgr. Gabriel Piquet, Pastor Niemöller, etc.

When the two non-commissioned officers of the S.S. opened the door of workshop 24 Georg Elser was planing a board. They lied to him about the object of their coming: 'We've been ordered to bring you to the crematorium. The chief of the block wants you to repair a door.'

'Good,' said Elser without surprise as he had already done several repairs in the camp, 'I'll go with you.' He carefully collected the shavings, wiped his plane, took off his apron and put on his jacket.

The vast parade ground which the three men crossed was empty at this hour of the morning. In Liberty Street, the central thoroughfare of the camp, a few prisoners were doing various jobs. A cool wind blew from the west. Large clouds darkened the sky. A few drops fell as the three men went through the central doorway dominated by a watch-tower. They turned to the right and followed the enclosing canal. They did not speak. The two S.S. men wore faces of marble. However, that morning, they admitted, they were upset. Their tread was heavy. They felt, perhaps for the first time, a painful sensation of unease. Franz Lechner said that he had nausea, that his head swam as if he had 104 degrees of fever. Georg Elser noticed nothing. Lost in his usual reverie he walked unconcerned to the crematorium. He walked to his death, preceding by twenty-five days the man who had ordered it and whom he had wanted to kill on November 8th 1939.

When they arrived at the crematorium, several prisoners marked with the green triangle on their pyjamas (common-law criminals) were coming out. At sight of the two S.S. men in black uniform they drew back to let them pass and froze to attention, cap in hand. All recognised the 'Zither player'.

At the threshold to the crematorium two more 'green triangles' detailed to the maintenance and replenishment of the furnaces also stood at attention. Beyond them was the section chief, flanked by an S.S. man whom neither Fritz nor Lechner knew. He was a non-commissioned officer, a stranger to Dachau. He saluted them with a *Heil Hitler*. Fritz and Lechner responded, clicked their heels, turned round and quickly went out, leaving Elser to his fate.

They took a few steps in silence. As they again approached the canal Lechner said to Fritz, 'I am sickened by this execution.'

'Disgusting,' murmured Fritz, lowering his head.

'He was a good chap. . . .'

'I'm sure of it,' returned Fritz, his voice choked with emotion.

The two S.S. men regained their posts without another word. On entering the Bunker of Honour, Fritz went alone to workshop 24. Meditatively he regarded the place where Elser worked. His eyes fell on the zither which lay on a table near the door. With a finger he made the strings vibrate; then, frightened, he brought down his hand to stop the sound. He remained so for a moment, then put the zither under his arm and went out. In the corridor he passed Lechner, who noticed the instrument and said, 'You're right.'

Fritz went back to the crematorium. Something had snapped in him. He would never again be the same man. His face was grey, his eyes were set, his lips had a bitter twist. Had he become conscious suddenly of the vast criminal horror that stamped the whole Black Order for ever, that Order to which he had belonged for nearly eight years? If Franz Lechner's evidence is to be believed it is certain.

Fritz entered the furnace room. The two 'green triangles' stood to attention. Fritz did not see them. He saw only the blood-stained body of Georg Elser, lying naked on its stomach on an iron trolley. The back of his skull was smashed: bullets in the nape of the neck. Beside him two other naked bodies were likewise ready to disappear into the flames.

The S.S. man did not say a word. The two 'green-triangles' were petrified, cap in hand, faces without expression, eyes empty. Fritz approached Elser's remains. Gently he placed the zither on the body. He could not avoid a slight bump which caused the instrument to vibrate. The musical sound for an instant drowned the dull roar of the furnaces heating at full blast. Fritz started and left the crema-

Above The Munich bierkeller while Hitler spoke. (*Keystone*)
Below The bierkeller shortly after Hitler's departure.

Arthur Nebe,
head of Kripo.

Georg Elser
sketches his bomb
for the Gestapo.
(*Bundesarchiv Koblenz*)

torium on the run; So disappeared the author of the carnage in the beer hall, Georg Elser, the 'zither player'.

Paris–Arcachon–La Plagne
November 1971–August 1972

NOTES TO CHAPTER 15

1. Lucien Corosi, *L'Attentat manqué de la Bürgerbräu*, in *Miroir de l'Histoire*, December 1969.
2. *Völkischer Beobachter* of November 9th 1939.
3. Anton Hoch, *Das Attentat auf Hitler im München Bürgerbräukeller 1939*, in *Vierteljahreshefte für Zeitgeschichte, Heft 4/69*.
4. See note 3.
5. The investigation disclosed the contrary: Elser procured all his materials in Germany.
6. Arthur Nebe's objective enquiry proves the contrary.
7. Elser was not in Dachau at this time.
8. Elser's testimony has been quoted by W. Shirer, *The Third Reich*; Terence Prittie, *Germans Against Hitler*; Charles Wighton, *Heydrich*; Alan Bullock, *Hitler*; Payne Best, *The Venlo Incident*; and repeated by many historians careless of the sources. We add the remarks of the Czech journalist Nicolas Koyetski and of Sachsenhausen Camp guard Michael Eccarius to Edouard Callic, *Himmler et son empire*. Finally Pastor Niemöller has given *Der Spiegel* the narrative of Elser's new version, a version confirmed by Franz Lechner, a guard at Dachau.
9. Kopnikov was then held at the camp of the *Combined Services Detailed Interrogation Centre (C.S.D.I.C.)* situated some thirty kilometres from Hanover at Bad Neundorf.
10. Testimony of S.S. Sergeant Franz Lechner on the Bavarian television for the film *L'Attentat*.

Appendix I
The Structure of the R.S.H.A.

On September 17th 1939, Hitler signed the decree creating the over-all directorate of Reich security, the R.S.H.A. (*Reichssicherheits-hauptamt*), placing S.S. General Heydrich at the head of it.

After the war S.S. General Heinz Jost said to me: 'After the creation of the R.S.H.A. Heydrich made an extraordinary ascent. His liberty of action was complete. Only an 'order from the Führer' could restrain him. He knew himself to be indispensable to the Reichsführer S.S. Heinrich Himmler, who called him his spring (*Triebfeder*). He saw him every day to discuss the reports on the other Reich leaders, and it was always Heydrich who decided the measures to be taken so as to strengthen his own position or under-mine that of Himmler. Heydrich recognised the value of this ambi-guous situation and exploited it as much as he could. He said to me, "It's very useful sometimes to have someone in front of you . . . to catch the blows." I must make it clear that Himmler, to my know-ledge, was not duped. He only rarely dropped his mask of cordiality towards his alleged subordinate, whom he did not like, however, but undoubtedly feared.'

In this we probably find the reason for Himmler's surprising decision never to subordinate to Heydrich the concentration camps and certain other S.S. organisms. Heydrich was, in truth, head of the R.S.H.A., but it was Kurt Daluege who, under the direct orders of Himmler, commanded the regular uniformed police (*Orpo*); it was to Oswald Pöhl that Himmler entrusted the admini-stration of the concentration camps; it was Theodor Eicke, chief commandant of the S.S. 'death's head' (*S.S. Totenkopfsturmbanne*), whom he asked to undertake the supervision of those camps.

To understand how much importance the S.S. in general and Heydrich in particular attached, after the declaration of war, to the 'total mobilisation of the political attention of the people', it is enough to read closely Heydrich's article 'Information Service for the People. Mobilisation against treason and calumny', published in the Bulletin of National Socialist Education dated September 1939.

Heydrich there explained in detail of what this 'service' consisted and wrote, 'Only the Germans deeply and fully conscious of the popular responsibilities incumbent on everyone can bring valuable aid to the organisms of State security.' He showed that in the interest of this 'people's information service' all the police, security and information services should be grouped in a single service, the R.S.H.A.

So was born the most unimaginable 'bureaucracy of terror' history has known.

The organisation of the R.S.H.A. was far from simple. The S.S. leader Dieter Wisliceny stated at Nuremberg, 'For a beginner it was practically impossible to find his way in the labyrinth of bureaux, offices, services, sections and sub-sections . . .'

The supreme head of the R.S.H.A. was Reinhard Heydrich (until his death in June 1942). Himmler took over temporarily then appointed Dr. Ernst Kaltenbrunner (January 1943–April 1945). The staff of the R.S.H.A. was composed of aides-de-camp, a secretariat, a press office, a service for the special affairs of the International Organisation of Criminal police: Interpol (Dr. Thomas then after 1944 Dr. Zindel), a service in charge of the Institute of Sports of the Sipo, a service for the inspection of Security Police and S.D. schools (Bruno Streckenbach, then from 1943 Erwin Schulz and from 1944 Dr. Fischer).

The R.S.H.A. comprised six (later seven) main divisions or offices or services (*Amt*, plural *Amter*.) See diagrams, pages 300-3.

Amt I

Personalabteilung, Ausbildung, Organisierung was concerned with the entire R.S.H.A. personnel and its training.

It was at first directed by Dr. Werner Best (until 1940), who was also responsible for counter-espionage. His successors were Bruno Streckenbach (1940–43), Erwin Schulz (1943–44) and Erich Ehrlinger (1944–45).

Amt II

Haushalt und Wirtschaft was in charge of administrative, economic and juridical matters for the whole R.S.H.A. It had as successive heads Dr. Werner Best (until 1940), Dr. Nockmann (1940–43), Preitzel (1943–44), Spacil (1944–45). The assistant chief (1939–41) was Dr. Franz A. Six, born in 1909, professor at the University of Königsberg, author of a thesis on *The Political Propaganda of the N.S.D.A.P. in the Struggle for Power*. He belonged to Lina and Reinhard Heydrich's intimate circle.

Amt III

Deutsche Lebensgebiete: Sicherheitsdienst-Inland (*S.D. Inland*) was the internal security information service. It was a Party organism entirely controlled by the S.S. The active information service within the Reich was divided into five sections and numerous sub-sections concerned amongst other things with questions relating to public opinion, the attitude of the population, ethnic minorities, race, public health, cultural, scientific, artistic, religious, journalistic matters, etc. Section III-D, for instance, under Willy Seibert, was specially detailed to deal with economic questions, the supervision of industries and industrialists, provisioning, commerce, man-power, etc.

Amt III was directed by a brilliant economist, Otto Ohlendorf, born in 1907, enrolled in the Party since May 28th 1925 (number 6531), gold medallist of the Party, first S.A., then one of the first S.S. (Card number 880). He had for assistants Dr. Karl Gengenbach (III-A), Dr. Hans Ehlich (III-B), Dr. Spengler (III-C), Willy Seibert (III-D), etc. In his first official note Ohlendorf says, 'The S.D. is an information service. It has the duty of informing the heads of services about the general situation and public opinion about events and the popular reactions to them.'

The desire of the S.D. was above all to be informed of all rumours. They sought to determine, for instance, if the anti-Bolshevik sentiment of the population had been modified since the signature of the German–Soviet non-aggression pact. The S.D. also collected exact information about the conduct of soldiers' wives, about opinion regarding food restrictions, etc. The S.D. started what all industrialised countries were twenty-five years later to utilise daily: public-opinion polls.

Amt IV

Geheime Staatspolizei: Gestapo (state secret police) was an organism not of the Party but of the State (Chancellery of the Reich Ministry of the Interior), having executive power (the right to arrest) in political matters, whose extent was as vast as it was varied; its object was the pursuit of adversaries of the regime and repression in all its forms.

The Gestapo very often paid no attention to decisions of the courts, civil or military, and carried out quite arbitrary executions. To the protests of the Minister of Justice, Franz Gürtner, Heydrich retorted that the mission of the Reichsführer S.S. was to guarantee the safety of the state and that the executions he carried out were justified by this fact alone. Heydrich's assistant, Dr. Werner Best, wrote, 'No juridical impediment can limit the defence of the state, which must adapt itself to the strategy of the enemy. This is the task of the Gestapo, which claims the rights of an army and which, like an army, cannot permit juridical rules to obstruct its initiative in the struggle.' After Franz Gürtner's death in January, 1941, the Secretary of State Franz Schlegelberger, much too cowed to stand up to Heydrich, little by little ceded all his powers to the R.S.H.A.

From the beginning to the end the Gestapo was directed by the Bavarian, Heinrich Müller, born in 1900, who would be rewarded for his zeal by being successively made Brigadeführer S.S. (December 16th 1940), Gruppenführer S.S. (November 29th 1941), then Obergruppenführer S.S., and finally recommended on November 3rd 1944, for the Knight's Cross of the Iron Cross with the following citation: 'In short, it is established that Müller enabled the Government, during these last ten years, by his work in the struggle against the enemy and by his personal and material contribution of every kind, successfully to achieve its re-arming and permit public life to be pursued normally and without appreciable friction.' The last words have an unconscious black humour which is unendurable when one thinks of the hundreds of thousands of people who fell into the clutches of the Gestapo to 'enable public life to be pursued normally and without appreciable friction'.

The man rightly nicknamed 'Müller-Gestapo' was assisted until 1943 by Walter Huppenkothen, then by Willy Krichbaum (1943), Panzinger (1944) and Dr. Humbert Achamer-Pifrader (1944–45).

The Gestapo comprised six sections, themselves divided into a large number of sub-sections. In five and a half years of existence

Amt IV of the R.H.S.A. would undergo many internal transformations although its organisation and specific powers stayed the same.

Section IV-A (opponents, sabotage and protection service) was directed by Panzinger.

Section IV-B (churches, sects, Jews and gypsies) was directed by Hartl, then, from 1943, by Roth. Sub-section IV-B4 (Jewish affairs, evacuations, recovery of goods held by 'enemies of the people and of the Reich', forfeiture of German nationality), which would in 1941 become sub-section IV-A4b, was directed by Adolf Eichmann, assisted by Rolf Günther, Franz Novak, Friedrich Suhr (replaced in 1942 by Otto Hunsche), Fritz Wöhrn, Paul Blobel, Arthur Harder, etc.

Section IV-C (records, preventive detention, press and N.S.D.A.P.) was directed by Dr. Fritz Rang, then, from 1943, by Emil Berndorff.

Section IV-D (sphere of influence of Greater Germany) was directed by Dr. Erwin Weinmann, then, from 1943, by Dr. Fritz Rang (of section IV-C). Their assistants were G. A. Nosske and Lischka.

Section IV-E (counter-espionage) was directed from 1939 to 1942 by Walter Schellenberg himself; then, (under Schellenberg's control) by Walter Huppenkothen, assisted by Dr. Hammer. Sub-section IV-E1 (counter-espionage administration and delivery of agents' identity cards) was successively directed by Bläsing (1939), Lindow (1940) and Renken (from 1942 on). Other sub-sections dealt with economic affairs in general, and economic and political counter-espionage. Counter-espionage for the Western sector (IV-E3) was directed successively by Dr. Karl Schäfer, Helmuth Knochen and Herbert Fischer; for the Northern sector (IV-E4) by Dr. Schaumbacher and Wilhelm Clemens; for the Eastern sector (IV-E5) by Joseph Kubitzky and Dr. Häusler; for the Southern sector (IV-E6) by Dr. Schmitz, then by Rauch.

Section IV-F (passport service and aliens' police) was directed by Councillor Krause from beginning to end.

Amt V

Kriminalpolizei or *Kripo* (criminal police) was a State department, like the Gestapo, having executive power (right of arrest) in criminal matters. Its direction was entrusted to a noted criminologist who was the head of Kripo from 1933; Arthur Nebe, born in 1894, a complex and very secretive person who enrolled in the Nazi party, the S.A. and the S.S. before 1931, but who nevertheless gave cover to and encouraged the successive military plots against Hitler. Note that, during repressive operations, the collaboration of Amt IV (Gestapo) and of Amt V (Kripo) was carried on under the sole direction of the Security Police (*Sicherheitspolizei* or *Sipo*).

Arthur Nebe had for assistant H. Werner, who also directed section V-A (policy in criminal and preventive matters).

Amt VI

Sicherheitsdienst-Ausland: *SD-Ausland* or *Auslandsnachrichtendienst* (Security Service and Intelligence Abroad, otherwise known as S.S. Secret Service abroad) was an organism of the Party entirely controlled by the S.S. It was directed from 1939 to 1941 by Heinz Jost, then until the end by Walter Schellenberg.

When in 1944 the Abwehr was absorbed by the S.S. (Canaris being appointed to another post before being arrested on July 22nd 1944, and subsequently hanged) a section VI-Mil was created. Its chief was Walter Schellenberg himself, with the following assistants: Dr. Martin Sandberger (VI-Mil-A); Eugen Steimle (VI-Mil-B); Major G. Ohletz (VI-Mil-D1); Otto Skorzeny (VI-Mil-D2); Lieutenant-Colonel Böning (VI-Mil E and G); Major Partl (VI-Mil, Instruction Regiment and special mission D); S. Sansoni (VI-Mil N, Information and transmissions), assisted by two S.S. officers, Mansolf and Marks.

In 1939 Amt VI was divided into six sections (then eight in the course of the following years).

Section VI-A, directed by Dr. Gerhard Filbert, then (from 1943 on) by Herbert Müller, dealt with the general organisation of the S.D., missions abroad, the security of couriers, material and the supervision of sections. Amongst those detailed to control and protect the S.D. detachments in the districts of the Reich while on foreign assignments one notes the names of S.S. chiefs: Bernhard and Sandberger (VI-A, West), Lehmann (VI-A, North), von Salisch (VI-A, East), Lopper (VI-A, South), Jobst Thiemann (VI-A, Centre) and Franz Goering, alias Wilhelm Thorwald, Claus Thomas, Wilhelm Tobias, for 'special missions'.

Section VI-B was in charge of espionage in Western Europe. It was directed in 1943 by Eugen Steimle and his assistant Dr. Wilhelm Höttl, alias Walter Hagen. It comprised six sub-sections: France, Belgium, Holland and Luxembourg (VI-B1). In France section VI-B1a was directed by Dr. Helmuth Knochen. Vatican and Italy (VI-B2), North Africa (VI-B3), Spain, Portugal and South America (VI-B4), directed by Lothar Fendler. Balkans (VI-B5) which would in 1943 become VI-E. Switzerland (VI-B6) directed by Sturmbannführer S.S. Felfe.

Section VI-C, espionage in the Russian and Japanese zones of influence, at first directed by Dr. Gräfe, then by Rapp (1943) and Dr. Henge (1944). Sub-section VI-C13: Iran, was directed by Roman Gamotha. In 1941 Schellenberg created a sub-section VI-CZ (Zeppelin) specialising in the problems of Soviet prisoners of war, directed by Walther Kurreck, assisted by Walter Weissberger, Huhn, Dr. Wallrabe and Brummerloh, at Auschwitz; by Erwin Sakuth at the Soldau, Wissokoje and Jablon camps.

Section VI-D: espionage in the Anglo-American zone of influence, directed from 1943 by Dr. Paeffgen.

Section VI-E: until 1943 entrusted with locating ideological adversaries abroad. It was directed by Dr. Hammer and his assistant Loose. From 1943 onward section VI-E dealt with espionage in Southern Europe, under the direction of Major Wanck, assisted by Dr. Wilhelm Höttl alias Walter Hagen, especially in the Balkans, Italy and the Vatican.

Section VI-F: technical requirements of the entire S.D., at first directed by Alfred Naujocks, assisted by Bernhard Krüger. From January 1941, Krüger took charge. He was replaced by Walter Fauff, then by Hermann Dörner (1943) and Lieutenant-Colonel Böning (1944–45).

In 1942 Walter Schellenberg created section IV-G, the scientific research service, directed at the end by R. Schmied; and Section IV-S, entrusted with the preparation and execution of 'physical, moral and political sabotage' (such as the kidnapping of Mussolini from the Gran Sasso, of the son of the Regent Horthy and the Ardennes offensive) which was directed from beginning to end by Otto Skorzeny, aided by Radl.

Amt VII

Weltanschauliche Forschung. Written documentation service, created in July 1940 by Professor Franz A. Six. He was replaced in 1944 by Dr. Paul Dittel with Günther Burmeister as assistant.

In the beginning the R.S.H.A. was a very complete organisation, well balanced and efficient, under the personal direction of Heydrich. It prefigured quite well the great modern secret service organisations. In proportion as Heydrich lost interest in police, security and intelligence matters in order to concentrate more and more on politics and aim at supreme power, the R.S.H.A. lost its effectiveness. It was still worse after the death of its chief and creator in June 1942: the R.S.H.A. became a veritable bureaucratic monstrosity.

As Jacques Delarue stresses [National Archives, Microcopy T-354. Rrf. SS/T. 354]: 'The R.S.H.A. was to reveal itself an un-wieldly mechanism in practice. The excessive departmentalisation imposed on it by the rules of secrecy greatly hampered its efficiency. Furthermore, the segregation of the intelligence and executive sectors, the fact that intelligence passed through so many hands before reaching the person who was to act upon it gave those at the top a false perspective . . . This over-bureaucratised conception of police work resulted in numerous mistakes committed by the German security services and in the inefficacy of many of its measures, even among its most repressive. Paradoxically, the over-organisation of the R.S.H.A. was the reason for its failures.'

It has rightly been said that the R.S.H.A. was exclusively the work of Reinhard Heydrich. He directed it with a fist and heart of iron and was able to adapt it skilfully to the needs of a widespread conflict. In fact it must be stated that Heydrich conducted, parallel with the Wehrmacht's, his own war. This can never be sufficiently emphasised. Assassination, blackmail and terror were his arms, the arms of the R.S.H.A. in this war conducted by the S.S.

In 1957, in the U.S.A., I found Heydrich's dossier in the archives of the S.S. There was a formulary, undated, unsigned and incomplete, bearing the heading: 'Record of proposal No—— for the award of the Croix de Guerre first class with swords.' This proposal probably originated in the Reich Chancellery or the O.K.W. which is to say Hitler himself.

The content of the proposal was drafted as follows: 'The Chief of the Security Police (Sipo), Obergruppenführer S.S. and General of Police Reinhard Heydrich, appointed Protector of Bohemia and Moravia [September 1941], has not only assumed the sole responsibility for Sipo within the country but has also directed and completely reorganised the S.D. in such a way that the Wehrmacht, engaged mainly in Poland but also in other operational theatres, has been relieved of police duties which devolved upon it in enemy countries. By his action Heydrich has well served military interests.

He can also be credited with the introduction and multiplication of units of Sipo, of the S.D. and the S.S. *Totenkopfsturmbanne* (Death's Head units); in doing this he has guaranteed the security of the Greater Reich in all its internal domains as well as in the occupied territories and enabled the Wehrmacht to concentrate solely on purely military activities. In this also he has rendered a signal service to military strategy. By. . . .'

Satan alone knows to where Heydrich would have extended his responsibilities and power if, as we have already stressed, death by assassination had not ended this prodigious ascent towards supreme dominion.

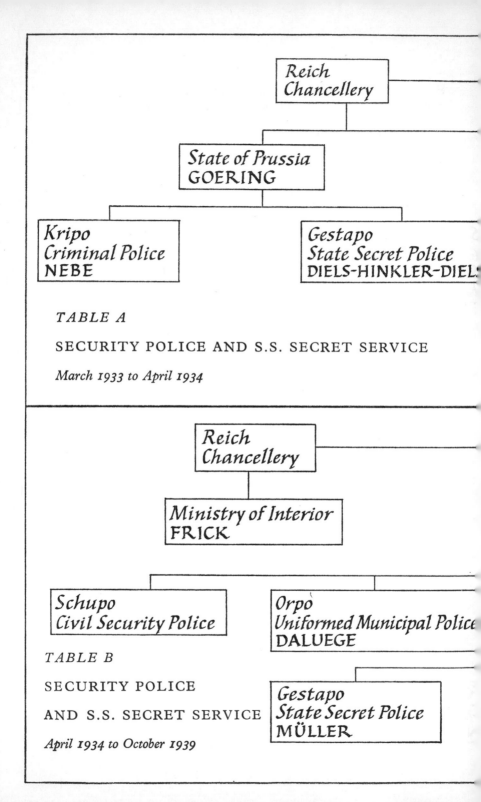

Reich Chancellery

State of Prussia GOERING

Kripo Criminal Police NEBE

Gestapo State Secret Police DIELS-HINKLER-DIEL:

TABLE A

SECURITY POLICE AND S.S. SECRET SERVICE

March 1933 to April 1934

Reich Chancellery

Ministry of Interior FRICK

Schupo Civil Security Police

Orpo Uniformed Municipal Police DALUEGE

TABLE B

SECURITY POLICE

AND S.S. SECRET SERVICE

Gestapo State Secret Police MÜLLER

April 1934 to October 1939

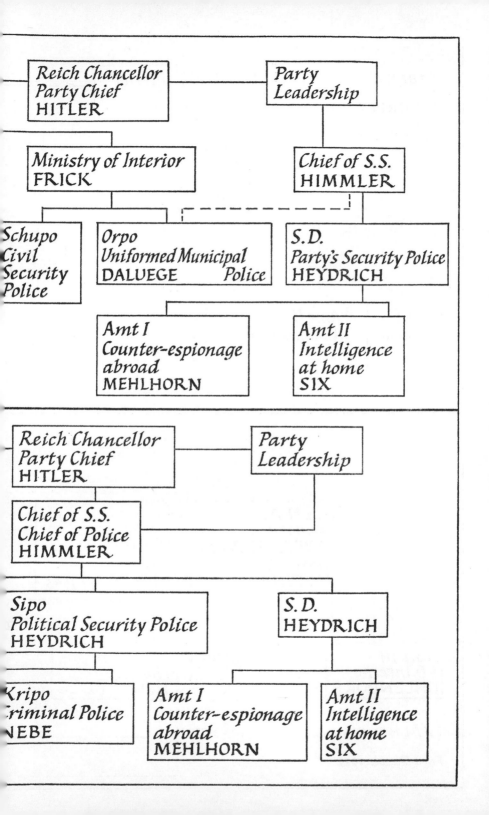

TABLE C
SECURITY POLICE
AND S.S. SECRET SERVICE

From October 1939

Ministry of Interior FRICK

Orpo DALUEGE

S. D.

| Amt I Personnel | Amt II Administration | Amt VII Written records | Amt III Interior |

R.S.H.A. Security
HEYDRICH *Oct 1939–May 1942*
HIMMLER *May 1942–Jan 1943*
KALTENBRUNNER *Jan 1943–Apr 1945*

S. D.

| Amt III SD Interior OHLENDORF | Amt VI SD Exterior JOST–SCHELLENBERG |

TABLE D S.S. SECRET SERVICE

From October 1939

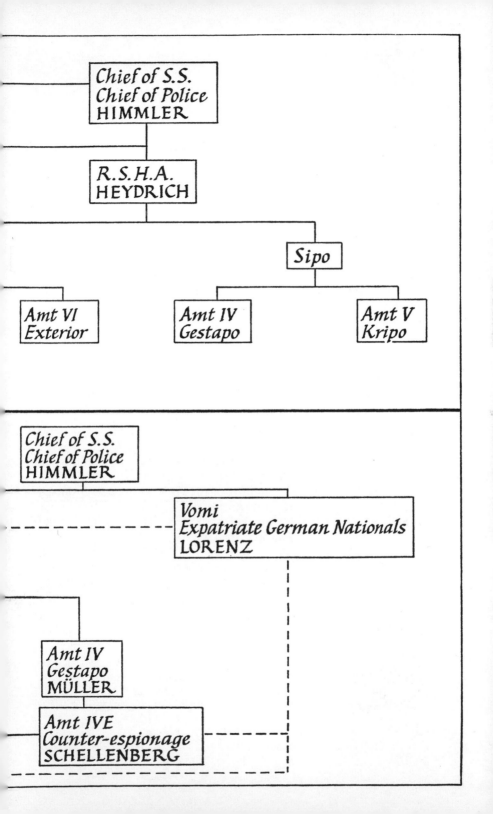

Appendix II
Chronology

1889 April 20	Birth of Adolf Hitler at Braunau, Austria.
1900 April 28	Birth of Heinrich Müller at Munich.
October 7	Birth of Heinrich Himmler at Munich.
1904 March 7	Birth of Reinhard Heydrich at Halle (Saxony).
1910 January 16	Birth of Walter Schellenberg at Sarrebruck.
1919 September 16	Hitler enrolls in the D.A.P. (German Workers Party).
1920 August 7/8	Founding of the N.S.D.A.P. (Nazi Party).
1921 July 29	Hitler president of the N.S.D.A.P.; he becomes the 'Führer'.
1923 March	At Munich creation of the *Stabswache*, germ of the S.S.
May	The *Stabswache* becomes the *Stosstrupp Adolf Hitler*.
November 8/9	The failure of the Hitler–Ludendorff putsch in Munich.
1924 December 20	Hitler leaves prison. He has practically finished *Mein Kampf*.
1925 November 9	The *Stosstrupp Adolf Hitler* becomes the S.S.
1926 April	Berchtold becomes chief of the S.S.
July 4	Hitler delivers to the S.S. the 'Flag of Blood', (the standard of the Swastika from the failed putsch).
1929 January 6	Himmler is named *Reichsführer S.S.* The S.S., which then numbered only 280 men, is attached to the staff of the S.A.
1931 January	Ernst Röhm becomes chief of staff of the S.A.
April	Heydrich expelled from the Navy.
June 14	First meeting of Himmler and Heydrich.

1931 July 14	Heydrich enters the S.S.
October 5	Creation of the S.S. secret service (S.D.).
1933 January 30	Hitler becomes chancellor of the Reich.
February 27	Reichstag fire.
March 5	Election: 238 seats for the N.S.D.A.P.
March 5	Opening of the Dachau concentration camp.
March 9	Himmler Prefect of Police in Munich.
March 17	Hitler dubs his S.S. guard *Leibstandarte S.S. Adolf Hitler*, commanded by Sepp Dietrich.
March 21	Heydrich appointed *Oberführer S.S.*
March 23	Parliament votes full powers to Hitler.
April 27	Goering founds the *Gestapo* in the state of Prussia.
Late December	Himmler controls all the police of Germany except those of Prussia and Schaumburg-Lippe.
1934 February 24	Arrest of the Polish spy Sosnowski and his accomplices.
April 10	Himmler named chief of the *Gestapo*. He installs himself in Berlin, along with Heydrich.
June 30	Night of the Long Knives.
July 1	Röhm killed in his cell in Munich.
July 2	Schellenberg enters the S.D.
July 20	The S.S. becomes independent of the S.A.
August 2	Death of Field Marshal Hindenburg.
August 19	Hitler voted Führer of the Third Reich by plebiscite.
Autumn	Naujocks exposes the Czech Major Horvath.
November 7	The staff of the S.S. installed in Berlin.
1935 January 1	Admiral Wilhelm Canaris becomes head of the *Abwehr* (Military intelligence).
January 23	Naujocks and Gröthe assassinate Formis in Czechoslovakia.
February 18	Benita von Zollikopfen-Altenkligen and Renate von Natzmer, of the Sosnowski affair, beheaded in Berlin.
March 14	Hitler re-establishes compulsory military service in Germany.
1936 March 7	The German army reoccupies the Rhineland.

June 17	Himmler chief of all police. Heydrich chief of Sipo and Daluege chief of Orpo.
December	Heydrich receives General Skoblin in Berlin: the Tukhachevsky affair begins on the German side.
December 21	Abwehr–S.S. secret service agreement on division of jurisdictions, the so-called 'Pact of the Ten Commandments'.
1937 June 11	Marshal Tukhachevsky condemned to death, executed the next day.
1938 January/February	Von Blomberg and von Fritsch affair.
February 4	Hitler Commander-in-Chief. The former general staff of the *Reichswehr* becomes the *Oberkommando der Wehrmacht (O.K.W.)*.
March 12/14	Invasion of Austria: *Anschluss*.
September 29	Munich agreements.
November 29	Dr. Emil Hacha becomes President of the Czechoslovak Republic.
1939 March 13	Hitler–Mgr. Tiso meeting in Berlin.
March 14	Hitler–Hacha meeting in Berlin.
March 15	Hitler's entry into Prague.
August 23	German–Soviet non-aggression pact.
August 31	Gleiwitz provocation led by Naujocks.
September 1	Invasion of Poland.
September 3	Declaration of war by England and France on Germany.
September 27	Hitler's decree creating the R.S.H.A.
October 21	Schellenberg meets Best and Stevens in Holland.
October 30/31	Schellenberg's second meeting with Best and Stevens.
November 7	Third meeting. Heydrich instructs Naujocks to assure 'the safety' of Schellenberg.
November 8	Attempt on Hitler's life at the *Bürgerbräukeller* in Munich.
November 9	Naujocks kidnaps Best and Stevens in Venlo. The Dutch officer Dirk Klop, alias Lieutenant Coppens, is mortally wounded. The author of Munich attempt identified: Georg Elser.
November 10	Arthur Nebe questions Elser for the first time.

November 19   Schellenberg promoted to S.S. Brigadier
General. Naujocks receives from Hitler's
hands the Iron Cross first class.

November 20   Arthur Nebe, chief of the Criminal Police,
obliged to hand Elser over to the Gestapo.

Appendix III
Sources

I cannot here cite all the testimony collected orally or in writing; it will easily be understood why certain survivors preferred to preserve their anonymity.

Amongst those I can mention are S.S. Generals Walter Schellenberg, Heinz Jost and Sepp Dietrich; the Abwehr Generals Erwin von Lahousen and Hans Piekenbrock, Admiral Conrad Patzig, Colonel Oscar Reile, Captain Richard Protze, Colonel Moravec of the Czech Secret Service, the English Colonel Scotland, etc.

As regards Schellenberg's Memoirs, published in England (1956), in France (1958) and in Germany (1959), it should be stated that the German and English are more complete than the French. I have been able to read in its entirety the original manuscript which runs to three thousand typed pages. The various publishers have, with good reason, cut repetitions (numerous) and details (often fascinating and revealing but unnecessary to non-specialists). My quotations from the Schellenberg Memoirs are by courtesy of André Deutsch Ltd., London

For the documentation as a whole I refer the interested reader to the bibliography published at the end of my two books, *Hitler et l'Ordre noir* and *Canaris*.

THE CHIEF UNPRINTED SOURCES ARE:

1. At Munich, in the Institute of Contemporary History (*Institut für Zeitgeschichte, München. I.Z.M.*).
2. At Coblenz, in the State and Military Archives (*Bundesarchiv-Militärarchiv, Koblenz. B.A.M.*).
3. At Bonn, in the Political Archives of the Ministry for Foreign Affairs (*Politisches Archiv des Auswärtigen Amt, Bonn. P.A.A.A.*).
4. At Freiburg-im-Breisgau, at the Central Office for Research in

Military History (*Dokumentenzentrale des Militärgeschichtlichen Forschungsamt, Freiburg-im-Breisgau. D.M.F.*).

5. In Berlin, at the Principal Archives and Secret Archives of the State of Prussia (*Hauptarchiv, Ehem. Preuss. Geheimes Staatsarchiv, Berlin. H.A.*).

6. At Hamburg, at the Centre for Research into the History of National Socialism. (*Forschungstelle zur Geschichte des Nationalsozialismus, Hamburg. F.G.N.*).

Numerous documents used in the various trials of war criminals at Nuremberg (thirteen in all) have not been published. They are to be found in Munich (*I.Z.M.*).

THE CHIEF PRINTED SOURCES ARE:

Trial of the chief war criminals by the International Military Tribunal at Nuremberg, in 42 volumes (*T.M.I.*).

International Military Tribunal: The Trial of the German Major War Criminals, 22 volumes (*I.M.T.*).

Trials of German War Criminals before the Nuremberg Military Tribunals, 15 volumes (T.W.C.).

Nazi Conspiracy and Aggression, 10 volumes (N.C.A.).

Documents on German Foreign Policy, 1918–1945, 10 volumes (D.G.F.P.).

A valuable book must be added: *Rangliste des Reichsführers S.S.*, a work containing the biographies of ten thousand S.S. officers, printed specially for Himmler and Heydrich in an edition of only a hundred copies.

AMONGST THE PUBLISHED BOOKS CONSULTED:

Alexandrov, V.—*Le Front noir.*
Alquen, Gunther d'—*Die SS Historie.*
Amort, C. & Jedlicka, I.M.—*On l'appelait A-54.*
Andolenko (General)—*Histoire de l'armée russe.*
Baur, Hans—*J'étais pilote de Hitler.*
Benès, Edouard—*Memoirs.*
Bennecke, H.—*Die Reichswehr und das Röhm-Putsch.*
  Hitler und die SA.
Benoist-Méchin, J.—*Histoire de l'armée allemande*, 6 volumes.
Best, Payne—*The Venlo Incident.*
Best, Werner—*Die Deutsche Polizei.*
Bloch, Charles—*La Nuit des longs couteaux.*

Boberach, Heinz (Editor)—*Meldungen aus dem Reich* (A selection of confidential reports of the S.D., 1939–44).
Bonnet, Georges—*De Munich à la guerre.*
   Le Quai d'Orsay sous trois républiques.
   La Défense de la paix, 2 volumes.
Brascher, D.—*Die nationalsozialistiche Machtergreifung.*
Brissaud, André—*Hitler et l'Ordre noir.*
   Les SS.
   Canaris.
Brone, Pierre—*Les Procès de Moscou.*
Buchheim, Hans—*SS und Polizei im NS-Staat.*
   Die SS—Das Herrschaftsinstrument.
Buchheit, Gert—*Ludwig Beck.*
   Der Deutsche Geheimdienst.
   Le Complot des généraux contre Hitler.
Bullock, Alan—*Hitler: A Study in Tyranny.*
Burckhardt, Carl—*Ma Mission à Dantzig.*
Callic, Edouard—*Himmler et son empire.*
Castellan, Georges—*Le Réarmement clandestin du Reich.*
   L'Allemagne de Weimar.
Ciano, Galeazzo—*Diario, 1937–1938.*
   Diario, 1939–1942, 2 volumes.
Conquest, Robert—*The Great Terror: Stalin's Purge of the Thirties.*
Crankshaw, Edward—*Gestapo.*
Dallin, D. J.—*Soviet Espionage.*
Dalton, Hugh—*The Fateful Years, 1931–1945.*
Decaux, Alain—*Nouveaux dossiers de l'Histoire.*
Delarue, Jacques—*Histoire de la Gestapo.*
Deriabine, P. & Gibney, F.—*Le Monde secret.*
Destrem, Maja—*L'Eté 1939.*
Diels, Rudolf—*Lucifer ante portas.*
Dietrich, Otto—*Zwölf Jahre mit Hitler.*
Domarus, M.—*Hitler, Reden und Proklamationen.*
Eichstadt, Ulrich—*Von Dollfuss zu Hitler.*
Erasmus, J.—*Der geheime Nachrichtendienst.*
Erickson, John—*Soviet High Command.*
Fischer, Louis—*Vie et mort de Staline.*
François, Jean—*L'Affaire Röhm-Hitler.*
François-Poncet, André—*Souvenirs d'une ambassade à Berlin.*
Gallo, Max—*La Nuit des longs couteaux.*
Gamelin, Maurice—*Servir.*

Garder, Michel—*Histoire de l'armée soviétique.*
Gaucher, Roland—*L'Opposition en U.R.S.S., 1917–1967.*
Gisevius, H. B.—*Jusqu'à la lie,* 2 volumes.
  Où est Nebe?
Goebbels, Joseph—*The Goebbels Diaries.*
  Combat pour Berlin.
Goering, Emmy—*Memoiren.*
Gorbatov, A. V.—*Les Années de ma vie.*
Goerlitz & Quint—*Hitler,* 2 volumes.
Guérin, Alain—*Le Général gris.*
Haffner, Sebastian—*Le Pacte avec le Diable.*
Hagen, Walter—*Le Front Secret.*
Halder, Franz—*Hitler as Warlord.*
Heiber, Helmut—*Goebbels.*
Heiden, Konrad—*Histoire du national-socialisme.*
Höhne, Heinz—*L'Ordre noir, histoire de la SS.*
Hossbach, F.—*Zwischen Wehrmacht und Hitler.*
Hoch, Anton—*Das Attentat auf Hitler im Münchner Bürgerbräu-keller 1939,* in: *Vierteljahrshefte für Zeitgeschichte, Heft 4/1969.*
Houbart & Rankovitch—*Guerre sans drapeau.*
Jacobsen & Jochmann—*Ausgewählte Dokumente zur Geschichte des Nationalsozialismus.*
Kaltenbrunner, Ernst—*Spiegelbild einer Verschwörung.*
Keitel, W.—*Field-Marshal Keitel's Memoirs.*
Kessel, Joseph—*Les Mains du miracle.*
Kotze, H. von.—*Hitlers Sicherheitsdienst im Ausland.*
Krivitsky, Walter—*J'étais l'agent de Staline.*
Manvell, R. & Fraenkel, H.—*Doctor Goebbels: His Life and Death.*
  Heinrich Himmler.
  Hermann Goering.
Mayda, G.—*Monaco 1939, una bomba contro Hitler* (*Storia,* Dec. 1969).
Mourin, Maxime—*Les Complots contre Hitler.*
Nekritch, Alexandre—*L'Armée Rouge assassinée.*
Newman, Bernard—*Real Life Spies.*
Nicolai, W.—*Geheime Mächte.*
Niekisch, E.—*Das Reich der niederen Dämonen.*
Nikouline, Lev—*Maréchal Toukhatchevsky,* in: *Octobre,* n° 2 to 5, 1963.
Noël, Léon—*L'Agression allemande contre la Pologne.*
Nord, Pierre—*L'Intoxication.*

Orb, H.—*Die Deutsche Spionage.*
Orcival, François d'—*Le Danube était noir.*
Orlov, Alexandre—*L'Histoire secrète des crimes de Staline.*
Papen, Franz von—*Memoirs.*
Peis, Gunther—*Naujocks, the Man Who Started the War.*
Pleltenberg, Malte—*La Tragédie des généraux.*
Poretski, E. K.—*Les Nôtres. Vie et mort d'un agent soviétique.*
Prittie, Terence—*Germans Against Hitler.*
Rauschning, Hermann—*Hitler m'a dit.*
Reile, Oscar—*Die Geheime Ostfront.*
Reitlinger, Gerald—*SS, Alibi of a Nation, 1922–1945.*
Ribbentrop, Joachim von—*De Londres à Moscou.*
Röhm, Ernst—*Die Memoiren des Stabschefs Röhm.*
  Die Geschichte eines Hochverräters.
Schellenberg, Walter—*The Schellenberg Memoirs.*
Schmidt, Paul—*Ma figuration auprès de Hitler.*
Serge, Victor—*De Lénine à Staline.*
Shirer, W.—*The Rise and Fall of the Third Reich.*
Soltikow, Michael—*Sosnowski, l'espion de Berlin.*
Strasser, Otto—*Hitler et moi.*
  Die Deutsche Bartholomäusnacht.
Ströbinger, Rudolf—*L'Espion aux trois visages, A-54.*
Tokaev, G. A.—*Le Paradis de Staline.*
Toscano, M.—*Fonti memorialistiche e documentarie per la storia diplomatica della seconda guerra mondiale.*
Tukhachevsky—*Ecrits sur la guerre.*
Uralov, Alexandre (A. Avtorkhanov)—*Le Régime de Staline.*
Wheeler-Bennett, J. W.—*Nemesis of Power.*
  Munich, Prologue to Tragedy.
Wighton, Charles—*Heydrich.*
Wulf, Josef—*Heinrich Himmler.*
  L'Industrie de l'horreur.
Zoller, Albert—*Douze ans auprès de Hitler.*

AMONGST THE JOURNALS AND REVIEWS CONSULTED:

Völkischer Beobachter (the National Socialist Party daily).
Das Schwarze Korps (the S.S. weekly).
Die Deutsche Polizei (the Sipo and S.D. review).
Befehlsblatt der Sicherheitspolizei und des S.D. (official journal of Sipo and S.D.).

NS—Schulungsbriefe (September 1939).
Pravda (June 11th 1937 and June 15th 1937).
Cahiers du communisme (special number of November 1961; The XXIInd Congress of the Soviet Communist Party).
Der Spiegel.
Stern.
Historia (Italy).
Miroir de l'histoire.
Perspectives polonaises.
Die Nachhut (the Abwehr Veterans' review).

Index